A Musician Looks at the Psalms

BY DON WYRTZEN

ZondervanPublishingHouse

Grand Rapids, Michigan

A Division of HarperCollins*Publishers*

A Musician Looks at the Psalms
Copyright © 1988, 1991 by Don Wyrtzen
All rights reserved

Requests for information should be addressed to:
Zondervan Publishing House
1415 Lake Drive S.E.
Grand Rapids, Michigan 49506

Library of Congress Cataloging-in-Publication Data

Wyrtzen, Don.
    A musician looks at the Psalms / Don Wyrtzen.
        p.   cm.
    Includes indexes.
    ISBN 0-310-36361-6 (pbk.)
    1. Bible. O.T. Psalms—Meditations. 2. Music in the Bible
—Meditations. 3. Devotional calendars. I. Title.
BS1430.4W97   1991
242'.5—dc20   90–15582
                                                        CIP

Printed in the United States of America

91 92 93 94 95 / AM / 10 9 8 7 6 5 4 3 2 1

Dedicated to my parents,
Jack and Marge Wyrtzen,
whose precious gifts to me
are reflected in this book.

From my dad comes the gift
of his love for the Scriptures.
From my mom came her
emotional sensitivity.

Thanks, Dad, and my loving
tribute to you, Mom,
for all of life's melodies
you have shared with me.

Contents

Foreword

Most people know Don Wyrtzen only as a musician—a gifted composer and master of the keyboard. It has been my privilege to know him as a personal friend. For over two decades, I have appreciated the man's life, which has depths and dimensions he is much too modest to promote.

Hidden within the heart of this artist is a wellspring of fresh creativity that seems bottomless. From it flows imagination, spontaneity, insight, vulnerability, humor, realism, tenderness, and a dozen other qualities seldom found within the same individual. The combination of these traits has resulted in what I call "that Wyrtzen touch." Whatever he puts himself into results in a work that pulsates with such an inimitable style, it makes me smile with amazement. I find him exceedingly refreshing in our day of predictable duplications and same-song, second-verse compositions. To put it plain and simply, Don Wyrtzen is rare.

Unknown to most, he has been pondering the ancient hymnbook of the Psalms for years. With persistent faithfulness he has invested untold hours not only reading the psalmist's words, but feeling the ebb and flow of his emotions. As only a musician of Don's caliber could do, he has slipped silently into the studio and listened to the varied strains of thought as he studied the harmonious chords and changing rhythms of the original masterwork as they flowed from the psalmist's fingers. Unhurried, he allowed these observations to linger until they emerged into a natural transition that led into the issues of life we face today. The result is now in your hands: *A Musician Looks at the Psalms*.

This is not "just another daily devotional" to be thumbed through and tossed aside. It is a well-arranged composition from the hands of an artist, who decided to write his lyrics on the pages of a book instead of a musical score. It will soon become your close companion.

For each day of the calendar year, you will find a brief exposition of a psalm, a relevant development of the theme with today's world in mind, and a sensitive prayer that will give you a boost into the real world . . . just enough to make you wish for more.

I commend my long-time friend, Don Wyrtzen, for providing this volume for all of us to enjoy. I commend you for choosing it from among thousands of others you could have selected. Believe me, you will not be disappointed! It will be a source of much encouragement and comfort. Furthermore, it is the only book available with "that Wyrtzen touch."

Chuck Swindoll
Pastor, Author, Radio Bible Teacher

Notes from the Composer

On the inception of the work and the key players

On my way to a concert at Grace Youth Camp in Western Michigan in the summer of 1984, I was stressed out. Playing the piano and sharing with an audience was the last thing I wanted to do. Earlier in the year I had lost two of the dearest people in the world to me—my mom and my pastor, and my spirits were at an all-time low. How could I be expected to bring hope to others when I couldn't even help myself?

I did then what I've done many times before and since. I turned it all over to the Lord. Later, sharing intimately about the death of my mom with the group of campers, we mutually experienced some exciting new insights from Psalm 40:1–3: "I waited patiently for the LORD; he turned to me and heard my cry. He lifted me out of the slimy pit, out of the mud and mire; he set my feet on a rock and gave me a firm place to stand. He put a new song in my mouth, a hymn of praise to our God. Many will see and fear and put their trust in the LORD."

Listening attentively that night were Roy and Sandy Irving. Roy is editor of the renowned Sunday school magazine, *Power for Living*. After the concert, he told me that he had been deeply touched and requested an interview. The germ of a wonderful idea was born in his mind that night, but it was almost a year later before he suggested to me that I consider writing a very personal devotional journal based on the Psalms. He felt that a composer trained in theology could make a unique contribution.

The idea grew on me. I had studied the Psalms with the brilliant Hebrew scholar, Dr. Bruce Waltke, had taught them to a large Sunday school class at Calvary Church in Grand Rapids, Michigan, and had read them voraciously for years. Not only that, but much of the praise music I was writing was inspired by the Psalms. I decided to accept the challenge.

The process became biblical therapy for me. As I jotted down notes on planes, in motels, at home on the weekends, I found that I was writing in order to better grapple with reality, to find emotional equilibrium, and to cope with midlife concerns. Gradually I realized that I was experiencing more consistency, stability, and security in life—that there was real in-depth change taking place.

If I'm the composer of this magnum opus, Roy Irving is the orchestrator. As the project art director, Roy's sensitive visual ideas have brought to life the musical structure I superimposed on the Psalms. Without him, this score would never have been heard. I am so honored to feature the exquisite nature photography of Roy's son, Gary Irving, a superb young talent.

Making my words really sing is senior editor Anne Severance. She is truly a verbal virtuoso, a semantic Paganini. She helped me rewrite the manuscript and pulled out of me a lot of deeply personal material. What a beautiful sensitive Christian she is and what an encouragement she has been to me.

My family has been extremely supportive and caring during this project. My wife Karen, God's special gift to me, helped enormously with the selection of pictures and offered invaluable feedback on the manuscript itself. I thank my terrific kids, D.J. and Kathy, for letting me make this large time investment. They grew up bumping their heads underneath the piano while Daddy wrote his music. Standing by while I hammered out a book has been a new experience for them.

My publisher, Zondervan Publishing House, believed in the concept from the beginning. Bob DeVries and Cheryl Forbes caught the vision and accepted the manuscript for publication. Julie Link helped me get off the ground with her editorial expertise. Bruce Ryskamp, Joe Allison, and Phil Bandy committed their administrative and marketing skills to spreading the word. Nia Jones has been my faithful contact with the publishing house, serving as confidante, comrade, and cheerleader! Jim Buick, president of the Zondervan Corporation, has become a dear friend and encourager, along with other premiere musicians, artists, and Christian leaders who have supported me in this venture. And how can I thank Chuck Swindoll for launching this project on such a high note?

May all the glory, honor, and praise go to our Lord and Savior, Jesus Christ.

Don Wyrtzen
Brentwood, Tennessee

Prelude

by Don Wyrtzen

The Psalter, the ancient hymnal of Israel, gives a magnificent picture of reality. These lyricists and composers wrestled with the nitty-gritty of life in the ancient world. They wrote incredibly honest and beautiful songs about their struggles and triumphs. Some of what they wrote seems messy to a purely rationalistic mind, but it all rings true to a full view of reality.

I believe the Lord wants us to relate to Him with our whole beings, with the totality of our personalities. But many of us intellectualize Christianity. We approach it much as we would a crossword puzzle in *The New York Times*. We are quite satisfied if all the little squares are filled in properly, both horizontally and vertically. If everything fits, matches, goes together, we feel content. However, a vital relationship with the Lord is based on more than head knowledge! He wants to get inside our hearts too—our psyches, our *personas*.

I also believe that intellectualized Christianity is too brittle and rigid for life. Brittle things tend to snap! Modern life is unpredictable, constantly changing, and complex. Both our external and internal worlds keep shifting and moving. Life seems to have a rhythm—work to rest, tension to resolution, and dissonance to consonance. We even tend to think in terms of black versus white and of relative versus 13 absolute.

What do we need? What will give us comfort and direction in our complex modern society? We need an adequate view of reality! Intellectual precision, sound doctrine, and impeccable theology are essential, but they are not enough. They are basic blocks in the structure of reality, but they are not the whole building. Those of us who have bought into that system, to the neglect of other crucial areas of our personality, have often found our lives bankrupt sooner or later.

The Lord isn't interested in a half-hearted, casual relationship. Hear His compelling command: "Love the LORD your God with all your heart and with all your soul, and with all your strength" (Deuteronomy 6:5). He demands that we love Him with our hearts, the seat of our love and emotions; with our souls (*Nephesh*), the center of our personalities and self-consciousness; and with our strength, our physical bodies.

This is at the fountainhead of living on the basis of the Law. It was in love that the Israelites were to obey the Law, because of an awesome respect (fear) and reverence for the Lord Christ. The Messiah taught us that the whole Law and the Prophets hang on two great commandments—loving God with our whole beings, and loving our neighbors as ourselves (Matthew 22:37–40).

The love of God was displayed, not only in the Law, but also on a grand and glorious scale through His "one and only Son" (John 3:16). The thrill of the gospel is that it enables us, as never before, to live on the basis of these two great commandments. As we do, we come to know the Lord with our whole beings.

As I've written this journal, I have identified with these ancient songwriters. Their sharing with me, under the power and inspiration of the Holy Spirit, has taken me to new heights and depths of reality. They have pulled, stretched, challenged, and comforted me.

The motifs and musings that follow are personal. These are not an exegetical and theological treatise. They are written from an artistic, musical, and emotional perspective. All 150 psalms are included, with a few key thoughts for each day of the year.

I believe that art must be perceived in terms of both form and content. Form refers to how something is said; content relates to what is said. Form relates to style; content relates to substance. There should be congruity between the form, and the content (i.e., you don't depict a thunderstorm with a piccolo solo!). Form is very important, though often neglected. I don't think it was an accident that Psalm 51, 14 David's magnificent poem of confession, was written in poetic form. Poetry is much more passionate and multi-layered than prose. So both form and content are highly significant in this journal.

A sonata or symphony (a sonata for orchestra) generally has three parts: exposition of the theme, development of the theme, and recapitulation of the theme. I have loosely followed that format in my journal.

The book itself is a three-part form—prelude, body, postlude. For each day there are three sections:

- **Theme:** usually several key verses from each psalm.
- **Development:** some personal thoughts on those verses, and
- **Personal prayer:** an attempt to apply by faith a biblical concept for each day.

I've also included some traditional hymns and contemporary lyrics along the way.

Where possible, I have tried to tie in a musical perspective, because I believe that music can be seen as a metaphor for life. What's wrong with many of us is that the song has gone out of our lives!

I have given each psalm its own title, using modern musical forms—sonatas, fugues, variations, rhapsodies, dirges, marches, hymns, etc.—to enhance the meaning of the text. I have also tied in some of the literary forms of the psalms—descriptive praise, individual and national lament, imprecatory, enthronement, etc.—which have only recently been discovered. The beautiful layout of this book highlights its artistic structure.

But this is a personal, devotional journal. If taken to heart a little at a time, it will enable you to take a giant step toward authenticity and harmony in your life.

King David, the chief musician, says, "The law of the LORD is perfect, reviving the soul. The statutes of the LORD are trustworthy, making wise the simple. The precepts of the LORD are right, giving joy to the heart. The commands of the LORD are radiant, giving light to the eyes. The fear of the LORD is pure, enduring forever. The ordinances of the LORD are sure and altogether righteous. They are more precious than gold, than much pure gold; they are sweeter than honey, than honey from the comb. By them is your servant warned; in keeping them there is great reward" (Psalm 19:7–11).

Adoration

May I love You, Lord, with all my heart,
With my whole life, not just in part;
May I love You, Lord, with all my soul,
Make loving You my highest goal.

May I love You, Lord, with all my might,
Fill my being with radiant light;
May I worship You more than anything,
Filled with glorious praise I'll sing.

May I bow before You, Lord, on high,
As Your holy name I glorify;
May I worship You on bended knee,
King of Kings who reigns in majesty.

May I learn to know You more each day,
With my family walking by the way;
May I worship You more than anything,
Filled with glorious praise I'll sing.

Words and music by Don Wyrtzen.
© 1984 by Singspiration Music.

January

PSALMS 1–23

*"As a composer, my calling
is to set God's Truth to music
in simple, powerful form."*

Ode to Joy *First Movement—in Minor*

■ **Theme**   *Blessed is the man who does not walk in the counsel of the wicked or stand in the way of sinners or sit in the seat of mockers (v. 1).*

■ **Development**   Deep inside, I long to be happy. At the core of my being I crave fulfillment, meaning, and significance. The mind-set I choose and lifestyle I live can only partly satisfy these longings.

To get a clear picture of happiness, I need to come to grips with what sort of behavior brings unhappiness. Taking advice from the ungodly, hanging around with sinners, and socializing with scoffers will sap my life of meaning and joy.

The people close to me—arrangers, composers, vocalists, and instrumentalists—strongly influence me. They have a subtle yet pervasive effect on my life. How easy it would be for me to impress them with my gifts and abilities in an attempt to "make it big" in records, films, or television. I don't want to compromise my commitment to Christian music, but if I'm not careful, I will walk, then stand, and ultimately sit with people who couldn't care less about God.

If I choose friends from a secular environment, my personal values will gradually change, the song of my life will shift to a minor key, and I'll lose a deep sense of personal joy. I need to keep my motives pure in my professional dealings; I don't want to become a clone of someone I admire.

■ **Personal prayer**   *Lord, help me not to be brainwashed by materialistic society, but give me a deep sense of personal joy in knowing You.*

Ode to Joy *Second Movement—in Major*

■ **Theme**   *But his delight is in the law of the LORD, and on his law he meditates day and night (v. 2).*

■ **Development**   My mind is the key to my happiness, joy, and personal meaning. I am "transformed by the renewing of my mind" (Romans 12:2). I must delight in the magnificence of the Law. I must revel in the glory of biblical truth so that it shapes my thinking and changes my life.

I must meditate on it, fantasize about it, and be imaginative with it. I often struggle with low self-esteem and feel inadequate. But I know that when I'm weak, the Lord gives me strength. My source of strength and adequacy is the Lord, not I. As I learn to pray more honestly, I will apply the Word more personally. Inspired by the Word, my life will burst forth with song.

What made the ancient Jews distinct from the surrounding nations? The magnificence and glory of the Mosaic Law. What will make my life ring true today in the modern world? God's truth, the Holy Scripture! I must move beyond a cognitive perception of it and relate it to my total personality. I must delight in it!

■ **Personal prayer**   *Heavenly Father, I'm moved by the lyric poetry of Your Word. May my life become a motif of praise as I learn to love Your truth.*

Ode to Joy

Third Movement—Righteousness in Three Parts: Planted, Productive, Prosperous

■ **Theme**   *He is like a tree planted by streams of water, which yields its fruit in season and whose leaf does not wither. Whatever he does prospers (v. 3).*

■ **Development**   When water flows through a pipe, the pipe remains unchanged; but when it flows through a tree, the tree receives nourishment and is changed. For a tree is a living organism.

In this passage we learn three things about this tree: It is planted; it is productive; and it is prosperous. This beautiful, flourishing tree is a stunning simile for the righteous person. The chaff of verse 4 is an apt word picture for the person who throws his life away.

When I read this passage, I think of my friend, D. J. DePree, founder of the Herman Miller furniture firm. His love for the Word enlightens his life. He is the only man I know who is equally competent in biblical studies, in business, and in the arts. He has walked with the Lord for over seventy years. Perhaps his greatest contribution is his Sunday school teaching, which he's still doing in his nineties.

I want to be like D. J. DePree:
● Planted—firmly rooted and stable.
● Productive—marked by effectiveness.
● Prosperous—showcasing God's blessing.

■ **Personal prayer**   *Lord, make my life a well-watered tree rather than chaff that the wind blows away.*

Ode to Joy Recapitulation

■ **Theme**   For the LORD watches over the way of the righteous, but the way of the wicked will perish (v. 6).

■ **Development**   This psalm presupposes two destinies: the destiny of the righteous and the destiny of the unrighteous. The godly person, living on the basis of the law of the Lord ends up holy and happy. The ungodly person, living on the basis of a secular environment, ends up condemned and doomed. And the Lord deeply cares about both.

We will hear a lot more from this righteous person. He is the man of prayer who speaks most often in the Psalms.

Psalm of My Life

Like worthless chaff the wind blows away,
   Scorched by the bright desert sun through the day,
No root below, no fruit borne above,
   My life was thirsting for rains of His love.

While roaming far away on my own,
   I stood with sinners with hearts cold like stone,
I sat with scoffing cynics at play,
   Until my life changed direction one day.

While meditating day and night,
   His Word brought pleasure and highest delight,
It quenched my thirst and nurtured my soul,
   It satisfied me and made my life whole.

Then, like a lovely well-watered tree,
   Nourished by rivers that flow endlessly,
Weighed down by luscious fruit from His hand,
   My full life prospered for Him in the land.

Words and music by Don Wyrtzen.
© 1975 by Singspiration Music.

■ **Personal prayer**   Lord, remind me of life's destinies. Help me choose righteousness over unrighteousness.

King of Kings and Lord of Lords

■ **Theme** *"I have installed my King on Zion, my holy hill." I will proclaim the decree of the LORD: He said to me, "You are my Son; today I have become your Father" (vv. 6–7).*

■ **Development** "King of Kings and Lord of Lords . . . and He shall reign forever and ever." My ear keeps playing Handel's *Messiah* as I approach Psalm 2, and I am overwhelmed by its majesty and glory. My friend Larry McGill had a similar experience when he sang Handel's *Messiah* with four thousand others. During the "Hallelujah Chorus," he was so overcome with the beauty and intricacy of the music as well as the message that tears flowed down his cheeks and he was unable to sing.

God chose King David, the chief musician, to be the greatest king in Israel's history. But God also chose David's great Son to be King of kings. His kingdom will be established and His reign will be forever. Verses 6 and 7, the centerpiece of this psalm, speak of the coronation of the King and the pledge of adoption given to David's heir. As Christ, the Messiah, fulfills this, He becomes the basis for missionary ventures throughout the world.

As I enter the throne room of God through this psalm, the nations of the world come into focus and perspective. But in a more compelling manner, I am overwhelmed by the dignity, solemnity, and majesty of this King of all the universe. May I learn to give Him my full allegiance and loyalty today. May I learn to worship Him, adore Him, glorify Him, and enjoy Him! But may the awesomeness of His majesty not rob me of personal intimacy with Him.

■ **Personal prayer** *Thank You, Lord, that I can approach Your throne of grace with confidence and can receive Your grace and help as I need them.*

Elegy in the Night First Movement

■ **Theme**   *I lie down and sleep; I wake again, because the* LORD *sustains me. I will not fear the tens of thousands drawn up against me on every side (vv. 5–6).*

■ **Development**   Anxiety is deep and profound. Fear controls and dominates. Long nights become theatening. Children cause distress and personal grief. Big questions start to press upon me, and I start to feel that God has withdrawn from me. Sometimes in the middle of the night, I awake, disturbed over the changes and uncertainties in the music business; at other times I feel uncertain if I don't have my wife's approval of a major issue. How vulnerable and needy I am.

At times like this I'm learning to pour out my soul to my heavenly Father. I'm learning that spirituality begins with honesty. I'm learning to express myself emotionally to God. I don't want to have just a cognitive relationship to Him. I want to learn to share my total personality with Him: the mood swings, the ups and downs, the consonance as well as the dissonance of my life, the harmony as well as the disharmony. There is no resolution without tension. And this is true whether in symphonic form or in the structure of my own life.

King David experienced all these textures in his full but turbulent life. He even had to cope with a son who, though so full of promise and potential, out of rebellion was trying to kill him. Yet somehow David was able to roll all of this trauma over on the Lord. He entrusted his troubles to the Lord—overwhelming as they were—and turned over and got a good night's sleep. He learned that faith could flourish in the soil of fear and that anxiety could be transformed into tranquility.

■ **Personal prayer**   *Teach me, Lord, how to honestly lament. Then when You miraculously deliver me, I can really praise You.*

Elegy in the Night   Second Movement

■ **Theme**   *Answer me when I call to you, O my righteous God. Give me relief from my distress; be merciful to me and hear my prayer. Let the light of your face shine upon us, O LORD. You have filled my heart with greater joy than when their grain and new wine abound. I will lie down and sleep in peace, for you alone, O LORD, make me dwell in safety (vv. 1, 6–8).*

■ **Development**   King David had a melancholic cast to his psyche. Artistic, sensitive, and creative by nature, he also tended to be a perfectionist. But unlike many creative people, who often feel inadequate because they can't do everything perfectly, he didn't allow his perfectionism to add to his guilt. Instead he allowed the nightmares of his life to motivate him to express himself intuitively as well as intellectually. Recently, I wrote a theme which I called "Elegy In the Night." I was hurting so much when I wrote it, I expressed my emotions musically but not lyrically. I don't know if I'll ever be able to find the words for that melody.

When humiliated, exasperated, surrounded by lies, and filled with doom and gloom, David took all of this to God in prayer. He also wrote songs about all of it—songs that reveal the innermost working of his soul and lead other believers into profound, personal worship.

In distress, David learned to pray more meaningfully, to trust God more implicitly, and, as a result, to compose more freely and imaginatively. As David learned to bring his experiences into harmony with his artistic temperament, God led him to a deep wellspring of peace and contentment. The New Testament insight on this is 1 Peter 5:7: "Cast all your anxiety on him because he cares for you."

■ **Personal prayer**   *Just as the dominant seventh pulls toward a deeply satisfying resolution in the tonic chord, may the tensions of my personal life be resolved in You, O Lord, my Deliverer.*

Morning Song

■ **Theme**   *In the morning, O Lord, you hear my voice; in the morning I lay my requests before you and wait in expectation. . . . But let all who take refuge in you be glad; let them ever sing for joy. Spread your protection over them, that those who love your name may rejoice in you (vv. 3, 11).*

■ **Development**   Living in the complexity of the modern world puts me under a lot of stress. My mind continually mulls over unresolved personal conflicts, domestic hassles, competitiveness at work, and the pressure to perform. All of this rises to the surface very early in the morning. For me, many days are blue Mondays.

Often beneath creativity lies a fragile psyche. When I immaturely demand the respect and admiration of my colleagues, an honest, too-objective criticism deeply hurts me. I have experienced undue depression because I have placed too much value in myself instead of in the Lord.

Sensitive, artistic, and high-strung, King David also experienced severe depression early in the morning. Yet he didn't wallow in despair nor nurture his black moods. Instead he started his day with God by offering daily sacrifices at God's threshold. He met God there, spoke with Him, and committed all of his troubles to the Lord.

David approached God with great expectation. He didn't deny his many problems, but he broke free of his loneliness. He realized he was not alone in the world but part of a company of believers who could join him in praise. God responded by covering him, encircling him, and caring for him. And the sun came up, and the black clouds were blown away.

■ **Personal prayer**   *Dear Lord, I praise You and thank You that I am not alone in the universe. Because of the presence of Christ in my life, I can live today with deep peace and joy.*

Kyrie—"Lord Have Mercy!"

■ **Theme** O LORD, *do not rebuke me in your anger or discipline me in your wrath. Be merciful to me, LORD, for I am faint; O LORD, heal me, for my bones are in agony. My soul is in anguish. How long, O LORD, how long? . . . The LORD has heard my cry for mercy; the LORD accepts my prayer* (vv. 1–3, 9).

■ **Development** The painful, heart-wrenching discipline of the Lord caused David to cry out for mercy. But the heavenly Father, an example to all fathers, had to discipline His son. Hebrews 12:5–6, the classic New Testament commentary on discipline, says, "My son, do not make light of the Lord's discipline, and do not lose heart when he rebukes you, because the Lord disciplines those he loves, and punishes everyone he accepts as a son."

Deeply troubled and alarmed, David almost lost heart. His conscience was uneasy, and he was exhausted and depressed. Even his prayer had died away. He could only weep.

Unlike David, I sometimes deny such feelings, or at least compound my problems with rationalization. I find it hard to be vulnerable enough to face my predicament, to come to grips with my life, and to share my hurt and pain with brothers or sisters in Christ who are close to me.

David faced squarely the reality of his messed-up life. He cried out to his heavenly Father for mercy and discovered that his walk with the Lord must begin with reality. He moved from petition to praise and found answered prayer. Then he wrote this moving psalm for those of us who have a hard time admitting, much less expressing, the deep hurt and pain of our lives. When we do as David did, God goes to work in our lives, giving us authentic reasons to praise Him.

■ **Personal prayer** *Lord, make the tough things of my life a black velvet backdrop against which You showcase the diamond of Your grace.*

Song of the Slandered Saint
Suggested by Spurgeon

■ **Theme**   O LORD my God, I take refuge in you; save and deliver me
from all who pursue me, or they will tear me like a lion and rip me to pieces
with no one to rescue me. . . . O righteous God, who searches minds and
hearts, bring to an end the violence of the wicked and make the righteous
secure. . . . I will give thanks to the LORD because of his righteousness and
will sing praise to the name of the LORD Most High (vv. 1–2, 9, 17).

■ **Development**   Betrayed, hounded, and unjustly accused as a result
of Saul's jealousy and rivalry, David broke forth with the plea, "Lord it
isn't fair!" I can remember a producer who accused me of too much
self-confidence and arrogance when actually I had many self-doubts. I
felt I had been judged unfairly.

David didn't just complain. He moved on to honest prayer and
finally to praise. He came down on the side of God instead of on the
side of despair. Deep in his soul, David knew that the "Judge of all the
earth will do right" (Genesis 18:25). He found security in God's
righteousness (v. 9). He practiced in the ancient world what the
apostle Paul later taught: "Do not be anxious about anything, but in
everything, by prayer and petition, with thanksgiving, present your
requests to God. And the peace of God, which transcends all
understanding, will guard your hearts and your minds in Christ Jesus"
(Philippians 4:6–7).

27

■ **Personal prayer**   O Lord Most High, may I not wallow in despair
today, but may I completely trust Your righteousness and fairness.

How Majestic Is Your Name in All the Earth

■ **Theme**   O LORD, our Lord, how majestic is your name in all the earth! You have set your glory above the heavens. From the lips of children and infants you have ordained praise . . . (vv. 1–2).

■ **Development**   Psalm 8, a consummate example of what a hymn should be, celebrates the glory and the grace of God. Its major thesis, "How excellent is your name," shows that God's glory is more than a theological concept; it is also linked to an emotional component— joy. C. S. Lewis, in *Reflections on the Psalms*, reminds us that "to glorify God is to enjoy Him."

Majesty combined with intimacy characterizes our relationship with God. On one hand, we can relate to Isaiah, who witnessed the holiness of God: "Woe to me!" he cried. "I am ruined! For I am a man of unclean lips, and I live among a people of unclean lips, and my eyes have seen the King, the LORD Almighty" (Isaiah 6:5). On the other hand, God wants us to approach His throne with confidence so that we may receive mercy and find grace (Hebrews 4:16).

That the Sovereign of the Universe desires a close, personal relationship with me is almost beyond comprehension. He is my heavenly Father, and I am His child.

■ **Personal prayer**   Lord, may I move from sterile, inattentive worship to an intimate relationship with You. May I learn to enjoy Your presence!

The Majesty of Man

■ **Theme**   *You made him a little lower than the heavenly beings and crowned him with glory and honor (v. 5).*

■ **Development**   When compared to the vastness of the universe, I am infinitesimal. Yet even though I am dwarfed by the magnitude of God's creation, I have profound meaning and significance because I am made in God's image (Genesis 1:26–27). Because His glory is revealed not only in nature but also in me, I possess majesty. Even though I may not like certain things about myself (my height, my weight, my age), I need to remember that I am a reflection of the image of God.

Humanism has deified man and attempted to make him the "measure of all things." I sometimes overreact to this and think that I am nothing. But I am only a little lower than the angels in God's hierarchy. I am crowned with glory and honor. I reflect God's glory just as much as the starry heavens do.

Unlike the animals, which also reflect God's incredible imagination, I have a sense of my own existence and I can communicate. But even more significant, I can pray directly to the Lord of Hosts. Because I'm part of God's family, the universe isn't meaningless and empty; it is my home.

In size, I may be infinitesimal, but in worth I am infinitely valuable because I reflect God's glory.

■ **Personal prayer**   *Lord, help me to think soberly and objectively about myself. May I not get so wrapped up in my weaknesses that I forget that Your glory and majesty are revealed in me.*

Triumphal March

■ **Theme**   *I will praise you, O LORD, with all my heart; I will tell of all your wonders. I will be glad and rejoice in you; I will sing praise to your name, O Most High. My enemies turn back; they stumble and perish before you. For you have upheld my right and my cause; you have sat on your throne, judging righteously* (vv. 1–4).

■ **Development**   This psalm, a stirring lyric to a triumphal march, celebrates a glorious victory in battle. Although flushed with the new wine of success, David didn't use the occasion to boast; instead he broke forth in praise, celebrating God's actions and His Person.

David was happy about his victory, but he also saw the bigger picture. As God worked in David's personal life and daily experiences, he also works in history through great redemptive acts. David knew that the Lord would ultimately triumph and usher in a worldwide reign of justice.

This psalm assures me that I can live in confidence, knowing that God has a firm hold on history. Things are not careening out of control! He holds the momentous events of the future as well as the ordinary events of my daily life in His hands. I recall when I really tasted success for the first time. A top-notch London symphony played my scores for a recording session. I had to fight to retain my composure as I conducted the orchestra. That experience boosted my sagging self-image.

As I taste the sweet elixir of success from time to time, may I not become drunk with personal pride. May I be reminded that God is the One who has composed the score and has personally orchestrated my life.

■ **Personal prayer**   *O Lord, Most High, I praise You for being in control of history, including the details of my life today.*

A Mournful Lament

■ **Theme** *Why, O LORD, do you stand far off? Why do you hide yourself in times of trouble? In his pride the wicked does not seek him; in all his thoughts there is no room for God. His victims are crushed, they collapse, they fall under his strength. You hear, O LORD, the desire of the afflicted; you encourage them, and you listen to their cry, defending the fatherless and the oppressed, in order that man, who is of the earth, may terrify no more (vv. 1, 4, 10, 17–18).*

■ **Development** When I desperately need God, where is He? I feel the terror of being abandoned. God seems far away, as if He is in hiding. How must I react when I'm in this kind of corner?

First, *I can lament.* As David did, I can pour out my soul to God and let my raw emotions flow out to my Creator.

Second, *I can face reality.* In verses 2–11, the psalmist described a wicked tyrant who is boastful, greedy, blasphemous, and atheistic. Yet he appeared to be prosperous, stable, and happy. This harmony between evil and success seems grossly unfair! But the psalmist faced squarely the tyranny of this wicked ruler and confronted God with His responsibility.

Third, *I can pray.* The psalmist prayed for God to remember the helpless, to see their trouble and grief, and to break the power of this evil man. This response is an excellent model for me to follow when I face problems. God is much greater than any problem, so I need not fear that I'm asking too much.

Fourth, *I can praise.* David expressed faith that the Lord hears, listens, encourages, and defends. As he worshiped the Lord of eternity, his terror diminished.

I too must learn to lament, to face reality, to pray, and to praise. I must free myself of empty cliches and repetitive, time-worn phrases. When I'm honest with my heavenly Father, I will begin to praise Him with my whole being.

31

■ **Personal prayer** *Instead of internalizing anxiety and anger, may I learn to lament to You, O Lord, my King forever.*

Finding Refuge

■ **Theme**   In the LORD I take refuge. How then can you say to me: "Flee like a bird to your mountain." . . . The LORD is in his holy temple; the LORD is on his heavenly throne. He observes the sons of men; his eyes examine them. . . . For the LORD is righteous, he loves justice; upright men will see his face (vv. 1, 4, 7).

■ **Development**   David's friends advised him to flee to a mountain cave for safety. He was being pursued—perhaps by Saul or by Absalom. But instead of giving in to panic, he placed his faith in the Lord as his refuge.

I'm a peacemaker. I'll go to any lengths to avoid conflict, and as a result I experience much distress in interpersonal relationships. Not only I—people today flee pain and stress through the misuse of work (even the Lord's work), sex, drugs, alcohol.

The Lord is in residence, not in flight. He is always there as a refuge and shelter for His people. His city has foundations; His temple is secure. Instead of wallowing in fear, David exercised faith and found a complete and satisfying security in the righteousness and justice of God.

When I feel trapped, I must trust God and believe in the freedom that comes from His truth (John 8:31–32). Because of His just rule, the wicked will go down in judgment and ruin, but I will behold Him face to face. The child of God always has a happy ending to look forward to.

■ **Personal prayer**   O Lord, as I live in the middle of the rootlessness and complexity of modern life, may I find my refuge and shelter in You.

Double-Tonguing

■ **Theme** *Help, LORD, for the godly are no more; the faithful have vanished from among men. Everyone lies to his neighbor; their flattering lips speak with deception. . . . The words of the LORD are flawless, like silver refined in a furnace of clay, purified seven times (vv. 1–2, 6).*

■ **Development** In music, the effect of double-tonguing is delightful. In life, it is devastating and cruel. James tells us that "no man can tame the tongue. It is a restless evil, full of deadly poison" (3:8). The music industry is notorious for its hype and its manipulation of people. Since the art form of music is so subjective and since aesthetic taste is so personal, relationships between people are very important. Unfortunately, positive, healthy relationships can easily degenerate into negative, unhealthy "politics."

The untamed tongue of Psalm 12 lies, flatters, deceives, and boasts. Empty talk, smooth talk, and double talk take the place of satisfying communication, and deceit and manipulation rule. I'm amazed at how deceitful my own heart is. As I read Crabb's *The Marriage Builder,* I see how often I use manipulation for my own ends in our marriage. Often I don't even realize it! By nature I am unaware of my own deceitfulness.

In stark contrast stand the flawless and pure words of the Lord, a wealth of silver refined in God's crucible.

I want my life to be permeated with God's words, not marked by an uncontrollable tongue. If I'm controlled by the Spirit, I won't manipulate people. I will minister to them. And I will experience fullness in place of emptiness, wholeness in place of fragmentation, and fellowship in place of loneliness.

■ **Personal prayer** *Help me, Lord, to minister to people rather than manipulate them.*

Dirge of Depression to Descant of Delight

■ **Theme**   *How long, O LORD? Will you forget me forever? How long will you hide your face from me? How long must I wrestle with my thoughts and every day have sorrow in my heart? How long will my enemy triumph over me? . . . But I trust in your unfailing love; my heart rejoices in your salvation. I will sing to the LORD, for he has been good to me (vv. 1–2, 5–6).*

■ **Development**   How long? Repeated four times, this question indicates that David was distressed with God, with himself, and with his enemy. Much good can come from tension. For example, the music from stringed instruments is a result of tension. For me there is nothing quite like the glorious resolution of the rising tension produced in a Beethoven symphony.

David was restless. His mind was in turmoil, and he felt dejected. His enemy seemed to be ascending, threatening his kingship and causing personal humiliation. God seemed distant. The friendship between David and his Lord had clouded over.

But things are not always as they seem. Part of David's genius was his ability to transcend such difficulties. Without tension there can be no resolution. The tension in David's life came from his difficulties with the enemy and his devotion to God. This conflict led to personal maturity, which he attained because he maintained intimacy with God.

His dirge of depression became a descant of delight. Like an eagle, David soared to new heights. His life took flight when he pledged himself to God's unfailing love, when he chose to praise and thank God, when he realized that God had a higher purpose. "His ways are not our ways, and his thoughts are not our thoughts" (Isaiah 55:8–9). A spiritual metamorphosis took place when David wrapped himself in God's love instead of in his besetting circumstances. He reached the loftiest height of all when he started to sing of God's goodness.

34

■ **Personal prayer**   *Lord, I want to trust in Your unfailing love, rejoice in Your salvation, and sing of Your goodness today.*

Discord of Depravity

■ **Theme**   *The fool says in his heart, "There is no God." They are corrupt, their deeds are vile; there is no one who does good. . . . All have turned aside, they have together become corrupt; there is no one who does good, not even one (vv. 1, 3; also Romans 1).*

■ **Development**   The mood of this piece is arrogant. The theme is total depravity—leaving God out of life. The motifs are materialism, secularism, exploitation, and corruption. The essence of living in the flesh is to live as if God doesn't exist. I know of a prominent evangelist who arrogantly decided no longer to call God his Father.

What happens when we leave God out of our lives? Psalm 14 graphically and poetically answers the question.

Denying God begins a downward progression. Suppressing the truth leads to idolatry, self-destructiveness, and gross immorality. Error replaces truth, behavior becomes totally depraved, and people are oppressed.

Apostates think they are wise, but they are fools. When we choose the foolish route of denying God, we end up in rebellion against God, in alienation from others, and in personal corruption because we have killed off the source of all love and meaning for our lives.

This psalm is discordant and dissonant until the last verse, when David returns to the theme of salvation. The Lord will restore the fortunes of His people and make them glad. We don't need to be mannequins—lifeless and stripped of all love and meaning.

■ **Personal prayer**   *Heavenly Father, make me fully aware that it is Your existence alone that fills my life with love and gives it meaning.*

Rhapsody of Righteousness

■ **Theme** LORD, *who may dwell in your sanctuary? Who may live on your holy hill? He whose walk is blameless and who does what is righteous* (*vv. 1–2*).

■ **Development**   Psalm 15 portrays a man of integrity who stands in bold contrast to the depraved man of Psalm 14.

Because he is a man of worship and sacrifice, his sins are covered by the blood. Therefore he has nothing to hide and he deceives no one. He is marked by five sterling characteristics:

1. *Integrity* (v. 2)
2. *Truth* (v. 3)
3. *Allegiance* (v. 4)
4. *Honor* (vv. 4–5)
5. *Stability* (v. 5)

One of the most authentic people I know is my friend, Bill Rigg. He is filled with quiet, steadfast conviction. When he spoke at the funeral service for his fifteen-year-old son, Jim, I saw unbelievable pain, but I also saw the reality of Jesus Christ.

I want God to create these personality strengths in me. They will be God's gift to me when I place complete trust in Him.

■ **Personal prayer**   *Lord, I pray that You will produce transparency, authenticity, and integrity in my life.*

Song of Security   In Life and in Death

■ **Theme**   *Keep me safe, O God, for in you I take refuge. I said to the* LORD, *"You are my Lord; apart from you I have no good thing." . . . Therefore my heart is glad and my tongue rejoices; my body will also rest secure, because you will not abandon me to the grave, nor will you let your Holy One see decay. You have made known to me the path of life; you will fill me with joy in your presence, with eternal pleasures at your right hand* (vv. 1–2, 9–11).

■ **Development**   How can I be secure in life when I know I will someday die and when I feel at times that I am only an animal, a machine, or a combination of molecules? Death fascinates me, yet I was shocked by my mother's sudden death. Death seems to be an assault on humanity, impossible to grasp and comprehend.

Though very aware of my mortality and fallenness, I know that I bear God's image. As Augustine reminds me, my heart has a God-shaped vacuum that will never be satisfied apart from the Lord. In short, my security must be in Him. My profound need to be loved and accepted must be met by God.

How will He meet my deep longing for security?

1. He assigns me my portion and makes my lot secure (v. 5).
2. He gives me a delightful inheritance (v. 6).
3. He helps me face hard facts at night (v. 7).
4. His presence is at my right hand (v. 8).
5. He gives me a glad heart and a joyous tongue (v. 9).
6. He watches over my body—even after death (v. 9, also Acts 2:22–37).
7. He makes known to me the path of life, fills me with joy in His presence, and gives eternal pleasures at His right hand (v. 11).

Therefore, I will place my faith in these promises and let the Lord be my reference point. I will let Him integrate, authenticate, and inform my life. As He brings wholeness, my insecurities will be transformed into peace and rest.

■ **Personal prayer**   *Lord, I praise You because I am one of Your loved ones. Help me to count on the fact that because I am in You, no one could be more secure.*

My Everything

Lord, You are my everything, My highest joy and prize;
  You meet my needs in every way with grace that satisfies.
Lord, You are my everything, My food and drink today;
  You lead to brooks and meadows green and guide in a
    special way.

Since I am your own precious sheep,
  You watch me even when I sleep!
You have become my All-in-all, You always lift me when I
    fall.
  Lord, you are my everything, My highest joy and prize;
You meet my needs in every way with grace that satisfies.

Lord, You are my everything, my highest joy and prize;
  You meet my needs in every way with grace that satisfies.
Lord, You are my everything, my Shelter, Refuge, Friend;
  You are my great inheritance, Whose blessings never end.

You give me wisdom in the night, You fill me with
    complete delight;
  Your presence fills my heart with joy,
Which nothing ever can destroy.
  Lord, You are my everything, My highest joy and prize;
You meet my needs in every way with grace that satisfies.

Words and music by Don Wyrtzen. © 1981.

Prayer for Justice

■ **Theme**   *Hear, O LORD, my righteous plea; listen to my cry. Give ear to my prayer—it does not rise from deceitful lips. May my vindication come from you; may your eyes see what is right . . . I call on you, O God, for you will answer me; give ear to me and hear my prayer. Show the wonder of your great love, you who save by your right hand those who take refuge in you from their foes. Keep me as the apple of your eye; hide me in the shadow of your wings (vv. 1–2, 6–8).*

■ **Development**   I want to pray with the same warmth, intimacy, and immediacy with which King David prayed. He unveiled his inner self, crying out to God and pleading for refuge. The old gospel song says it so well:

> *Under His wings I am safely abiding,*
> *Tho' the night deepens and tempests are wild;*
> *Still I can trust Him, I know He will keep me,*
> *He has redeemed me and I am His child.*
>
> *Under His wings, under His wings,*
> *Who from His love can sever?*
> *Under His wings my soul shall abide,*
> *Safely abide forever.*
>
> *Under His wings, O what precious enjoyment!*
> *There will I hide till life's trials are o'er;*
> *Sheltered, protected, no evil can harm me,*
> *Resting in Jesus I'm safe evermore.*

Words by William O. Cushing. Music by Ira D. Sankey.

Once again, David confronted his problem head-on and talked honestly to God about his callous, arrogant, and murderous enemies who were frustrating him on every side.

He ends with an exquisitely beautiful verse: "And I—in righteousness I will see your face; when I awake, I will be satisfied with seeing your likeness" (v. 15).

■ **Personal prayer**   *Help me, Lord, to give up my quest to find satisfaction in anyone but You. Make me intensely aware that only You can totally satisfy.*

Doxology

■ **Theme**   *I love you, O Lord, my strength. The Lord is my rock, my fortress and my deliverer; my God is my rock, in whom I take refuge. He is my shield and the horn of my salvation, my stronghold. I call to the Lord, who is worthy of praise, and I am saved from my enemies (vv. 1–3).*

■ **Development**   The psalms contain more lament than praise. Uninhibited praise is usually preceded by authentic lament. Perhaps today our praise and worship are shallow and superficial because we have not learned to lament. Unlike David, we have little or no concept of how profound our personal need is.

Miraculously delivered from his enemies and from Saul (see 2 Samuel 8, 22), David broke forth in this moving song with intense feeling. Because of his artistic discipline, he was able to hone this experience into a carefully crafted psalm of beautiful structure and symmetry:

Doxology (vv. 1–3)
Metaphors of deliverance (vv. 4–6)
Theophany (vv. 7–15)
Personal application (vv. 16–45)
Doxology (vv. 46–50)

This song deals with David's dramatic deliverance from Saul and from his enemies, but it also deals with the quintessential Deliverer to come, the Messiah. In Romans 15:9, Paul applies Psalm 18:49 directly to Christ, our Messiah.

Psalm 18 comforts and encourages me. Like David, I can be set free—physically and emotionally. The liberation of my personality will occur as I place more and more trust in Christ, my Deliverer, rather than in human effort unempowered by God.

■ **Personal prayer**   *I praise You, Yahweh, for being my Rock, my Savior, and my Deliverer. May You be exalted in my life today, and may I sing praises to Your Name.*

Glorious Proclamation

■ **Theme**   *The heavens declare the glory of God; the skies proclaim the work of his hands. . . . The law of the LORD is perfect, reviving the soul. The statutes of the LORD are trustworthy, making wise the simple. . . . May the words of my mouth and the meditation of my heart be pleasing in your sight, O LORD, my Rock and my Redeemer (vv. 1, 7, 14).*

■ **Development**   No nobler, more majestic psalm has ever been written about God's revelation than Psalm 19. It tells us how God took the initiative to reveal Himself to us—a concept beyond my comprehension. He did not leave us in darkness; He communicated through the sky and the Scripture.

Creation reveals God's invisible qualities. His power and divine nature can be seen clearly in what He has made (Romans 1). He holds each of us accountable for our response to this revelation. If we respond favorably, He sends more revelation (Acts 10). If we suppress this truth, we have no excuse!

Our heavenly Father, a creative virtuoso, dazzles us with His power and might. Yet because He wants to be close to us, He bridged the distance between us with His Word, making possible an intimate relationship. His Word is perfect, restorative, and trustworthy (v. 7). It brings wisdom, joy, radiance, and light (vv. 7–8). His ordinances are pure, eternal, sure, and righteous (v. 9). They are more precious than gold and sweeter than honey (v. 10). Living on the basis of the Law has its own great reward (v. 11).

The compelling message of the contemporary lyric "But Greater Still" convinces me that the value of God's Word defies description. Its worth to me is intensely personal. It nourishes my soul and its truth sets me free.

■ **Personal prayer**   *O Lord, my Rock and my Redeemer, may the words of my mouth and the meditation of my heart be pleasing in Your sight.*

But Greater Still

God speaks to me in creation and my heart sings His praise,
    He paints His revelation in a thousand different ways;
His handiwork reveals His glory in its intricate design,
    His infinite creativity is a miracle divine.

The skies tell me of His glory—what a dazzling display!
    They give a silent witness of His presence every day;
The skies tell me a moving story by the interplay of light,
    Their message reaches everywhere on a starry summer
        night.

But greater still is His perfect Word so rich with wealth
        untold,
    It's sweeter than a honeycomb, worth more to me than
        gold,
So may my life always please my Lord in every simple way,
    And may I praise His precious name in thoughts and
        words today.

Words and music by Don Wyrtzen.
© 1981 by Singspiration Music.

Invocation   *Prayer Before Battle*

■ **Theme**   *May the LORD answer you when you are in distress; may the name of the God of Jacob protect you. . . . May he give you the desire of your heart and make all your plans succeed. We will shout for joy when you are victorious and will lift up our banners in the name of our God. May the LORD grant all your requests. . . . Some trust in chariots and some in horses, but we trust in the name of the LORD our God* (vv. 1, 4–5, 7).

■ **Development**   Knowing he faced a life-or-death struggle, David prepared for battle by offering prayers and sacrifices. The congregation prayed for him, and David voiced his certainty of God's answer (vv. 6–8).

The focus of David's cry for help was the Name of the Lord, which he knew had power. Any hope for conquest, and all protection, support, and help, come only from that Name. The most formidable weapons of the ancient world were impotent against the Name of the Lord.

I too face confrontation—in the big hassles of life and the small hassles of daily living. I don't want to rely on modern insights or popular solutions. They are sterile and useless. Only the Name of the Lord can give me relief and support. I don't want it to be the last place I go for help. I don't have the resources to make it on my own. I'm a dependent person. When I am weak, then I am strong. As Sandi Patti sings so gloriously, "There is power in the Name of the Lord."

43

■ **Personal prayer**   *Lord, keep me from placing my trust in the might of men; remind me that Your Name is the only reliable source of strength.*

Victory March

■ **Theme**   O LORD, *the king rejoices in your strength. How great is his joy in the victories you give! You have granted him the desire of his heart and have not withheld the request of his lips. . . . For the king trusts in the LORD; through the unfailing love of the Most High he will not be shaken. . . . Be exalted, O LORD, in your strength; we will sing and praise your might (vv. 1–2, 7, 13).*

■ **Development**   After pouring out my soul in lament and prayer, I need to wait patiently for the Lord to answer. As He answered David, He will also answer me. In Psalm 21, a glorious royal hymn, David celebrated the Lord's answer to his petition in Psalm 20. The Lord brought victory rather than defeat, gave life instead of death, and blessed him by granting him his heart's desire.

Even under pressure, David modeled stability and security. I too need to grasp that my safety, steadiness, and confidence are based on God's loyal love (Romans 8:35–39). David's faith, centered squarely on the rock-solid, permanent, eternal love of the Lord, stabilized and strengthened him.

David didn't win the battle with his own strength, expertise, or military genius. But that didn't diminish his exhilaration. To celebrate God's victory, David wrote glorious music. Like David, I too will praise when I lift up my life to the Lord, and He will bring music back into my life.

■ **Personal prayer**   *Lord, may I learn to "throw a party" to celebrate Your glory, majesty, and unfailing love.*

Song of the Suffering Servant
First Movement—The Eloquence of Darkness: Part I

■ **Theme**   My God, my God, why have you forsaken me? Why are you
so far from saving me, so far from the words of my groaning (v. 1)?

■ **Development**   When I face an obstacle that I can't go over, under,
or around, I need to acknowledge my pain and helplessness. Denial
and fantasy only compound my problem with dishonesty. I need to
look squarely at my situation and admit my inability to resolve it.

The parallels between this psalm and Christ's crucifixion are
astounding. This exquisite lyric poetry portrays deep personal shame
and intense suffering. Reading it makes me feel vicariously what Christ
went through to win my redemption on the darkest day in history.
Since Christ lived the experiences described here and quotes it in the
New Testament, I believe this lament applies to Him.

Throbbing with urgency and immediacy, the first movement of
this psalm (vv. 1–21) eloquently portrays darkness in several related
themes:

First, *David cried out to God* (vv. 1–2). "My God, my God, why
have you forsaken me?" According to gospel accounts, Christ said
these exact words at the height of His agony on the cross (Matthew
27:46; Mark 15:34).

Second, *David remembered history* (vv. 3–5). He praised the Lord
and affirmed His holiness by citing the experiences of his fathers who
trusted God through adversity and were delivered.

Third, *David described Christ's experience of shame* (vv. 6–8).
Scorned and despised, He was mocked by a blood-thirsty crowd that
was cynical and cruel.

Fourth, *David reflected on God's care* (vv. 9–11). The Hebrew
word for trust means "to lie prone—completely helpless." David
trusted God from the beginning—even from birth. He pleaded for
God to be close because there was no one else to help.

■ **Personal prayer**   Help me, Father, to identify my suffering and need
with the Savior. Help me, by faith, to become aware that when I participate
in His sufferings, I also share in His glory.

Song of the Suffering Servant
First Movement—The Eloquence of Darkness: Part 2

■ **Theme**   *Many bulls surround me; strong bulls of Bashan encircle me. Roaring lions tearing their prey open their mouths wide against me (vv. 12– 13).*

■ **Development**   Continuing the theme of suffering, David portrayed a fifth scene of darkness: Christ's intense suffering on the cross. He pictured the mocking crowd as a menagerie of wild animals. They were like ravenous wolves closing in on their prey. Murder, sin, and hate filled their wild eyes.

Verses 16–18 describe in uncanny detail the Roman execution— piercing the hands and feet, counting the bones, people staring and gloating, soldiers dividing the garments and casting lots for them.

Sixth, David pleads for immediate help (vv. 19–21). He prays intensely for God to come close and deliver him from these wild, murderous, unclean predators.

What a model for me to follow when I am called to suffer. Romans 8:17–18 says it all, "Now if we are children, then we are heirs—heirs of God and co-heirs with Christ, if indeed we share in his sufferings in order that we may also share in his glory. I consider that our present sufferings are not worth comparing with the glory that will be revealed in us."

It is easy to live under the mistaken notion that if I do the will of God, my life will be a paragon of perfection, free from anxiety and trauma. But I need to recognize that I may suffer *because* I am doing the will of God. This happened to David, and it happened to Christ in Gethsemane and on the Cross.

My goal in life should be holiness, not happiness. But grabbing hold of this concept in our affluent society is difficult at best. The fullest, most richly textured life is the holy life. Only the refiner's fire produces pure gold. The holy life yields the richest, most enduring rewards.

46

■ **Personal prayer**   *Lord, though I live in a pagan, materialistic culture, may I commit my life to the higher value of holiness over happiness. Let me experience a deep wellspring of joy, no matter what happens.*

Song of the Suffering Servant
Second Movement—The Joyful Feast

■ **Theme**   *I will declare your name to my brothers; in the congregation I will praise you (v. 22).*

■ **Development**   After the powerful lament of verses 1–21, the Lord miraculously hears and delivers. Heart-wrenching, soul-searching lament is the basis for the true praise of God.

In the Old Testament economy, this praise and worship was accomplished through prayer, sacrifice, a commemorative feast, and vows of service to God (Leviticus 7:16). Joy was not to be kept private. Servants, poor people, and especially Levites were to be invited to the feast (Deuteronomy 12:17–19). The whole congregation was to celebrate what God had done for them.

David threw a party in the Lord's honor. He got carried away with expressions of thanksgiving and praise (vv. 27–31). He sang a stirring canticle of blessing, and his worship found its ultimate focus in God's eternal kingdom—where the poor will be fed, where nations will bow down before the Lord, and where His righteousness will be proclaimed to people yet unborn.

■ **Personal prayer**   *Lord, may I move today from lament to praise, from darkness to light, and from ordinary business to celestial celebration.*

Satisfaction

■ **Theme**   The LORD *is my shepherd, I shall not be in want (v. 1).*

■ **Development**   Perhaps the most creative and artistic person in the Bible, David was a virtuoso harpist, a military genius, a capable administrator, and a cultural innovator. He led a sweeping renaissance of Jewish culture. Perhaps his most enduring literary achievement was to write and/or compile this psalm, the most-loved and well-known of all. It comforts, satisfies, and meets the deepest longings of the human heart.

It starts straightforwardly with the simple words, "The LORD is my shepherd." "Lord" is emphatic here. It is the *Lord* who makes our faith distinctive. No other person fits: not Mohammed, not Buddha, not Gandhi. "My" personalizes the relationship, revealing intimacy and closeness.

"Shepherd" is the most comprehensive and intimate metaphor in the Psalms. The shepherd lives with his flock and is everything to it— guide, physician, and protector.

The last phrase, "I shall not be in want," means that God will fulfill my deepest personal needs and that I will find meaning and true identity in Him. In short, I don't need God plus anything or anyone. All my emotional and psychological longings for significance and security will find fulfillment in the Lord.

48

■ **Personal prayer**   *Thank You, Lord, that You meet all my needs and that you are the key to my wholeness and fulfillment.*

Rest

■ **Theme**   *He makes me lie down in green pastures, he leads me beside quiet waters, he restores my soul (v. 2).*

■ **Development**   Just as the ark of the covenant went ahead of Israel to find places of rest, so the Lord guides us to refreshment and relaxation. He provides green pastures and quiet waters. He doesn't want us to work nonstop.

I need to be intellectually "driven" in my work. I used to work on a fairly regular basis with the London Symphony musicians doing recording projects. On many occasions I would fly all night to London, write music the first day, record the following day, write all that night, and record the next day. By that time, I was more like a zombie than an arranger-composer, badly in need of rest.

A shepherd thinks in terms of the needs of his flock just as a father thinks in terms of the needs of his family. God has taken on a flock, a family. He is involved with us, bound up with us, and deeply concerned about meeting our innermost personal needs. Modern psychology has pointed out how essential it is for normal emotional development that we have an adequate father. Ultimately, only our heavenly Father is adequate.

I want the Lord to balance my life today, to define my lifestyle and my priorities, to deliver me from neurotic activity and workaholism, and to keep me from trying to meet my own needs through work and achievement instead of through Him.

49

■ **Personal prayer**   *Lord, help me to turn over to You the pressure and stress that I feel. Teach me to relax in Your Spirit.*

Guidance

■ **Theme**   *He guides me in the paths of righteousness for his name's sake (v. 3).*

■ **Development**   The Lord not only renews my life physically and emotionally, but He also guides me in paths of righteousness. I need to trust the authority of Scripture as my rule of faith and behavior. I need to commit myself to doing God's will, whatever it is. And I need to walk closely with God so I know Him intimately. If I trust Him and nurture and cultivate intimacy with Him, He makes my paths smooth and straight (Proverbs 3:5–6).

Living righteously and blamelessly has its own reward. If we place God's authority and our commitment to and intimacy with Him in proper perspective, He leads us by the hand through life and manages our affairs. What a comfort to know that the Lord is right in front of me, removing obstacles!

Why does the Lord do this for me? "For his name's sake." The Lord takes His Name very seriously. We are to uphold His holy Name. When we do, God makes us new. In Ezekiel 36:22, 26 the Lord says, "It is not for your sake, O house of Israel, that I am going to do these things, but for the sake of my holy name. . . . I will give you a new heart and put a new spirit in you; I will remove from you your heart of stone and give you a heart of flesh."

■ **Personal prayer**   *Sovereign Lord, I lift up Your holy Name today. Renew my spirit and give me a new heart.*

February

PSALMS 23–30

*Like David and my dad, I want
the kind of personal integrity and
uprightness that I can depend on
for protection.*

Comfort

■ **Theme**   *Even though I walk through the valley of the shadow of death, I will fear no evil, for you are with me; your rod and your staff, they comfort me (v. 4).*

■ **Development**   The greatest insult to humanity is the specter of death. At certain moments the fear of it grips and mystifies us. When it does, we need to come to the soothing, timeless truth of Psalm 23:4.

I will never forget the night my mom died. We had just experienced a joyous reunion with my parents over the Christmas holidays. Because of a business trip, I had left my family in northern Michigan for a skiing vacation and returned home. When I arrived, I heard the phone ringing. My close friend Bob Steed told me my mom had gone to be with the Lord. I was shocked! That long night became a melange of crying, reminiscing, praying, and fitful sleeping. But I didn't feel alone; I felt the Lord walking with me through my grief.

The valley of the shadow is a dark ravine. Yet, like the green pastures (v. 3), it too is a right path. People today fear death, so they don't talk about it very often. But the Bible discusses it in very comforting terms as part of the nature of reality.

In verse 4, the lyric switches from "he" (vv. 2–3) to "you," a much more personal pronoun. I am to fear no evil for "you are with me." Instead of walking ahead of me, the Lord now walks alongside me, as an escort. He is not distant and impersonal. He is my companion—even in death. His presence overcomes the worst thing that remains: fear.

Armed as He walks beside us, our Shepherd and Companion protects us with His rod and staff. The rod—a cudgel or short, heavy club—symbolized defense. The staff, which the shepherd used to help him walk or to round up the flock, symbolized control. The Lord defends us even in death and gives us His security.

■ **Personal prayer**   *Lord, I thank You that You walk beside me as my Friend and Companion. I thank You that You are at my side even at the moment of death.*

Interlude

■ **Theme**   *Where, O death, is your victory? Where, O death, is your sting? The sting of death is sin, and the power of sin is the law. But thanks be to God! He gives us the victory through our Lord Jesus Christ (vv. 55–57).*

■ **Development**   The apostle Paul gave us the New Testament picture of death in 1 Corinthians 15:55–57 and in 2 Corinthians 5:7–9. The more we see death from the biblical perspective, the more our fear will melt away. The events described in Psalm 23:4 happen instantaneously. In the light of eternity, death is just a walk through the gates of glory to a forever of eternal joy.

Originally written for Dr. W.A. Criswell, pastor of First Baptist Church in Dallas, Texas, the song, "Finally Home," has brought peace and comfort to hundreds of people. Dr. Criswell's daughter, Anne, first sang the chorus coupled with a chorus of "The Glory Song" because we didn't have any verses yet. John W. Peterson, one of my mentors and a noted songwriter, encouraged me to write verses that would describe a human's fear of death and provide the background for this glorious chorus. I wrote the lyrics and music; the Lord gave the song His special touch.

■ *Personal prayer*   *Lord, I thank You and praise You that someday I will wake up in glory and discover that I've finally arrived Home.*

Finally Home

When alarmed by the fury of the restless sea,
   Towering waves before you roll;
At the end of doubt and peril is eternity,
   Though fear and conflict seize your soul:

When surrounded by the blackness of the darkest night,
   O how lonely death can be;
At the end of this long tunnel is a shining light,
   For death is swallowed up in victory!

But just think of stepping on shore and finding it heaven!
   Of touching a hand and finding it God's!
Of breathing new air and finding it celestial!
   Of waking up in glory and finding it home!

Words by L. E. Singer and Don Wyrtzen. Music by Don Wyrtzen.
Copyright © 1971 by Singspiration Music.

Celebration

■ **Theme**   *You prepare a table before me in the presence of my enemies. You anoint my head with oil; my cup overflows (v. 5).*

■ **Development**   As great art so frequently does, verse 5 throws us a curve. What do a table, oil, and a cup have to do with sheep? The answer is—nothing. The songwriter simply changed his imagery from that of a shepherd to one of even greater intimacy and closeness: the friend.

The threat of verse 4 becomes the triumph of verse 5. We transcend the depths of the valley to the heights of a victory celebration. The Lord not only leads through the dark valley, but He provides a feast for us as well. Our enemies are present, but they are captives.

I felt a genuine sense of injustice when another musician was chosen to do a project that had been promised to me. When I realized my vulnerability to jealousy, I committed the entire matter to the Lord in prayer. Later I became involved in two other projects, which were so well received that my music ministry was given an enormous boost.

The Lord, our Host, provides abundantly. He sets a beautiful table, anoints us with costly perfume, and fills our cups to the brim. In other words, He more than meets our needs.

How limited is our faith! The Lord, our Friend and Host, wants to supply us *abundantly.* Believers, of all people, should not be running scared. As the old Sunday school song says, "My cup is full and running over."

■ **Personal prayer**   *Lord, thank You for bringing truth and beauty into my life. Thank You that I don't have to live in poverty but can be satiated by Your glorious riches.*

Prosperity

■ **Theme** *Surely goodness and love will follow me all the days of my life, and I will dwell in the house of the LORD forever (v. 6).*

■ **Development** The modern perspective on success and prosperity is often very narrow, defined only in materialistic terms. But David defined true prosperity in Psalm 23:6. Rather than being pursued by enemies, the believer is pursued by the Lord's prosperity. The Lord's goodness and love define that prosperity. The most richly textured Hebrew word for love, *hesed*, is used here. It's also used to describe Hosea's miraculous love for his prostitute wife and to describe God's love for Israel even when she worshiped idols. Similar to *agape,* the Greek word for love used in the New Testament, *hesed* describes God's loyal, unfailing, unconditional love. This love is hard for us to comprehend because human love so frequently has mixed motives.

Even though He knows everything there is to know about us (Psalm 139), God loves us. Even though we stand naked before Him, He fully accepts us. The Lord's love for us is also the core of the gospel message. That I can be fully exposed and yet totally accepted is the thrill of the gospel.

When we learn to accept this love, we will be able to love ourselves, which is the foundation for self-worth. Then we'll also be free to love other people, which is the basis for friendships, marriage, and a fulfilled family life. In the arms of our heavenly Father, we are vulnerable—yet fully safe.

I am beginning to be aware of God's love for me. I see wonder in ordinary things and I accept them as gifts of God's grace. God's love is so vast, it is impossible for me to fully comprehend.

What a promise the last phrase is: "I will dwell in the house of the LORD forever!" Death is not a threat to me. I don't go into oblivion, buried beneath the sod. I have no cause for despair. "I will dwell in the house of the LORD forever!" I wonder what resplendent music the chief musician wrote for that!

■ **Personal prayer** *I praise You, Lord, that I don't have to live in fear— even of death—because You have promised I can dwell in Your house forever.*

The King of Glory Processional

First Movement—The Lord's Creativity

■ **Theme**   *The earth is the LORD's, and everything in it, the world, and all who live in it; for he founded it upon the seas and established it upon the waters (vv. 1–2).*

■ **Development**   The creative power of God inspires awe. I'm filled with reverent wonder as I contemplate it. To think that He spoke and worlds came into being! In contrast to God, I work with raw materials that He created. My creativity is derived from His. I put the wrapping paper and ribbon on His packages.

Several years ago, Karen and I traveled to Brazil. Along with lecturing and ministering to missionaries, we scheduled some sightseeing. I will never forget the awesome Iguacu Falls. There in the majestic grandeur of cascading water, I saw the omnipotence of the almighty God. I shouted spontaneously, "How great Thou art!"

Because the Lord made the earth and everything on it, He owns it. He founded the earth (Genesis 1) and established it upon the waters. The heathen nations feared the restless, perilous, foaming seas, But even the violent waters belong to God and reflect the variety and depth of His creative imagination.

The Lord didn't create the earth and then abandon it. He is intimately involved with sustaining it. He watches over what belongs to Him. My Lord doesn't like loose ends! He not only sustains His creation; He watches over me too and allows me to reflect His creativity!

■ **Personal prayer**   *I praise You, Lord, for Your incredible imagination and creativity. I thank You that I can, in a very small way, imitate it.*

The King of Glory Processional

Second Movement—The Lord's Holiness

■ **Theme**   *Who may ascend the hill of the LORD? Who may stand in his holy place? He who has clean hands and a pure heart, who does not lift up his soul to an idol or swear by what is false. He will receive blessing from the LORD and vindication from God his Savior (vv. 3–5).*

■ **Development**   David speaks eloquently about God's holiness and our need for purity which, in today's language, we would call integrity. He concludes that only a person marked by integrity can stand before God's absolute holiness.

Isaiah understood that purity is the prerequisite for knowing God. When exposed to the stunning radiance of God, he said, "I am a man of unclean lips, and I live among a people of unclean lips, and my eyes have seen the King, the LORD Almighty" (Isaiah 6:5). Jesus Himself taught that only the pure in heart would see God (Matthew 5:8). And the apostle Paul drove home the same point when he said, "I want you to be wise about what is good, and innocent about what is evil" (Romans 16:19). We cannot begin to know the holiness of God until we cultivate purity in our personal lives.

The quest for purity and integrity challenges believers today. Modern technology provides easy and private access to seductive entertainment. Nuances of temptation common today were unknown in the ancient world. Yet even so, David's words remain true today. Integrity is the prerequisite for knowing God and being able to stand before His holiness.

■ **Personal prayer**   *Heavenly Father, my desire is to have clean hands and a pure heart today. By Your Spirit, change me into a person of integrity and purity.*

The King of Glory Processional

Third Movement—The Lord's Might

■ **Theme**   *Lift up your heads, O you gates; lift them up, you ancient doors, that the king of glory may come in. Who is he, this King of glory? The LORD Almighty—he is the King of glory (vv. 9–10).*

■ **Development**   The dramatic scene at the end of Psalm 24 may have been enacted as the processional arrived at the city gates. Begun in Egypt, this stately march ascended to Zion and broke forth into a dazzling festival of praise.

There have been a number of times in my life when a musical experience has also become a spiritual experience. During the World's Fair in New York, I directed a mass choir of a thousand Christian women. As I fought to keep my composure, my heart overflowed with praises for God.

As the ancient doors swung open, the spotlight focused on the King of glory riding through the gates. He was a King of towering stature, strong and mighty in battle, the Warrior of Warriors! No doubt the marching band started to sing and play the song of Miriam and Moses: "The LORD is a warrior; the LORD is his name" (Exodus 15:3).

What pageantry and excitement they had in their worship! Not lifeless, boring, predictable rituals. They exulted praise to the King of glory. They celebrated His creativity (24:1–2), His holiness (24:3–6), and His might (24:7–10). What a battle cry for us today as we look forward to seeing the King of glory face-to-face!

■ **Personal prayer**   *Lord, teach me to worship You with genuine fervor and vitality. May I be excited by Your presence rather than embalmed by lifeless liturgy.*

A Personal Hymn for the Congregation First Motif—Protection

■ **Theme**   *To you, O LORD, I lift up my soul; in you I trust, O my God. Do not let me be put to shame, nor let my enemies triumph over me. . . . Guard my life and rescue me; let me not be put to shame, for I take refuge in you. May integrity and uprightness protect me, because my hope is in you (vv. 1–2, 20–21).*

■ **Development**   Although written as a hymn for the whole congregation, Psalm 25 is very personal. And, like many of David's artistic creations, it is highly structured. Crafted around the Hebrew alphabet, it is difficult to outline. But David seems to have focused on four basic motifs: protection from his enemies, guidance for his life, forgiveness from sin, and hope for deliverance.

Knowing that only integrity and uprightness could protect him from his enemies, David asked for forgiveness from past sins. And knowing that only those whose hope is in the Lord could walk in integrity, he asked for guidance and placed his hope in God.

Integrity is a word that beautifully encompasses honor, sincerity, and wholeness. My dad, who lives consistently on the basis of his convictions, personifies integrity. He advances his evangelism on biblical principles and is not easily distracted from reaching his goals. By daily example, he teaches me that if my hope is truly in the Lord, not in secular thinking and methods, I will be able to cultivate personal integrity and be protected. Like David and my dad, I want the kind of personal integrity and uprightness that I can depend on for protection.

60

■ **Personal prayer**   *Lord, may I be preoccupied with You rather than with the enemies who surround me. Mark my life with integrity and uprightness.*

A Personal Hymn for the
Congregation   Second Motif—Guidance

■ **Theme**   *Show me your ways, O LORD, teach me your paths; guide me in your truth and teach me, for you are God my Savior, and my hope is in you all day long. . . . Good and upright is the LORD; therefore he instructs sinners in his ways. He guides the humble in what is right and teaches them his way (vv. 4–5, 8–9).*

■ **Development**   Pagans had an irrational approach to guidance. They trusted magical pointers and omens. David, in stark contrast, had an intimate walk with his Lord. When David cried out to God, he received guidance and direction. In this psalm, David lists four characteristics necessary for knowing God's will: discernment, persistence, obedience, and reverence.

Discernment is the ability to distinguish good from evil (Hebrews 5:14). Because God's will is always true and good, those who have poor discernment—who cannot distinguish between good and evil, right and wrong—cannot know God's will.

But knowing right from wrong doesn't come naturally; it takes a lifetime of learning. Without a persistent search for truth, we will never know God's will. David demonstrated persistence by keeping his eyes "ever on the LORD" (v. 15). His hope was in the Lord "all day long" (v. 5).

Obedience doesn't come naturally either, but it is another prerequisite for knowing God's will. David modeled obedience by being good, upright, humble, and teachable (vv. 8–9). To obey God's will is to obey His Word. As the prophet told King Saul, "To obey is better than sacrifice, and to heed is better than the fat of rams" (1 Samuel 15:22). Therefore, persistence in studying Scripture is essential.

Because "the LORD confides in those who fear him" (v. 14), those who want to know God's will need to learn reverence. David viewed the Lord with awe and respect, and the Lord became his friend. God promises guidance to those who walk intimately with Him.

■ **Personal prayer**   *Lord, may I walk closely and intimately with You so that I will experience Your guidance and direction in my life.*

A Personal Hymn for the
Congregation   Third Motif—Forgiveness

■ **Theme**   *Remember not the sins of my youth and my rebellious ways;*
according to your love remember me, for you are good, O LORD. Good and
upright is the LORD; therefore he instructs sinners in his ways. . . . Turn to
me and be gracious to me, for I am lonely and afflicted. The troubles of my
heart have multiplied; free me from my anguish. Look upon my affliction
and my distress and take away all my sins (vv. 7–8, 16–18).

■ **Development**   David readily admitted his sins; he didn't hide
behind rationalization. His honestly reflected a clear-cut, ethical value
system that today's world seriously lacks. It is rare to hear someone say,
"I lied!" We often hide behind highfalutin' phrases and euphemisms;
Charles Van Doren vividly illustrates this. Instead of saying, "I lied,"
he said, "I've been involved in an incredible delusion." This was his
statement after he was found to be cheating in television quiz scandals.

Guilt had been eating away at David, and his troubles had
multiplied. He knew that only the Lord could relieve him of his
affliction and so he cried out for the Lord to "take away all my sins"
(v. 18). Confession is still the only way out of anxiety caused by sin
and guilt. A clear conscience leads to good health. A solid theology is
the best psychology.

As New Testament Christians, we need never surrender to the
erosion of unresolved guilt. We can claim the apostle John's promise:
"If we confess our sins, he is faithful and just and will forgive us our
sins and purify us from all unrighteousness" (1 John 1:9).

■ **Personal prayer**   *To You, O Lord, I lift up my soul. Deliver me from*
trouble today and take away all my sins.

A Personal Hymn for the Congregation Fourth Motif—Hope

■ **Theme**   To you, O LORD, I lift up my soul; in you I trust, O my God (vv. 1–2).

■ **Development**   Instead of feeling anxious because of the stress of his life, David had a sense of well-being and security. Because his confidence was in the Lord, he had no fear. He did not base his hope on his own righteousness; he based it on the loyal love (*hesed*) of the Lord. He didn't trust sacred formulas and structures; he trusted the faithfulness of God. David was fully aware of the graciousness and dependability of his Lord. For him to place his confidence in anything or anyone else would be groundless.

Only the Lord can provide the deep inner sense of security, which, I believe, we all long to feel. God doesn't promise insulation from all harm. Nor does He guarantee that ungodly people will not prosper or succeed. But He does promise to take us through the storms of life if we place our trust in Him, not ourselves. We must risk the life of faith to become truly secure.

David was high-strung, sensitive, and fragile, yet he exhibited unusual strength and authority. What really informed his leadership was bedrock security that came from his trust in the Lord.

■ **Personal prayer**   Lord, I thank You that You are fully aware of all my insecurities. I turn them all over to You today, because I choose to place my complete trust in You.

Devotional Leitmotifs

First Leitmotif—Personal Integrity

■ **Theme**   *Vindicate me, O LORD, for I have led a blameless life; I have trusted in the LORD without wavering. Test me, O LORD, and try me, examine my heart and my mind (vv. 1–2).*

■ **Development**   Psalm 26 is all about personal integrity. Integrity signifies soundness, completeness, and honesty. People with these characteristics identify with Yahweh and keep themselves separate from sinners.

The psalmist petitioned the Lord for two things: vindication and examination. On the basis of his integrity, he asked to be delivered and avenged. He also asked to be critically examined. He wanted his heart and his mind tested because he was confident of his integrity. His life had not been dominated by ulterior motives, nor had he played political games. He had been singular in his purpose to trust the Lord.

How I need to cultivate total openness before the Lord! Transparency is the prelude to genuine spiritual intimacy. Because David experienced this, he was a man after God's own heart (Acts 13:22). No higher compliment could ever be paid!

■ **Personal prayer**   *Lord, may my life be an open book before You!*

Devotional Leitmotifs

Second Leitmotif—Separation from Sinners

■ **Theme**   *For your love is ever before me, and I walk continually in your truth. I do not sit with deceitful men, nor do I consort with hypocrites; I abhor the assembly of evildoers and refuse to sit with the wicked (vv. 3–5).*

■ **Development**   David demonstrated his integrity in two specific ways: his separation from sinners and his identification with Yahweh. The structure of David's life rested on two pillars: God's love and God's truth.

David kept God's unconditional love before him. Knowing that God would love him no matter what he thought of himself or what behavior he engaged in, David walked confidently through life.

He also walked continually in God's truth. Because he knew that friends and associates would play a major role in shaping his attitudes and values, he chose them carefully. Deceivers, hypocrites, evildoers, and other wicked people were not part of his group. It wasn't that he disapproved of them socially, but rather that he would not align himself with them spiritually. For as Solomon warned his young son, "Do not go along with them, do not set foot on their paths" (Proverbs 1:15). Their way of life leads to spiritual death.

I need to model David in his careful choice of personal friends and confidants because they do influence my value system. In this David showed great wisdom because his friends affirmed him and kept him on track.

■ **Personal prayer**   *O Lord, lead me to friends who will encourage me and lead me closer to You.*

Devotional Leitmotifs
Third Leitmotif—Identification with Yahweh

■ **Theme** *I wash my hands in innocence, and go about your altar, O LORD, proclaiming aloud your praise and telling of all your wonderful deeds. I love the house where you live, O LORD, the place where your glory dwells (vv. 6–8).*

■ **Development** Picture in your mind an open court with singers marching around the altar. Before the priests approached this altar, they stopped at the laver for cleansing. David put himself in this picture and used it to personalize his praise.

David loved to "let go" in praise of the Lord. He told of God's wonderful deeds, and he did it loudly in songs of thanksgiving. He loved the Lord's house because the glory of the Lord dwelt there.

Recently I attended The Praise Gathering, where Ronn Huff led ten thousand of us in singing Michael W. Smith's "Great Is the Lord." The voices of the mass choir—accompanied by brass, percussion, and organ—lifted us right out of our seats. Then, without accompaniment, we sang "Great Is Thy Faithfulness." What a sense of the Lord's presence!

In praising the Lord and expressing love for His house, David clearly identified himself with Yahweh. He proved this by his actions: He offered acknowledgment to His Lord.

Like David, I want to continually praise the Lord with my imagination, animation, and with everything I've got. Above all, I want to avoid boredom in God's house. With words and music I want to bring excitement about the Lord to His dwelling place.

66

■ **Personal prayer** *Lord, as I identify with You and with Your house, help me find my own personal identity.*

Devotional Leitmotifs
Fourth Leitmotif—Petition for Redemption

■ **Theme**   *Do not take away my soul along with sinners, my life with bloodthirsty men, in whose hands are wicked schemes, whose right hands are full of bribes. But I lead a blameless life; redeem me and be merciful to me. My feet stand on level ground; in the great assembly I will praise the Lord (vv. 9–12).*

■ **Development**   David prayed for deliverance from the fate of sinners and petitioned the Lord to redeem him. He trusted Yahweh to spare him from the fate inevitably coming to the wicked.

David's beautiful prayer unveiled his true character. In it we see his authenticity, integrity, and deep humility. Wholehearted in his commitment, David would continue to walk along the path he had chosen. His life was characterized by loyalty and righteousness.

Assured of God's deliverance, he ended the psalm by praising and blessing the Lord, adding his voice to a choir of believers whose lives ring true to reality because they trust the Lord.

Making music is part of the fellowship that binds believers together. The enjoyment of music is enhanced when we listen with another person. If we participate in a vocal or instrumental ensemble, our pleasure is even greater. Ultimately, personal involvement is the key to the joy of music. Just as David got involved musically with the congregation, we too must get involved personally in making music for the glory of God.

■ **Personal prayer**   *Lord, I thank You for Your loyal love. Continue to build integrity and humility into my life as I place my trust in You.*

Freedom

First Variation—Freedom from Fear

■ **Theme** *The LORD is my light and my salvation—whom shall I fear? The LORD is the stronghold of my life—of whom shall I be afraid? When evil men advance against me to devour my flesh, when my enemies and my foes attack me, they will stumble and fall. Though an army besiege me, my heart will not fear; though war break out against me, even then will I be confident (vv. 1–3).*

■ **Development** My wife, Karen, and I were with our beloved pastor, George Gardiner, when he lost his two-year bout with cancer and went to be with the Lord. Shortly before his homegoing, he shared with me his paraphrase of Psalm 27:1–2: "The Lord is my light and my radiation—whom shall I fear? The Lord is the stronghold of my life—of whom shall I be afraid? When cancer advances against me to devour my flesh, even then will I be confident."

Fear can cripple us and keep us in bondage. Some of us allow anxiety, a type of fear common in modern culture, to dominate us and keep us from developing our full potential.

In two fitting and beautiful metaphors that describe the Lord, David gave the antidote to fear: light and salvation.

Light is an appropriate symbol for truth, goodness, and joy. When the Lord is our centerpiece, His light will dispel the darkness of our fear. Amen!

The Lord also *saves us* from our enemies. When they advance and attack, the Lord will make them stumble and fall. David built a crescendo in verse 3. He asserted his freedom from fear and his overwhelming confidence.

Like Pastor Gardiner, we can face courageously whatever confronts us if we remember that the Lord has already conquered fear. Worry will disintegrate if we remember that He is our light and salvation.

■ **Personal prayer** *Lord, help me to find rest in perceiving You as my Light and my Salvation instead of continuing to be overcome by fear.*

Freedom
Second Variation—Freedom to Praise

■ **Theme**   *One thing I ask of the LORD, this is what I seek: that I may dwell in the house of the LORD all the days of my life, to gaze upon the beauty of the LORD and to seek him in his temple. For in the day of trouble he will keep me safe in his dwelling; he will hide me in the shelter of his tabernacle and set me high upon a rock. Then my head will be exalted above the enemies who surround me; at his tabernacle will I sacrifice with shouts of joy; I will sing and make music to the LORD (vv. 4–6).*

■ **Development**   Worship is another antidote for worry. David understood that praising the Lord was the one thing that could dispel fear (v. 4). There is safety and security in the Lord's sanctuary.

From the simple tent in the wilderness to the glory of Solomon's temple, Israel had been preoccupied with worshiping Yahweh. David did not isolate himself. He faced trial within the context of a community of believers. God's house was his place of safety.

David did not visit God's house merely to observe. He got personally involved in singing and making music to the Lord. His answer to deep, personal fear and insecurity was to make music for God's glory.

We must not let the pressure of modern life squeeze the song out of our lives. A sure way to let that happen is to sing only when we feel like it—when we're inspired. We must learn to sing in the night, when we're hurting and when we're afraid. Getting involved, moving on with your life, being forced out of yourself are the keys to transcending personal pain. Renewal and recovery come when we praise God for His sovereign control.

Then, the joy of the Lord will come flooding in, bringing with it His serenity and safety. Isaiah says it so beautifully, "You will keep in perfect peace him whose mind is steadfast, because he trusts in you" (Isaiah 26:3).

No matter what today may bring, "I will sing and make music to the LORD" (Psalm 27:6). This is the secret of tranquility in daily life.

69

■ **Personal prayer**   *Lord, no matter what my circumstances turn out to be today, help me to sing and make music to Your holy Name!*

Freedom

Third Variation—Freedom from Rejection

■ **Theme**   *Hear my voice when I call, O LORD; be merciful to me and answer me. My heart says of you, "Seek his face!" Your face, LORD, I will seek. Do not hide your face from me, do not turn your servant away in anger; you have been my helper. Do not reject me or forsake me, O God my Savior. Though my mother and father forsake me, the LORD will receive me. Teach me your way, O LORD; lead me in a straight path because of my oppressors. Do not turn me over to the desire of my foes, for false witnesses rise up against me, breathing out violence (vv. 7–12).*

■ **Development**   To David, ultimate rejection would be to have the Lord turn His face from him. Acutely aware of the gulf between his own impurity and God's absolute holiness, David appealed to God's mercy and pleaded to be spared from rejection.

Rejection is incredibly difficult to deal with, especially when it comes from those ordinarily close to us, such as family members or friends. This happens to many people, and it causes all kinds of emotional and psychological pain. But even when rejected by loved ones, we can attain intimacy because the Lord never turns His face from those who seek Him.

One of the keys to successful songwriting is to be able to handle rejection. Songs are subjective; unlike numbers, lyrics and music have nuances, so there can be a wide range of opinions about the value of a particular song. Perhaps it takes more courage than talent to be a songwriter. Rejection is painful, though, especially the personal rejection in a wife-husband, parent-child relationship.

David's point here is that even when we are rejected by those who are supposed to love us, the Lord will not reject us. Someone I love may push me off a cliff, but God has suspended Himself like a net to catch me. For believers, the Lord is always our safety net.

■ **Personal prayer**   *Thank You, Lord, that You have suspended a safety net beneath me. Continue to deliver me from the fear of falling.*

Freedom

Fourth Variation—Freedom to Be Patient

■ **Theme**   *I am still confident of this: I will see the goodness of the LORD in the land of the living. Wait for the LORD; be strong and take heart and wait for the LORD (vv. 13–14).*

■ **Development**   The final thought of this magnificent psalm is a statement of faith. David had the assurance that God was worth waiting for, and he had freely placed his confidence in the goodness and fairness of the Lord. He knew that the Lord would have the last word.

Relocation can be a traumatic experience for a family. Our move from Grand Rapids, Michigan, to Nashville, Tennessee, caused us to experience many conflicting emotions—sometimes feeling uprooted, confused, or excited! I believe it is possible to do the right thing yet feel strange doing it because of inward resistance to the Lord's will. The only way to gain perspective is to wait on the Lord.

Fear can render us ineffective and lifeless. But God gives us the answer to this phantom of the night: Himself. He is our Light and our Salvation. Therefore, we need not be dominated by fear or rejection. We are free to praise and to be patient. Praise brings the shining light of His presence into our lives to replace darkness. And confidence in the Lord builds patience.

Faith stands in bold contrast to fear. When we seek the Lord, He delivers us from all our fears (Psalm 34:4).

■ **Personal prayer**   *Lord, help me to place my complete confidence in You and to wait for You. Give me the ability to trust in Your overwhelming goodness.*

Bursting Out in Song
A Mournful Melody

■ **Theme**   *To you I call, O LORD my Rock; do not turn a deaf ear to me. For if you remain silent, I will be like those who have gone down to the pit. Hear my cry for mercy as I call to you for help, as I lift up my hands toward your Most Holy Place. Do not drag me away with the wicked, with those who do evil, who speak cordially with their neighbors but harbor malice in their hearts. Repay them for their deeds and for their evil work; repay them for what their hands have done and bring back upon them what they deserve (vv. 1–4).*

■ **Development**   Forced to look into the eyes of death, David pleaded for salvation. He asked the Lord to distinguish between himself and the wicked and requested that he not face a common death with them. He prayed specifically for three things: (1) that the Lord would hear him and help him; (2) that the Lord would not identify him with hypocritical sinners; (3) that the Lord would be fair in rendering judgment.

What strength there is in placing our trust in the goodness and justice of God! When Abraham prayed for Sodom, he spoke profoundly when he said, "Will not the Judge of all the earth do right?" Focusing our faith in the Lord and His righteousness answers a myriad of unsettling philosophical questions. One of the most profound is the question of our final destiny.

■ **Personal prayer**   *Lord, I praise You that I can leave my eternal destiny in Your hands. I believe in Your righteousness and justice.*

Bursting Out in Song
A Joyful Melody

■ **Theme**   *Since they show no regard for the works of the* LORD *and what his hands have done, he will tear them down and never build them up again. Praise be to the* LORD, *for he has heard my cry for mercy. The* LORD *is my strength and my shield; my heart trusts in him, and I am helped. My heart leaps for joy and I will give thanks to him in song. The* LORD *is the strength of his people, a fortress of salvation for his anointed one (vv. 5–8).*

■ **Development**   In these verses, David expressed supreme confidence that the Lord would answer his prayer and would eventually overthrow the wicked.

This confidence put David in a mood to praise the Lord. He praised the Lord for three things: (1) for hearing his prayer; (2) for being his strength and shield; (3) for being the salvation of Israel.

David made these points with increasing intensity. Like a mighty musical crescendo climaxing with cymbals crashing, he burst out in song and praise. His heart leaped, and he was filled with thanksgiving. Convinced that the Lord was his strength, his salvation, and his song, David worshiped the Lord in the beauty of holiness.

There is no better way to express ardent emotion than through music. Music allowed David to express the inexpressible.

I find that when I'm overburdened with melancholia (feeling "down"), thinking about God's goodness helps me. I like to substitute praise songs for negative thoughts, so I wrote a little chorus, "He Satisfies My Life" to concentrate on the theme: "God is good."

> *As I lift my voice in praise my heart sings,*
> *For He satisfies my life with good things.*
> *I can't describe the joy that He brings,*
> *For He satisfies my life with good things.*

Words and music by Don Wyrtzen.
© 1985 by Singspiration Music.

73

■ **Personal prayer**   *May joy rise in my heart so that I may burst out in songs of praise to him!* (Psalm 28:7, TLB).

Bursting Out in Song
An Entreating Melody

■ **Theme**   *Save your people and bless your inheritance; be their shepherd and carry them forever (v. 9).*

■ **Development**   David was much more than an average citizen. He was the prototype of the Messiah. Because of his special position, David bestowed God's grace on the people. This concept reached full maturation in Christ of the New Testament "who has blessed us in the heavenly realms with every spiritual blessing" (Ephesians 1:3).

The final verse of this psalm is a prayer that has become part of the "Te Deum," a celebrated song of praise, rejoicing, and thanksgiving. In it, David importunes God for the salvation, blessing, and sustenance of His people. Using the shepherd motif again, David asked the Lord to lift up His people and carry them forever. Isaiah used similar comforting words: "In his love and mercy he redeemed them; he lifted them up and carried them all the days of old" (Isaiah 63:9).

David started in minor but ended in major. He began in the dark but ended in the light. He went from being low in spirit to being high with joy. He moved from lamentation to praise. What an appropriate model for worship and prayer!

Like David, I want to be able to honestly pour out my soul to my heavenly Father, trusting that He will carry me. What comfort this will bring when I feel stress from the complexity of modern life!

I am trying not to take for granted God's gifts of grace in my life. Grace involves even more than His gift of salvation.

■ **Personal prayer**   *Lord, I thank and praise You for Your grace, for Your salvation, for the blessing of Your inheritance, and for shepherding me forever.*

Majesty   His Splendor

■ **Theme**   Ascribe to the LORD, O mighty ones, ascribe to the LORD glory and strength. Ascribe to the LORD the glory due his name; worship the LORD in the splendor of his holiness (vv. 1–2).

■ **Development**   Our Lord's absolute holiness, transcendence, and majesty are incomprehensible and unfathomable to mere mortals. For this reason, David threw logic and analysis to the wind and allowed the flow of Hebrew poetry to take over in Psalm 29. Reminiscent of the Song of the Sea (Exodus 15), the oracles of Balaam (Numbers 23–24), and the Song of Deborah (Judges 5), this psalm lets us feel through poetry the towering majesty of the Lord.

The scene opens with angels singing themes of true worship and adoration. In them we see that declaring the greatness of God involves the total personality.

It may be true that we have a more intimate relationship with God than the angels do. Angels are awestruck by the greatness of God, but they do not experience the thrill of the gospel as we do. God took the initiative to relate to us personally through Jesus Christ. Though we are "a little lower than the angels" in God's hierarchy, we have a unique entrée to Him.

Like the angels, I am to be filled with love and wonder at the mention of His name. I am to worship Him for the splendor of His holiness. Through meditation, prayer, music, and poetry, I can do this. And because of who God is and what He does, I will do it. A.W. Tozer called worship "the missing jewel of evangelicalism." Instead of learning about worship from religious leaders, I need to learn about it from the angels who are uninhibited and unrestrained in their praise of God.

■ **Personal prayer**   Lord, make me aware of Your holiness and transcendence and teach me how to reflect them back to You.

Majesty His Storm

■ **Theme**   *The voice of the* L*ORD* *is over the waters; the God of glory thunders, the* L*ORD* *thunders over the mighty waters. The voice of the* L*ORD* *is powerful; the voice of the* L*ORD* *is majestic. The voice of the* L*ORD* *breaks the cedars; the* L*ORD* *breaks in pieces the cedars of Lebanon. He makes Lebanon skip like a calf, Sirion like a young wild ox. The voice of the* L*ORD* *strikes with flashes of lightning. The voice of the* L*ORD* *shakes the desert; the* L*ORD* *shakes the Desert of Kadesh. The voice of the* L*ORD* *twists the oaks and strips the forests bare. And in his temple all cry, "Glory!" (vv. 3–9).*

■ **Development**   The magnificence of nature reflects the power and might of God (Romans 1:20). All of nature trembles at the sound of His voice. It calmed the raging sea of Galilee and caused Jesus' disciples to exclaim, "Who is this? He commands even the winds and the water, and they obey him" (Luke 8:25). And it made everyone in the temple shout, "Glory!"

In our day, we think of man as being bigger than he is and of God as being smaller than He is. This distortion makes us lose perspective on what is important and causes us to major on minor issues. We major in minor issues when we reduce the mystery of the Godhead to a rationalistic system, when we get wrapped up in external behaviors rather than in internal reality, and when we explain Christianity in numbers rather than by an intimate relationship with the Lord. We need to hear again the voice of almighty God as it resounds like tympani rolling, cymbals crashing, and brass bands playing fanfares— all climaxing in one eruption of praise and a mighty crescendo of glory.

■ **Personal prayer**   *Lord, give me an acute awareness of Your power and might. And give me a foretaste of heaven by letting me experience some of Your glorious presence now.*

Majesty His Salvation

■ **Theme**   The LORD sits enthroned over the flood; the LORD is enthroned as King forever. The LORD gives strength to his people; the LORD blesses his people with peace (vv. 10–11).

■ **Development**   The Hebrew word for *flood* (v. 10) appears just one other time in the Old Testament—in Genesis 6. Psalm 29:10 means, therefore, that our Lord has the power to unleash the violent forces of nature just as He did during Noah's flood (Genesis 6–11).

The Lord Jesus, God-Incarnate, used His voice to display supernatural power. He said to the churning sea, "Quiet! Be still!" Then the wind died down, and it was completely calm (Mark 4:39). He also used His voice to raise Lazarus from the dead, "Lazarus, come out!" And the dead man obeyed (John 11:43–44). God speaks with awesome authority and might.

Verse 11 gives us a glimpse into the future. The Lord will give, and the Lord will bless. The Lord uses His voice, not for a gratuitous show of force, but as an instrument of judgment and salvation.

Franz Delitzch, a brilliant nineteenth-century Old Testament scholar, viewed the closing words "with peace" as a rainbow arching over the psalm. We can either experience the *force* of God's wrath or the *peace* of His salvation. We can choose between the awesome power He uses against His enemies or the compassionate intimacy He offers to His children.

■ **Personal prayer**   Lord, I am fully aware that You are enthroned as King forever. I praise You for giving me strength, blessing, and peace.

Joy Comes in the Morning *Outburst of Praise*

■ **Theme**   *I will exalt you, O LORD, for you lifted me out of the depths and did not let my enemies gloat over me. O LORD my God, I called to you for help and you healed me. O LORD, you brought me up from the grave; you spared me from going down into the pit. Sing to the LORD, you saints of his; praise his holy name. For his anger lasts only a moment, but his favor lasts a lifetime; weeping may remain for a night, but rejoicing comes in the morning (vv. 1–5).*

■ **Development**   Restoration follows confession. David wrote Psalm 30 after experiencing this glorious truth.

Perhaps the most innovative, imaginative, and creative person in Scripture, David was vulnerable to the sin of pride. To chasten David for arrogantly numbering the fighting men of Israel (1 Chronicles 21), God allowed him to be placed near death.

David was aware of the contrasts between sorrow and joy, the momentary and the eternal, the troubles that weigh little and the glory that outweighs everything (2 Corinthians 4:16–18). He praised God that His anger lasts only for a moment but that His favor lasts for a lifetime (v. 5).

David experienced momentary personal pleasure with Bathsheba (2 Samuel 11). This affair produced unalterable consequences for David, Bathsheba, and their families. Yet because David had an intimate relationship with God, he confessed his sin (Psalm 51). God responded by restoring and renewing him (Galatians 6:1).

What an encouragement to those who have given in to temptation and are living with the inevitable stress! The answer is confession, which leads to restoration and praise.

■ **Personal prayer**   *Lord, teach me how to keep short accounts with You. Teach me also to regularly praise Your precious Name.*

Joy Comes in the
Morning   *Outburst of Confession*

■ **Theme**   *When I felt secure, I said, "I will never be shaken." O LORD, when you favored me, you made my mountain stand firm; but when you hid your face, I was dismayed. To you, O LORD, I called; to the LORD I cried for mercy: "What gain is there in my destruction, in my going down into the pit? Will the dust praise you? Will it proclaim your faithfulness? Hear, O LORD, and be merciful to me; O LORD, be my help" (vv. 6–10).*

■ **Development**   David had turned from God and was leaving Him out of his life. But when God turned His face from him, David felt cold, raw fear. He saw his unfaithfulness as frailty and his carefree lifestyle as carelessness.

Reciting his psychological disintegration, his personal destruction, and his feelings of deep insecurity, David cried out for mercy. At the end of himself, David abandoned his independence, his cleverness, and all his human resources, realizing that the solidarity of his kingdom depended on God's favor, not on his own ingenuity (vv. 6–7). Knowing that he had been out of tune with God, David tightened the strings of his life through a mighty outburst of confession.

In numerous ways my inadequacy comes to the surface every day. I reveal it when I'm threatened by competition, when I'm defensive with Karen, or when I desire to simplify the mysteries of life. I'm just learning to admit my inadequacy by not denying it. I'm even learning to rejoice in it, though a bit guardedly I admit, because Paul teaches us, "When I am weak, then I am strong" (2 Corinthians 12:9–10). Dependence on the Lord is the key to security.

Without the Lord we are dust (v. 9). David's artistic and administrative genius, apart from God's special touch, were no match for the pressures and complexities already apparent in the ancient world.

79

■ **Personal prayer**   *Lord, forgive me for leaving You out of my life, for trying to "go it alone." I confess my tendency toward self-sufficiency and now thrust myself upon You for mercy and help.*

Joy Comes in the
Morning   Outburst of Joy

■ **Theme**   *You turned my wailing into dancing; you removed my sackcloth and clothed me with joy, that my heart may sing to you and not be silent. O LORD my God, I will give you thanks forever (vv. 11–12).*

■ **Development**   David's richly textured personality and artistic temperament were expressed on many emotional levels. In this psalm he was as uninhibited in his praise as when he "danced before the Lord with all his might" (2 Samuel 6:14). David wasn't shy about expressing the intensity of his joy.

In the first movement of this psalm, David felt the exuberance of praise (vv. 1–5). In the second movement, he felt the depression of guilt over his sin (vv. 6–10). In this movement, after a moving confession, David felt the exhilaration and freedom of forgiveness, and it culminated in an outburst of joy (vv. 11–12).

What colorful contrasts David experienced: from wailing to dancing; sackcloths of despair to garments of joy; sounds of silence to songs of joy; independence to dependence; disintegration to integration; cynicism to caring; and from needing no one to trusting God. He exchanged a growing insecurity for unshakeable confidence. No wonder he vowed to praise the Lord and to give thanks to Him forever!

I also feel stark contrasts, fluctuating mood swings, and mixed motives in my life. I've conducted some of the finest musicians in the world, but I'm often plagued by self-doubts. I deeply desire to glorify God in writing this book. But I'm also conscious of my concern about how I'm coming across to you. Even though many would consider my life to be quite *successful*, I sometimes wonder how *significant* it has been. But I'm learning to persistently praise God in the midst of it all, and every once in a while, like C.S. Lewis, I'm surprised by joy.

■ **Personal prayer**   *Dear Father, may I not continue to be content with my self-centered and self-contained life. May I not eat husks when I can feast at Your banquet table.*

March

PSALMS 31–39

My guilt has overwhelmed me like a burden too heavy to bear. —Psalm 38:4

David Faces Crisis Rejection!

■ **Theme**   *Be merciful to me, O LORD, for I am in distress; my eyes grow weak with sorrow, my soul and my body with grief. . . . Because of all my enemies, I am the utter contempt of my neighbors; I am a dread to my friends—those who see me on the street flee from me. I am forgotten by them as though I were dead; I have become like broken pottery. . . . But I trust in you, O LORD; I say, "You are my God." My times are in your hands; deliver me from my enemies and from those who pursue me. . . . Love the LORD, all his saints! The LORD preserves the faithful, but the proud he pays back in full. Be strong and take heart, all you who hope in the LORD* (vv. 9–24).

■ **Development**   David knew what it was like to experience discouragement, despair, grief, and gloom. When he was depressed, he felt isolated and rejected. The picture he paints in Psalm 31:9–13 is black, and his use of graphic and descriptive nouns—distress, sorrow, grief, anguish, groaning, affliction, contempt, dread, and terror— helps us feel what he felt.

I'm certain that we all struggle with the pain of rejection. I feel rejected spiritually when I don't sense God's presence in my life. I feel rejected domestically when Karen and I disagree. And I feel rejected professionally when someone doesn't like a new song I've written.

David's response to his rejection is a model for me today. Once again, he prayed and praised. After affirming his faith in the Lord and praying for deliverance from his enemies, for the shame and death of the wicked, and for his own purity, he moved again to a crescendo of praise (vv. 19–24). The first pair of verses speaks eloquently of God's care for His own (vv. 19–20). The next pair personalizes the message. David praised the Lord for His wonderful love and indescribable mercy (vv. 21–22).

Four brief, but powerful concepts end this psalm of crisis: Love the Lord! Be faithful! Be humble! Be strong and take heart!

■ **Personal prayer**   *Lord, help me to wait for You! Help me to put my faith in what I know rather than in what I feel!*

Whiter Than Snow   *Forgiveness*

■ **Theme**   *Blessed is he whose transgressions are forgiven, whose sins are covered. Blessed is the man whose sin the* LORD *does not count against him and in whose spirit is no deceit. . . . Then I acknowledged my sin to you and did not cover up my iniquity. I said, "I will confess my transgressions to the* LORD" *—and you forgave the guilt of my sin (vv. 1–2, 5).*

■ **Development**   In the Psalter, David composed many variations on the theme of forgiveness. Psalm 32 zeroes in on the exhilarating emotional release that comes from forgiveness after confession.

David gave two reasons for personal contentment and happiness: First, we are happy (blessed) when our sins are forgiven; second, we are happy when we are counted righteous. The New Testament teaches that forgiveness and imputation of personal righteousness hinge on Christ's atonement for our sin. (David's faith prefigured Christ's sacrifice. See Romans 4:6–8.)

Like many of us, I too often choose short-term gratification over long-term benefits. My eating habits are an example. I'd rather have an ice-cream cone now than be in great physical shape later. There is pleasure now but misery later when I feel guilty.

As David continued to sin, his bones wasted away but his conscience remained very much alive. He groaned all day long from the weight of God's heavy hand on him. He had all of the symptoms of guilt. But when he confessed his sins and acknowledged his transgressions, he experienced complete forgiveness.

Why do I sometimes continue in my sin? Why don't I listen to my conscience and follow David's example? When I face reality and acknowledge and confess my sin, I, like David, experience the exhilaration of forgiveness. I feel healthier, too.

■ **Personal prayer**   *Lord, wash me and I shall be whiter than snow.*

Whiter Than Snow   *Deliverance*

■ **Theme**   *Therefore let everyone who is godly pray to you while you may be found; surely when the mighty waters rise, they will not reach him. You are my hiding place; you will protect me from trouble and surround me with songs of deliverance (vv. 6–7).*

■ **Development**   When the mighty waters of trouble rise and I am about to go under, I can cry out, "Lord save me!" And He will. Peter also experienced deliverance in Matthew 14:28–33.

David was going through deep waters when he wrote Psalm 32. In danger of going under, he sought the Lord, and the Lord miraculously delivered him. Through this, David learned that trusting in the Lord was the only safe place to be and his only real security. The Lord protected David from trouble and surrounded him "with songs of deliverance."

Music can be the perfect vehicle of comfort and protection. One day when I was flying in a small plane through vicious, clear-air turbulence, I had an anxiety attack and began hyperventilating. I started to sing to myself Joe Park's "He Holdeth Me." Then I remembered Moses' magnificent blessing, "The eternal God is your refuge, and underneath are the everlasting arms" (Deuteronomy 33:27). As the Lord lovingly replaced my anxiety with the security of His arms, I became calm.

Saved from adversity, David composed his own songs of deliverance so that others could worship with him. How marvelous that he shared his discovery! What a motivation for me to make music that celebrates my deliverance.

■ **Personal prayer**   *Lord, thank You that I am safe in You, and that You deliver me from the complex problems of life today!*

Whiter Than Snow *Joy*

■ **Theme**   *I will instruct you and teach you in the way you should go; I will counsel you and watch over you. Do not be like the horse or the mule, which have no understanding but must be controlled by bit and bridle or they will not come to you. Many are the woes of the wicked, but the LORD's unfailing love surrounds the man who trusts in him. Rejoice in the LORD and be glad, you righteous; sing, all you who are upright in heart! (vv. 8–11).*

■ **Development**   David progressed from sin to joy. Not only did he find exhilaration in forgiveness; he also found great joy in fellowship with the Lord. David felt God's chastening, then he experienced God's care.

Wicked people, because they don't understand or obey the truth, are like horses and mules; they can be controlled only by uncomfortable bits and bridles. Consequently, they experience many woes. In contrast, the righteous are surrounded by the Lord's unfailing truth and love. The Lord promises to instruct, counsel, and watch over us, which will keep us out of trouble. But we must depend on Him for guidance, which requires an intimate relationship with Him.

What a promise for us as we face life's day-to-day stresses! What a reason for celebration, singing, and joy! The Lord's truth leads to personal freedom. And that freedom results in a deep sense of joy.

■ **Personal prayer**   *Heavenly Father, I praise You for counseling me and watching over me. When I contemplate Your unfailing love, my heart is filled with joy and I want to make music.*

Hymn of Praise *Beauty*

■ **Theme** *Sing joyfully to the LORD, you righteous; it is fitting for the upright to praise him. Praise the LORD with the harp; make music to him on the ten-stringed lyre. Sing to him a new song; play skillfully, and shout for joy (vv. 1–3).*

■ **Development**   The psalmist starts this magnificent hymn of praise with a plea for music-making executed with excellence. The Lord wants to hear a *new* song, and He wants to hear it played *skillfully*. He despises frozen forms and sacred clichés because rituals lose their meaning and traditions turn stale.

Having reviewed hundreds of unsolicited music manuscripts, I can honestly say that most of them are imitative and derivative rather than truly creative and innovative. The Lord is unimpressed with echoes; He rewards uniqueness.

The very nature of music is to change—and true artists, by definition, grow steadily, change constantly, and create regularly. By doing so, they remain contemporary and relevant. Genuine art reflects the Lord's beauty and skill, so sincerity alone is never enough. The Lord wants freshness and good technique as well as fervor.

When I sing a new song, play my instrument with skill, and shout for joy, the Lord will lift me out of my own small, circumscribed world, and I will join with all true believers and heaven's angels in sacred song!

Praising God through artistic expression enhances my inner beauty the way a diamond tiara enhances the outward beauty of a lovely woman.

■ **Personal prayer**   *Dear Lord, may I use my voice and my instrument to bring glory to Your Name today.*

Hymn of Praise Truth

■ **Theme**   Let all the earth fear the LORD; let all the people of the world revere him. For he spoke, and it came to be; he commanded, and it stood firm (vv. 8–9).

■ **Development**   I find profound personal comfort in order and design. I observe it in nature when I drive up the Maine coast and when I scan a symphony score by Mozart. Even though I admire the sensitivity of modern existentialists and can empathize with their despair, like the sweet psalmist of Israel, I find security in knowing that God has a specific plan for the universe and one for my life too.

I cannot begin to understand the truth of God's power, but I see it in the wonder of creation and in the creative acts of history. Only the plans of the Lord are sure. They stand firm through all generations.

The geopolitical manipulations of earth's rulers succeed or fail according to God's overarching plan. Nebuchadnezzar, Darius, Alexander the Great, Caesar, Napoleon, Hitler—all were mere instrumentalists contributing to God's score for the universe. The Lord is the Master Orchestrator of history.

■ **Personal prayer**   I praise you, Lord, for Your powerful Word. Thank You for using it to create the universe and to act in history.

Hymn of Praise   Love

■ **Theme**   The LORD loves righteousness and justice; the earth is full of his unfailing love. . . . But the eyes of the LORD are on those who fear him, on those whose hope is in his unfailing love (vv. 5, 18).

■ **Development**   God not only sees all people and everything they do from His exalted position in the heavens, He also sees their inward thoughts and motives. No one can hide from Him!

When God sees reliance upon self rather than on Him, He withholds His reward. The use of huge armies, great personal strength, and the latest technology will lead to death, not victory.

The only hope for the arrogant and autonomous is for them to place their trust in the Lord, who watches over those who fear Him, and to place their hope in His love.

The Lord doesn't really need articulate people, as Joseph proved before Pharaoh. The Lord doesn't really need strong people, as the young shepherd boy David proved before Goliath. And the Lord doesn't really need brilliant people. Paul tells us that God chooses "the foolish things of this world to shame the wise" (1 Corinthians 1:27).

If I place my confidence in my own cleverness, energy, charm, or other human resources, I will fail. Real inner strength to meet the challenges of my life come only when I give the Lord reverence and when I trust totally in His unfailing love of righteousness.

■ **Personal prayer**   I praise You, Lord, that Your love for justice and righteousness will finally win and that I don't have to harbor bitterness and resentment over today's injustices.

Hymn of Praise Holiness

■ **Theme** *We wait in hope for the LORD; he is our help and our shield. In him our hearts rejoice, for we trust in his holy name. May your unfailing love rest upon us, O LORD, even as we put our hope in you (vv. 20–22).*

■ **Development** The psalmist concluded this majestic hymn of praise by leading his congregation in asserting their faith in the holiness of the Lord!

They asserted their faith by waiting in hope for the Lord (v. 20), by rejoicing in Him (v. 21), and by praying for the Lord's loyal love (v. 22). Their finale is a promise that they have placed all of their hope in the Lord.

Wait, rejoice, petition—what a paradigm for personal praise! Praise must be the top priority in our lives.

When Isaiah saw the Lord face to face, he trembled in fear because of his sins. In Isaiah 6, we can only imagine the utter majesty and glory of the Lord, which Isaiah saw. But even *this* tiny glimpse of God's holiness (Psalm 33) can result in uninhibited praise and worship. "Through Jesus, therefore, let us continually offer to God a sacrifice of praise—the fruit of lips that confess his name" (Hebrews 13:15).

> To be what You want me to be, dear Lord,
>   I'll live for eternity;
> To be more like Your Son, dear Lord—
>   I've only just begun.
>
> To be what You want me to be, dear Lord,
>   I'll live so the world can see
> The image of Your Son, dear Lord—
>   Unite our hearts as one.

Words and music by Don Wyrtzen.
© 1972 by Singspiration Music.

89

■ **Personal prayer** *Lord, I praise You for filling my heart with joy because I have trusted in Your holy Name.*

Song of Exaltation   Extolling the Lord

■ **Theme**   *I will extol the* LORD *at all times; his praise will always be on my lips. My soul will boast in the* LORD; *let the afflicted hear and rejoice. Glorify the* LORD *with me; let us exalt his name together (vv. 1–3).*

■ **Development**   David knew how to praise the Lord. The rich texture of his highly sensitive personality made exaltation the focus of his life. As my mentor, he teaches me three facets of worship.

First, I am to extol the Lord. Praising Him must become second nature to me, part of the daily rhythm of my life. Praise must be an inner voice of worship, not a lifeless liturgy.

How do I do this? Sometimes, I paraphrase Scripture when I write poetry about the Lord and compose songs for His glory. I call upon His name in prayer and sing songs of praise to Him. No matter where I am, I try to glorify His name in simple, practical ways.

Second, I am to boast in the Lord. At dinner parties and other social occasions, my conversation must be dominated by stories of the great things God has done for me, not by what I have done for myself. Discussions about who I know, where I have been, and what I have done reveal my insecurity. Only by putting the spotlight on the Lord and focusing on Him will I find true security.

Third, I am to glorify the Lord. As C.S. Lewis observed, "to glorify is to enjoy." Ironically, the overstimulation of modern life leads to boredom. I need to move away from the emptiness the world offers to find the fulfillment of the Lord. Enjoying the Lord in the company of my brothers and sisters in Christ enhances this joy.

■ **Personal prayer**   *Dear Lord, I extol You, I boast in You, and I glorify You. In Your precious Name, Amen!*

Song of Exaltation   Seeking the Lord

■ **Theme**   *I sought the LORD, and he answered me; he delivered me from all my fears. Those who look to him are radiant; their faces are never covered with shame. This poor man called, and the LORD heard him; he saved him out of all his troubles. The angel of the LORD encamps around those who fear him, and he delivers them (vv. 4–7).*

■ **Development**   The elusive monster of fear lurks in the shadows, waiting to claw my soul to shreds. As one prone to melancholia, I see its ugly face often: when I'm struggling with the emotional stress of a difficult relationship, when I'm afraid failure is just around the corner, when success seems too hard to handle, and on days when free-floating anxiety is getting the best of me.

Ironically, the Lord delivers from fear all those who fear Him. So when I am afraid, I need to seek the Lord, who will hear me and save me from all my troubles.

Furthermore, the Lord promises me radiance. I can hold my head high and look straight ahead because He has covered my shame. Forgiveness leads to transparency, and transparency to intimacy. And, as if that were not enough, He gives me inner beauty that is reflected in outer radiance. Praise His holy Name!

■ **Personal prayer**   *I praise You, Lord, for replacing fear and trouble with peace and radiance.*

Song of Exaltation
Tasting the Lord's Goodness

■ **Theme**   Taste and see that the LORD is good; blessed is the man who takes refuge in him. Fear the LORD, you his saints, for those who fear him lack nothing. The lions may grow weak and hungry, but those who seek the LORD lack no good thing (vv. 8–10).

■ **Development**   Many who believe they have "tasted the Lord" have only a superficial knowledge of Him. They say they have tried Him, think they know all about Him, and claim they have been disappointed in Him. But "tasting the Lord" involves more than a casual glance, a brief encounter, or a simple, memorized formula. To taste the Lord, I need to embrace Him, to relate to Him with my whole being!

I need also to fear the Lord. To do this, I must concentrate on Him, not on myself. Narcissism subtly kills spiritual intimacy. Because I am very sensitive, I tend to be neurotic. Instead of looking outside myself and to the Lord, I tend to turn inward, which leads to despair. I would do better to focus less on self, serve others, and trust the Lord more. When I respect Him as I should, I will lack nothing.

Even the king of the jungle grows weak from hunger. But the one who seeks the Lord lacks no good thing. Those who have the Lord have no need for anything else, for He alone is complete. As a result, the anxiety I feel about competitiveness will dissolve. And my struggles for power and prestige will be replaced by knowing intimately the One who holds all power and deserves all prestige.

■ **Personal prayer**   Help me to taste and see Your goodness, Lord. Help me to find all the power and prestige I need in my relationship with You.

Song of Exaltation
Fearing the Lord

■ **Theme**   *Come, my children, listen to me; I will teach you the fear of the* LORD. *Whoever of you loves life and desires to see many good days, keep your tongue from evil and your lips from speaking lies. Turn from evil and do good; seek peace and pursue it (vv. 11–14).*

■ **Development**   I am to reject the lie that there is fulfillment outside the will of God. Reverence for the Lord is the only way to personal enrichment. From David, I learn that two big changes will occur in my life when I reverence God.

First, I will speak the truth. Deception comes easily and naturally for me. I never had to learn to lie. When I was a kid, I remember calling the operator just to say something rude and brash to her. When she called back, my dad answered the phone. He asked me if I had made the call. I lied. Even though it was easy to lie, deceiving my dad wasn't wise. As David says, if I commit myself to speaking the truth, I will have many good days and a long life.

Second, I will do good and pursue peace. The fringe benefits will be personal fulfillment and spiritual enrichment because my goals and behavior will be in harmony with the will of God.

93

■ **Personal prayer**   *Lord, teach me to speak the truth and to turn from evil. I can't do it on my own, so empower me, that I may experience the fulfillment that comes from doing Your will.*

Song of Exaltation

Crying out to the Lord

■ **Theme**   The eyes of the LORD are on the righteous and his ears are attentive to their cry; the face of the LORD is against those who do evil, to cut off the memory of them from the earth. The righteous cry out, and the LORD hears them; he delivers them from all their troubles. The LORD is close to the brokenhearted and saves those who are crushed in spirit (vv. 15–18).

■ **Development**   A certain comfort comes from crying, and there is virtue in ventilation. Before I can really praise the Lord, I must lament honestly and deeply. I must be vulnerable enough to let my wife and children see me cry because genuine spirituality begins with honesty about my own feelings.

Not long ago as Karen, Kathy, D.J., and I prayed for a bereaved family, I cried. I was so overcome with sadness for this good friend, I lost control in the middle of the prayer. I felt embarrassed and uncomfortable because I like to be in control. But crying was the best and most natural thing for me to do in order to give God complete control. I must remember that I do not live in exile, estranged from God, where there is darkness and no hope.

Though not denying the reality of sin, pain, suffering, and death, I need to embrace the greater reality—that the Lord is Victor over these. He has conquered the negatives of my life. He is my Savior and Deliverer. When I begin to see this, laborious lament is transformed into uproarious praise.

■ **Personal prayer**   Thank You, Lord, that You are close to the brokenhearted and that You save those who are crushed in spirit.

Song of Exaltation
Finding Safety in the Lord

■ **Theme**   A *righteous man may have many troubles, but the* LORD *delivers him from them all; he protects all his bones, not one of them will be broken. Evil will slay the wicked; the foes of the righteous will be condemned. The Lord redeems his servants; no one will be condemned who takes refuge in him (vv. 19–22).*

■ **Development**   This promise was fulfilled beautifully after Jesus' death. Following Roman custom, the two condemned malefactors were removed from their crosses after having had their legs broken. But when they came to Jesus, "they did not break his legs" (John 19:33).

The Lord not only cares about me psychologically but physically as well. My psyche and my body reflect His image.

The Lord kept me safe on a particularly dangerous, icy road when I was in college. As I crested the hill, I saw that two other cars had already collided at the bottom. Naturally I braked hard, which was enough to propel me down the hill faster into the other two cars. Although I was badly shaken, no one was hurt. The Lord protected and delivered me that day.

David here vividly contrasts the wicked and the righteous. The wicked are slain by evil, but foes of the righteous are condemned. The Lord redeems His own. No one who finds refuge in the Lord is condemned. As a righteous person, I may have many troubles, but the Lord will deliver me from all of them.

This great worship anthem, "Song of Exaltation," gives six specific steps toward personal fulfillment. I am to *extol* the Lord; *seek* the Lord; *taste* the goodness of the Lord; *fear* the Lord; *cry out* to the Lord, and *find safety* in the Lord. The key is in the object—the Lord! Faith in any person other than the Lord is foolishness.

■ **Personal prayer**   *Lord, I praise You that no matter what my external circumstances will ever be, I am safe in Your care!*

Limited Perspective
Impatience with God—First Movement

■ **Theme**   *May those who seek my life be disgraced and put to shame; may those who plot my ruin be turned back in dismay. . . . Then my soul will rejoice in the LORD and delight in his salvation. My whole being will exclaim, "Who is like you, O LORD? You rescue the poor from those too strong for them, the poor and needy from those who rob them"* (vv. 4, 9–10).

■ **Development**   David was impatient. The Lord, it seemed, was not listening to his prayers. While his enemies plotted against him, David tried to come to grips with God's seeming silence. The striking contrasts of his poetry reflect the ups and downs of his life.

David was being hassled and harassed, but his real problem was his limited perspective. One of the key issues in life is time. When we get preoccupied with "now," we lose perspective. When we get hung up on the present, we lose sight of the future.

I'm in mid-life now. At times I become overly concerned about time. How much time do I have left? Is what I'm doing important? Have I accomplished anything significant in my life? Since only God sees the big picture, we need to place complete trust in His will. His plan encompasses the whole universe, but it also includes me in detail as an individual.

■ **Personal prayer**   *Dear Father, forgive me for being angry and impatient with You. Help me to place my complete faith in You and Your plan.*

Limited Perspective
Impatience with God—Second Movement

■ **Theme** *Yet when they were ill, I put on sackcloth and humbled myself with fasting. When my prayers returned to me unanswered, I went about mourning as though for my friend or brother. I bowed my head in grief as though weeping for my mother. . . . I will give you thanks in the great assembly; among throngs of people I will praise you (vv. 13–14, 18).*

■ **Development** The Lord had not yet answered David's prayer. Ruthless witnesses accused him. When he stumbled, they attacked maliciously. When he faltered, they gathered in glee. David had every human reason to get angry at God, but he responded by praising and thanking Him.

David went public with his confession. He worshiped in the company of believers, shared the reality of his plight, and told of his decision to trust God no matter what. His brothers and sisters participated in both his pain and his praise.

How often we hide when we are hurting! How often we pretend all is well when everything is falling apart! How often we try to maintain an image of stability when the foundation of our lives is crumbling! What emotional energy we waste building façades!

I come from a background that rewards performance. Consequently, even when my world seems to be falling apart around me, "the show" goes on. Even when I'm despondent and on the emotional brink, I still try to play or speak. But I'm learning to open up to a few trusted friends. I'm gradually learning that being vulnerable is how we share our lives and our love.

David shared honestly and candidly. He wasn't afraid to cry in front of his family, and that was one of the secrets behind his powerful praise.

■ **Personal prayer** *Dear Father, I praise and thank You. I know You will answer my prayers in Your perfect time.*

Limited Perspective
Impatience with God—Third Movement

■ **Theme**   *Vindicate me in your righteousness; O LORD my God; do not let them gloat over me. . . . May those who delight in my vindication shout for joy and gladness; may they always say, "The LORD be exalted, who delights in the well-being of his servant." My tongue will speak of your righteousness and of your praises all day long (vv. 24, 27–28).*

■ **Development**   Still grappling with the silence and distance of the Lord, David longed for vindication. He wanted to see his enemies defeated, disgraced, and put to confusion.

But instead of letting his sorrow get him down, David lifted up praise to the Lord. Though still concerned for his own acquittal, he concentrated on worship!

And when he praised, his ambivalence melted away. I am just beginning to pray when I'm sad, to give thanks when I'm sorrowful or suffering, and to praise God when I'm experiencing pain. After praise and worship, David had a small problem and a big concept of God, instead of a big problem and a small concept of God.

Praise always brings with it a proper perspective, one that is unlimited.

■ **Personal prayer**   *Lord, may my tongue speak of Your righteousness and Your praises all day long.*

A Musical Play
Act One: Portrait of Wickedness

■ **Theme**   *An oracle is within my heart concerning the sinfulness of the wicked: There is no fear of God before his eyes (v. 1).*

■ **Development**   In this surprising oracle, David defined the wicked as those who lack the fear of God. In contrast to the righteous, who recognize their sin and fear God, the wicked flatter themselves too much to detect or hate their sin.

Their self-delusion and recklessness affects their communication, and they are deceitful. Even at night they plot evil schemes and sinful courses of action. They completely lack spiritual values. Their thoughts, wills, and feelings are all corrupt, and this interior rottenness leads to corrupt behavior.

I think of pornographers who exploit women and children for money and power. Of drug runners who pander to the needs of addicts. And of abusers of all types who use their strength to dominate innocent victims.

Apart from God, man is powerless to help himself. He doesn't even know he needs help. Wallowing in his own corruption, he desperately needs God's love and righteousness, but he doesn't know it.

99

■ **Personal prayer**   *O God, I thank You that because of Your grace, I don't need to wallow in wickedness.*

A Musical Play
Act Two: Paradigm of Righteousness

■ **Theme**   Your love, O LORD, reaches to the heavens, your faithfulness to the skies. Your righteousness is like the mighty mountains, your justice like the great deep. O LORD, you preserve both man and beast (vv. 5–6).

■ **Development**   When words are inadequate to define the love of God, the music of poetry helps me express it. So do analogies. David used word pictures of finite things—the heavens, skies, mountains, and seas—to explain infinite things—love, faithfulness, righteousness, and justice.

This is how John Walvoord pictures love:

> Love was when God became a man
> Locked in time and space
>   without rank or place;
> Love was God born of Jewish kin,
> Just a carpenter with some fishermen.
>
> Love was when Jesus walked in history—
> Lovingly He brought a new life that's free;
> Love was God nailed to bleed and die
> To reach and love one such as I.

Words by John E. Walvoord. Music by Don Wyrtzen.
© 1974 by Singspiration Music.

After describing God's unsearchable, inexhaustible, and unfathomable love, David becomes more intimate. He tells of the pricelessness of God's unfailing love and affirms that all men, whatever their station in life, can find security, "refuge in the shadow of your wings"; sustenance, "feast on the abundance of your house"; and satisfaction, "drink from your river of delights." He is the Fountain of life, the Source of all light and joy.

What cause for rejoicing and singing today! What themes to inspire magnificent music-making!

100

■ **Personal prayer**   O Lord, help me to feast at Your table and drink from Your fountain that I may be filled with eternal joy.

A Musical Play
Act Three: Prayer of Confidence

■ **Theme**   *Continue your love to those who know you, your righteousness to the upright in heart (v. 10).*

■ **Development**   Overwhelmed by the stark contrast between human depravity and divine grace, David was driven to prayer. He pleaded for God's continued love and righteousness and for protection from arrogant and wicked men. Then he painted a word picture of the final doom of evildoers who lay fallen, thrown down, and unable to rise.

Ready to fight wickedness (Act One) and to embrace God's grace (Act Two), David gets caught up in urgent prayer (Act Three).

What are the lessons for me today? My life should be totally different from the person who has "no fear of God before his eyes." I don't want to be flippant about the holiness of God, casual about the grace of God, or unduly wise about evil. As Vance Havner so aptly said, "I don't want to be guilty of playing marbles with diamonds."

My life should be a paradigm of God's righteousness because my personality is being radically transformed by God's grace. Therefore, I can join David in this timeless prayer of confidence.

■ **Personal prayer**   *O Lord, make me a paradigm of Your righteousness. May Your grace transform my life today.*

Harmonic Progressions
Harmony in Wisdom

■ **Theme**   *Trust in the LORD and do good; dwell in the land and enjoy safe pasture. Delight yourself in the LORD and he will give you the desires of your heart. Commit your way to the LORD; trust in him and he will do this: He will make your righteousness shine like the dawn, the justice of your cause like the noonday sun. Be still before the LORD and wait patiently for him; do not fret when men succeed in their ways, when they carry out their wicked schemes. Refrain from anger and turn from wrath; do not fret—it leads only to evil (vv. 3–8).*

■ **Development**   Jesus said, "Blessed are the meek for they will inherit the earth" (Matthew 5:5). David said this in Psalm 37:11: "But the meek will inherit the land and enjoy great peace."

Like the flowers of the field, the wicked are only temporary; they eventually wither and die. Therefore, we are not to fret over them. Instead, David gives five steps to personal peace, wisdom, and tranquility:

First, we are to "trust in the Lord and do good." When we do this, we will experience deep inner security.

Second, we are "to delight in the Lord." When we do, a spiritual metamorphosis takes place and His desires become ours.

Third, we are "to commit our way to the Lord." We are to entrust our lives to our Lord's care.

Fourth, we are "to be still before the Lord." We are to wait patiently for the Lord to work out His plans and not be impressed with the success of others.

Fifth, we are "to refrain from anger." We are to resist anger by turning away from it.

Those of us who follow these five imperatives will experience a deep peace and inner serenity, but not a total absence of upheaval in our personal lives. The storms of life are only on the surface; underneath is the calm of His security and strength. The Lord promises that those who follow the path of patient faith will inherit the earth and enjoy great peace.

102

■ **Personal prayer**   *Dear Lord, I praise You for Your promise of deep personal security. Help me not to continue to search for it elsewhere.*

Harmonic Progressions
Dissonance in Wickedness

■ **Theme**   *Better the little that the righteous have than the wealth of many wicked; for the power of the wicked will be broken, but the* LORD *upholds the righteous* (vv. 16–17).

■ **Development**   Wise people are righteous; foolish people are wicked. They stand in bold contrast to each other in this psalm. David described the wicked vividly. They plot against the righteous. They attack by drawing the sword and bending the bow. They slay poor, needy, and righteous people. They are violent and hostile.

The Lord, however, will have the last word. He will laugh at the wicked. He knows their day is coming. He turns their own weapons against them. He breaks their power and renders their wealth useless. He predicts their final denouncement. Like the flowers of the field, they will vanish and disappear.

The righteous, on the other hand, will be upheld. Their inheritance will endure forever. Even in days of famine, they will enjoy plenty.

Though the wicked often prosper while the righteous suffer, in the end God will uphold His justice. He will destroy the wicked and bless the righteous. In the long run, it pays to serve the Lord and to live righteously. Personal fulfillment is a fringe benefit.

■ **Personal prayer**   *I praise You, Lord, for Your power and justice. I thank You that You will eternally reward personal righteousness.*

Harmonic Progressions
Consonance in Righteousness

■ **Theme**   *I was young and now I am old, yet I have never seen the righteous forsaken or their children begging bread. They are always generous and lend freely; their children will be blessed. . . . The mouth of the righteous man utters wisdom, and his tongue speaks what is just. The law of his God is in his heart; his feet do not slip (vv. 25–26, 30–31).*

■ **Development**   Would I like to give generously, experience the Lord's blessing, and look forward to an eternal inheritance? Would I like stability and steadiness in my personal life?

What would it be like to be blessed physically, materially, and to have inner security? Is it possible that I could speak wisdom, proclaim justice, and generally integrate God's truth into my personality? Could I ever be the focus of the Lord's delight? Because God's Word is my reference point for the nature of reality, the more I absorb and obey it, the more I fulfill my destiny. Then I can become an accomplished, complete person.

These are the blessings and benefits the Lord gives to the righteous, to those who fill their hearts with the law of God. Their "feet do not slip."

What promises! My security and wealth don't lie in uncertain riches but in the Lord Himself. Therefore, I'm able to give and lend constantly, and I can be a lasting blessing to society through the family that I lead. What a comfort to know that even though I experience ups and downs, the Lord's hands hold me steady! The Lord Himself establishes my steps and delights in my way. He makes harmony out of my life.

■ **Personal prayer**   *Lord, fill my heart with Your law so that my feet will not slip.*

Harmonic Progressions
Finale: Interplay Between Harmony and Disharmony

■ **Theme**   *I have seen a wicked and ruthless man flourishing like a green tree in its native soil, but he soon passed away and was no more; though I looked for him, he could not be found. . . . The salvation of the righteous comes from the LORD; he is their stronghold in time of trouble. The LORD helps them and delivers them; He delivers them from the wicked and saves them, because they take refuge in him* (vv. 35–36, 39–40).

■ **Development**   In tying up the loose ends of this moving psalm, David lets us see the final end of the wicked and righteous person. The last verses are a moving finale, an exciting interplay between harmony and disharmony.

The wicked lie in wait for the righteous, but the Lord renders them impotent. The metaphor used to picture the wicked, ruthless man is a flourishing green tree. But that tree soon withers, dies, falls down, and rots. It vanishes without a trace.

Hitler, architect and Führer of Germany's Third Reich, became a broken man. On April 39, 1945, in a bomb shelter of the Chancellery, Hitler and his wife, Eva Braun, swallowed poison. Aides burned their bodies with gasoline.

In bold contrast, the righteous are exalted. They possess the land. They have a glorious future because their salvation comes from the Lord. The Lord helps them, protects them, and delivers them in times of trouble. He is their shelter and their refuge.

This uplifting psalm ends with peace, serenity, and calm objectivity—a totally different mood from the fretful impatience and anxiety David expresses at the beginning of this psalm.

■ **Personal prayer**   *Lord, I live in a frantic society and experience stress and pressure. Be my refuge and shelter.*

Dirge of Discouragement Guilt

■ **Theme**   O LORD, *do not rebuke me in your anger or discipline me in your wrath. For your arrows have pierced me, and your hand has come down upon me. Because of your wrath there is no health in my body; my bones have no soundness because of my sin. My guilt has overwhelmed me like a burden too heavy to bear (vv. 1–4).*

■ **Development**   Our heavenly Father is very attentive. He disciplines the children He loves (Proverbs 3:11–12). David was experiencing the profound, searing devastation of internal guilt. It gnawed away at him.

Since he feared God's anger and wrath, David cried out for mercy. Emotional tension erupted into physical illness because his guilt was so overwhelming.

We must never assume that all sickness is punishment, although I believe that sometimes physical illness is directly related to guilt over irresponsible behavior. Here we have a clear-cut case of illness resulting from sin. David said, "My wounds fester and are loathsome because of my sinful folly." He was paying the wages of sin with mental anguish and physical agony.

What is the bottom line of sinful behavior? David said, "I am feeble and utterly crushed. I groan in anguish of heart." Authentic lament almost always precedes genuine praise. I admire David's honesty. His life throbbed with reality and authenticity.

■ **Personal prayer**   *I thank You, Lord, for giving me a sensitive conscience that serves as a spiritual gyroscope for my life.*

Dirge of Discouragement Isolation

■ **Theme** *All my longings lie open before you, O Lord; my sighing is not hidden from you. My heart pounds, my strength fails me; even the light has gone from my eyes. My friends and companions avoid me because of my wounds; my neighbors stay far away (vv. 9–11).*

■ **Development** The more David needed the support of friends, the less attention he received from them because of his abnormality. He was caught in the same vicious cycle many of us find ourselves in. Sin has led to guilt; guilt has led to emotional and physical illness, illness has led to suffering and pain, and pain has led to isolation and loneliness. David was like a modern-day AIDS victim. He said, "My friends and companions avoid me because of my wounds; my neighbors stay far away" (38:11).

David felt the effects of alienation. Estranged from his heavenly Father as well as his community of friends, David—like many of us—was lonely and despondent. He was at a point where only the Lord could meet his incredible need. He was ready and open for a deep work of God in his life.

■ **Personal prayer** *I cry to You, Lord, out of my deep loneliness and despair. Please come to me, minister to me, and fully meet my need!*

Dirge of Discouragement *Patience*

■ **Theme**   *I wait for you, O LORD; you will answer, O Lord my God. For I said, "Do not let them gloat or exalt themselves over me when my foot slips" (vv. 15–16).*

■ **Development**   Despite David's instability and anxiety, he was able to wait on God. Though mired in a morass of sin, guilt, and suffering, he still exercised faith. David faced his sin squarely and confessed his iniquity. His sensitivity to the inner voice of God's Spirit had not been seared, and he did not have a jaded conscience.

Once Karen and I attended a bullfight in Mexico City. We were in a large stadium surrounded by thousands of very excited Latin people. We watched as the first bull was manipulated by the matador with his banderillas. In time, the bull was outmaneuvered and killed. Seeing blood flow the first time made us queasy. But after seeing ten bulls killed in a similar way, we weren't as queasy. I believe we can become anesthetized to sin in much the same way. David wasn't like this. He was still deeply troubled by his sin and was beyond making excuses or rationalizations for it.

All of this is testimony to the fact that David was God's child. Heathen people are not profoundly troubled by their sin. The fact that David felt God's chastening hand was one more proof that he was a son. Guilt is also tacit evidence for the holiness of God, the absolute standard by which all ethics and values are measured.

■ **Personal prayer**   *Heavenly Father, I confess my sin before You today. Bind my wandering heart to You. Amen.*

Dirge of
Discouragement   Calling on God

■ **Theme**   O LORD, do not forsake me; be not far from me, O my God. Come quickly to help me, O Lord my Savior (vv. 21–22).

■ **Development**   At the end of this penitential psalm, David cried out to God. He could no longer endure being alone.

David had an intimate knowledge of his Lord. He knew Him by His deepest, most personal name—*Yahweh*. He was also related to God by covenant. He knew the Lord as his Master and Savior, and addressed the Lord from these perspectives in verses 21–22.

David had three final requests: that the Lord would not forsake him; that the Lord would be close; and that the Lord would come quickly to help.

Being right all the time is really important to me. Therefore, saying "I'm sorry" isn't easy for me. But I'm learning that I don't have to be so perfectionistic and that being vulnerable can be quite liberating. I'm just beginning to learn how to be released through repentance. Apologizing brings real freedom to my life; repentance provides the only true resolution for my guilty conscience.

■ **Personal prayer**   Lord, I identify with David, the ancient King of Israel. Please don't forsake me; be close, and come quickly to help. To get right to the point: Forgive my sin.

Aria on Anxiety
Verbalizing Feelings

■ **Theme**   *I said, "I will watch my ways and keep my tongue from sin; I will put a muzzle on my mouth as long as the wicked are in my presence." But when I was silent and still, not even saying anything good, my anguish increased. My heart grew hot within me, and as I meditated, the fire burned; then I spoke with my tongue (vv. 1–3).*

■ **Development**   David learned to verbalize his feelings, to communicate his anxiety, and to articulate his inner thoughts.

Silence and stillness had made David sick. Not facing reality had increased his anxiety. He had become a pressure cooker, and the lid was ready to blow off!

I'm a goal-oriented person. When my goal is blocked, I become anxious. Often I deny or block out how I'm really feeling, which forces my feelings to escalate out of control. I have found that feelings, good or bad, must be acknowledged or they will destroy me.

David didn't acknowledge his feelings in front of the wicked. He restrained himself from venting them in the wrong company. Unrestrained ventilation could be misconstrued by unbelievers as disloyalty or even blasphemy.

He took his pent-up protest to the Lord. Lament as well as praise was an integral part of his prayer. His relationship with the Lord was honest and down-to-earth—the way I want mine to be today.

■ **Personal prayer**   *Help me, Lord, to watch my ways and to keep my tongue from sin. Help me to bring my gravest concerns to You.*

Aria on Anxiety
Assessing Life's Brevity

■ **Theme** *"Show me, O LORD, my life's end and the number of my days; let me know how fleeting is my life. You have made my days a mere handbreadth; the span of my years is as nothing before you. Each man's life is but a breath. Selah. Man is a mere phantom as he goes to and fro: He bustles about, but only in vain; he heaps up wealth, not knowing who will get it"* (vv. 4–6).

■ **Development** Life is brief. Like a vapor, a mist, a breath, it is soon over. James says, "Why, you do not even know what will happen tomorrow. What is your life? You are a mist that appears for a little while and then vanishes" (James 4:14).

Our busyness makes us think we are more important than we really are. Yet in all of our bustle and activity, we are still mere phantoms. We have little control over the destiny of our heaped-up wealth. Our lifespan is nothing before God. And life itself is empty without Him.

Mid-life is a time of critical evaluation for most of us. We are preoccupied with time. Accomplishments and achievements are carefully scrutinized as we look to the future. How much time do I have left? becomes a nagging question for us to answer. The dangerous temptation to live for false gods results in the emptiness we are so frantically fleeing.

David, too, was aware of time's passing. What caused him to number his days? What made him suddenly look at things from God's point of view? The answer: *intense suffering.* Extreme pain opened David to a deep work of God in his life. Suffering is God's megaphone to reach those of us with deaf ears.

■ **Personal prayer** *Lord, help me to become aware of just how fleeting my life really is. Help me to make today really count for You.*

Aria on Anxiety
Experiencing Discipline

■ **Theme**   *But now, Lord, what do I look for? My hope is in you. Save me from all my transgressions; do not make me the scorn of fools. I was silent; I would not open my mouth, for you are the one who has done this. Remove your scourge from me; I am overcome by the blow of your hand. You rebuke and discipline men for their sin; you consume their wealth like a moth—each man is but a breath"* (vv. 7–11).

■ **Development**   After experiencing the shattering cruelty of friends (Psalm 38), David felt the crushing severity of the Lord.

Overcome by God's heavy-handed treatment, David prayed to be released from the pressure. Despondent, he cried out to God, pouring out his soul about how brief and fragile life is.

Though nearly overwhelmed by his own mortality, David knew that salvation came from the Lord. He affirmed that faith by crying out "My hope is in you!"

The year 1984 was one of profound loss for me. Norman Johnson, our senior editor at Singspiration Music, went to be with the Lord. Then shortly after his death, my mom died. A few months later, my pastor, Reverend George Gardiner, passed away. These losses caused me to realize how fleeting life is and how near eternity is. Just the timespan of the twinkling of an eye separates us from God.

God isn't a sado-masochist, but He has built suffering and adversity into the mysterious nature of reality. God used pain and hardship to give David perspective—on his transient life on earth and on his hope for eternity. In other words, dissonance is an essential element of harmony. For it is the tension between consonance and dissonance that creates music.

■ **Personal prayer**   *Lord, no matter how dark and grave my circumstances become, help me to affirm my faith and trust in You. And I trust You to make music even out of the disharmony of my life.*

April

PSALMS 39–50

*With consummate creativity, the psalmist
portrays Christ in all His beauty as a
bridegroom arrayed for his bride.* —Psalm 45

Aria on Anxiety
Petitioning God's Help

■ **Theme**   *"Hear my prayer, O LORD, listen to my cry for help; be not deaf to my weeping. For I dwell with you as an alien, a stranger, as all my fathers were. Look away from me, that I may rejoice again before I depart and am no more (vv. 12–13).*

■ **Development**   David, feeling alienated and estranged from God, cries out for help. He even wonders if the Lord hears his weeping, for he feels like an outcast—a foreigner in Israel, a mere passing guest or sojourner. For the moment, all he can see is his own death looming before him.

As a Christian music executive in a secular world, I have felt this kind of alienation. Then I remind myself that I'm just a pilgrim here.

Despite David's desperation, alienation, and estrangement, he prays, and this prayer is a testimony of his bedrock faith and trust in God. Though he can't put his circumstances together rationally, he still clings to an existential relationship with God.

The most natural thing for a believer to do in times of despair and despondency is to turn to the heavenly Father. All true spirituality begins with this basic kind of honest lament.

■ **Personal prayer**   *Heavenly Father, I may be a stranger in this world, but I don't want to be a stranger to You. Don't let me blend with the voices of the world, but help me to sound a clear note of faith in the midst of doubt and disillusionment.*

Sonatina of Sacrifice   *Joy*

■ **Theme**   *I waited patiently for the LORD; he turned to me and heard my cry. He lifted me out of the slimy pit, out of the mud and mire; he set my feet on a rock and gave me a firm place to stand. He put a new song in my mouth, a hymn of praise to our God. Many will see and fear and put their trust in the LORD (vv. 1–3).*

■ **Introduction**   In three magnificent movements treating the subjects of joy (vv. 1–4), thanksgiving, (vv. 5–10) and prayer (vv. 11–17), David has flawlessly crafted a sonatina on the sacrifice of praise.

■ **Development**   Most likely the psalmist has recently been near death, for he uses the metaphor of a deep pit, lined with slime, to describe his precarious position. But the Lord hears his cry and delivers him—and what a deliverance! Now David's feet are firmly planted on a rock.

Released from distress, he moves quickly from anxiety to a joyous celebration of God's power. This fresh vision of God gives David exciting material for a "new song." He may have arranged an old hymn—and discovering its genius—added fresh color and new insights. Or perhaps, in the rush of creativity and exhilaration, he composed an entirely new song. Inner joy results in music!

This event, and other miraculous deliverances in David's life, have been the inspiration for many of his great hymns of praise shared with his congregation and recorded for generations to come. As a result, thousands "fear and put their trust in the Lord." Worship becomes witness! I also will be used of the Lord today to the extent that I place my faith and trust in Him and lead others to do so. This is the source of both my joy and my music.

■ **Personal prayer**   *Lord, help me not to seek joy and happiness apart from You. And may the songs that come from the deep springs of my heart point others to the Source of all satisfaction.*

Sonatina of Sacrifice   Thanksgiving

■ **Theme**   Many, O LORD my God, are the wonders you have done. The things you planned for us no one can recount to you; were I to speak and tell of them, they would be too many to declare. Sacrifice and offering you did not desire. . . . Then I said, "Here I am, I desire to do your will, O my God; your law is within my heart" (vv. 5–8).

■ **Development**   Caught up in the vortex of an exhilarating experience with the Lord, David breaks forth with thanksgiving. As his imagination soars, he is reminded of many other miraculous works God has wrought in behalf of His people. David's whole being, permeated with God's truth, is turned to His will, and the psalmist discovers that God desires the sacrifice of a pure heart and attitude rather than external, and sometimes empty, liturgies.

In music ministry it is easy to depend upon natural gifts, experience, and craftsmanship as a substitute for real inspiration. But David's time with the Lord becomes the deep reservoir out of which flow his hymns of praise.

Elated with this discovery, David can't keep still in "the great assembly" (v. 9). His lips, unsealed, proclaim the righteousness of God reigning in his heart, and he shares four major themes with the congregation: God's faithfulness, salvation, love, and truth. Suddenly David finds himself in the middle of a revival resulting from his own praise and thanksgiving!

116

■ **Personal prayer**   Lord, fill me with Your steadfast love and perfect truth so that the music I write will reflect my gratitude.

Sonatina of Sacrifice   Prayer

■ **Theme**   *Do not withhold your mercy from me, O* LORD; *may your love and your truth always protect me. For troubles without number surround me; my sins have overtaken me, and I cannot see. They are more than the hairs of my head, and my heart fails within me. Be pleased, O* LORD, *to save me; O* LORD, *come quickly to help me. . . . You are my help and my deliverer; O my God, do not delay* (vv. 11–13, 17).

■ **Development**   My sins always catch up with me. Like a pebble dropped into the water that creates ever widening circles, an act of sin has expanding consequences. The Lord forgives and erases the guilt, but He does not change history. Much of my pain emanates from the effects of sin that have continued past the original act.

David too is hurting. Overwhelmed by the number of his sins ("more than the hairs of my head") and the extent of his troubles, he is about ready to give up. Yet he cries out for mercy and for the protection of God's loyal love and flawless truth.

David may be down about his own sin, but he's very much aware of the sins of others as well, and he still has energy left to pray about the enemies who pursue him relentlessly. He petitions the Lord for their confusion, shame, and disgrace (vv. 14–15). In contrast, he also prays for the salvation, help, and deliverance of those who seek the Lord. This dual theme reminds us that, above all, God alone is worthy to be "exalted and magnified" (v. 16).

David closes his exquisite "Sonatina of Sacrifice" by focusing on the majesty and glory of God. Like David, I recognize that the Lord is my "help and deliverer."

■ **Personal prayer**   *Lord, may I seek You, rejoice and be glad in You, and may You always be exalted and magnified in my life and work.*

A Madrigal on Mercy
A Fundamental Principle Stated

■ **Theme**   *Blessed is he who has regard for the weak; the* LORD *delivers him in times of trouble. The* LORD *will protect him and preserve his life; he will bless him in the land and not surrender him to the desire of his foes. The* LORD *will sustain him on his sickbed and restore him from his bed of illness (vv. 1–3).*

■ **Development**   The message of these verses from Psalm 41 is found in miniature in Matthew 5:7 where the Lord Jesus says, "Blessed are the merciful for they will be shown mercy." David asserts the maxim of God's moral law that He will deliver the person who shows regard for the weak.

It is encouraging to see a growing response to human need. Many musicians donate the proceeds of their concerts to the underprivileged in cities where they perform. When motivated by love for the Lord, these merciful acts will not go unrewarded.

In fact, David is very specific about the four blessings the Lord bestows on the compassionate person: protection, security, strength, and good health. How practical and down to earth!

The Lord protects and preserves the life of the sympathetic and empathetic person. He also "blesses him in the land" and provides a profound sense of security. He further gives him strength over his foes; his enemies neither intimidate nor dominate him. Finally, He heals those who show compassion to the poor and needy.

■ **Personal prayer**   *Lord, make me more sensitive to hurting people. Open my eyes and my heart to their needs and let me be a channel of Your blessing in their lives.*

A Madrigal on Mercy
A Fundamental Principle Supported

■ **Theme**   *I said, "O LORD, have mercy on me; heal me, for I have sinned against you." My enemies say of me in malice, "When will he die and his name perish?" Whenever one comes to see me, he speaks falsely, while his heart gathers slander; then he goes out and spreads it abroad. All my enemies whisper together against me. . . . Even my close friend, whom I trusted . . . has lifted up his heel against me. But you, O LORD, have mercy on me (vv. 4–7, 9–10).*

■ **Development**   Most highly creative, artistic people are a bit fragile. Beneath the surface is a sea of insecurity. I have seen some of the top people in the industry demonstrate some pretty unChristlike characteristics when threatened by competition from within the ranks.

It's easy to understand why David is down in the pits again. Not only are his enemies hovering like vultures, just waiting for his death and denunciation, but he has just learned that he can't even count on his friends! Though they come to visit while he is on his sickbed, pretending concern, they spread malicious rumors about him the minute they leave. Even the friends with whom he has shared intimate confidences have betrayed him.

Though vengeance belongs to Jehovah alone, perhaps David is contemplating the punishment of traitors, one of the duties of a just monarch. David illustrates and supports God's principle that He will deliver those who are merciful. David believes his enemies have been held at bay because of his own integrity.

A glorious doxology concludes this madrigal on mercy and serves as a fitting close to the First Book of Psalms. It is a veritable outburst of praise comprising a double "Amen!"

■ **Personal prayer**   *Dear Lord, it's tough to forgive those who deliberately set out to malign me. But because You have been merciful to me, I long to show mercy to others. Give me the grace to do it! Amen and Amen.*

Longing and Lament
Thirsting for God

■ **Theme**   *As the deer pants for streams of water, so my soul pants for you, O God. My soul thirsts for God, for the living God. When can I go and meet with God? . . . These things I remember as I pour out my soul: how I used to go with the multitude, leading the procession to the house of God, with shouts of joy and thanksgiving among the festive throng (vv. 1–2, 4).*

■ **Development**   This ancient temple singer, perhaps exiled in the north, has a deep longing for God and His house. His longing takes the form of an insatiable thirst, much like that of a deer foraging for water in a dry and arid land. He has been separated from God, estranged from the sanctuary, and is in desperate need of intimacy and fellowship.

His only solace is the memory of the great festivals in God's sanctuary. He remembers the pulsating excitement of public worship when throngs of worshipers filled the air with shouts of praise and songs of joy. He remembers being brought to the core of his own reality through his interaction with the living God.

My life resonates to the song this Levite is singing. How many times have I attempted to fill the vacuum of my life with substitutes for God? How often have I felt emptiness deep inside my soul because I have become separated from Him? How typical of me to misuse God's precious gifts from a desire for sensual pleasure, only to block deep personal intimacy! And what am I left with? A profound thirst and longing for the living God. Only He can satisfy my deepest longings. All the rest is a disappointingly empty cup.

■ **Personal prayer**   *Lord, teach me to fill my life with You so that I will be fully satisfied.*

Longing and Lament
Overwhelmed with Despair—I

■ **Theme**   *Why are you downcast, O my soul? Why so disturbed within me? Put your hope in God, for I will yet praise him, my Savior and my God. . . . Deep calls to deep in the roar of your waterfalls; all your waves and breakers have swept over me. By day the LORD directs his love, at night his song is with me—a prayer to the God of my life (vv. 5, 7–8).*

■ **Development**   My soul is rooted in eternity, but my mind and body are often under severe pressures of the here and now. It is difficult to sustain creative energy over a long time. I live in fear of deadlines. I struggle with balancing my priorities, with handling money wisely, with proper investment of time, with handling difficult and demanding relationships. When I feel I'm in over my head, this psalm brings consolation.

This psalm writer knew the debilitating effect of depression and despair. In verse 7, his mind must have been in turmoil as he portrays an alien scene. Perhaps churned by a spring storm, the Jordan River rages. As the troubled waters hiss and spew, the river becomes a metaphor for all that is overwhelming and uncontrollable in the psalmist's life, and he feels that he has lost his footing and is in danger of drowning.

Still, his hope is in God. Verse 8 is the centerpiece, the psalmist's confession of faith. The one ray of light in the darkness is his confidence that the Lord loves him. All of the psalmist's anxiety is channeled through prayer to the God of his life. The song of the Lord is with him—and with me—even in the deepest waters and through the darkest night.

■ **Personal prayer**   *Lord, when I feel as if I'm sinking under unbelievable burdens, teach me to sing, to pray, and to feel Your inexhaustible love!*

Longing and Lament
Overwhelmed with Despair—II

■ **Theme**   *Why are you downcast, O my soul? Why so disturbed within me? Put your hope in God, for I will yet praise him, my Savior and my God. . . . You are God my stronghold. . . . Send forth your light and your truth, let them guide me. . . . Then will I go to the altar of God, to God, my joy and my delight. I will praise you with the harp, O God, my God (42:11; 43:2–4).*

■ **Development**   Just about the time I think I have gained the victory over some black mood, some writer's block, some unworthy goal, the whole thing comes crashing down around me, and I am back to square one. In this rut of defeat, my prayers sound very much like those of this psalmist: "Why have you rejected me? Why must I go about mourning, oppressed by the enemy?" (43:2).

This psalmist has a right to his depression. Ungodly people have accused him unjustly, and he prays to the Lord for vindication—for a declaration of his innocence.

But dark moods can give way to positive praying. Like the psalmist, I can't allow my mind to camp on negative ideas and feelings, but I can pray for God's light and truth to guide me. "Let them bring me to your holy mountain, to the place where you dwell" (43:3).

In the sanctuary, in the presence of my fellow believers, I'll praise the Lord with acoustic and electric instruments, with sophisticated rhythms, with innovative harmonies and soaring melodies—all reveling in the ineffable glory of God! In this way I, too, will be able to experience His transcending, transforming power.

■ **Personal prayer**   *Lord, in the darkness of my circumstances, help me to be aware that consummate joy and delight are centered in You.*

Longing and Lament
Overwhelmed with Despair—III

■ **Theme**   *Why are you downcast, O my soul? Why so disturbed within me? Put your hope in God, for I will yet praise him, my Savior and my God (v. 5).*

■ **Development**   Psalms 42 and 43 are actually one sadly beautiful poem. The two parts are unified by a plaintive refrain heard three times—42:5; 42:11; 43:5. It is the lament of a temple singer in the ancient world. Its bitter-sweet song is startlingly relevant to our situation today.

This psalmist knew how to pray. He expresses his feelings honestly, admitting that his inner life is restless and insecure. Some deep longings have gone unmet, and he doesn't pretend otherwise, skimming over the surface of his personal needs.

But he doesn't stop with this candid appraisal of his life, refusing to wallow in his hopelessness. He utters a full-throated confidence in God and vows that he will again praise the Lord and will turn his whole being to face Him.

Unlike a modern man, who gives up in despair or clings obstinately to some flimsy philosophy, this believer chooses to declare his faith in the one, true, living God of the universe. To pretend faith in an unworthy or imaginary object is foolishness. But to place our hope in God, no matter how uncertain and insecure we may be, is the path to praise.

■ **Personal prayer**   *O Elohim, I pray that my hope will be in You, even when I feel most helpless. May I never turn my face away from You!*

Unfailing Love   Then . . .

■ **Theme**   *We have heard with our ears, O God; our fathers have told us what you did in their days, in days long ago. With your hand you drove out the nations and planted our fathers; you crushed the peoples and made our fathers flourish. It was not by their sword that they won the land, nor did their arm bring them victory; it was your right hand, your arm, and the light of your face, for you loved them (vv. 1–3).*

■ **Development**   This psalm begins with a rousing recital of past victories in the history of Israel: Nations were driven out, peoples were crushed, enemies were pushed back, soldiers were victorious, foes were trampled. Israel's ancestors flourished as a theocracy—a nation united under the living God—in the midst of paganism and idolatry.

The psalmist articulates the secret of the overwhelming success of the armies of Israel: "I do not trust in my bow, my sword does not bring me victory; but you give us victory over our enemies, you put our adversaries to shame. In God, we make our boast all day long, and we will praise your name forever" (44:6–8). They fought in the Name of the Lord. That Name alone empowered them!

Names or song titles are also pivotal in capsulizing the meaning and power of a lyric. The Chief Musician, David, would have loved "How Great Thou Art!" or "His Name Is Wonderful." There is incomparable force and energy in the Name of the Lord.

What is the secret of effectiveness and power for me today? I must choose not to live independently of God, but make Him central in my life. I must resist an easy, casual commitment to Christ, but reflect in my daily walk the personality of the One whose Name I bear. That Name will give me the power to withstand temptation, endure criticism, and witness boldly.

■ **Personal prayer**   *O God, may I boast, not in my own gifts and abilities, but in You. And may I praise Your Name forever!*

Unfailing Love   Now . . .

■ **Theme**   *But now you have rejected and humbled us; you no longer go out with our armies. You made us retreat before the enemy, and our adversaries have plundered us. You gave us up to be devoured like sheep and have scattered us among the nations. . . . My disgrace is before me all day long (vv. 9–11, 15).*

■ **Development**   If ever there were a passage written in the minor key, it's this one. Hear the litany of defeat in the action words of these verses: *rejected, humbled, plundered, scattered, devoured.* Israel, God's favored nation, now faces demoralization and destruction.

Neighboring nations scoff and scorn; they gloat over the ill fortunes of Israel. They thumb their noses at these people who have apparently been abandoned by their God.

I heard my friend, Chuck Swindoll, give a moving message on integrity the other night. In it, he said that God tests His servants in two major ways—through adversity and through prosperity. Because we are children of the heavenly Father, He sometimes disciplines or chastens us. That's "tough love."

But how do we handle rejection and defeat? How do we react when our faith doesn't seem to be getting results? Is our relationship to God a hoax?

This psalm does not give us neat, tidy answers to those questions. The mystery of God's grand design looms in the distance. In the immediate situation God's people are suffering. Rather than causing them to forsake their faith, however, it drives them to their knees in profound prayer.

125

■ **Personal prayer**   *O God, in the reversals and discordant moments of my life, help me to hear Your faithful love calling me to repentance and renewal.*

Unfailing Love   *Why?*

■ **Theme**   *Awake, O LORD! Why do you sleep? Rouse yourself! Do not reject us forever. Why do you hide your face and forget our misery and oppression? . . . Rise up and help us; redeem us because of your unfailing love (vv. 23–24, 26).*

■ **Development**   Why me, Lord? The psalmist reflects my own twentieth-century struggle to see God when the lights are turned out. The people of Israel are experiencing the crush of rejection, and they are as perplexed as I with the mysteries of my own life. Why has this happened? What have I done? I've been on the job, faithfully serving Him, laboring in the place He's assigned me. Doesn't He know I'm hurting? Doesn't He care? Is He asleep?

The history of God's people, both past and present, seems to fluctuate between periods of blessing and periods of defeat. At these times, is God really withdrawing in wrath or does He just refuse to be hurried? During a furious squall on the Sea of Galilee, as waves threatened to capsize the disciples' boat, Jesus slept peacefully on a cushion in the stern (Mark 4:37–38).

God's timetable is often different from ours. Suffering may not be a punishment, only a battle-scar—the price paid for serving the Lord in a hostile environment, in a world at war with God.

When it seems as if the boat is sinking, we can cling to the reality of His unfailing love. "Who shall separate us from the love of Christ? Shall trouble or hardship or persecution or famine or nakedness or danger or sword? . . . No, in all these things we are more than conquerors through him who loved us" (Romans 8:35, 37).

126

■ **Personal prayer**   *O God, may my impatience not prevent me from constantly trusting in Your steadfast love no matter how bleak my circumstances appear.*

The Love Song   *Verses for a King*

■ **Theme**   *My heart is stirred by a noble theme as I recite my verses for the king; my tongue is the pen of a skillful writer (v. 1).*

■ **Development**   No writer should write until a fire burns deep inside. If one feels no strong conviction, no genuine emotion, no real compulsion, there is nothing to say!

This verse gives us a glimpse of the process of composition in the ancient world. In this messianic psalm, the inscription tells us the name of the tune—"Lilies." The composers are the sons of Korah; their subject, the wedding of the King of kings.

No wonder this musical artist's heart is "stirred"! Moved by the most noble theme of all times—the marriage of Christ to His bride, the Church—the psalmist's words flow quickly and fluently. With consummate creativity he portrays Christ in all His beauty as a bridegroom arrayed for his bride.

Now deeply involved—intellectually, emotionally, and spiritually—the psalmist's tongue becomes "the pen of a skillful writer," and he articulates an eloquent lyric. As his heart responds and his thoughts are engaged, the sacrifice kindled upon his lips overflows upon the page. Truly, this is an inspired work, though crafted with great artistry. Sincerity, especially among biblical writers, is never a substitute for skill.

What a mandate for a Christian artist! What a mission statement for the Christian writer! What goals to live for! What a target to shoot toward! And all centering in a depiction of the Messiah that is intensely personal, beautiful, and artistic.

■ **Personal prayer**   *Lord, give me a vision of Your Son that will set my heart on fire. Then my songs and my writings will burn with joy, praise, and beauty.*

The Love Song   Verses for the Groom

■ **Theme**   *You are the most excellent of men and your lips have been anointed with grace, since God has blessed you forever. Gird your sword upon your side, O mighty one; clothe yourself with splendor and majesty. In your majesty ride forth victoriously in behalf of truth, humility and righteousness; let your right hand display awesome deeds. . . . You love righteousness and hate wickedness; therefore God, your God, has set you above your companions by anointing you with the oil of joy (vv. 2–4, 7).*

■ **Development**   When I read the words of this beautiful psalm, I'm reminded of my own marriage to Karen. July 14, 1963 was a spectacular day for an outdoor wedding on the lawn of Word of Life Inn. With Schroon Lake and the majestic Adirondack Mountains as our backdrop, we recited our vows from memory. This groom was typically nervous and apprehensive, but anticipated a glorious future with his beautiful bride.

The warrior King described by the psalmist is the "most excellent of men," the model for all men of God. He is to ride forth in splendor and majesty, "in behalf of truth, humility, and righteousness."

His kingdom will be everlasting. It will be characterized by righteousness and justice. The King Himself is incomparable. He is anointed with the oil of joy; His robes are scented; His house is adorned with inlaid ivory; and His rooms are filled with the glorious music of strings. His honored women are the daughters of kings, the chiefest of whom is the royal bride beautified in robes of gold.

Hebrews 1 shows us that this is God's Son, the "heir of all things" and the Creator of the universe. This King is the Son who is the "radiance of God's glory and the exact representation of his being, sustaining all things by his powerful word" (1:3). He is the model for all believers, but particularly for all who would aspire to be men of God.

■ **Personal prayer**   *Lord, I worship You in all of Your magnificence and transcendent beauty. Make me more like You in truth, humility, and righteousness.*

The Love Song   *Verses for the Bride*

■ **Theme**   *Listen, O daughter, consider and give ear: Forget your people and your father's house. The king is enthralled by your beauty; honor him, for he is your lord. . . . I will perpetuate your memory through all generations; therefore the nations will praise you for ever and ever (vv. 10–11, 17).*

■ **Development**   The dignity of biblically ordained marriage in the ancient world is certainly foreign to the psychology of many modern marriages. This scene from the royal wedding depicts clearly the parting with the old and the new beginning required of this princess bride. The husband too must make a break from his childhood home, separating both physically and emotionally from parents, in order to give himself to his wife (Genesis 2:24).

This is to be an all-encompassing relationship, and no sacrifice is too great to ensure its success. Karen, for example, left her home and family in Topeka, Kansas to join me in New York. She then accompanied me to Dallas so I could further my education in both music and theology. She moved our young family to Grand Rapids, Michigan, and later to Nashville, Tennessee, to pursue various ministry opportunities the Lord opened up for us. None of these adjustments has been easy or problem-free, but like her biblical sister, Sarah, she has chosen to honor her husband at great personal sacrifice (1 Peter 3:6).

This evidence of her love supports me daily, but I recall too that radiant young woman on our wedding day. Like that royal bride in this psalm, Karen was accompanied by friends and approached our improvised altar "with joy and gladness."

In conclusion, new glories are promised to couples who are yielded to the Lord. This bride and groom will be blessed with sons who will become princes to "perpetuate their memory through all generations." This is a foretaste of the Messiah who will bring "many sons to glory" (Hebrews 2:10, 13) and who will "reign forever."

129

■ **Personal prayer**   *Lord, I thank You for Karen and for the beautiful relationship of marriage which illustrates so clearly Your relationship to Your bride, the Church.*

A Mighty Fortress
Part 1—God's Power Over Nature

■ **Theme**   *God is our refuge and strength, an ever-present help in trouble. Therefore we will not fear, though the earth give way and the mountains fall into the heart of the sea, though its waters roar and foam and the mountains quake with their surging (vv. 1–3).*

■ **Development**   How does one face the possibility of world catastrophe? How does one guard against internal disintegration of the personality in view of pressure to conform to the false standards of society? The answer is found in God alone, not in God plus anything else.

In our lifetime we may never personally experience earthquake, volcanic eruption, or tornadic winds—all evidences of the physical universe in turmoil. While these natural calamities are devastating, equally distressing and disrupting are the more common upheavals caused by marital conflict, financial reverses, illness, and the death of friends or loved ones.

When that which seems unchangeable and impregnable falls, God is my stability. He is my refuge—"my shelter and protection from danger." He is my strength—"my vigor, mental and moral power, firmness and courage." He is my ever-present help in trouble.

As a high-strung, sensitive, emotional person, I need to be constantly reminded of these truths. Worry is an inappropriate response for God's child. Anxiety, mental distress, and emotional agitation yield to trust in the unshakable, immutable, omnipotent God of the universe. He is the Master of all of nature, and I must make Him the Master of my troubled soul.

130

■ **Personal prayer**   *O Lord, I praise You that I do not have to fear anyone or anything because You are my Refuge and Strength.*

A Mighty Fortress
Part 2—God's Protection of His City

■ **Theme**   *There is a river whose streams make glad the city of God, the holy place where the Most High dwells. God is within her, she will not fall; God will help her at break of day. Nations are in uproar, kingdoms fall; he lifts his voice, the earth melts. The LORD Almighty is with us; the God of Jacob is our fortress (vv. 4–7).*

■ **Development**   The city of God is a rich metaphor, a symbol of peace, tranquility, and contentment. It denotes Jerusalem, Zion, any place where God dwells. The New Testament vision is of a heavenly community, rather than an earthly locality, where believers praise the Lord forever. God fills that place with His glory and peace. Fear, darkness, and vulnerability will be foreign there.

But how do I live now with daily stresses and nightly fears that claw at my soul? How do I cope with anxieties and pressures that keep me restless and uneasy? I must latch on to the exciting reality that the Lord is with me *now!* The God of Jacob is my fortress *now!*

> A mighty fortress is our God,
> A bulwark never failing;
> Our helper He amid the flood
> Of mortal ills prevailing.
> Dost ask who that may be?
> Christ Jesus it is He—
> Lord Sabaoth His name,
> From age to age the same,
> And He must win the battle.

Words and music by Martin Luther.

131

■ **Personal prayer**   *O Lord, may I catch a vision of that city of God where there is no anxiety, no fear, no stress, and may I realize that I may dwell with You—now—in peace.*

A Mighty Fortress
Part 3—God's Omnipotence

■ **Theme**   *Come and see the works of the LORD, the desolations he has brought on the earth. He makes wars cease to the ends of the earth; he breaks the bow and shatters the spear, he burns the shields with fire. "Be still, and know that I am God; I will be exalted among the nations" (vv. 8–10).*

■ **Development**   Christ commanded the violent surging waters, "Peace, be still!" When the last chapter of world history has been written, in the same way God will put an end to violence, war, and to all of the effects of sin in the universe.

In this vision of the end of time, desolations have been brought on the earth, wars have ceased, and instruments of war have been eliminated. God's judgment has prevailed and the world has become forcibly disarmed. At that time He will be exalted among the nations and in the earth. Man's hopes will be dashed, but God will be exalted in all of His majesty and glory.

What should be my response to this vision? Once fully aware that God is my fortress, my shelter, my protection, I must learn to be still and know that God is God and that He has provided our redemption through Christ.

In the end, He is all that matters in time and eternity.

■ **Personal prayer**   *O Lord, as You will finally be exalted among the nations and in the earth, be exalted in my life now and help me to be still before You.*

Exultation!

■ **Theme**   *Clap your hands, all you nations; shout to God with cries of joy. . . . God has ascended amid shouts of joy, the LORD amid the sounding of trumpets. Sing praises to God, sing praises; sing praises to our King, sing praises (vv. 1, 5–6).*

■ **Development**   This psalm, a hymn to the Great King, gives us a graphic picture of drama in worship. These ancient believers allowed themselves to be caught up in worship. They praised the Lord with every aspect of their being—intellectually, emotionally, and physically. They learned how to worship God with each of the five senses— sight, sound, smell, taste, and touch. This psalm pulsates and resonates with excitement!

Note the verbs which give movement and power to this psalm: "Clap your hands!" "Shout to God with cries of joy!" "Sing praises!" (Note, too, that these verbs are in the imperative. Lackluster worship is not acceptable.) Why such jubilation? Because the King has "subdued nations" (v. 3); He has chosen our inheritance (v. 4), and now He "has ascended amid shouts of joy" (v. 5).

This is a royal procession. As God ascends, accompanied by trumpet fanfares, the people form a great choir of highly involved worshipers, all praising the Lord in song and with musical instruments.

We need to attend church as dynamically involved worshipers rather than spectators. Church services are not sitcoms that "couch potatoes" view for entertainment. They should be dynamic encounters with God—challenging, convicting, and somewhat uncomfortable!

I want to lay aside personal inhibition and apathy and catch the spirit of these ancient worshipers. When I see God as they saw Him, high and lifted up, I will be euphoric in my praise and will long to exalt Him with every means at my disposal.

■ **Personal prayer**   *Dear Lord, I long to praise You with vigor and unrestrained passion. Unfetter my personality, enhance my sensitivity, and enlarge my creativity so that I can be profoundly involved in lifting You high!*

Chorus of Praise

The King in Zion

■ **Theme**   *Great is the* LORD, *and most worthy of praise, in the city of our God, his holy mountain. It is beautiful in its loftiness, the joy of the whole earth. Like the utmost heights of Zaphon is Mount Zion, the city of the Great King. God is in her citadels; he has shown himself to be her fortress (vv. 1– 3).*

■ **Development**   The Glory of the Lord . . .

Something has happened which has inspired the psalmist to exude praise. Perhaps the Lord has once again miraculously delivered the nation from annihilation. He sings out lustily and full-throatedly, "Great is the Lord, and most worthy of praise!" What a motif for today!

The songwriter revels in encomiums of praise to Zion, the city of our God. Nothing less than the most majestic expressions of highest praise will suffice in this setting—a city that is lofty and magnificent, "the joy of all the earth." God Himself is her fortress, her sure defense.

Why are all nations charmed by this city of Jerusalem? Why is it pivotal and strategic? Because it represents the place where God dwells. Blessings flow forth from her to all the earth.

What is here for me to learn today? First, that the best place for me is where God is. I will discover my identity, security, and stability in Him. Second, the source of personal blessing is God Himself. I must allow Him to become the hub, the center, the fulcrum of my life, just as Jerusalem is the spiritual crossroads of all nations on earth.

■ **Personal prayer**   *Dear Lord, You are most worthy of my praise. Nothing charms me like the irresistible picture of the New Jerusalem where I will someday dwell with You.*

Chorus of Praise
The Nations in Retreat

■ **Theme**   When the kings joined forces, when they advanced together, they saw her and were astounded; they fled in terror. Trembling seized them there, pain like that of a woman in labor. You destroyed them like ships of Tarshish shattered by an east wind. As we have heard, so have we seen in the city of the LORD Almighty, in the city of our God: God makes her secure forever (vv. 4–8).

■ **Development**   The protection of the Lord . . .

Assyrian warriors were renowned for their iron courage and enormous strength. Yet, at the sight of Jerusalem, the city of God, Sennacherib's vassals trembled! Even with their awesome power, they were no match for this impregnable fortress, defended by God Himself.

Strong metaphors describe their panic: "Pain like that of a woman in labor"; "like ships of Tarshish shattered by an east wind" (vv. 6–7). There is no rational explanation for such a disaster—only the terrible majesty and strength of God, who provided supernatural protection and providence for His people.

How frail I am in my humanity. I must not let myself be intimidated by minor fears or even by problems of more significant proportions. The same God who routed the Phoenician armies and battered their ships at sea is available to me today to set my anxious heart at rest. "If [that] God be for [me], who can be against [me]?" (Romans 8:31).

135

■ **Personal prayer**   O Lord, I come to You as a little child, thanking You once again for Your protection and care.

Chorus of Praise

■ **Theme**   *Within your temple, O God, we meditate on your unfailing love. Like your name, O God, your praise reaches to the ends of the earth; your right hand is filled with righteousness. Mount Zion rejoices, the villages of Judah are glad because of your judgments (vv. 9–11).*

■ **Development**   The praise of the Lord . . .

What a beautiful model for a praise song. The psalmist ponders the unfailing love of the Lord. The Hebrew word *hesed* is a magnificent Old Testament word for God's loyal, covenant love. Much like the Greek word *agape* in the New Testament, it describes the fact that God loves us no matter what, no strings attached. His love is unconditional and persistent.

In our self-centered society—where even love must often be earned through good performance, wealth, beauty, or status—it is refreshing to know that the real world of the spirit is governed by a God of grace and stubborn love.

Supporting me today are the pillars of God's loyal love and His eternal faithfulness. When I meditate on that, I am encouraged and strengthened. I have a choice. Either I can succumb to fears of rejection and failure, or I can lean against God's promises.

136

■ **Personal prayer**   *O God, I praise You for Your great faithfulness and stubborn love, even when I am tempted to try to "earn" my place with You and with my peers.*

Chorus of Praise
The Review of Zion

■ **Theme**   *Walk about Zion, go around her, count her towers, consider well her ramparts, view her citadels, that you may tell of them to the next generation. For this God is our God for ever and ever, he will be our guide even to the end (vv. 12–14).*

■ **Development**   The posterity of the Lord . . .

Because the Lord has delivered Israel, they celebrate and worship with exuberance. Having been confined within the walls of the city, they are now free to walk outside. There, in the exhilaration of newfound freedom, they behold and admire the city's undamaged towers, walls, and pristine palaces.

Reviewing the city, they are reminded that the Lord is their high tower forever. He will continually protect and deliver them and will guide them forever. More importantly, they are to "tell of [these things] to the next generation."

What a responsibility! Through the medium of music, I have God's mandate to share my faith and my gifts with those who will come after me.

New music inevitably builds on what has gone before. Bach, the master musician of the Baroque period who worked for the glory of God, has inspired many musicians centuries after his death. I praise the Lord for other church musicians who have been my mentors— Don Hustad, John W. Peterson, Ralph Carmichael, and others.

Now, maybe it's my turn. There is a "musical discipleship" involved. I must contribute to the lives of younger composers, arrangers, and orchestrators. As a communicator seasoned in the faith and in the medium, I must pass the baton of God's truth and His values to generations to follow.

■ **Personal prayer**   *Dear Lord, help me to be faithful, through the witness of my music, to "tell the next generation" of Your protection and guidance all the days of their lives.*

Meaning in Wealth?

■ *Theme*   *Hear this, all you peoples; listen, all who live in this world, both low and high, rich and poor alike. . . . Why should I fear when evil days come, when wicked deceivers surround me—those who trust in their wealth and boast of their great riches? . . . For all can see that wise men die; the foolish and the senseless alike perish and leave their wealth to others. . . . But man, despite his riches, does not endure; he is like the beasts that perish (vv. 1–2, 5–6, 10, 12).*

■ **Development**   The futility of trusting in wealth. . . . I've talked to a lot of secular musicians, and most of them say the same thing: When success comes, big money is at first a turn-on; after that, it can be real trouble. The Christian music scene has also suffered many excesses: inflated budgets, out-of-control production expense, political hype, unreasonable contracts, outrageous lifestyles, etc. This psalmist agrees and shoots down the theory that the acquisition of wealth guarantees happiness and immortality.

He begins with a solemn introduction in which he proposes to grapple with this age-old problem of meaning in life. Then he asks a question: Why should I fear an enemy who trusts in wealth? No man can buy human life. Life is so valuable and the price so high that no amount of money can buy off death. In the end all men, whatever their station, die and leave their accumulation of possessions behind.

In our blatantly materialistic society, many of us expend a lot of time and energy chasing "the bucks" while denying the reality of our own appointment with death. Since money cannot buy my life or happiness, I need to discover the true Source.

■ *Personal prayer*   *O Mighty One, Lord God, help me not to buy into the world's view that money and status bring meaning to life when that is Satan's lie, camouflaging the profound truth that You are our only real meaning.*

Meaning in Wealth?

■ **Theme**   *This is the fate of those who trust in themselves, and of their followers, who approve their sayings. Like sheep they are destined for the grave, and death will feed on them. The upright will rule over them in the morning; their forms will decay in the grave, far from their princely mansions. But God will redeem my life from the grave; he will surely take me to himself (vv. 13–15).*

■ **Development**   The final end of those who trust in wealth . . .

What a graphic picture of death the psalmist paints! Those who are trusting "in themselves"—in their own resources—for salvation are destined for the grave. At the moment of death, even wealthy, influential persons will be as helpless as sheep herded together. According to one poet, "death pastures them," and their ultimate resting place is "far from their princely mansions."

What a contrast with the godly and upright! I'm impressed by three promises in this passage: (1) The godly will have dominion—"the upright will rule over them" (v. 14). (2) The souls of the upright will be ransomed from the place of the dead—"God will redeem my life from the grave" (v. 15). (3) The Lord Himself will receive the righteous—"he will surely take me to himself" (v. 15). When phobias and fears about death assail me, these verses are a comfort and a lifeline.

Enoch walked with God on a regular basis, and one day, he continued walking right into His presence. Elijah was caught up in a chariot of fire. Our Lord ascended into the clouds. One day, each one of us who knows the Lord will walk through a door into eternity. We will be "absent from the body, but present with the Lord" (2 Corinthians 5:8).

■ **Personal prayer**   *Lord, I thank You that because you have conquered death, I don't need to live in fear of it. I'm looking forward to the day when You will take me to Yourself.*

Meaning in Wealth?

■ **Theme**   *Do not be overawed when a man grows rich, when the splendor of his house increases; for he will take nothing with him when he dies, his splendor will not descend with him. Though while he lived he counted himself blessed—and men praise you when you prosper–he will join the generation of his fathers, who will never see the light of life. A man who has riches without understanding is like the beasts that perish (vv. 16–20).*

■ **Development**   The finite nature of wealth . . .

I must admit that I, along with many others, have been charmed by "tinseltown." The accouterments of success seem so appealing that it's pretty easy to fall for those less-than-subtle advertising ploys touting fancy foreign engineering or the architectural wonders of some luxury house. Even in church we sometimes focus on the trappings— lavish sanctuaries, fine pipe organs, plush carpeting. When materialism and personal pride fuse together, we're all in grave danger of neglecting or even forgetting God!

Thoughts of death and the prospect of eternity, however, can abruptly change one's focus, perspective, and priorities. The psalmist reminds us that, no matter how imposing the wealthy and powerful may appear, "they can't take it with them."

In this life the wealthy often inspire awe, admiration, and praise. But this adulation will be short-lived. The possessions that are the basis of their pride and self-aggrandizement will not survive past the grave. Verse 20 describes the final state of the man who leaves God out of his life. Without understanding, he is like the beasts that perish. His power, influence, and wealth won't carry any weight in eternity.

■ **Personal prayer**   *Lord, may I learn to live always, not for this life only, but with "eternity's values in view."*

True Worship

■ **Theme**   *The Mighty One, God, the* Lord, *speaks and summons the earth from the rising of the sun to the place where it sets. From Zion, perfect in beauty, God shines forth. Our God comes and will not be silent; a fire devours before him, and around him a tempest rages. He summons the heavens above, and the earth, that he may judge his people: "Gather to me my consecrated ones, who made a covenant with me by sacrifice." And the heavens proclaim his righteousness, for God himself is judge (vv. 1–6).*

■ **Development**   The Lord appears . . .

Through the words of the psalmist, can we see the Lord in the beauty of His holiness? He is transcendent—beyond and above us. He is the Mighty One, who spoke the world into existence and orders the universe. He is the Perfect One. He is the Righteous One. He is also *Yahweh*, unchangeable and faithful. It is this One who is coming to judge the earth.

From Zion, the glorious place where God dwells, He comes, surrounded by fire and fierce energy. He does not remain silent, for He comes to judge His covenant people who have been negligent in their worship. He sees their hearts and knows that their practices have been deficient and their attitudes flippant.

Our worship practices, like our relationship with the Lord, should reflect both majesty and intimacy. Unfortunately, we usually emphasize one or the other. We worship God in His majesty, but are not intimate with Him, or we cultivate intimacy and neglect reverence. There is a holy balance toward which we should strive. In our services, there should be times of fervor in which we may even loudly proclaim His praises with clapping of hands. At other times, deeply moved by God's holiness, we approach Him in quiet meditation.

Our Lord is absolutely holy. He is also jealous. He covets genuine worship and praise. He is very serious about His Personhood and disdains my inattentiveness and casual approach to my relationship with Him. As He addresses His people Israel, He is also speaking to me.

141

■ **Personal prayer**   *Dear Lord, help me to sense Your absolute holiness and transcendence. And may this glorious vision of You lead me to fall at Your feet in total adoration.*

True Worship

■ **Theme**   "Hear, O my people, and I will speak, O Israel, and I will testify against you: I am God, your God. I do not rebuke you for your sacrifices or your burnt offerings, which are ever before me. I have no need of a bull from your stall or of goats from your pens, for every animal of the forest is mine, and the cattle on a thousand hills. . . . Sacrifice thank offerings to God, fulfill your vows to the Most High, and call upon me in the day of trouble; I will deliver you, and you will honor me" (vv. 7–10, 14–15).

■ **Development**   The Lord condemns empty liturgy . . .

I stand amazed in His presence! This transcendent Lord, this Sovereign God, who is beyond us and above us is also around us and within us and desires fellowship with us!

Ritualism can never take the place of relationship. Obedience, faithfulness, and calling on God in trouble all flow from an intimate relationship with Him. Now, God comes into court to arraign His own covenant people, intellectually strong and orthodox in their beliefs, but faulty in their motives and attitudes.

While Israel has practiced sacrifice and observing the Law, she has assumed that her offerings benefited God, as if He were somehow in debt to them. They have grown independent and cold, and their fervor has cooled. In point of fact, God owns everything, including the cattle on a thousand hills.

Adoration of God is not scoring brownie points with Him. He is eternally self-existent and does not need our puny offerings, our gifts, our talents. But wonder of wonders, He longs to have us know Him well, closely, intimately and to worship Him—not for what He gets out of it, but because He is waiting to bless and deliver us!

■ **Personal prayer**   O Lord, You are high and holy, yet You invite me into Your presence. You tell me to call on You in trouble. Lord, You are my friend.

True Worship

■ **Theme**   But to the wicked, God says: "What right have you to recite my laws or take my covenant on your lips? You hate my instruction and cast my words behind you. . . . You use your mouth for evil and harness your tongue to deceit. . . . These things you have done and I kept silent. . . . But I will rebuke you and accuse you to your face. Consider this, you who forget God. . . . He who sacrifices thank offerings honors me, and he prepares the way so that I may show him the salvation of God" (vv. 16–17, 19, 21–23).

■ **Development**   The Lord speaks against hypocrisy . . .

Sometimes I'm guilty of going through the motions—responding automatically to expectations when my mind is preoccupied with other concerns.

But God's indictment against the people in this passage involved more than a warning against simple preoccupation. Israel was engaged in full-fledged disobedience! While Israel was giving verbal assent to the Law, she was in reality breaking it right and left. In fact, she went beyond disobedience to the point where she defended dishonesty (v. 19), condoned adultery (v. 18), and participated in slander, speaking against her own brothers and sisters and despising familial ties (v. 20).

Because the Lord had been silent to this point, Israel assumed that He was satisfied with mere lip service. But God's outlook isn't like man's. Man places a high premium on outward appearance, but God looks at the attitude of the heart.

It isn't enough for me to have a thorough knowledge of the truth. I must cultivate intimacy with the Lord. Otherwise, all I will have is an empty religion rather than a transforming relationship.

■ **Personal prayer**   Dear Lord, transform my mind and heart. May Your Truth not just spring automatically from my lips, but may it transfigure my life.

May

PSALMS 51–64

With his life on the line, David doesn't panic, but cries out to God. —Psalm 54

Fugue on Forgiveness
Subject: Prayer of Confession

■ **Theme**   *Have mercy on me, O God, according to your unfailing love; according to your great compassion blot out my transgressions. Wash away all my iniquity and cleanse me from my sin. For I know my transgressions, and my sin is always before me. Against you, you only, have I sinned and done what is evil in your sight (vv. 1–4).*

■ **Development**   The background of this splendid poem on forgiveness is David's sin of adultery with Bathsheba (2 Samuel 11). Bold phrases showcase the intensity of David's confession: "blot out my transgressions" (v. 1); "wash away all my iniquity" (v. 2); "cleanse me from my sin" (v. 2). David is crying out for full forgiveness. Aware that he does not deserve God's mercy, he nevertheless appeals to God's unfailing love and compassion.

David feels the crushing weight of his guilt. Further compounding the problem is the fact that he has been engaged in a cover-up for at least a year. The death of the child conceived out of wedlock and the prophet Nathan's confrontation are the catalysts for his confession, and David acknowledges that his sin is ultimately against God and God alone.

The thesis of this remarkable outpouring from the heart of a king is that anyone—man or woman, peasant or potentate—may appeal to God for forgiveness and be restored to a life of joy and service.

I, too, am painfully aware that intimacy with God comes only when I am brutally honest with the Lord about specific sins in my life. I start making headway when I give up self-deception and stop playing games with myself and the Lord. Reality, not rationalization, leads to growth.

146

■ **Personal prayer**   *Lord, deliver me from impotence and guilt. On the basis of Your unfailing love and grace, set me free and fill my life with Your joy.*

Fugue on Forgiveness
Counter-Subject: Prayer of Petition

■ **Theme**   *Cleanse me with hyssop, and I will be clean; wash me, and I will be whiter than snow. Let me hear joy and gladness; let the bones you have crushed rejoice. Hide your face from my sins and blot out all my iniquity. Create in me a pure heart, O God, and renew a steadfast spirit within me. Do not cast me from your presence or take your Holy Spirit from me. Restore to me the joy of your salvation and grant me a willing spirit, to sustain me (vv. 7–12).*

■ **Development**   Nearly three thousand years after David's downfall, we don't have to look far to find his successors—fallen leaders dragged down by their sinful nature into moral bankruptcy. Unfortunately this condition is no longer limited to the secular world. In the Christian arena, too, we have been concerned with image rather than reality. We have evaluated success on the basis of external symbols rather than on internal purity. We have some Christian leaders who look great on the outside, but are dying inside.

In this very personal petition to the Lord, David acknowledges that he can't possibly correct his basic sinful nature. Only the God who created him can cleanse, renew, and restore. David's body, wracked with physical and emotional pain, must learn how to rejoice again. His crushed spirit longs to hear, once more, the music of God's joy and gladness. He asks to become a new creation, both psychologically and judicially, and prays, in this Old Testament context, that the Holy Spirit not be taken from him. Likely he is remembering Saul, who has lived as such an exile, deposed from God's blessing.

I also need a deep work of God in my life. Like David, I yearn for radical spiritual surgery—cleansing, restoration, a purified heart, the transforming power of the Holy Spirit, and the antidepressant of being filled with the joy of my salvation!

■ **Personal prayer**   *Lord, cleanse me from sin today and fill my crushed spirit with the joy of the Holy Spirit.*

Fugue on Forgiveness

Answer: Prayer of Praise

■ **Theme**   *Then I will teach transgressors your ways, and sinners will turn back to you. Save me from bloodguilt, O God, the God who saves me, and my tongue will sing of your righteousness. O Lord, open my lips, and my mouth will declare your praise. You do not delight in sacrifice, or I would bring it; you do not take pleasure in burnt offerings. The sacrifices of God are a broken spirit; a broken and contrite heart, O God, you will not despise* (vv. 13–17).

■ **Development**   You can feel the beat of David's heart in this deeply personal interaction with the Lord. He has been locked into a pattern of deceit, God has allowed him to be crushed, and now he pleads for mercy and forgiveness.

Yet David knows that the justice and honor of the heavenly Father demand nothing less than His child's utter brokenness. You can hear the resonant chords of his broken heart as he pleads, "Save me from bloodguilt, O God, the God who saves me!" (v. 14).

In exchange for mercy and forgiveness, David pledges himself to three actions: (1) to teach sinners the ways of God so convincingly that they will repent; (2) to praise God in song, as genuine praise always springs from honest, heart-wrenching lament; (3) to worship God through the sacrifice of contrition. David offers up his broken heart.

David concludes this magnificent fugue on forgiveness with a prayer for prosperity. He believes that meaningful worship leads to national prosperity, beginning with the purity and righteousness of its leaders.

148

■ **Personal prayer**   *Lord, my heart breaks when I consider my own willfulness and waywardness. Teach me to teach others about You, to praise You, and to sacrifice. Above all, lead me into a genuinely honest relationship with You.*

Fantasia on Faith
In Minor: Deceit's Discord

■ **Theme**   *Why do you boast of evil, you mighty man? Why do you boast all day long, you who are a disgrace in the eyes of God? Your tongue plots destruction; it is like a sharpened razor, you who practice deceit. You love evil rather than good, falsehood rather than speaking the truth. . . . Surely God will bring you down to everlasting ruin: . . . The righteous will see and fear; they will laugh at him, saying, "Here now is the man who did not make God his stronghold but trusted in his great wealth and grew strong by destroying others!" (vv. 1–3, 5, 6–7).*

■ **Development**   This psalm was written because of the treachery of a man named Doeg (1 Samuel 21–22), who was an informer during the reign of David. Doeg's career as a terrorist was built on slander, deceit, and intrigue. The tongue of this self-satisfied, clever man revealed his evil, corrupt character. His words, sharp as a razor, were used to destroy people and bring disgrace to God.

God will not put up with this kind of behavior forever, then or now. The unsaved can learn a lesson from Doeg. Their ruin, like his, is inevitable. In an act of final judgment, God will bring them to "everlasting ruin" (v. 5) and they'll learn, too late, that great wealth, obtained at the expense of destroying others, will not buy a reprieve in the day of judgment.

Probing my own deceitful heart, I find that this psalm stirs my conscience. I'm so often controlled by mixed motives and false goals. This affects my speech. How much easier it is for me to be critical rather than creative, to put down rather than to build up, to be a troublemaker rather than a peacemaker. Deceit always creates discord. Only a truthful tongue can sing in harmony!

■ **Personal prayer**   *O Lord, purify and purge me of deceit. Cleanse me on the inside so that my tongue sings only truth.*

Fantasia on Faith
In Major: Faith's Fantasy

■ **Theme**   *But I am like an olive tree flourishing in the house of God; I trust in God's unfailing love for ever and ever. I will praise you forever for what you have done; in your name I will hope, for your name is good. I will praise you in the presence of your saints (vv. 8–9).*

■ **Development**   What a difference between Doeg, the traitor, and David, the man of faith! What bold contrasts exist in the psalms: the wicked versus the righteous, the transient versus the permanent, adversity versus prosperity.

David uses the metaphor of a flourishing olive tree to depict God's blessing on his life. His faith is strong because his roots go down deep into the soil of God's unfailing love. Because of this inner security, David is able to praise God *for what He has done.* He is also freed to praise God *for who He is,* for His incomparable attributes, His "good name." In that Name David places his eternal hope.

I love David's last statement in this psalm: "I will praise you *in the presence of your saints.*" For ancient worshipers, private praise always led to public worship. Individualism did not obliterate their sense of community.

So many of us are loners, but how we need each other! Isolation, alienation, and aloneness result in weakness. The fellowship of brothers and sisters in Christ lends strength. God doesn't want us to be spiritual "Lone Rangers."

150

■ **Personal prayer**   *Your unending, unfailing love, O God, inspires me to proclaim my faith in You wherever your saints gather for worship.*

Sonatina on Wickedness

■ **Theme**   *The fool says in his heart, "There is no God." They are corrupt, and their ways are vile: there is no one who does good. . . . Will the evildoers never learn—those who devour my people as men eat bread and who do not call on God? . . . Oh, that salvation for Israel would come out of Zion! When God restores the fortunes of his people, let Jacob rejoice and Israel be glad! (vv. 1, 4, 6).*

■ **Development**   "The fool says in his heart, 'There is no God.' " This recurring theme is hammered home in the irreverent lyrics of rock musicians as well as in the various pseudo-religious movements so prevalent today. Many live today as if God didn't exist!

The thesis of this psalm, almost identical to Psalm 14, is that people are universally corrupt. What a contrast to modern-day humanism, which boasts of the inherent goodness of man!

In the first movement (vv. 1–3), David describes the human race as "fools," "corrupt," "vile," "turned away." He further grieves, "There is no one who does good, not even one" (v. 3). How refreshing to find many godly people in the music industry. One such musician is Steve Green, who is known not only for his soaring voice, but also for his strong conviction and personal holiness. David wishes he could find "even one"!

The second movement (vv. 4–5) portrays the wicked as ultimately "overwhelmed by dread" and despised by God. David can't believe the ignorance of those who persecute the righteous.

In the third and final movement David utters a plea for the salvation of Israel and declares his faith that God will restore the fortunes of His people.

As I think about the fact that Christ is coming back to this sinful world, my whole perspective changes. When people leave God out of their lives, they sour and become corrupt. I want to warn them that He may come today! But without spiritual reality at the core of my personhood, I too will sour and become corrupt. Only intimacy with the Lord and the eager expectation of His return will prevent this.

■ **Personal prayer**   *O God, act as my preservative from corruption. As I interact with unbelievers in my world, may I be salt and light. Come, Lord Jesus!*

Hymn of Confidence

■ **Theme**   *Save me, O God, by your name; vindicate me by your might. . . . Surely God is my help; the Lord is the one who sustains me (vv. 1, 4).*

■ **Development**   How do I respond under pressure? Am I paralyzed by fear? Do I panic? Do I try to escape? Do I withdraw? Do I become depressed? Do I use medication?

David, hotly pursued by his enemies, knows that he is in mortal danger. He has been betrayed by the Ziphites—ungodly, ruthless men—and has even been threatened by one who has loved him, King Saul. With his life on the line, David doesn't panic, but cries out to God.

His prayer is in two parts: "Save me, O God, by your name; vindicate me by your might." In the second part of this hymn, David asserts his trust in God: "Surely God is my help; the Lord is the one who sustains me."

Under fire, David faced the hard facts of his dilemma with confidence, but he was not alone. Nor does God abandon me to sort out my problems alone. The same Lord who delivered David "from all [his] troubles" is able to deliver me!

■ **Personal prayer**   *O God, when I am experiencing unbelievable pressure, help me to trust in Your name and in Your power—not in human solutions.*

Ballad of Betrayal
First Motif: Rejection

■ **Theme**   *If an enemy were insulting me, I could endure it; if a foe were raising himself against me, I could hide from him. But it is you, a man like myself, my companion, my close friend, with whom I once enjoyed sweet fellowship as we walked with the throng at the house of God (vv. 12–14).*

■ **Development**   One of the most painful experiences in life is betrayal by a close and trusted friend, one "with whom [you] once enjoyed sweet fellowship." Insult and persecution from enemies is to be expected; rejection by a beloved companion is almost unendurable! And this happens because human relationships are never free from impure motivations. It is human nature to use, exploit, and manipulate people for our ends. Often, all of this is denied until the association sours, the communication ceases, and the friendship dies. Then, when we see this person in the mall, we turn and go the other way!

As a warrior, David was often in danger. He had learned to live with "the terrors of death" (v. 4), "horror" (v. 5), "violence and strife" (v. 9), "threats and lies" (v. 11). But the ultimate blow is the rejection rendered by an intimate friend.

Destructive forces are loose in the city of David. Anarchy and confusion are the result of the betrayal of his trusted confidant who has become a traitor. To make matters worse, David has even worshiped with this rogue!

What do I learn from David's desperate cry? I learn to expect the unexpected, to stand firm in my belief that the Lord is orchestrating my life—its highs and lows, its dissonance and consonance. Further, I learn from my own suffering and anguish something of what Christ endured for me and that redemption comes at a terribly high price.

■ **Personal prayer**   *O God, help me to be honest with You about my feelings of injustice and unfairness. May times of persecution give me insight into the compassion and suffering of my Lord and Savior.*

Ballad of Betrayal
Second Motif—Affirmation

■ **Theme**   *Cast your cares on the LORD and he will sustain you; he will never let the righteous fall. But you, O God, will bring down the wicked into the pit of corruption; bloodthirsty and deceitful men will not live out half their days. But as for me, I trust in you (vv. 22–23).*

■ **Development**   In the midst of his gut-wrenching betrayal by a close friend, David feels the affirming hand of God on his life. I am reassured today, knowing that God has not changed and that He ministers to me in the same ways.

He hears my cry of distress—morning, noon, or night (v. 17). He is able to save me just as he saved David (v. 16). He is aware of the violence of the wicked because "men . . . never change their ways" (vv. 18–19). Even before I suspect treachery, the Lord knows the intent of the heart (v. 21).

The rich metaphors used in this psalm aptly depict a modern-day Judas. David's friend uses speech "as smooth as butter," but beneath the surface lies a ruthless, violent man. His words, "more soothing than oil," are "drawn swords." This situation is not new to David, for he mentions it on at least three other occasions (57:4, 59:7, 64:3).

What a God! He will not forsake the righteous (v. 22). I can "cast my cares" on the Lord and He will see me through my own Gethsemanes. David's final words in this psalm echo the song of my heart: "But as for me, I trust in you!"

■ **Personal prayer**   *O God, help me not to get so wrapped up emotionally with rejection that I miss the liberating power of Your affirmation.*

Polyphony of Pressure
David's Plight

■ **Theme**   *Be merciful to me, O God, for men hotly pursue me; all day long they press their attack. My slanderers pursue me all day long; many are attacking me in their pride. When I am afraid, I will trust in you. In God, whose word I praise, in God I trust; I will not be afraid. What can mortal man do to me? (vv. 1–4).*

■ **Development**   The publishing world is a pressure cooker. But all of twentieth-century life, whether in the corporate world or the kitchen, is a cauldron of frenetic activity, vigorous competition, and pressing decisions. We're all on the run. Seldom, however, are Christians in America running for their lives, though many are quietly dying inside.

In this psalm David is acutely aware of his fight for survival. (See 1 Samuel 21 and Psalm 34.) During a visit to Gath, he faces the possibility of daily attack. His enemies, all conspirators and killers, twist his words and plot to harm him. Simply speaking, David is on the run. He is a fugitive, living like a scavenger on the edge of society. He is fighting for his life. He even has to pretend insanity! But because of his intimate relationship to the Lord, his response isn't typical. Instead of giving in to fear, he chooses faith.

As I face the stresses and tensions of modern life, I want to respond like King David. Instead of groveling in fear and intimidation, I choose to pray, to trust, to exercise faith, and to praise the Lord. How I respond under pressure reveals my true character. My neighbors are watching!

■ **Personal prayer**   *O God, may I not be intimidated by other people. When I'm afraid, let me learn to trust more in You, for "what can mortal man do to me"?*

Polyphony of Pressure
God's Protection

■ **Theme**   *Record my lament; list my tears on your scroll—are they not in your record? Then my enemies will turn back when I call for help. By this I will know that God is for me. In God, whose word I praise, in the LORD, whose word I praise—in God I trust; I will not be afraid. . . . For you have delivered my soul from death and my feet from stumbling (vv. 8–11, 13).*

■ **Development**   Every tear we shed is recorded "on God's scroll"! What a comfort to David, whose back was to the wall. The king was a brilliant soldier and a military genius who exuded power and strength. But he wasn't afraid to cry!

Like a highly skilled recording engineer who uses digital sampling, God accurately records every sigh, every whisper, every heartbeat, every tear—from the moment of my birth cry to the present. He knows me intimately. He is the complete and perfect Engineer, always attuned to my condition.

Though under severe stress, David is a real model for me. He places his complete trust in the Lord and in His Word. He is so confident of deliverance that he speaks in the past tense: "You *have delivered* my soul from death and my feet from stumbling" (v. 13).

David wasn't victimized by his circumstances. He didn't let pressure overwhelm him. His conscious choice made all the difference. He chose to praise the Lord and to trust His supernatural powers of protection. David's decision drove away his fear and enabled him to see his deliverance as an accomplished fact.

■ **Personal prayer**   *Father, I am moved, not only by Your vigilant protection, but by Your tenderness. Not a whisper goes unheard! What can I do but praise Your Name?*

Triumphant Song
Prayer of Deliverance

■ **Theme**   *I cry out to God Most High, to God, who fulfills his purpose for me. He sends from heaven and saves me, rebuking those who hotly pursue me; God sends his love and his faithfulness. . . . Be exalted, O God, above the heavens; let your glory be over all the earth* (vv. 2–3, 5).

■ **Development**   Again I see myself reflected in David. This time he has fled from King Saul and is hiding in a cave (1 Samuel 22, 24). There are times when I feel like escaping from the world and going into hiding "until the [present] disaster has passed."

In fact, when I was attending a Christian high school, I was under pressure to be a campus leader. Secretly I wanted to blend in with the crowd, or better still, to be left alone. I still struggle with feelings of shyness and social ineptitude, so I can relate to David's cave.

Instead of giving up or giving in, David prays in that dark hiding place. His prayer is a harmony in four parts.

Part One: "Lord, have mercy!" He calls on the mercy of God and huddles under "the shadow of his wings" (v. 1).

Part Two: He believes that God has a plan, uniquely designed for him, and that He will "fulfill his purpose" (v. 2).

Part Three: He acknowledges his helpless state and describes his adversaries as predators with teeth like "spears and arrows" and tongues like "sharp swords" (v. 4).

Part Four: Seeing beyond his present plight, David looks forward to a time when he will be vindicated and avenged and to that day when the Lord will establish His righteousness and glory over the earth! (v. 5).

When David finds himself in hot water, he prays. When he is between a rock and a hard place, he prays. When he is under extreme pressure, he prays. I'd like to be more like this warrior who prayed!

■ **Personal prayer**   *My prayer, O God Most High, is that Your purpose will be fulfilled in my life and that Your glory may shine through my personality.*

Triumphant Song
Prayer Celebrating God's Love and Faithfulness

■ **Theme**   My heart is steadfast, O God, my heart is steadfast; I will sing
and make music. Awake, my soul! Awake, harp and lyre! I will awaken the
dawn. I will praise you, O Lord, among the nations. I will sing of you
among the peoples. For great is your love, reaching to the heavens; your
faithfulness reaches to the skies. Be exalted, O God, above the heavens; let
your glory be over all the earth (vv. 7–11).

■ **Development**   David is counting on victory, so he celebrates God's
love and faithfulness. As the chief musician in Israel, he can't
conceive of a better way to adore his Lord than through music and
song. Because his faith is steadfast, he feels no fear but plans to
"awaken the dawn" with singing. How interesting, since depression
and despair are most acutely felt by many people in the early morning
hours.

On a crescendo of praise, David's imagination soars as he exults in
purest praise of his Lord. He vows to sing of Him to all peoples. He
eloquently proclaims the greatness of God's love and worshipfully
celebrates His faithfulness which reaches to the skies. "Be exalted, O
God, above the heavens; let your glory be over all the earth" (v. 5).

David didn't bow down in defeat to his intolerable circumstances.
Instead, he made an artistic choice to lift his voice in song, celebrating
God's incomparable love and faithfulness!

■ **Personal prayer**   O God, I praise You for giving me reason to awaken
the dawn. May I start each day with You, sharing the melody of your love
and faithfulness with others I meet today.

Appassionata for Justice
The Charge

■ **Theme** *Do you rulers indeed speak justly? Do you judge uprightly among men? No, in your heart you devise injustice, and your hands mete out violence on the earth. Even from birth the wicked go astray; from the womb they are wayward and speak lies. Their venom is like the venom of a snake, like that of a cobra that has stopped its ears, that will not heed the tune of the charmer, however skillful the enchanter may be (vv. 1–5).*

■ **Development** Many of us struggle with bitterness over dishonesty, injustice, and unfairness in life. From the perspective of the immediate, life *is* often unfair. I know what it's like to be set up for humiliation in a public business meeting—to feel like a sheep among wolves because of the surprise element.

Our God is a God of righteousness and justice. Abraham correctly assumes that the "Judge of all the earth" will do right (Genesis 18:25). On this basis David poses two critical questions: "Do you rulers indeed speak justly?" and "Do you judge uprightly among men?" (v. 1).

The questions are obviously rhetorical and intended to cause self-assessment in the hearers. A scathing denunciation follows. David's accusation rings out: "You devise injustice!" (v. 2). "Your hands mete out violence!" (v. 2). "[You] speak lies!" (v. 3). And there is more. These judges are as venomous as snakes and as indifferent to correction as cobras who pay no heed to their charmers.

David is right in denouncing these ancient judges. God places a high premium on justice, since this is an aspect of His own character. Still, Jeremiah 17:9 reminds us that the human heart is desperately deceitful.

David's haunting questions linger in my mind like an unwelcome refrain. Am I honest and aboveboard in all my dealings? Am I a just executive? As a husband and father, do I give Karen and the kids a fair hearing? I'm glad our God is a just—and merciful—Judge!

■ **Personal prayer** *Dear Lord, search my heart and, by the power of Your Holy Spirit, point out any wicked way in me. I want to reflect Your character with integrity.*

Appassionata for Justice
The Verdict

■ **Theme** *Break the teeth in their mouths, O God; tear out, O LORD, the fangs of the lions! Let them vanish like water that flows away; when they draw the bow, let their arrows be blunted. Like a slug melting away as it moves along, like a stillborn child, may they not see the sun. Before your pots can feel the heat of the thorns—whether they be green or dry—the wicked will be swept away (vv. 6–9).*

■ **Development** I know just how David feels! How often have I been tempted to judge others as they have judged me. It's especially easy to spot a weakness in someone else when I too am guilty—like knocking lack of discipline in overeating when I've put on a few pounds myself.

David doesn't check his emotions here. He pronounces his verdict on these unjust judges, using bold strokes and vivid imagery. He demands that their teeth be smashed and their fangs pulled out so they will not be able to communicate their lies. He hopes they will vanish like water on a hot day. He wants their words to be as ineffectual as blunted arrows. He desires that they simply melt away like slugs (snails) in a drought. He wants them to die suddenly like a stillborn child who never sees the light of day. He wants their destruction to be swift. Maybe they will even be swept away like astronauts in a blinding explosion!

In anticipating the fulfillment of a geopolitical kingdom on earth, David expects that all enemies who threaten the establishment of God's kingdom on earth will be destroyed swiftly and violently. Here he savors the sweet taste of revenge.

The New Testament, however, gives us an entirely different perspective. We are to leave the final judgment of scoundrels to God and wait patiently for His kingdom to be established on earth. "Vengeance is mine. I will repay," says the Lord (Hebrews 10:30 RSV).

160

■ **Personal prayer** *Lord, may I entrust the ultimate end of my enemies to You. Remove from me the bitterness of revenge.*

Appassionata for Justice
The Vindication

■ **Theme**   *The righteous will be glad when they are avenged, when they bathe their feet in the blood of the wicked. Then men will say, "Surely the righteous still are rewarded; surely there is a God who judges the earth" (vv. 10–11).*

■ **Development**   Immanuel Kant, noted German philosopher, believed that the universal notion of justice was proof of God's existence. He also believed it was proof of a literal heaven. Why? Because he didn't observe justice being fully fulfilled on this earth. It is also tacit evidence for a place of eternal punishment. Why? Because Hitler, for example, never got the punishment he deserved during his lifetime.

David is encouraged that God's justice will be carried out. In these verses he resorts to wild, strong imagery to carry the intensity of his thoughts. He longs to see the righteous "bathing their feet in the blood of the wicked." Such a military coup would bring him great satisfaction.

David is also convinced that injustice will not prevail forever. The righteous will be rewarded. Men will see that God does judge the earth finally and righteously. So ends David's passionate plea for justice and vindication.

What personal comfort and intellectual solace I can derive from the fact that God will someday set all things straight! The finale of a Beethoven symphony will seem inconsequential in comparison to this!

■ **Personal prayer**   *Dear Lord, I thank You that by definition You are just. Help me to leave final judgments with You.*

A Mighty Fortress
Conspiracy and Treachery

■ **Theme**   *Deliver me from my enemies, O God; protect me from those who rise up against me. Deliver me from evildoers and save me from bloodthirsty men. . . . O my Strength, I watch for you; you, O God, are my fortress, my loving God (vv. 1–2, 9).*

■ **Development**   As I read these hymns penned by David, the greatest warrior-king Israel ever produced, I'm reminded that my own life seems somewhat tame by comparison. While David, the shepherd boy, stalked and killed fierce predators that threatened his flock, I only struggle with fierce competition in the music industry. Still a lad, he fought the giant Goliath with a slingshot, five smooth stones, and the Name of the Lord. Some of the giants in my life loom large to me, but budget hassles, contract negotiations, and balancing priorities are not so dramatic. Assuming manhood, David seemed forever engaged in the fight for survival, while I attempt to keep creative energy alive and wrestle with significance and meaning in life.

Inspired by yet another attempt on his life, this time by crazed and jealous King Saul, David prays for deliverance from the treachery of evildoers. As is so often the case in an assassination attempt, conspiracy is involved (v. 3). But David's wife, Michal, foils the plan, warns David, and helps him escape through a window.

In my daily routine, it isn't often "fierce and bloodthirsty men" who conspire against me and rob me of life and vitality, but tight schedules, family crises, and creative dry spells. In these mundane moments, too, God provides an "open window" of deliverance, a way out.

162

■ **Personal prayer**   *O God, I praise You for "open windows" and that You continue to stand as my Strength and Fortress in every circumstance of my life.*

A Mighty Fortress
Justice and Peace

■ **Theme**   *But do not kill them, O Lord our shield, or my people will forget. In your might make them wander about, and bring them down. . . . But I will sing of your strength, in the morning I will sing of your love; for you are my fortress, my refuge in times of trouble. O my Strength, I sing praise to you; you, O God are my fortress, my loving God (vv. 11, 16–17).*

■ **Development**   While David expects justice to be done, he is motivated by more than revenge and vindication. He longs for the punishment of his enemies to *reflect God's sovereignty.* Is this the same David who envisioned a blood bath of the wicked (58:10), exhorted God to defang the lions and blot them up like water that evaporates in the sun (58:6–7)?

Now the psalmist implores God to stay His hand of execution (v. 11), but allow his enemies to wander as fugitives so that "it will be known to the ends of the earth that God rules over Jacob" (v. 13).

I pause to reflect: Do I desire that God be glorified . . . even more than I desire to see my competitors get their deserts? Am I motivated by pride to seek credit for peacemaking, or do I point others to Him?

Notice the bold contrast in verse 16. David is carried away into paeans of praise. So moved is he by his Sovereign Lord that he promises to extol His virtues "in the morning." And, to emphasize his intent, David repeats his promise: "I will sing of your strength, in the morning I will sing of your love; for you are my fortress, my refuge in times of trouble" (v. 16).

■ **Personal prayer**   *O Lord God Almighty, You are King of kings, my All in all. May I never be guilty of seeking revenge for injustices, but desire to point all people—even my opponents—to You.*

Military March   *Deliverance*

■ **Theme**   *But for those who fear you, you have raised a banner to be unfurled against the bow. Save us and help us with your right hand, that those you love may be delivered (vv. 4–5).*

■ **Development**   Being a passionate person, I'll have to admit that there have been times when I've been angry with God. When bad things happen, when my goals are blocked, when nothing seems to work out, I feel angry! In turn, my attitude is displeasing to my heavenly Father, and he deals with me like the obstinate child I am.

David is keenly aware that God is sovereign and has absolute control over victories and defeats. The big threat here is probably the nation of Edom, which invaded Judah while David was fighting in the north (2 Samuel 8, 1 Kings 11, and 1 Chronicles 18).

This major defeat is the result of God's anger kindled against His people. The very earth has been shaken and David pleads with the Lord to "mend its fractures" (v. 2). "You have been angry—now restore us!" he cries.

When God is angry with me and I have felt the earthquake of His displeasure, there is only one hope—to ask for restoration and renewal. Battling with God is no contest. To withdraw or to move farther away is to prevent healing and intimacy with Him. "Let [me] draw near to God with a sincere heart in full assurance of faith, having [my] heart sprinkled to cleanse [me] from a guilty conscience" (Hebrews 10:22).

■ **Personal prayer**   *O God, continue to save me and help me with Your right hand. I am so grateful that Your great love and mercy outweigh Your anger.*

Military March   Triumph

■ **Theme**   *God has spoken from his sanctuary: "In triumph I will parcel out Shechem and measure off the Valley of Succoth. Gilead is mine, and Manasseh is mine; Ephraim is my helmet, Judah my scepter. Moab is my washbasin, upon Edom I toss my sandal; over Philistia I shout in triumph"* (vv. 6–8).

■ **Development**   When I moved my family from Grand Rapids, Michigan, to Nashville, Tennessee, feelings of disorientation, dislocation, and disruption were almost overwhelming. Yet I felt the move was part of God's plan for our lives. Perhaps He wanted us to face our deepest soul longings that can only be fulfilled in Him, not in friends or familiar surroundings. He puts us in the place where He wants us!

The psalmist reminds us that because the tribes of Israel belong to God, He will deliver His own and subjugate their enemies. They will be put in their place. God, the Lord of the manor, will parcel out the lands precisely as it suits Him.

To Israel He assigns the lands of Shechem, the Valley of Succoth, Gilead, Manasseh, Ephraim (His helmet of defense), and Judah (His place of rule).

Israel's enemies will become their slaves. Moab will be reduced to the level of a washbasin! God will toss His sandal to Edom! Philistia will hear God's shout of triumph!

Note that all of these lands already belong to God. The Israelites are merely sojourners, tenants, and stewards of all that the Lord has given to them. This gives them both security and an awesome responsibility.

■ **Personal prayer**   O God, I thank You for providing our home, of which we are only "tenants" for the time You have given us on this earth. May I never forget that, whatever my address, my real dwelling place is with You!

Military March   Trust

■ **Theme**   *Who will bring me to the fortified city? Who will lead me to Edom? Is it not you, O God, you who have rejected us and no longer go out with our armies? Give us aid against the enemy, for the help of man is worthless. With God we will gain the victory, and he will trample down our enemies (vv. 9–12).*

■ **Development**   In the ancient world, David believes that supernatural power supersedes natural resources. Divine victory comes through trusting and praising God. Human defeat is the result of fearing man and cowering before him. The answers to David's problems almost always come through prayer and praise—a recognition of God's sovereignty.

This is a reminder to me when I'm intimidated by obstacles to success and tempted to depend solely upon human resources—my mind, my talent, the corporation, the weekly paycheck, the marketing team, the sales force, and the professional musicians with whom I work.

In this passage, David asks some questions I might ask myself: "Who will lead me to this heathen, fortified city?" (*Am I intimidated by the size and strength of the opposition, or do I trust God to make up for my inadequacies?*) "Who will lead me to Edom?" (*Dare I face my competition without prayer for direction?*) "Is it not You, O God?" (*Are You on my side, Lord? Or, more importantly, Am I on Your side?*).

David then declares that human help is worthless and ends this military psalm by pleading with God for aid against the enemy. His faith is strong. God *will* give the victory. Technology and human ingenuity are no match for the incomparable power of God. Without His inspiration, no matter how well-trained or gifted or knowledgeable I may be, I'll fail. Under His banner, I march to sure and certain victory!

166

■ **Personal prayer**   *Lord, help me neither to trust in my own abilities and connections nor to flinch in the face of overwhelming obstacles, but to depend upon Your supernatural power.*

Hiding in Thee
Lead Me to the Rock That Is Higher Than I

■ **Theme**   *Hear my cry, O God; listen to my prayer. From the ends of the earth I call to you, I call as my heart grows faint; lead me to the rock that is higher than I (vv. 1–2).*

■ **Development**   Far from home, David is feeling overwhelmed, inadequate, and insecure. Isolation makes one an easy target for discouragement and depression.

From time to time, I've felt this way on a business trip. Differences in time zones, jet lag, and unfamiliar surroundings exacerbate those feelings. And calling home isn't always the answer, since problems crop up there too! It's not easy to be God's man in today's world.

Nor was it easy for David. But he didn't allow himself the luxury of sliding into despair. He called on God who "neither slumbers nor sleeps (Psalm 121:4). He asked the Lord to lead him to a place of safety, a high refuge—one that he could never attain by himself. Only then will he feel truly safe.

Though I may travel to "the ends of the earth" on business for my company, I'm as close to my Lord as my next prayer.

■ **Personal prayer**   *Lead me today, Father, to "the Rock that is higher than I"!*

Hiding in Thee
I Long to Dwell in Your Tent Forever

■ **Theme**   *For you have been my refuge, a strong tower against the foe. I long to dwell in your tent forever and take refuge in the shelter of your wings. For you have heard my vows, O God; you have given me the heritage of those who fear your name (vv. 3–5).*

■ **Development**   There are times when even strong men feel weak and undone. Such a time was in 1984, when a series of losses changed my life radically and decimated my emotional energy.

David candidly admits his weakness—both physically and emotionally. Now he simply wishes to retreat for a time into the sanctuary of the tent of the Lord. He is likely referring to the Tabernacle, that magnificent portable temple of God, built of acacia wood overlaid with gold and hung with blue, purple, and scarlet curtains of finest linen. It was here that God's shekinah Glory dwelt in the Holy of Holies, His presence abiding with David's forebears during their sojourn in the wilderness. Now, so far from home, David longs for such a physical manifestation of his Lord.

David made his vows before God, just as I dedicated my life to His service on Word of Life Island when I was a kid. I share David's spiritual inheritance—unlimited and inalienable. In reality, then, I already possess the power of God's attributes if I lay claim to them, confessing my own unworthiness and weakness.

In these times of retreat, when I'm at the end of myself, I find Him in a fresh experience of worship. The 1984 episode had the positive effect of causing me to reevaluate my life critically and forced me to face "false gods" squarely. It was the beginning of a turning point in my ministry!

■ **Personal prayer**   *O God, may I dwell in Your place of safety forever. There may I experience the profound fulfillment of my deepest longings.*

Hiding in Thee

Increase the Days of the King's Life

■ **Theme**   *Increase the days of the king's life, his years for many generations. May he be enthroned in God's presence forever; appoint your love and faithfulness to protect him. Then will I ever sing praise to your name and fulfill my vows day after day (vv. 6–8).*

■ **Development**   When David prays, "Increase the days of the king's life, his years for many generations." I understand his concern. America is a nation preoccupied with aging.

It's uncomfortable to reach midlife. Because I have prematurely silver hair, some people think Karen is my daughter instead of my wife! Even my dad, who is now in his seventies, likes to tell people that he's my brother. Not only that, but I'm surrounded by highly talented, young musicians in an industry dominated by youth.

While much of Western society worships at the shrine of youth, touting wrinkle creams, beauty spas, and fitness clubs as the secret to its preservation, King David knows that there is only one lasting solution. I know it too. To abide in the presence of God forever is to enjoy eternal life—both in duration and in quality. What an answer to deep personal fears and insecurities!

Since this psalm most likely also alludes to the coming Messiah, these blessings will be fulfilled to overflowing in the Person of the King of kings and Lord of lords!

No wonder David's intense emotion erupts in exuberant praise. "Then will I ever sing praise to Your name" (v. 8). He pledges his faithfulness "day after day." The mandate for the believer is a deep, abiding sense of the Lord's love and faithfulness.

■ **Personal prayer**   *O Lord, You have numbered my days. Don't let me be so concerned with my own aging process that I miss the blessings of intimate relationship with You, now and in the life to come.*

Hymn in Three Stanzas
First Stanza: Waiting in Silence

■ **Theme**   *My soul finds rest in God alone; my salvation comes from him. He alone is my rock and my salvation; he is my fortress, I will never be shaken. How long will you assault a man? Would all of you throw him down—this leaning wall, this tottering fence? They fully intend to topple him from his lofty place; they take delight in lies. With their mouths they bless, but in their hearts they curse (vv. 1–4).*

■ **Development**   David's life wasn't a bed of roses. He faced an inordinate amount of adversity. He learned, however, to be still under stress—to rest in the Lord.

Rests in music are crucial. A musical rest is a sign that, for a specified time, the music ceases. Contrasts in the arts are highly significant; hence, rests are often as important as the notes. Intervals of silence between tones enhance the beauty and texture of the music. So, also, in life!

The psalmist's calm security and implacable stability come from God. David perceives his Lord as his Rock, his Salvation, his impregnable Fortress. Therefore, he cannot be moved or distracted by the taunts of the wicked.

His enemies, of course, see him in a different light. They view him as vulnerable—"a leaning wall," "a tottering fence" (v. 3). Shouting curses and lies, they will attempt to topple David from his lofty position.

Unbelievable strength is drawn, however, in rest—waiting in silence which implies utter trust that the rope will hold, the fortress will stand, the walls won't cave in. Not only does salvation come from God, but He gives me those still moments when I gain strength from the battle.

■ **Personal prayer**   *O God, I thank You for intervals of silence when, if my soul really listens, I can hear, not the mockery of the world, but Your still, small voice.*

Hymn in Three Stanzas
Second Stanza: Trusting in God

■ **Theme**   Find rest, O my soul, in God alone; my hope comes from him. He alone is my rock and my salvation, he is my fortress, I will not be shaken. My salvation and my honor depend on God; he is my mighty rock, my refuge. Trust in him at all times, O people; pour out your hearts to him, for God is our refuge (vv. 5–8).

■ **Development**   David has a very personal relationship with God. This intimacy is observed in his use of the pronoun *my*. Note the phrases: "*my* soul," "*my* hope," "*my* salvation," "*my* fortress," "*my* honor," "*my* mighty rock," and "*my* refuge." God was not an abstract theological concept to David, but his source of hope, safety, deliverance, and unshakable faith.

On the basis of his experiential knowledge of God, David pleads with other believers to trust in God, to pour out their hearts to Him, and to rely on Him as their shelter from danger.

This biblical picture of man is in sharp contrast to the bleak portrait painted by secular existentialism. Yes, *apart from God*, I am fragile and vulnerable. But *in union with God*, I am complete and fulfilled!

> *Rock of Ages, cleft for me,*
> *Let me hide myself in Thee;*
> *Let the water and the blood,*
> *From Thy riven side which flowed*
> *Be of sin the double cure,*
> *Cleanse me from its guilt and power.*

Words by Augustus M. Toplady. Music by Thomas Hastings.

■ **Personal prayer**   O God, my Rock and my Refuge, once again I express my trust in You. I pour out my heart to You. I thank You for filling the vacuum of my soul with the hope of Your salvation.

Hymn in Three Stanzas
Third Stanza: Expecting His Reward

■ **Theme**   *Lowborn men are but a breath, the highborn are but a lie; if weighed on a balance, they are nothing; together they are only a breath. . . . Though your riches increase, do not set your heart on them. One thing God has spoken, two things have I heard: that you, O God, are strong, and that you, O Lord, are loving. Surely you will reward each person according to what he has done (vv. 9–12).*

■ **Development**   I have a tendency to be impressed with a person's status, his level of achievement, her impeccable credentials. David shows us how futile it is to place too much emphasis on human accomplishment. Why? Because all people, regardless of rank or position, are "but a breath."

Another common fallacy in affluent America is our fascination with money-making. We have only to watch the stock market to see that money is an inadequate object for our faith. In a roller-coaster economy, a person who sets his heart on getting rich is skating on thin ice. Both human ingenuity and material prosperity are meaningless when weighed against the majesty and might of God.

Where, then, is the real power in life, the real reward? David shows us the answer in two facets of God's diamond-like character: "You, O God, are strong. . . . You, O Lord, are loving." On the basis of these two attributes, He will control events so that perfect justice prevails in the end. We can trust that kind of God to reward us accordingly.

■ **Personal prayer**   *O God, I thank You that, though I am so weak, You are strong. Even more astounding is that You love me and are planning to reward me "according to what [I] have done."*

Plainsong of Praise
My Soul Thirsts for You

■ **Theme**   O God, you are my God, earnestly I seek you; my soul thirsts for you, my body longs for you, in a dry and weary land where there is no water (v. 1).

■ **Development**   The desert sands are hot, the heat excruciating, the land parched and dry. David is thirsty. His mouth is as dry as a potsherd. This experience prompts him to reflect on his deep thirst for God.

This first verse of his song is an affirmation of David's faith: "O God, you are my God." The prayer that follows is expressed in three motifs: "Earnestly I seek you." "My *soul* thirsts for you." "My *body* longs for you." His whole being is in touch and in love with God. Nothing that "dry and weary land" can provide will satisfy the driving hunger and thirst of his soul.

My song "Longing for God" was born out of a hunger and thirst in my soul much like David's:

> Like a dry and thirsty land,
> I long for You, O Lord!
> My parched and hungry soul
> Longs for Your quenching Word!
>
> May I find You in sweet fellowship,
> May I see You in great preaching,
> May my heart be moved with Your love,
> May Your Spirit work in teaching!
>
> In the shadow of Your wings
> I sing songs in the night;
> In the darkness of this world
> I cling to You for light.
>
> Words and music by Don Wyrtzen.
> © 1980 by Singspiration Music.

173

■ **Personal prayer**   Dear Lord, my whole being longs for You today. Please come and let me drink deeply of the Living Water.

Plainsong of Praise
I Will Praise You as Long as I Live

■ **Theme**   *I have seen you in the sanctuary and beheld your power and your glory. Because your love is better than life, my lips will glorify you. I will praise you as long as I live. . . . My soul will be satisfied as with the richest of foods; with singing lips my mouth will praise you. . . . Because you are my help, I sing in the shadow of your wings (vv. 2–5, 7).*

■ **Development**   Once David had beheld the power and glory of his Lord, he was never the same again. Deeply moved by the presence of God in the sanctuary, he was inspired to write some of the loftiest and most sublime praise music ever written.

Because the love of God also means more to me than life itself, I will praise Him "as long as I live."

Like David, I know the deep satisfaction of composing praise music—a satisfaction much like that of rich food that satisfies physical hunger.

I long for the kind of divine obsession that drove David to meditate on the name of the Lord through the watches of the night. As "my soul clings" to Him, whether in the sanctuary or in the shadows of my life, I pray that my music will be a reflection of His power, glory, and love.

> *As long as I live, He will be supreme,*
> *As long as I live, He will be my theme;*
> *As long as I live, this will be my dream—*
> *Jesus, the Source of lasting joy.*
>
> *Jesus, the Source of lasting joy,*
> *Giving life abundantly;*
> *Jesus, the Source of lasting joy,*
> *He's my only security.*

Words and music by Don Wyrtzen.
© 1982 by Singspiration Music.

■ **Personal prayer**   *Dear Lord, I want to praise You as long as I live! Kindle in me a fire of passion until the words and music flow through my purified soul.*

Plainsong of Praise
They Who Seek My Life Will Be Destroyed

■ **Theme**   *They who seek my life will be destroyed; they will go down to the depths of the earth. They will be given over to the sword and become food for jackals. But the king will rejoice in God; all who swear by God's name will praise him, while the mouths of liars will be silenced (vv. 9–11).*

■ **Development**   There is more than one way to "destroy" life. A sarcastic comment can cut like a sword. When it is premeditated, the wound is even deeper. Gossip, often without basis in fact, can be a lethal weapon. "The tongue is a small part of the body. . . . Consider what a great forest is set on fire by a small spark" (James 3:5).

It's much easier to be a critic than a creator—to pick apart someone's work rather than to put together something new. How insidious we are with our criticism! "So and so is terrific, *but* . . ." These negative evaluations tear down those who are made in God's image and destroy the creative process as well. The church needs to become much more tolerant of creative people. Art doesn't flourish in the harsh winds of criticism. A bitter spirit can't break forth into beautiful song.

King David knew all about verbal swordplay as well as physical attack. His enemies were ever lurking in the shadows. In this psalm he has been personally absorbed in praising God until some incident or memory triggers his thoughts about his enemies, and he is forced to contemplate the judgment of the wicked. The destroyers will themselves be destroyed and swallowed up into the depths of the earth. They will be devoured by the sword and their bodies will be thrown to the jackals. "The mouths of liars will be silenced" (v. 11). It seems a fitting punishment for the crime.

What a contrast for King David and contemporary Christians as well! We who have been delivered spontaneously burst forth into affirmations of belief in God's Name and songs of praise. When the Lord meets our needs, as He works in our lives, when He defuses the venomous words and deeds of our critics, we praise Him!

175

■ **Personal prayer**   *Dear Lord, I rejoice in Your holy Name and thank You for helping me deal with criticism. Turn the words of my critics into praises to You!*

Drone-Pipe of Judgment
Drone of Complaint

■ **Theme**   *Hear me, O God, as I voice my complaint; protect my life from the threat of the enemy. Hide me from the conspiracy of the wicked, from that noisy crowd of evildoers. They sharpen their tongues like swords and aim their words like deadly arrows. They shoot from ambush at the innocent man; they shoot at him suddenly, without fear. They encourage each other in evil plans, they talk about hiding their snares; they say, "Who will see them?" They plot injustice and say, "We have devised a perfect plan!" Surely the mind and heart of man are cunning* (vv. 1–6).

■ **Development**   A drone-pipe is the lowest tone on the bagpipe, used for accompaniment. It is often used as a pedal point, a long sustained bass note against which changing harmonies sound.

Like so many of David's psalms, my prayers often take on the monotonous tone of complaint. Here David is overwhelmed by the malicious schemes of that "noisy crowd," the wicked. "They shoot from ambush at the innocent man!" (v. 4). What a natural tendency it is to counter-attack—to "sharpen our tongues like swords" and "aim our words like deadly arrows!" (v. 3).

Yet beneath the apparent bitterness and complaining is a drone, an insistent pedal point: "Hear me, O God. . . . Hear me, O God. . . . Hear me, O God." David's emphasis is not on his grumbling, but on God!

Caught in the crossfire of slanderous speech and hidden snares, he acknowledges the Sovereign Lord as his ultimate Arbiter, the supreme Peacemaker. David may drone on indefinitely about his woes, but he always turns to the Lord for protection and justice.

■ **Personal prayer**   *Hear me, O God! If I must be monotonous, let it be in singing Your praises!*

June

PSALMS 64–74

*We are often like the trumpet player in the
orchestra who wants to set his own tempo
instead of following the conductor. —Psalm 74*

Drone-Pipe of Judgment
Prophecy of Praise

■ **Theme**   *But God will shoot them with arrows; suddenly they will be struck down. He will turn their own tongues against them and bring them to ruin; all who see them will shake their heads in scorn. All mankind will fear; they will proclaim the works of God and ponder what he has done. Let the righteous rejoice in the LORD and take refuge in him; let all the upright in heart praise him! (vv. 7–10).*

■ **Development**   When I'm tempted to question certain inequalities in my world, I need to be reminded that the administration of a just God promises perfect objectivity and lack of prejudice . . . *someday.* Such a God can be counted on to balance the scales.

Ironically the very people who are bringing me the most grief, those who dare to wage war against God, will be brought down by their own words and schemes. God is in control!

Over and over again, I read the psalmist's litany of grievances, his pleas for protection, and, at last, his songs of praises. I've wondered sometimes just why God felt it necessary to be quite so repetitious in recording His Word.

In music, repetition is vital. Beethoven was a master at taking a little bit of material—sometimes just one short theme—and repeating it in a kaleidoscope of musical variations. The psalmists did the same thing. They hammered away at similar motifs and themes repeatedly. Perhaps the ancient Israelites were like us—slow learners! Like the ocean, music is cyclical—it thrives on thematic repetition, development, and variety.

God is teaching me—pounding out the truth in every heartbeat, in every rhythmic cycle of nature, in the echoes of His love—that He is the Sovereign Lord of my life. *Someday* He will be feared and respected by all mankind because of His swift enactment of justice. *Someday* all the righteous will rejoice and take refuge in Him. *Someday* "at the name of Jesus every knee [will] bow . . . and every tongue confess that Jesus Christ is Lord" (Philippians 2:10–11).

■ **Personal prayer**   *O Lord, I rejoice in You today. My heart leaps in recognition of another continuous theme—the insistent, steady reminder of Your love!*

Concerto of Gratitude
His Blessing

■ **Theme** *Praise awaits you, O God, in Zion; to you our vows will be fulfilled. O you who hear prayer, to you all men will come. When we were overwhelmed by sins, you forgave our transgressions. Blessed are those you choose and bring near to live in your courts! We are filled with the good things of your house, of your holy temple* (vv. 1–4).

■ **Development** "God is so good; God is so good; God is so good . . . He's so good to me."

The words of this contemporary chorus reflect the view of ancient believers who celebrated this life-sustaining affirmation in conjunction with the barley harvest (Leviticus 23). This psalm holds the key to the "utter fulfillment, blissful happiness, and complete contentment" available to modern-day believers as well.

In meditation, I review God's blessings on my life—salvation, answered prayer, Christian fellowship. I'll never forget the night my mom led me to the Lord as a kid of seven. I was afraid and upset. She comforted me with Christ's words in John 6:37: "All the Father giveth me shall come to me; and him that cometh to me I will in no wise cast out" (KJV). Upon accepting that promise, peace and serenity displaced my childish fears. Since then, I have felt God's hand of provision— once when Karen and I were down to our last nickel and an unexpected royalty check put food on our table! And we continue to grow in Christ with our brothers and sisters—Larry, Jan, Dick, Carol, Don, Shay, and Stan—as we meet together weekly for prayer.

Finally, like the temple-worshipers, I have been *chosen* and brought "near to live in [his] courts!" What sublime happiness awaits me for the rest of my life and through all eternity. "All the good things of [his] house" are mine! Where will I experience real happiness and a rich, inner satisfaction? Only in the presence of the Lord.

179

■ **Personal prayer** *O God, my Savior, thank You for saving me, for sustaining me, and for giving me all the good things of Your house.*

Concerto of Gratitude

His Power

■ **Theme**   *You answer us with awesome deeds of righteousness, O God our Savior, the hope of all the ends of the earth and of the farthest seas, who formed the mountains by your power, having armed yourself with strength, who stilled the roaring of the seas, the roaring of their waves, and the turmoil of the nations. Those living far away fear your wonders; where morning dawns and evening fades you call forth songs of joy (vv. 5–8).*

■ **Development**   We Americans are obsessed with power. We want to climb higher, run farther, move faster than any other generation in history. We'd like to climb on board the Concorde at lunch and arrive in London in time for dinner. Our psychologists delve into the recesses of inner space, while our scientists explore outer space. All America held its breath when Neil Armstrong stepped onto the moon! Sometimes, when I take the express elevator to the top of the World Trade Center in New York or the Sear's Tower in Chicago, I wonder if we are even guilty of erecting our own twentieth-century Towers of Babel.

As a kid I used to watch the Atlantic Ocean roar off the New Jersey coastline. I've observed Niagara Falls many times from different vantage points (including the excursion boat at the foot of the Falls)! And I've peered into the crater atop Mount St. Helens via videotape, helicopter, and television. God's omnipotence evidenced in nature dwarfs even the most splendid of man's puny achievements.

But this God of might and majesty is also intensely personal. He is intimate as well as infinite. He who "formed the mountains" and "stilled the roaring of the seas" hears every whispered prayer.

Such a God inspires me to hope. He "calls forth songs of joy" from my soul until I can hardly wait to transpose them to paper!

■ **Personal prayer**   *O God, my Savior, thank You for Your power, which not only formed the world, but keeps my spirit alive with joy!*

Concerto of Gratitude
His Provision

■ **Theme**   *You care for the land and water it; you enrich it abundantly. The streams of God are filled with water to provide the people with grain, for so you have ordained it. You drench its furrows and level its ridges; you soften it with showers and bless its crops. You crown the year with your bounty, and your carts overflow with abundance. The grasslands of the desert overflow; the hills are clothed with gladness. The meadows are covered with flocks and the valleys are mantled with grain; they shout for joy and sing (vv. 9–13).*

■ **Development**   Human striving and struggling to attain is often disappointing. Always wanting more and never being satisfied feeds on itself and produces greed, lust, and discontent. What a waste of energy!

In these exalted verses the psalmist tells us a simpler way to be happy. He points us to God who answers prayer, not in the abstract, but specifically and in intricate detail. He waters the land, enriches it abundantly, drenches its furrows, levels its ridges, softens it with showers, and blesses its crops. The carts are filled to overflowing with grain. Even the desert flourishes, and the hills are "clothed with gladness."

God is not only the consummate Husbandman; He knows all about the music business too! He knows what it takes to take a song from its germ idea through the various stages of development. Fine craftsmanship is imperative. Then comes reevaluating, rewriting, polishing. Once the song is complete, other musical disciplines come into play: making a demo, song plugging, arranging, orchestrating, and recording. No detail may escape our attention.

Nothing escapes His notice either. There is no matter too trivial to take to the Lord in prayer. Whatever my need—whether shepherding a single song through the recording process, developing a major new recording artist, or fulfilling my role as husband and father—my God has all the answers. His concern for every minute detail of my work and existence prompts me to shout for joy!

■ **Personal prayer**   *O God, my Savior, thank You for caring about every aspect of my life and answering my smallest prayer with Your bounty.*

181

Call to Remembrance
Come and See What God Has Done!

■ **Theme** *Shout with joy to God, all the earth! Sing to the glory of his name; make his praise glorious! . . . Come and see what God has done, how awesome his works in man's behalf! . . . For you, O God, tested us; you refined us like silver. You . . . laid burdens on our backs . . . but you brought us to a place of abundance (vv. 1–2, 5, 10–12).*

■ **Development** "Come and see what God has done," exhorts the psalmist. Israel is encouraged to remember past victories and to join in a song of deliverance. Strong verbs signal the personal involvement of surrounding nations: "Shout for joy!" "Sing to the glory of his name!" "Make his praise glorious!"

Israel has reason to rejoice. God has performed "awesome works"—the parting of the Red Sea, the routing of rebels and the overthrow of dangerous enemies, the provision of His presence in times of severe testing and trial. The Israelites have come through a painful process of purification much like the refining of silver. ("You, O God, tested us; you refined us like silver" v. 10.) To remove impurities, the smelter must fire his furnace to at least 1,761° F. According to Pliny in his *Historia Naturalis*, "the ore was washed and sieved five times, fused with lead and then cupelled for pure silver."

I too have known the Refiner's fire. The loss of my mom, my pastor, and a close friend in a single year was a devastating experience. My song "When Thou Passest Through the Waters," a spiritual based on Isaiah 43:2, was a comfort to me during that difficult time.

God is faithful to lead us through the fire and water to a "place of abundance" (v. 12). Jesus says, "I have come that they may have life, and have it to the full" (John 10:10). I find a place of fullness and intimacy with my Lord when I follow where He leads.

■ **Personal prayer** *Dear Lord, I praise You for walking with me through the fire and water of purification so that I may enjoy You forever in the "place of abundance."*

When Thou Passest Through the Waters

When thou passest through the waters, I will be with thee,
When thou passest through the waters, I will be with thee;
And through the rivers, they shall not overflow thee,
When thou walkest through the fire, thou shalt not be
  burned.

When thou passest through the waters, I will be with thee,
When thou passest through the waters, I will be with thee;
And through dark trials, they shall not overwhelm thee,
When suffering for His sake, thou art glorified.

Words and music by Don Wyrtzen.
© 1979 by Singspiration Music.

Call to Remembrance
Come and Listen!

■ **Theme**   *Come and listen, all you who fear God; let me tell you what he has done for me. I cried out to him with my mouth; his praise was on my tongue. If I had cherished sin in my heart, the LORD would not have listened; but God has surely listened and heard my voice in prayer. Praise be to God, who has not rejected my prayer or withheld his love from me!* (vv. 16–20).

■ **Development**   What did an Old Testament believer do when he was in the furnace of God's testing, when he was on a "guilt trip"? He fulfilled his vows to the Lord. He went to the temple to present burnt offerings as a sacrifice for sin. Why? Because "without the shedding of blood there is no forgiveness" (Hebrews 9:22).

Karen and I once had an interesting conversation with a well-known songwriter having a hard time accepting the gospel. The Old Testament sacrifices seemed primitive and barbaric to him, and he could not conceive of a loving God sacrificing His own Son!

Each time a choice animal was killed and the white wool stained crimson with its life blood, the worshiper received a graphic message of substitutionary death. God's refrain echoed again and again: "I love you. I love you. I love you." The ancient believer saw with his own eyes the staggering cost of sin and the amazing grace that guarantees our redemption.

God's full forgiveness follows *sincere* repentance. "If I had cherished sin in my heart, the Lord would not have listened" (v. 18). But the Lord does listen to the psalmist's heartfelt confession and pours out His love in response.

Twenty centuries later, you and I have the benefit of the gospel message that was foretold in those Old Testament rites: "For God so loved the world that He gave his one and only Son, that whoever believes in him shall not perish but have eternal life" (John 3:16). Therefore, I am filled with joy and thanksgiving because I am forgiven, cleansed, and absolved from guilt! I am now free to accept myself because the Lord accepts my prayer and does not withhold His love from me.

184

■ **Personal prayer**   *O Lord, I can't keep silent! You inspire me to write and to sing songs of thanksgiving for the miracle of Your love and forgiveness!*

Shine on Me

■ **Theme**   *May God be gracious to us and bless us and make his face shine upon us, that your ways may be known on earth, your salvation among all nations. May the peoples praise you, O God; may all the peoples praise you (vv. 1–3).*

■ **Development**

> The LORD bless you and keep you;
>   the LORD make his face shine upon you
>   and be gracious to you;
> The LORD turn his face toward you
>   and give you peace (Numbers 6:24–26).

So Aaron and his sons blessed the Israelites in ancient times. This familiar benediction has been blessing people for generations.

In this passage the composer uses the metaphor of light: "May God . . . make his face shine upon us" (v. 1), followed by a trio of eternal themes: God's grace (vv. 1–2), praise of the peoples (vv. 3–5), and God's blessing (vv. 6–7).

I can envision a scenario in which the worship leaders, the congregation, and God all play vital roles. It could go something like this:

Worship leader: O God, may Your unmerited favor rest upon us and may the light of Your countenance flood our hearts and minds with all spiritual understanding. Then we can be Your witnesses, bringing proof of Your salvation and love to all nations on earth.

Congregation: We lift our voices to You, O God! We are but one tribe, one nation among many who rejoice to see justice and perfect leadership. We express the utmost joy and gladness in You today.

God's blessing: "If my people, who are called by my name, will humble themselves and pray and seek my face and turn from their wicked ways, then will I hear from heaven and will forgive their sin and will heal their land" (2 Chronicles 7:14).

God is speaking. We must listen. As He shines upon us, we'll reflect His glory.

185

■ **Personal prayer**   *Joyful, joyful, I adore You, God of glory, Lord of light!*

Celebration of Conquest
Extolling God

■ **Theme**   But may the righteous be glad and rejoice before God; may they be happy and joyful. Sing to God, sing praise to his name, extol him who rides on the clouds—his name is the LORD—and rejoice before him. A father to the fatherless, a defender of widows, is God in his holy dwelling. God sets the lonely in families, he leads forth the prisoners with singing (vv. 3–6).

■ **Development**   The more intimately I come to know God, the more I am awed by His grace and goodness. Through David's eyes, I see even more clearly God's compassionate nature as well as His majesty and power.

This song accompanied a ritual procession celebrating God's conquests and victories in behalf of Israel. David begins by praying that God will show His awesome power to the wicked by "blowing them away" (v. 2). Then he moves almost immediately to praise, urging his followers to honor and extol the Lord for His tender care. He is the Father of the fatherless, the Defender of widows, the Caring One who sets the lonely in families, the Deliverer of prisoners.

I have a dad whom I respect and admire, so I don't know what it's like to be fatherless. But my friend, Margaret Clarkson, hymn writer par excellence, never knew her father, and I can read the depth of her pain in her lyrics. I will never be a widow, but my mother-in-law, Ruth Parr, lost her husband some time ago. I don't know exactly how she feels, but I hear her crying sometimes. I have a friend who has been in prison; and, while I haven't served a jail sentence, I imprison myself sometimes behind bars of isolation and remoteness, even with my family around me! But I know our heavenly Father can meet every one of these needs and so many more if we let Him, for He is our source of consummate security, shelter, and safety.

When I experience God in His gentleness, I am compelled to join in the chorus of praises to His Name. He is my Father, my Defender, my Provider, my Redeemer!

■ **Personal prayer**   O God, I rejoice before You today. May I continue to see You, not only as the omnipotent Rider of the Clouds, but as the tender Shepherd.

Celebration of Conquest
Remembering the Conqueror

■ **Theme**   *The mountains of Bashan are majestic mountains; rugged are the mountains of Bashan. Why gaze in envy, O rugged mountains, at the mountain where God chooses to reign, where the LORD himself will dwell forever? The chariots of God are tens of thousands and thousands of thousands; the Lord has come from Sinai into his sanctuary. When you ascended on high you led captives in your train; you received gifts from men, even from the rebellious—that you, O LORD God, might dwell there (vv. 15–18).*

■ **Development**   Sometimes I need to step back and look at where I've been before I can discern where I'm going or how I'm going to get there. Midway through the year is a natural time to take stock.

David must have felt much the same way, since so many of his psalms review Israel's glorious history—from her trek through the wilderness to her conquest of the Promised Land (vv. 7–10). He then describes the occupation of Canaan where wicked kings were routed and driven out (vv. 11–14).

This psalm brings to mind some of my own wilderness wanderings. It's easy to get lost on the pilgrim journey when you tend to live in a fog. Maybe I'm too laid back—not decisive enough. Or maybe I don't always discipline myself enough. But I'm thankful that even at these times, my Lord knows the way!

The climax of the passage depicts God ascending Mount Zion—a mighty conqueror with "thousands of thousands" (v. 17) of chariots, and leading "captives in [His] train" (v. 18). It also recalls the siege of Jerusalem by David's army and his establishing the Ark of the Covenant there.

My life gains fresh perspective when I count my victories and focus on the Conqueror. God Himself has escorted me through the wastelands, has cared for me tenderly when I am troubled and tired, and has even conquered death (vv. 19–20). Such a Conquering Savior demands my highest praise and adoration!

187

■ **Personal prayer**   *O God, thank You for reminding me of Your comforting presence through some tangled times. I praise You, my Savior, for rescuing me and leading me to the mountaintop where I will dwell with You forever!*

Celebration of Conquest
Assessing His Victory

■ **Theme**   *Your procession has come into view, O God, the procession of my God and King into the sanctuary. In front are the singers, after them the musicians; with them are the maidens playing tambourines. Praise God in the great congregation; praise the LORD in the assembly of Israel. . . . You are awesome, O God, in your sanctuary; the God of Israel gives power and strength to his people. Praise be to God! (vv. 24–26, 35).*

■ **Development**   I love a parade! I remember taking our kids, D.J. and Kathy, when they were small, to the Fourth of July parade in Cascade, a suburb of Grand Rapids, Michigan. There were homemade floats, decorated bikes (with streamers in the wheels), and even an old fire tender with water spewing forth in all directions. Parades are exciting!

God's triumphal entrance into Zion is pictured as a victory parade, complete with singers, dancers, and musicians. Led by the little tribe of Benjamin, they are all praising God in the assembly.

David ends this celebration psalm with a moving call to praise the God who "rides the ancient skies" and "thunders with mighty voice" (v. 33). God's power is awesome and He bestows strength on His people.

May my vision of the Lord increase to the magnitude of David's vision! May I resonate with the awareness that if I open up to Him and cultivate spiritual receptivity, I will receive more of His awesome power and strength in my life. Praise be to God!

■ **Personal prayer**   *O Lord, I join the artists, musicians, and singers of the ancient world in worshiping You in all of Your power, majesty, and glory!*

Ode to Hope   David Feels Low

■ **Theme**   *Save me, O God, for the waters have come up to my neck. . . . I am worn out calling for help; my throat is parched. My eyes fail, looking for my God. Those who hate me without reason outnumber the hairs of my head; many are my enemies without cause, those who seek to destroy me. I am forced to restore what I did not steal (vv. 1, 3–4).*

■ **Development**   There is nothing more disconcerting than being unjustly accused, since denial is the weakest form of defense. David finds himself in just such a no-win situation in this psalm.

His enemies, some of whom are important city officials, despise him, and even his own relatives have disowned him. He feels like a drowning man! "The waters have come up to my neck" (v. 1); "I sink in the miry depths" (v. 2); "I have come into deep waters; the floods engulf me!" (v. 2). His enemies sing cynical songs about him and mock him.

What's significant here is that David is suffering, not because of sin, but as a consequence of zealously following the Lord. He puts on sackcloth, signifying mourning, and pours out his heart to the Lord.

Music is probably the richest of all art forms because it speaks to all levels of the personality simultaneously. One doesn't relate to a powerful piece of music cognitively only, but emotionally and physically as well. Hence, we use music to speak the unspeakable, to express the inexpressible—sorrow, discouragement, anger, bitterness, joy. And we use it when words are not enough.

David uses poetic lament to vent his sense of personal injustice. I'm encouraged by his honesty. I am made aware again that not all suffering is the result of sin. Christ Himself suffered the greatest injustice of all, precisely because He was pure and righteous. Following Him sometimes leads me into uncomfortable circumstances. But I'm in good company!

■ **Personal prayer**   *Dear God, teach me how to embrace Your sufferings so I can share in the delights of Your kingdom, and may I use the gift of music to share the secrets of Your caring with others.*

Ode to Hope   *David Prays*

■ **Theme**   *But I pray to you, O LORD, in the time of your favor; in your great love, O God, answer me with your sure salvation. . . . Answer me, O LORD, out of the goodness of your love; in your great mercy turn to me. Do not hide your face from your servant; answer me quickly, for I am in trouble. Come near and rescue me; redeem me because of my foes (vv. 13, 16–18).*

■ **Development**   David prayed with great fervor. His intensity is equal to his need, graphically described in these phrases: "Rescue me from the mire, do not let me sink; deliver me . . . Do not let the floodwaters engulf me or the depths swallow me up or the pit close its mouth over me" (v. 15).

Ninety-nine out of a hundred persons will not go through the hard work of letting the Lord excise the pain from their lives. Denial, changing external behaviors, and maintaining proper images are attempted shortcuts to maturity for most people.

David refuses to resort to that kind of evasive maneuver. He is facing reality here, and I can learn something from his prayer. He appeals to the Lord on the basis of (1) His timing—"in the time of your favor" (v. 13); and (2) His purposes—"your sure salvation" (v. 13). Yet his overriding desire seems to be that God's justice prevail (v. 18). Maybe this is the secret to power in prayer. When selfish desires are yielded to the Lord, His Name is glorified and His purposes fulfilled.

So often I try to hurry God, or attempt to manipulate Him for my own ends. I need to be aware that I limit His work in my life when I confine Him to the present moment rather than the time span of eternity. When I'm in trouble, I need to pray for His name to be magnified *through* my circumstances, *in* His timing, *for* the salvation of souls.

■ **Personal prayer**   *Dear Lord, You are the Giver of life, but You are also my Lifesaver in times of deep trouble.*

Ode to Hope   The Lord Hears

■ **Theme**   *I will praise God's name in song and glorify him with thanksgiving. This will please the* LORD *more than an ox, more than a bull with its horns and hoofs. The poor will see and be glad—you who seek God, may your hearts live! The* LORD *hears the needy and does not despise his captive people* (vv. 30–33).

■ **Development**   Our Lord is like the shepherd who knows each individual sheep intimately and by name. He is also like the symphony conductor who not only hears the grand ensemble of the orchestra, but can also single out each individual part as well.

The ear of the Lord is tuned to the hearts of His people. "When he cries out to me, I will hear, for I am compassionate" (Exodus 22:27).

David is counting on that compassion. He comes before the Lord with singing, knowing that the sounds of thanksgiving will be more pleasing than burnt offerings—"an ox . . . or a bull with its horns and hoofs" (v. 31). In turn, this sacrifice of praise will be heard by all in the assembly, and the hearts of the people will be encouraged.

As the psalmist gains personal strength and hope in the very process of praising the Lord, he urges others to join him in the glad chorus. All is not lost! We are not alone in our pain and distress. He hears! He hears!

> O God, our help in ages past,
> Our hope for years to come,
> Our shelter from the stormy blast,
> And our eternal home.
>
> Under the shadow of Thy throne
> Thy saints have dwelt secure;
> Sufficient is Thine arm alone,
> And our defense is sure.

Words by Isaac Watts. Music by William Croft.

■ **Personal prayer**   *O God, You know the sounds of my distress. You hear me when I sing Your praises. May I never fail to hear Your voice— comforting, guiding, instructing, warning.*

Petition   O God, Save Me!

■ **Theme**   *Hasten, O God, to save me; O LORD, come quickly to help me. May those who seek my life be put to shame and confusion; may all who desire my ruin be turned back in disgrace. May those who say to me, "Aha! Aha!" turn back because of their shame (vv. 1–3).*

■ **Development**   For years I've dreaded deadlines. Enormous pressure builds when there is a full symphony recording session booked for tomorrow and the scores aren't done—even though there has been pacing and discipline. Often, there is only time for a hasty "Help, Lord!"

David is again in dire straits. His life is in danger and his reputation at stake (v. 2). God must act quickly, or David's adversaries will press their advantage. With his enemies breathing down his neck, he cries, "O God, save me!"

The apostle Peter had a similar experience in New Testament times. Like his Lord, he walked on the water. "But when he saw the wind, he was afraid, and beginning to sink, cried out, 'Lord, save me!'"

Along with David and Peter, I can praise the Lord for responding to life's emergencies with His grace and deliverance.

> *Fatherlike, he tends and spares us;*
> *Well our feeble frame He knows;*
> *In His hands, He gently bears us,*
> *Rescues us from all our foes.*

Words by Henry F. Lyte. Music by Henry Smart.

■ **Personal prayer**   *Hurry, Lord! I need the strength of Your presence right now . . . this hour . . . this minute! And hasten the coming of Your kingdom on earth, as it is in heaven.*

Petition   Let God Be Exalted!

■ **Theme**   But may all who seek you rejoice and be glad in you; may those who love your salvation always say, "Let God be exalted!" Yet I am poor and needy; come quickly to me, O God. You are my help and my deliverer; O LORD, do not delay (vv. 4–5).

■ **Development**   There is no trumped-up worship experience here — no empty ritual or phony liturgy. David is brutally honest with himself and with God in facing the reality of his plight. But he doesn't stay in the doldrums. He shifts his focus from problems to praise.

He revels in exalting the Lord and in expressing the love he feels for Him. The Lord is his Help and Deliverer. Though David is poor and needy, surely the Lord will come to his aid without delay.

As I actively seek the Lord, I find great joy in Him. I delight in my salvation, in the help and deliverance He offers. Thank You, Lord.

> Praise my soul, the King of heaven.
> To His feet thy tribute bring;
> Ransomed, healed, restored, forgiven,
> Evermore His praises sing.
>
> Praise Him for His grace and favor
> To our fathers in distress;
> Praise Him, still the same as ever,
> Slow to chide, and swift to bless.

Words by Henry F. Lyte. Music by Henry Smart.

■ **Personal prayer**   O God, may You be lifted to the highest position of praise, honor, and power in my life!

Lifestyle of Dependence
Confidence

■ **Theme**   In you, O LORD, I have taken refuge; let me never be put to shame. Rescue me and deliver me in your righteousness; turn your ear to me and save me. Be my rock of refuge, to which I can always go; give the command to save me, for you are my rock and my fortress. Deliver me, O my God, from the hand of the wicked, from the grasp of evil and cruel men (vv. 1–4).

■ **Development**   This psalmist is most likely an older person who has experienced the marvelous faithfulness of God for a lifetime. He knows his psalter well, for he quotes Psalms 22, 31, 35, and 40 and vows to continue praising God. He also asks for deliverance from the wicked men who seek to harm him and who mock him for his faith.

He has supreme confidence in the Lord's ability to save. He pictures the Lord as his Refuge, his Rock, and his Fortress. He knows that the only reliable place of safety and security is with the Lord.

I have observed some benefits of growing older in the Lord. For example, there is nothing so full of character as the time-worn, wrinkled face of one of God's prayer warriors, glowing with a radiance that no cosmetic on earth can bestow. The practice of praise produces inner beauty, seasons the spirit, develops prayer muscle. Older saints have learned the paradox that dependence upon the Lord is the secret to perfect freedom! Like the great hymns of the faith, these dear men and women of God grow more precious as time goes by.

194

■ **Personal prayer**   O Lord, You are my Refuge, my Rock, and my Fortress. May I learn to lean on You more completely.

Lifestyle of Dependence   Hope

■ **Theme**   *For you have been my hope, O Sovereign* LORD, *my confidence since my youth. From birth I have relied on you; you brought me forth from my mother's womb. I will ever praise you. I have become like a portent to many, but you are my strong refuge. My mouth is filled with your praise, declaring your splendor all day long. Do not cast me away when I am old; do not forsake me when my strength is gone (vv. 5–9).*

■ **Development**   This psalmist believes in the sovereignty of God— that the Lord, the Supreme Ruler of the universe, has everything under His control. Not only is He sovereign, but He *sustains.* From birth, through youth, into the middle years and beyond, the psalmist has felt His sustaining grace.

In music, we use the fermata (musical pause or hold) to indicate that a note is to be sustained or held. Breaking the rhythmic pace of a piece adds texture and variety. Sustained notes have emphasis because of their staying power. A person can likewise exhibit strong character through endurance, persistence, and continuance in habits of holiness.

Now that the psalmist is growing older, however, he is afraid. He fears losing his strength (v. 9). He fears his enemies (v. 10). He even fears the possibility that the Lord will forsake him (v. 11). Still, he is honest and forthright about his anxieties and cries to God who has always been his safe haven. He prays for "staying power" as he faces the challenges of aging.

As I grow older, I need to build my confidence on my own life history with the Lord. He has never failed to meet my needs. He has always taken care of me. He has proven Himself faithful and has been my confidence and hope "since my youth." I know I can rely on Him to take care of me today . . . and tomorrow.

■ **Personal prayer**   *O Lord, You are fully trustworthy. I rest myself in You for the remaining days of my life and into all eternity!*

Lifestyle of Dependence   Praise

■ **Theme**   *I will praise you with the harp for your faithfulness, O my God; I will sing praise to you with the lyre, O Holy One of Israel. My lips will shout for joy when I sing praise to you—I, whom you have redeemed. My tongue will tell of your righteous acts all day long, for those who wanted to harm me have been put to shame and confusion* (vv. 22–24).

■ **Development**   Repetition teaches and reinforces. This psalmist has learned how to praise the Lord by praising—repeatedly, continually, for a lifetime. He revels in the subject of his praise—God's faithfulness and righteousness (v. 16). He delights in the act of praise—"with the harp" (v. 22); "with the lyre" (v. 22); with "my lips" (v. 23); with "my tongue" (v. 24).

Musicians have a divine mandate to live a lifestyle of praise. I thrill to the variety of musical instruments mentioned in the book of Psalms and to the parts of the body used in praising the Lord. Hands clap and strum; lips shout; vocal chords resonate and sing; tongues confess and testify; feet dance! Our very bodies are created to perform a symphony of praise! As temples of the Holy Spirit, our bodies are sacred sanctuaries to be used for His glory, not for our selfish desires. Worship begins with the imagination and the heart, but it must expand outward until our very nerve endings tingle with praise.

The longer I live, the more evidence I gather of God's grace and glory. As I practice praise, I become more proficient in expressing my love and gratitude to Him. Like the elderly psalmist, I've experienced some dissonant moments when it appeared there was no resolution, only to find that God was orchestrating these events for my good. "And we know that in all things God works for the good of those who love him, who have been called according to his purpose" (Romans 8:28).

■ **Personal prayer**   *O Lord, teach me how to praise You and remind me to practice until my heart sings in perfect harmony with Your will.*

Solomon's Song   His Justice

■ **Theme**   *Endow the king with your justice, O God, the royal son with your righteousness. He will judge your people with righteousness, your afflicted ones with justice. . . . He will defend the afflicted among the people and save the children of the needy; he will crush the oppressor. He will endure as long as the sun, as long as the moon, through all generations (vv. 1–2, 4–5).*

■ **Development**   Solomon most likely composed both Psalm 72 and Psalm 127. In this first psalm, he is probably describing his reign as well as the millennial reign of Christ, for he speaks of righteousness, peace, and long-term prosperity.

While he has the good judgment to ask God's blessing on his own administration—"Endow the king with your justice, O God!" (v. 1)—it seems clear that Solomon is referring also to the coming messianic kingdom that will "endure as long as the sun, as long as the moon, through all generations" (v. 5).

As a musician and businessman, what can I learn from Solomon? First, I admire his verbal artistry. "He [Jesus] will be like rain falling on a mown field, like showers watering the earth. In his days the righteous will flourish; prosperity will abound till the moon is no more" (vv. 6–7).

But I am also deeply moved by Solomon's personal ethics. "He will judge your people with righteousness. . . . He will defend the afflicted among the people and save the children of the needy; he will crush the oppressor" (vv. 2, 4). Solomon is worthy of emulation in my business dealings and in the practice of my faith.

Without Christ's love in my heart, I might be tempted to lapse into neglect of the talented people who come through my office. But I operate my business on Christian principles, nurturing musical gifts for the glory of God, not for selfish gain. I look for opportunities to hear the unheard and to stand firmly against outside influences that would dilute the Christian message of our music. Living a life of integrity may not promote material rewards, but it promises spiritual prosperity!

197

■ **Personal prayer**   *Lord, reign in my heart and bring Your justice and righteousness to every area of my life!*

Solomon's Song   *His Rule*

■ **Theme**   *All kings will bow down to him and all nations will serve him. For he will deliver the needy who cry out, the afflicted who have no one to help. He will take pity on the weak and the needy and save the needy from death. He will rescue them from oppression and violence, for precious is their blood in his sight (vv. 11–14).*

■ **Development**   Solomon's reign was lengthy and far-reaching, extending from sea to sea and from the Euphrates River to the ends of the earth (v. 8). He received tribute from the kings of Tarshish and gifts from the kings of Sheba and Seba (v. 10). He was widely worshiped and revered.

One might imagine that mighty Solomon would have become corrupted and drunk with pride because of his great power and influence. Instead, he had a heart of compassion for the needy, the afflicted, and the helpless. He rescued them from oppression and violence. Motivated by a lofty concept of the worth of the individual, he was a great king with a servant heart much like that of One who came much later—our Savior, who knelt to wash His disciples' feet (John 13:5).

I would love to be remembered for several things: some of the songs I've written, the passion with which I approach music—attempts at soaring melodies, sophisticated harmonies, and unusual voicings. I love to communicate, to feel as if I'm playing an audience like a Stradivarius. But to be known as a competent musician with a servant's heart would be the highest accolade of all!

■ **Personal prayer**   *O Lord, may I lay aside my hang-ups with success and model myself after You, who willingly laid down Your crown and took up a cross . . . for me!*

Solomon's Song   His Adoring Subjects

■ **Theme**   *Long may he live! May gold from Sheba be given him. May people ever pray for him and bless him all day long. . . . May his name endure forever; may it continue as long as the sun. All nations will be blessed through him, and they will call him blessed. Praise be to the LORD God, the God of Israel, who alone does marvelous deeds. Praise be to his glorious name forever; may the whole earth be filled with his glory. Amen and Amen* (vv. 15, 17–19).

■ **Development**   I barely remember the coronation of Queen Elizabeth II of England, only that there was a lot of pomp and pageantry and that some magnificent music was played in Westminster Abbey. I loved the majesty of the pipe organ, combined with brass fanfares and undergirded by the strength and power of rolling timpani and clashing cymbals. And I'll never forget seeing the telecast showing the smiling faces and waving flags of the English subjects who lined the streets to celebrate her coronation day.

King Solomon was held in the highest esteem. He was blessed with personal gifts, agricultural prosperity, a solid, enduring reputation, and the respect of his peers. The Queen of Sheba alone brought him massive amounts of gold (1 Kings 10:10). The common folk praised him for paving the way for flourishing trade, peaceful alliances with neighboring nations, and the blessing of God on their land, which yielded unprecedented crops and herds.

Solomon's response to all of this takes the form of a majestic doxology. It is the second doxology in the book of Psalms and is a fitting close for Book II (Psalms 41–72). "Praise be to the LORD God, the God of Israel, who alone does marvelous deeds. Praise be to his glorious name forever; may the whole earth be filled with his glory. Amen and Amen" (vv. 18–19).

In 1741, at the London premiere of Handel's *Messiah*, King George II rose to his feet during the glorious "Hallelujah Chorus" in worshipful recognition of his Supreme Sovereign. Later, it was Queen Victoria who said, "Someday it shall be my joy to lay my crown at His feet!"

199

■ **Personal prayer**   *Lord, whatever honors or accolades come to me in this life I will gladly lay at Your feet!*

Prelude to True Prosperity
Stating the Paradox

■ **Theme**   *Surely God is good to Israel, to those who are pure in heart. But as for me, my feet had almost slipped; I had nearly lost my foothold. For I envied the arrogant when I saw the prosperity of the wicked. They have no struggles; their bodies are healthy and strong. They are free from the burdens common to man; they are not plagued by human ills* (vv. 1–5).

■ **Development**   If the Christian life promises blessing, why do godly people struggle while unbelievers enjoy prosperity? Some, in attempting to answer that question, have considered turning away from God.

Sheldon Vanauken, noted author of *A Severe Mercy*, was tempted to disown God when his wife was dying of cancer. My dad has a friend, a highly articulate, gifted evangelist, who abandoned his ministry after becoming disillusioned. And when I was in college, I too experienced some disharmony between mind and spirit and came close to a decision to get along without God in my life.

This psalm wrestles with those issues poignantly and poetically. Asaph, one of the chief singers, percussionists, and ministers in the ancient temple, almost walked away from God. He was one of the Lord's major spokesmen and a charismatic leader; yet he seriously considered packing it all in.

I believe spirituality begins with honesty. Part of that is being objective about one's true feelings. This psalm is a beautiful catharsis for Asaph. He pours out his hurting soul before his heavenly Father. The Lord, in His marvelous mercy and incomprehensible grace, hears.

200

■ **Personal prayer**   *O Father, how can I ever be objective about my feelings? I'm hurting, confused, and very frustrated. Please minister to me out of Your vast storehouse of grace.*

Prelude to True Prosperity
Viewing Life from What Is Seen

■ **Theme**   *Therefore pride is their necklace; they clothe themselves with violence. From their callous hearts comes iniquity; the evil conceits of their minds know no limits. They scoff, and speak with malice; in their arrogance they threaten oppression. . . . Therefore their people turn to them and drink up waters in abundance. They say, "How can God know? Does the Most High have knowledge?"* (vv. 6–8, 10–11).

■ **Development**   Has the Lord called us to happiness or to holiness? Is it possible to have harmony in life without dissonance? Asaph, in attempting to come to grips with adequate answers to those questions, is tempted to wander away from the Lord.

First, he draws his view of life from what he *sees*: The wicked are prospering and the godly are afflicted. To Asaph and to many modern worshipers, this seems contrary to the moral teaching of the Scriptures, since the Law and Proverbs boldly promise blessing for obedience (Deuteronomy 28; Proverbs 3). The more Asaph observes these apparent contradictions, the more his faith is shaken.

I too suffered from cognitive dissonance while in college. I believed what I saw—that the external symbols of success equaled success itself. Nor did I observe enough internal consistency and reality in Christendom. (It's easier to build a flourishing Christian empire than to nurture a sensitive, beautiful marriage, for example.) Behavioral conformity without spiritual renewal leads to performance without intimacy, breeds doubt rather than faith, and stresses illusion rather than reality.

Secular society and the media can also impact upon our Christian beliefs. For many people, newspapers and television—indeed, the whole non-Christian milieu—carry more clout than God's Word! Yet the Scriptures present the big picture, the long-term view. My own limited perspective often leads to an incorrect translation of God's meaning for my life. I don't want to be guilty of making the mistake Asaph almost made—selling the Lord short.

■ **Personal prayer**   *O Father, help me to have complete confidence in the authority of Your Word. You alone know my tomorrows and know the minor chords of my life can be used to produce a pleasant and harmonious melody.*

Prelude to True Prosperity
Being Consumed by Envy

■ **Theme**   *This is what the wicked are like—always carefree, they increase in wealth (v. 12).*

■ **Development**   How perplexing! Asaph takes the second step down the ladder of faith when he allows envy to dominate his thoughts. How easy to be drawn into this tangled web spun by the Master Deceiver. Sometimes the grass *does* seem greener on the other side of the fence!

Envy is sin. It's as simple as that. Yet I know of no more subtle addiction to which Christians, living in a highly commercialized world, can fall prey. We see the same ads as the wicked—the posh luxury resorts, the high-tech cars and gadgets, the designer clothing—and wonder why some who seem so undeserving get all the breaks—particularly when prosperity for obedience was promised in the Law! We might as well admit, along with Asaph, that we don't have it all together. Some things just don't add up.

In Isaiah 55:8–9, I receive a gentle rebuke: "For my thoughts are not your thoughts, neither are your ways my ways. . . . For as the heavens are higher than the earth, so are my ways higher than your ways, and my thoughts than your thoughts." The apostle Paul echoes this truth and adds a dimension of his own reaction: "We are hard pressed on every side, but not crushed; *perplexed,* but not in despair" (2 Corinthians 4:8).

Apparently the proper response to perplexity, at least for the Christian, is to trust in the Lord . . . anyway!

■ **Personal prayer**   *O Father, I bring my perplexities and unresolved conflicts to You. Help me not to envy the unrighteous who prosper, but to put my trust in You.*

Prelude to True Prosperity
Almost Dropping Out

■ **Theme**   *Surely in vain have I kept my heart pure; in vain have I washed my hands in innocence. All day long I have been plagued; I have been punished every morning (vv. 13–14).*

■ **Development**   What's the use? I can almost hear Asaph's rationale as he takes the third step down the ladder of faith to defection. "All day long I have been plagued; I have been punished every morning" (v. 14). "But as for me, my feet had almost slipped; I had nearly lost my foothold" (v. 2).

In Hebrew, the word *foot* includes the area from the knee to the sole. The picture is this: "My knees nearly buckled. My steps almost slipped out from under me." In effect, Asaph is saying, "I can't take it anymore!" He's about to take matters into his own hands and remove the Lord from the throne of his life.

In some ways John DeLorean, before his conversion to Christ, was the paradigm of the modern American man. One of the "beautiful people," he was bright, pragmatic, energetic, and innovative. But without Christ at the helm of his life, without his sights set on Christian values, without a proper perspective of the value of people, his empire came crashing down.

Fortunately for John, Asaph—and me—God is merciful and longsuffering, "not willing that any should perish, but that all should come to repentance" (2 Peter 3:9, KJV).

■ **Personal prayer**   *O Father, when everything in me screams, "I can't take it any more," help me to hold on!*

Prelude to True Prosperity
Returning to the Lord

■ **Theme**   If I had said, "I will speak thus," I would have betrayed your children. When I tried to understand all this, it was oppressive to me till I entered the sanctuary of God; then I understood their final destiny (vv. 15–17).

■ **Development**   Asaph now begins his journey back to the Lord by pondering "all this" (v. 16) and rejecting materialism—what is *seen*. Materialism is seriously flawed. It can put food *on* the table but will never guarantee fellowship *around* the table. It can provide a *house*, but not a *home*. It can adorn a woman with fine jewels, but never promises love. Materialism generates the notion of loving things and using people. Christianity produces love for people and subordinates things.

Asaph takes a second rung up the ladder of faith when he enters the sanctuary (v. 17). In that place of shelter and serenity, he experiences fellowship and he hears God's Word. With the temple as his support system, he's no longer trying to go it alone.

All Christians, including leaders, speakers, writers, and recording artists, need that kind of support. Since true prosperity is spiritual in nature, we find it only in fellowship with other "becomers." In concert, we give and receive empathy, accountability, inquiry, and care. The Enemy would love to encourage the "star syndrome" which places the "star" in a class by himself, above the limitations and restrictions governing everyone else. When that person becomes isolated in an ivory tower, when he believes his own stuff, when he becomes charmed by the press releases and his own notoriety, he is set up for a big fall. There is only one Superstar, the Lord Jesus Christ.

Asaph too begins to get the picture when he encounters God. The terminology used in his magnificent psalm stresses God's holiness, His "everlastingness," His transcendence. When Asaph finally sees God as He really is, the stunning revelation gives him a whole new perspective on life.

204

■ **Personal prayer**   O Father, give me a fresh revelation of Yourself. May I not neglect my worship experience, but gladly seek the fellowship of other believers in Your sanctuary.

Prelude to True Prosperity
Encountering the Living God

■ **Theme**   *When my heart was grieved and my spirit embittered, I was senseless and ignorant; I was a brute beast before you. Yet I am always with you; you hold me by my right hand. You guide me with your counsel, and afterward you will take me into glory. Whom have I in heaven but you? And earth has nothing I desire besides you (vv. 21–25).*

■ **Development**   After Asaph's encounter with the living God, he sees *himself* as he is: "senseless . . . ignorant . . . a brute beast"— hardly the picture of success as we know it. That's always the case. Meeting God and coming to know Him intimately exposes our limitations, our inadequacies, our weaknesses.

And now Asaph begins to understand the ultimates of life. Because he has caught a glimpse of God in His glory, his perspective is changed on everything, including death. "And afterward you will take me into glory" (v. 24). The alternative is to see life as the brutes or animals, who are locked by instinct into the material world.

Asaph then "lets go and lets God." He invites God to meet his needs for love and meaning. "My flesh and my heart may fail, but God is the strength of my heart and my portion forever" (v. 26). He concludes by fully committing himself to the Lord. In turn, God stamps upon Asaph His own character, heart, and mind.

■ **Personal prayer**   *O Father, give me Your thoughts, Your mindset, and Your perspective on my life. Please meet my profound longings for meaning and love as I commit myself fully to You.*

Asaph's Lament
Devastation: No Leaders in the Land

■ **Theme** *Why have you rejected us forever, O God? Why does your anger smolder against the sheep of your pasture? Remember the people you purchased of old, the tribe of your inheritance, whom you redeemed— Mount Zion, where you dwelt. . . . They burned your sanctuary to the ground; they defiled the dwelling place of your Name. they said in their hearts, "We will crush them completely!" They burned every place where God was worshiped in the land. We are given no miraculous signs; no prophets are left, and none of us knows how long this will be (vv. 1–2, 7– 9).*

■ **Development** "No prophets are left . . ." This mournful theme delivers Asaph's message of devastation. A nation or an individual without "prophets"—spiritual counsel—is a prime target for the Enemy.

Asaph groans over the fate of his people, who are suffering at the hands of enemy invaders. He describes, in graphic detail, the demolition of the sanctuary—the seat of worship and God's dwelling place. The aggressors have "smashed all the carved paneling," looted, and pillaged. In a final act of blasphemy, they burn the sanctuary and disperse the prophets. God's Word is not heard in the land, and no one knows how long the devastation will continue.

Though our church buildings are not in imminent danger of being razed, we might well ask ourselves why our pulpits and our people are not evidencing more power. Do we fail to lift up our spiritual leaders in our prayers? Do we criticize instead of encourage? Or is it that so many of our churches are "Laodicean"—neither hot nor cold (Revelation 3:15).

What is needed? Honest, courageous facing of our sin as God's people—individually and corporately. Repentance—crying out to God with contrite hearts. Forgiveness—accepting the covering of Christ's precious blood shed on the Cross. Renewal—allowing His spirit to change our lives to conform to His image. Witness—sharing the Gospel with the unsaved world.

■ **Personal prayer** *O God, may I be faithful to be in Your house, worshiping, praising, thanking You for our freedom to gather. Anoint Your servant, my pastor, with Your grace and blessing.*

Asaph's Lament
Disorientation: God's Tempo or Mine?

■ **Theme**   *How long will the enemy mock you, O God? Will the foe revile your name forever? Why do you hold back your hand, your right hand? Take it from the folds of your garment and destroy them! But you, O God, are my king from of old; you bring salvation upon the earth (v. 10–12).*

■ **Development**   Unlike the impotent gods of the ancient world, Asaph's God is fully involved, fully in control of His creation. Still, He doesn't move fast enough to suit the psalmist, for God does not bow to man's demands nor adhere to his timetable.

We are often like the trumpet player in an orchestra who wants to set his own tempo instead of following the conductor. We'd like for God to work *presto* (at a rapid rate) when the tempo of His plan may be *largo* (slow and dignified). A major aspect of being a world-class conductor, such as Herbert Von Karajan or George Solti, is to be in perfect control of the orchestra, setting the appropriate tempo to enhance the master score.

But Asaph has had it with waiting on God. "Why do you hold back your hand, your right hand?" he complains. He'd be much happier if the Lord would assert Himself and destroy the adversary— quickly and decisively.

As if to refresh His memory, Asaph outlines God's sovereign acts of the past: "You split open" the Red Sea; "You broke the heads" of sea monsters; "You crushed" Leviathan (a reference to Egypt); "You opened up springs" for the Israelites; "You set all the boundaries of the earth!" (vv. 13–17). Asaph wonders how such an active God can sit passively by and why He doesn't strike back in behalf of His people with dramatic force and energy.

But God always moves to accomplish His purposes with precise timing. What Asaph needed to learn and what I need to remember is that God's tempo is perfect. "But when the time had fully come, God sent his Son, born of a woman, born under law, to redeem those under law, that we might receive the full rights of sons" (Galatians 4:4).

207

■ **Personal prayer**   *O God, forgive my impetuous nature, my desire to rush things. Teach me that the greatest gifts come to those who wait patiently for You.*

Asaph's Lament
Deliverance: The Grand Finale

■ **Theme** *Remember how the enemy has mocked you, O LORD, how foolish people have reviled your name. Do not hand over the life of your dove to wild beasts; do not forget the lives of your afflicted people forever. Have regard for your covenant, because haunts of violence fill the dark places of the land. Do not let the oppressed retreat in disgrace; may the poor and needy praise your name. Rise up, O God, and defend your cause; remember how fools mock you all day long. Do not ignore the clamor of your adversaries, the uproar of your enemies, which rises continually (vv. 18–23).*

■ **Development** Everything in this psalm is building to a grand finale, a glorious resolution of the woes of these prophetless people.

The glory of the finale was mastered by Beethoven. He was able to build enormous tension before the final ending. He would often seesaw back and forth between tonic and dominant, throwing in a neopolitan sixth to build even more intensity. All of that energy set up an incredibly satisfying final chord. Today, in contemporary Christian music, David Clydesdale is a master of the big ending. Asaph's lament is moving toward such a climax here.

Pleading the cause of Israel, Asaph pours out his soul before God. He asks the Lord to remember His promise to His covenant people—"your dove"—who have suffered affliction. He argues a strong case in defense of the poor, the needy, and the oppressed. When God hears, defends, and delivers them from disgrace, then His people will be able to praise His Name.

The apostle James reminds us that "the prayer of a righteous man is powerful and effective" (James 5:16). Asaph is such a man, interceding for the helpless children of Israel. A note of triumph soars high above Asaph's lament, heralding God's grand finale of deliverance.

208

■ **Personal prayer** *O God, I take my stand with Asaph, a musician who interceded for his people. Deliver us from the clamor and uproar of sin in our lives as we anticipate Your glorious finale!*

July

PSALMS 75–89

If only my faith could soar on such wings!
"Lord, You haven't answered all my prayers yet,
but I believe You will." —Psalm 89

Victory Celebration   *Praise to God*

■ **Theme**   *We give thanks to you, O God, we give thanks, for your Name is near; men tell of your wonderful deeds. . . . As for me, I will declare this forever; I will sing praise to the God of Jacob. I will cut off the horns of all the wicked, but the horns of the righteous will be lifted up (vv. 1, 9–10).*

■ **Development**   Asaph's cup is overflowing. He is profuse in his praise and his thanksgiving, singing out the nearness of God's Name and his wonderful deeds as cause for celebration. In fact, in his ecstasy, he vows to praise the God of Jacob forever!

It is possible that God Himself is speaking in verse 10. He promises to cut off the defiance of the wicked and to lift up and exalt the righteous. Those of us who feel the sting of injustice and inequality understand the joy of God's intervention in our relationships.

I learn a couple of crucial things from these verses. First, I need to praise the Name of the Lord regularly. Second, I need to give thanks to Him for His sovereign acts in my life. Third, I need to rest in the fact that God will judge evil. Things are not careening out of control. My Lord, the Divine Arbiter, is the eternal evaluator of all things.

■ **Personal prayer**   *O Lord, I adore You and find exquisite comfort in the security of knowing You have everything under control.*

Victory Celebration
Judgment of God

■ **Theme**   You say, "I choose the appointed time; it is I who judge uprightly. When the earth and all its people quake, it is I who hold its pillars firm. To the arrogant I say, 'Boast no more,' and to the wicked, 'Do not lift up your horns; . . . do not speak with outstretched neck.' " No one from the east or the west or from the desert can exalt a man. But it is God who judges: He brings one down, he exalts another. In the hand of the LORD is a cup full of foaming wine mixed with spices; he pours it out, and all the wicked of the earth drink it down to its very dregs (vv. 2–8).

■ **Development**   When you're on a roll, and every song seems destined for the charts, it's easy to take the credit and forget the One who wrote the music.

The Lord despises arrogance. People in the music industry are especially vulnerable to pride. Caught up in their own self-importance, the proud are pictured in this passage as animals who strut about, lifting up their horns in "stiff-necked" rebellion.

God Himself will judge our performance. It is He who promotes and demotes, exalts and diminishes. It is only by His touch that any life produces the kind of music that is pleasing to His ear. Those who are consistently "out of tune" will find themselves confronting His wrath. It will be administered like a cup of strong, foaming wine which they will be forced to drink to the last dregs!

At the "appointed time," every person will stand before this righteous Judge. He shows no favoritism, nor is He impressed with credentials or sales records or hit tunes. He will judge "uprightly," with absolute integrity.

211

■ **Personal prayer**   O Lord, I will never stop speaking of You. I will never stop singing of You. And I'm grateful that You will judge my performance in this life with utter fairness.

Psalm of Sovereignty

■ **Theme**   In Judah God is known; his name is great in Israel. His tent is in Salem, his dwelling place in Zion. There he broke the flashing arrows, the shields and the arrows, the weapons of war. You are resplendent with light, more majestic than mountains rich with game (vv. 1–4).

■ **Development**   In these stirring lines, Asaph plays on two physical characteristics of the countryside to describe God—the "resplendent light" of the desert sun and the majestic mountains surrounding Jerusalem.

God's majesty and light have inspired hymnists through the ages. Think of the lexicon of praise hymns used in our worship: "Joyful, Joyful, We Adore Thee," "The Lord Is My Light and My Salvation," "Praise, My Soul, The King of Heaven," "How Great Thou Art," "Sing Praise to God Who Reigns Above," "Praise the Lord! Ye Heavens, Adore Him," "The Light of the World," "My Tribute," "Bless His Holy Name," and on and on. We can never exhaust the majesty and glory of His Name.

God displays His majestic power in His sovereign judgment of the wicked; "He broke the flashing arrows, the shields and the swords" (v. 3). "Valiant men . . . sleep their last sleep" (v. 5). "Both horse and chariot lie still" (v. 6). What a prophecy! One day all weapons of war will be obsolete (Isaiah 2:4).

I am moved by reverent awe for this God of ours to vow my allegiance to Him. He is capable of using His terrible might and majesty to chasten His children as well as to rout the Enemy. But there is another reason. He is also a God of infinite and unconditional love, dazzling radiance and light, and my only place of shelter is in the shadow of His mountain.

212

■ **Personal prayer**   How majestic is Thy name, O Lord! Light the dark corners of my life and give me a fresh vision of Your majesty!

A Song in the Night
Feeling Abandoned

■ **Theme**   *When I was in distress, I sought the Lord; at night I stretched out untiring hands and my soul refused to be comforted. I remembered you, O God, and I groaned; I mused, and my spirit grew faint. You kept my eyes from closing; I was too troubled to speak. I thought about the former days, the years of long ago; I remembered my songs in the night (vv. 2–6a).*

■ **Development**   Why is it that one's troubles seem so much worse at night? There have been times when I've been so disturbed I couldn't sleep. Tossing and turning, I've asked the same questions the psalmist asked so long ago: Does God still love me? Has He forgotten me? Can He hear my prayer? Is He mad at me? Has He turned His back on me forever?

Asaph feels utterly abandoned by God and cries out, but finds no comfort for his churning emotions. Recalling times in the past when God has acted in his behalf, he is puzzled now by God's silence. The Lord seems distant, remote, even angry. Asaph is experiencing deep, personal pain and begins a downward spiral on a decrescendo of depression (vv. 7–9).

Rejection breeds deep inner fear that can hold the spirit in a vise-like grip. In my midnight hours, irrational emotions sweep over me like waves in a turbulent sea.

My fellow musician did the right thing in venting his feelings. Asaph was learning some of the deep mysteries of life in God's school of suffering. He was learning to wait patiently for the Lord. He was learning that honesty precedes spirituality, and lament almost always precedes praise.

213

■ **Personal prayer**   *Lord, I'm hurting. Right now, in the soul-deep darkness of my night, I cry out for relief. Let me hear some note of hope.*

Then I Remembered

Troubled, I couldn't speak;
Worried, I couldn't sleep;
Rejected, unloved, my longings were unfulfilled.
I prayed to God for help,
"O Lord, don't You hear me?"
Distressed, I reached out my hands to Him,
His voice said, "Peace, be still!"

Then I remembered how He touched me
And He made me His heir,
How He's led me like a Shepherd
I'm a wonder of His care;
When I remembered all He had done for me,
I was lifted from despair—
He heard me, He touched me
And He answered my prayer.

Words and music by Don Wyrtzen.
© 1988 by Singspiration Music.

A Song in the Night
Remembering God's Miracles

■ **Theme**   Then I thought, "To this I will appeal: the years of the right hand of the Most High." I will remember the deeds of the LORD; yes, I will remember your miracles of long ago. I will meditate on all your works and consider all your mighty deeds. Your ways, O God, are holy. What god is so great as our God? You are the God who performs miracles; you display your power among the peoples (vv. 10–14).

■ **Development**   Asaph's deliverance from despair comes when he remembers that his God is a God of miracles, past and present. Asaph's joy erupts in this penetrating question: "What god is so great as our God?" (v. 13).

He recalls the astonishing events of the Exodus: Rain cascades in sheets; thunder rumbles; lightning rips the sky; the earth quakes; the waters writhe and convulse and are at last swept back into trembling walls, forming a conduit for the teeming masses of Israelites escaping Egyptian tyranny (vv. 16–20).

Meditation on these miracles prompts him to praise God for His incomparable holiness and majesty.

Asaph's conclusion is based on a critical evaluation of the past. The Lord has consistently met the needs of His people. The implication is that He will again rescue and deliver them. Hence, Asaph moves from a diatribe of despair to a doxology of hope.

—————————————————————————————— 215

■ **Personal prayer**   *O Lord, why do I ever worry and fret? Yesterday You died for me. Today You live for me. Tomorrow You come for me.*

Chords of Rebellion   *Disobedience*

■ **Theme**   *He decreed statutes for Jacob and established the law in Israel, which he commanded our forefathers to teach their children, so the next generation would know them, even the children yet to be born, and they in turn would tell their children. Then they would put their trust in God and would not forget his deeds but would keep his commands (vv. 5–7).*

■ **Development**   Teach the children . . . "so the next generation would know them . . . and they in turn would tell their children. . . ."

I'll never forget the first Scripture verses I learned as a child: John 3:16, John 1:12, Romans 3:23 and 6:23. Or the first songs: "Jesus Loves me," "For God So Loved the World," "Deep and Wide," "The Happy Day Express," and so many others.

Hundreds of generations after God gave that command to teach the children, my parents obeyed! Mom taught us most of the time, since Dad was a traveling evangelist. But when he was home, we kids got the whole nine yards—Bible reading, Scripture memory, singing, and prayers around the world!

Just as my parents warned me, Asaph now warns his audience about personal rebellion against God and disobedience of His Law. He tells of ancestors who forgot God and were slain in the wilderness because of His anger. He also tells of a nation graciously delivered when its people learned to obey.

As an example of disobedience, he relates the case history of the tribe of Ephraim. Intoxicated by self-confidence and human independence, they forgot God's miracles and spurned His law. Though armed to the teeth with bows and arrows, in battle they turned back.

What is the message for me from these verses? Once committed to the Lord, I must not turn back or I set myself up for personal disaster. If I rebel, He will crush me. If I allow a pattern of disobedience to develop, God will respond in anger—not because He has that right as my Creator, but because He cannot bear to see me destroy myself. I must go all the way with Him—the whole nine yards!

■ **Personal prayer**   *Dear Lord, so soon I forget Your wonderful works. Forgive my poor memory, my rebellion, and my disobedience. Don't let me stray from Your side.*

Chords of Rebellion   *Disloyalty*

■ **Theme**   *He did miracles in the sight of their fathers in the land of Egypt, in the region of Zoan. . . . But they continued to sin against him, rebelling in the desert against the Most High. They willfully put God to the test by demanding the food they craved. . . . But then they would flatter him with their mouths, lying to him with their tongues; their hearts were not loyal to him, they were not faithful to his covenant (vv. 12, 17–18, 36–37).*

■ **Development**   So often I'm like these willful wanderers of Israel. Instead of being grateful for God's gracious provision in the wilderness, they griped!

When they demanded food, "he rained down manna for the people to eat, he gave them the grain of heaven . . . he sent them all the food they could eat. . . . He rained meat down on them like dust. . . . They ate till they had more than enough, for he had given them what they craved" (vv. 24–25, 27, 29).

Despite all this, the children of Israel behaved like spoiled brats. They were negative, critical, and rebellious. When God chastised them, they returned to Him briefly before lapsing back into flattery and deceit. Yet He was merciful and chose not to destroy them, remembering "that they were but flesh, a passing breeze that does not return" (v. 39).

Yet who am I to condemn? I'm as ambivalent as they. The Lord calls me to consistency, but my walk with Him is cluttered with behavioral highs and lows. He asks that I be thankful for unexpected mercies and daily gifts of grace, but I demand more. Lord, forgive me!

217

■ **Personal prayer**   *Father, deliver me from the sins of ingratitude and greed. Above all, don't let me take Your goodness for granted!*

Chords of Rebellion   Desertion

■ **Theme**   *But they put God to the test and rebelled against the Most High; they did not keep his statutes. Like their fathers they were disloyal and faithless, as unreliable as a faulty bow. They angered him with their high places; they aroused his jealousy with their idols. When God heard them, he was very angry; he rejected Israel completely. . . . He chose David his servant and took him from the sheep pens; from tending the sheep he brought him to be the shepherd of his people Jacob, of Israel his inheritance. And David shepherded them with integrity of heart; with skillful hands he led them* (vv. 56–59, 70–72).

■ **Development**   Asaph continues to describe his rebellious people. They put God to the test, did not keep His statutes, and engaged in idolatry and spiritual adultery. Their heavenly Father reacted in anger and rejection. He abandoned the tabernacle of Shiloh and allowed the ark (covenant box) to be captured by the enemy. Young men were killed in war, leaving eager maidens with no one to marry; priests died violently, and widows were not able to mourn.

Then the Lord awoke "as from sleep" and saved them. He rejected the tribes of Joseph, Manasseh, and Ephraim in favor of Judah's Zion for the place of His sanctuary. He also reached down into the sheep pens and chose the country boy, David, to shepherd people instead of sheep. The young man was chosen because of two outstanding personality traits—skill and integrity. His hands were proficient and his heart was pure.

What a model King David is for me! I covet the delicate balance between a high level of professional skill and a deep sense of personal integrity. I admire his roots, his country values, and his poet's vision which he took with him all the way to the throne of Israel!

■ **Personal prayer**   *Dear Lord, bless my life with skill and integrity so that I can aspire to leadership with distinction.*

Lamentation Over Jerusalem   *The Holy City Defiled*

■ **Theme**   *O God, the nations have invaded your inheritance; they have defiled your holy temple, they have reduced Jerusalem to rubble. They have given the dead bodies of your servants as food to the birds of the air, the flesh of your saints to the beasts of the earth. They have poured out blood like water all around Jerusalem, and there is no one to bury the dead. We are objects of reproach to our neighbors, of scorn and derision to those around us (vv. 1–4).*

■ **Development**   Despite the animated promises of modern media evangelists, life sometimes delivers blows instead of blessings, even for the godly.

This psalm recaps the theme of Psalm 74—the devastation of the Holy City. The temple had been defiled. Saints had been slaughtered, the corpses left to be scavenged by the birds of the air. Blood was flowing like water around Jerusalem, and there was no one left to bury the dead. The heathen nations, filled with profane people, mocked and blasphemed the name of God.

Moved by the plight of his people, Asaph prayed with deep feeling that the Lord would not remember their sins, but would come to their aid once again. This was not a time of booming prosperity, but a time of national agony and personal suffering. The only hope was God's supernatural intervention.

This very day I can expect to encounter at least three obstacles that cause pain or distress—from mild discomfort and irritation to deep, personal anguish. And I will probably compound the trauma by adding guilt. It encourages me to learn that Asaph faced trouble, just as I do, yet was faithful to his commitment to the Lord.

219

■ **Personal prayer**   *O God, my life is a mess! I've come to the end of myself, and I don't know which way to turn. But I know that, wherever I might go, You are there!*

Lamentation Over
Jerusalem   *Prayer and Praise*

■ **Theme**   *How long, O LORD? Will you be angry forever? How long will your jealousy burn like fire? Pour out your wrath on the nations that do not acknowledge you, on the kingdoms that do not call on your name; for they have devoured Jacob and destroyed his homeland. . . . Before our eyes, make known among the nations that you avenge the outpoured blood of your servants. May the groans of the prisoners come before you; by the strength of your arm preserve those condemned to die. . . . Then we your people, the sheep of your pasture, will praise you forever; from generation to generation we will recount your praise (vv. 5–7, 10–11, 13).*

■ **Development**   Asaph is fed up! I sympathize with his frustration over the heathen nations who mock God. Christians in the marketplace constantly hear such complaints from skeptical colleagues and neighbors: "Where was God when the stock market crashed?" "How can a loving God let innocent people suffer?" Or even from Christians themselves: "Why did the Lord let this happen to me . . . after all I've done for Him?"

Still, Asaph doesn't lose faith here. He implores God to hear the "groans of the prisoners" and "avenge the outpoured blood of [his] servants" (vv. 10–11). This plea is not motivated by duty, but out of a sense of "desperate need." He longs to see the Lord glorified *through the affliction of the people.*

Joni Eareckson Tada is physically disabled because of a diving mishap when she was a kid. She is paralyzed from the neck down. Yet the Lord has graced Joni with profound insight and faith and has given her a far-reaching ministry that she didn't have before the accident. She's a very special person whose life has touched literally millions around the world!

This is the kind of answer Asaph and I long to hear from the Lord. Crippled by painful loss, emotional and psychological trauma, lack of love and acceptance, we cry out for ourselves and other sufferers: "Lord, I am weak, but You are strong!"

220

■ **Personal prayer**   *O Lord, help me to hear Your voice above the din of human confusion. Teach me that Your strength is made perfect in my weakness and let me praise You forever.*

Refrain of Restoration
Please Listen!

■ **Theme**   *Hear us, O Shepherd of Israel, you who lead Joseph like a flock; you who sit enthroned between the cherubim, shine forth before Ephraim, Benjamin and Manasseh. Awaken your might; come and save us. Restore us, O God; make your face shine upon us, that we may be saved* (vv. 1–3).

■ **Development**   A choir containing one person singing off-key is distracting and displeasing to the ear. But when the "out of tuneness" is between an individual and God, the very melody of life is destroyed!

For too long, the children of Israel have been off-key with the Lord. They have lost their reference point and have strayed into some atonal musical wilderness. Now the psalmist pleads for his people to be restored to God's favor. "Hear us! . . . Wake up! . . . Restore us, O God!" he cries out in spiritual agony. "Bring us back to our former condition with You!"

Hope is implied in the psalmist's plaintive refrain. While Asaph is addressing the eternal God who "sits enthroned between the cherubim," he perceives Him also as the tender "Shepherd of Israel."

Shepherds often soothed their restless flocks with music. David himself got his start singing his folk songs to sleepless sheep out in the desert on many a Mediterranean night.

Asaph and I long to hear harmony restored once more in the life of the flock and in our own hearts.

■ **Personal prayer**   *Shepherd of Israel, please listen! And let me hear the tender melody of Your love so I can tune my life to Your perfect pitch.*

Refrain of Restoration
Please Don't Be Angry!

■ **Theme** O LORD God Almighty, *how long will your anger smolder against the prayers of your people? You have fed them with the bread of tears; you have made them drink tears by the bowlful. You have made us a source of contention to our neighbors, and our enemies mock us. Restore us, O God Almighty; make your face shine upon us, that we may be saved* (vv. 4–7).

■ **Development** I like the emotional openness of these verses, since I tend to deny a lot of emotion. Like my ancient brothers and sisters, I need to become more transparent and vulnerable. Toughing it out with the aid of denial and pretense is dishonest and self-defeating. Beyond that, it's not biblical.

Here, in stunning hyperbole, Asaph portrays the response of Israel to the disciplining hand of God. "You have fed them with the bread of tears; you have made them drink *tears by the bowlful*" (v. 5)!

Though I seldom cry, I know that tears are often therapeutic. They give emotional release. They also cleanse and lubricate the ducts of the eye, and they can even dislodge foreign objects. Perhaps the faithless children of Israel are dislodging the foreign object of sin from their hearts as they weep tears of repentance. As a result of their penitent state, God will not be angry forever, but will restore them to full favor (v. 7).

When I recall that even "Jesus wept" (John 11:35), I am encouraged to allow the healing tears to flow!

■ **Personal prayer** *Shepherd of Israel, please don't be angry with me! Open me up emotionally and show me how my deepest needs can be met in You.*

Refrain of Restoration
Please Restore Prosperity!

■ **Theme**   *Your vine is cut down, it is burned with fire; at your rebuke your people perish. Let your hand rest on the man at your right hand, the son of man you have raised up for yourself. Then we will not turn away from you; revive us, and we will call on your name. Restore us, O LORD God Almighty; make your face shine upon us, that we may be saved (vv. 16–19).*

■ **Development**   In this psalm, the metaphor of a flourishing vine is used to picture Israel. At one time the vine was so abundant that it spread to the southern mountains, to the northern cedars of Lebanon, to the eastern Euphrates River, and to the western Mediterranean Sea. But now it has withered and died after being trampled by wild beasts and boars.

For the third time Asaph reiterates the refrain, "Restore us, O LORD God Almighty; make your face shine upon us, that we may be saved (v. 19). He promises faithfulness in exchange for restoration and salvation.

I need to remember that prosperity finds its genesis in the Lord. Secular success apart from God's hand on my life is a hollow victory. Without His blessing, life has no meaning. I want to be very much aware of how much my personal effectiveness depends on Him.

223

■ **Personal prayer**   *Shepherd of Israel, please prosper my soul and make my life a flourishing vine.*

Music for the Feast of
Tabernacles   *Let's Celebrate!*

■ **Theme**   *Sing for joy to God our strength; shout aloud to the God of Jacob! Begin the music, strike the tambourine, play the melodious harp and lyre. Sound the ram's horn at the New Moon, and when the moon is full, on the day of our Feast; this is a decree for Israel, an ordinance of the God of Jacob (vv. 1–4).*

■ **Development**   This psalm celebrates God's miraculous deliverance of His people from Egyptian bondage. In the wilderness He had met every need. On one occasion He had answered out of a thundercloud (Exodus 16:10). On another, He tested His people at Meribah (Numbers 20).

Now Asaph calls the people to a glorious festival which will memorialize these events. He commands them to sing joyfully and loudly. The choir is to be accompanied by an orchestra of tambourines, melodious harps, and lyres. The ram's horn will deliver its fanfare at the New Moon to usher in the Feast. God Himself has decreed this worship service as an ordinance and statute.

What do I learn from this joyous festival? I learn that part of my worship should memorialize God's supernatural acts in my life, such as the most recent time His truth set me free in my inner person. I learn that I need to get creatively involved in praising the Lord—reading Scripture aloud, praying the Word back to the Lord, or sharing the work of the Holy Spirit in my life with another person.

And one of the best ways to do this is through music.

224

■ **Personal prayer**   *God of Jacob, teach me to make music for Your glory today. Set me free to play skillfully, to sing worshipfully, and to dance joyfully.*

Music for the Feast of
Tabernacles *Hear, O My People*

■ **Theme**   *"Hear, O my people, and I will warn you—if you would but listen to me, O Israel! You shall have no foreign god among you; you shall not bow down to an alien god. I am the LORD your God, who brought you up out of Egypt. . . . But my people would not listen to me; Israel would not submit to me. So I gave them over to their stubborn hearts to follow their own devices. . . . If Israel would follow my ways, how quickly would I subdue their enemies and turn my hand against their foes!"* (vv. 8–14).

■ **Development**   Without the responsive ear of the listener, there is no music! There is a marked difference between passive hearing and active listening. Music depends on involved listeners: Choir members must hear their director's instructions; soloists must listen for their musical cues; symphony conductors must listen critically to create balance and ensemble in their orchestras. Audiences too must learn how to listen.

In this psalm God is saying, "Listen, my people, let me warn you." But the people are willful and independent. *They will not listen!* And God "gave them over to their stubborn hearts to follow their own devices" (v. 12).

What Israel missed by refusing to listen is parallel to my own loss if I miss God's cues for my life: freedom from enemies (v. 14), food for the table (v. 16). In fact, if I worship God in an exclusive relationship, I will be abundantly blessed with "the finest of wheat; with honey from the rock."

Unfortunately for the Israelites, God's hands were tied. Because of their stubborn rebellion, He could not bring the prosperity and peace they craved. How sad that so often I too go unrewarded because I don't listen.

■ **Personal prayer**   *God of Jacob, I'm much like those other people of Yours in my stubbornness and refusal to listen to Your instructions for abundant life. Speak loudly so your servant will hear and obey.*

Psalm of Justice
God Indicts Human Judges

■ **Theme**   *"How long will you defend the unjust and show partiality to the wicked? Defend the cause of the weak and fatherless; maintain the rights of the poor and oppressed. Rescue the weak and needy; deliver them from the hand of the wicked. They know nothing, they understand nothing. They walk about in darkness; all the foundations of the earth are shaken"* (vv. 2–5).

■ **Development**   God is speaking here. And when God speaks, we'd do well to listen! The question He asks probes my own twentieth-century conscience: "How long will you defend the unjust and show partiality to the wicked? . . . Rescue the weak and needy!"

Though God is addressing the legal magistrates He Himself has appointed over Israel, I need to assess my own attitudes and actions toward the oppressed, the weak, the fatherless, and the poor. As I encounter these needs in my daily life, do I turn a deaf ear, or do I respond with compassion and mercy?

It is the rare person who really shows compassion for needy, hurting people. In this society we're programmed to expect a person to shape up, take control, solve his or her own problems. We applaud self-reliance and scorn any show of dependence. But Bob MacKenzie, well-known music executive, brought a struggling young musician to Nashville at his own expense. That young man, Greg Nelson, is now one of the most outstanding producers in the industry!

God's structure of law and order is undermined when His people don't respond to the needs of others; His kingdom is advanced when they do!

I may not be an "elected official," but I am God's official representative within my own sphere of influence. And I'm accountable to Him to reflect not only His justice, but His mercy also.

■ **Personal prayer**   *O God, I thank You for allowing me the privilege of representing You in my world. Help me to emulate Your righteousness and kindness to all I meet.*

Psalm of Justice
God Is the Only Righteous Judge

■ **Theme**   God presides in the great assembly; he gives judgment among the "gods"; . . . Rise up, O God, judge the earth, for all the nations are your inheritance (vv. 1, 8).

■ **Development**   God is the Judge of human judges. He created justice, equity, and objectivity. Judges who practice law deceitfully, without awareness of God's solemn appointment, will perish. It is the Lord who presides in the great assembly.

Not only will God come down on the heads of human judges, but He will also judge all the earth. The nations of the world belong to God, who holds the inhabitants responsible for their ethics and conduct.

All of this confirms that I am not just a statistic in a cold, indifferent universe, nor merely part of the flow in an environment resulting from chance. I am a human being who fits into God's plans for all eternity. Therefore, I have rare value. Because I am precious to Him, my behavior has significance. I am responsible, so I must learn to live responsibly. Beyond that, I am unique because I am made in God's image. He has created me, saved me, and sealed me with His Spirit. What encouraging thoughts for today!

■ **Personal prayer**   O God, I thank You that You are impartial and just and that I can rest my case with You.

Asaph's Lament for Judah
O God, Do Not Keep Silent!

■ **Theme**   *O God, do not keep silent; be not quiet, O God, be not still. See how your enemies are astir, how your foes rear their heads. With cunning they conspire against your people; they plot against those you cherish. "Come," they say, "let us destroy them as a nation, that the name of Israel be remembered no more" (vv. 1–4).*

■ **Development**   Groaning is good! One of the keys to dispelling pain is to face it head on. Lament almost always precedes praise.

Asaph is in pain. Troubled by a coalition of disgruntled nations who are plotting to overthrow tiny Judah, he takes his complaints to God once again. Edomites, Ishmaelites, Moabites, Ammonites, Amalekites, and Philistines have allied themselves and, with the support of mighty Assyria, are threatening to roll over Judah like a tidal wave. Total annihilation is their objective.

The psalmist doesn't mince words. He wants God to get involved: "Do not keep silent! . . . Be not quiet! . . . Be not still!" In reverse order, he seems to be saying, "It's your move, Lord. Don't just speak to our enemies. Shout, if you have to!"

Still, Asaph has pled before, and his words alone seem impotent to produce the desired effect.

In facing personal pain, I've learned that, when words fail me, I can trust the Holy Spirit to help me. "[I] do not know what [I] ought to pray for, but the Spirit Himself intercedes for [me] with groans that words cannot express" (Romans 8:26).

228

■ **Personal prayer**   *Holy Spirit, speak for me. My own words are weak and powerless, but Your groans in my behalf will be heard and interpreted by the Father.*

Asaph's Lament for Judah
Do It to Them!

■ **Theme**   *Do to them as you did to Midian, as you did to Sisera and Jabin at the river Kishon, who perished at Endor and became like refuse on the ground. Make their nobles like Oreb and Zeeb, all their princes like Zebah and Zalmunna, who said, "Let us take possession of the pasturelands of God."* . . . *May they ever be ashamed and dismayed; may they perish in disgrace. Let them know that you, whose name is the* LORD—*that you alone are the Most High over all the earth* (vv. 9–12, 17–18).

■ **Development**   Asaph is a consummate lyricist. He uses vivid, picturesque imagery to express his feelings. What haunting Israeli melody accompanied this powerful lament? We can only imagine what it sounded like—plaintive, vigorous, intense.

The angrier Asaph grows, the more moving and dramatic his imagery. His lyric captures the intensity of his lament to the Lord: "Do to them as you did to Midian . . . to Sisera and Jabin at the river Kishon . . . to Oreb and Zeeb, Zebah and Zalmunna." Here, Asaph is referring to specific historical events: When the Lord delivered the Midianites into Gideon's hand (Judges 7); when Sisera met a grisly death through Deborah and Barak (Judges 4–5); and when Oreb and Zeeb (Midianite warriors) and Zebah and Zalmunna (Midianite kings) were crushed because they dared to oppose Him (Judges 8).

The next phrases simmer with excitement. Asaph asks God to make the enemy hosts like "tumbleweed . . . like chaff before the wind. As fire consumes the forest or a flame sets the mountains ablaze, so pursue them with your tempest and terrify them with your storm" (vv. 13–15).

The God I worship is the God of fire and storm as well as green pastures and still waters. He alone inspires the intricate composition of my life, and it involves tension along with release.

229

■ **Personal prayer**   *O God, with the power of Asaph's pen, I would compose rhapsodies to Your Name. I want the world to know that You alone are the Most High over all the earth!*

Pilgrim's Song   *Longing for God*

■ **Theme**   *How lovely is your dwelling place, O LORD Almighty! My soul yearns, even faints, for the courts of the LORD; my heart and my flesh cry out for the living God. Even the sparrow has found a home, and the swallow a nest for herself, where she may have her young—a place near your altar, O LORD Almighty, my King and my God. Blessed are those who dwell in your house; they are ever praising you. Blessed are those whose strength is in you, who have set their hearts on pilgrimage. As they pass through the Valley of Baca, they make it a place of springs; the autumn rains also cover it with pools. They go from strength to strength, till each appears before God in Zion (vv. 1–7).*

■ **Development**   How easy it is for contemporary society to accept the view that this life is all there is! We tend to put down as many roots as possible and pretend that this world is really our home.

The writer of this psalm has discovered his permanent roots. Driven by a deep inner compulsion to know God, he is drawn to the temple. He longs to make his home in the place "where God is." Just as the lark and the swallow—birds known for their sweet songs—have found nests for themselves, this unknown psalmist desires to "settle in," to nestle near the altar close to his God, where he can sing His praises continually.

Other believers, on pilgrimage to Jerusalem, must pass through the Valley of Baca, a once-arid region where the Lord has caused springs of water to flow. Refreshed and strengthened, these pilgrims move on to complete their journey.

I too must remember that I'm only a pilgrim. "This world is not my home." Instead of putting down roots in a particular city or community or vocation, I must keep in mind my eternal destination. My roots are in eternity, not in this life. But I need frequent renewal in God's refreshing springs and the fellowship and loving support of other pilgrims. I love the church because it is my place of stability, security, and sustenance as I continue the journey.

■ **Personal prayer**   *O Lord Almighty, help me to love Your place and Your people. May I draw strength from my fellow pilgrims, my brothers and sisters in Christ.*

Pilgrim's Song *Praying to God*

■ **Theme** *Hear my prayer, O LORD God Almighty; listen to me, O God of Jacob. Look upon our shield, O God; look with favor on your anointed one. Better is one day in your courts than a thousand elsewhere; I would rather be a doorkeeper in the house of my God than dwell in the tents of the wicked. For the LORD God is a sun and shield; the LORD bestows favor and honor; no good thing does he withhold from those whose walk is blameless. O LORD Almighty, blessed is the man who trusts in you (vv. 8–12).*

■ **Development** These verses are both a comfort and a challenge. I know I've been "set apart" to Christian service in the ministry of music, but sometimes low-grade motivation obscures my vision. The enchantment of conducting a professional orchestra for the first time, seeing my first published song, listening to my first record have faded, and I'm faced with the daily grind. I must work harder to keep the excitement and creative-energy level high.

The psalmist has no such fears or insecurities. His rock-solid devotion to God supersedes all other concerns. He knows He has been set apart ("anointed") by the Lord, and he is utterly committed to his calling (v. 9). In fact, if necessary, he is willing to serve in some menial position ("a doorkeeper") in the house of the Lord rather than to live in the lavish tents of the wicked (v. 10).

In verse 11 we learn the reason for such devotion. The Lord is pictured as a "sun and shield." He offers warmth, blessing, protection, and prosperity. He does not withhold anything good from those whose walk with Him is *blameless*—"a spotless walk, conduct ordered according to God's will, and a truth-loving mode of thought."

Now that the musical honeymoon is over, I need to be more committed, to persist and persevere in practicing my craft. I need to exercise discipline as I'm enjoying inspiration. I also need to follow the example of my ancient colleague—turn to my Source and spend more time in meaningful interaction with His people. Out of the rich texture of meaningful human relationships come songs that touch the heart.

■ **Personal prayer** *O Lord, today I rededicate my life to Your service. Be my Sun and Shield, and give me the satisfaction of knowing that my walk is worthy of my calling.*

Rhapsody on Renewal

Prayer for Revival

■ **Theme**   *You showed favor to your land, O Lord; you restored the fortunes of Jacob. You forgave the iniquity of your people and covered all their sins. You set aside all your wrath and turned from your fierce anger. Restore us again, O God our Savior, and put away your displeasure toward us. Will you be angry with us forever? Will you prolong your anger through all generations? Will you not revive us again, that your people may rejoice in you? Show us your unfailing love, O Lord, and grant us your salvation (vv. 1–7).*

■ **Development**   Life is often difficult and depressing for me. Work and family priorities go askew. I feel stressed out, disoriented, unbalanced. Why? Because I'm trying to make it on my own, taking God for granted, failing to follow His master score.

In art, as in life, balance and symmetry of form are crucial both in the creation and the reception of the work. Sir Georg Solti, maestro of the Chicago Symphony, is a master at juggling the intricacies of complex works and fashioning them into a glorious musical melange. Our lives need to be lived as art forms for God's glory.

This psalm, written by the Sons of Korah, begins by reciting ways in which the Lord has restored Israel—He has forgiven and covered their sins; He has set aside His wrath and turned from (changed His mind about) His anger toward them (v. 3).

The people need revival once again. They have failed to stay in tune with His will. They are out of sync with His plan. They need to right themselves, to shift their position until they are restored to harmony and balance in Him.

No one needs revival more than I. When the Lord dominates and controls my life, then and only then will I feel His incredible love and lasting joy . . . again!

■ **Personal prayer**   *O God my Savior, let me experience a renewal of my soul today so that Your love breaks out in every word and action of my life.*

Rhapsody on Renewal
Harvest Time

■ **Theme**   *I will listen to what God the* LORD *will say; he promises peace to his people, his saints—but let them not return to folly. Surely his salvation is near those who fear him, that his glory may dwell in our land. . . . The* LORD *will indeed give what is good, and our land will yield its harvest. Righteousness goes before him and prepares the way for his steps (vv. 8–9, 12–13).*

■ **Development**   When a dying church is rekindled, when a spirit is revived, when harmony is restored—there is a blend of elements that produces a symphony of grace. "Love and faithfulness meet together; righteousness and peace kiss each other" (v. 10).

Though I have a tendency to pretend that pain doesn't exist in my close relationships, when the Holy Spirit convicts me of some sinful attitude and I'm willing to repent, I know the ecstasy of freedom and release.

The psalmist is looking forward to this kind of answered prayer because he knows God always keeps His promises. For those who choose faith instead of folly, He will grant "harvest." Blessing is the effect of God's character colliding with culture (v. 12).

This kind of harmony is perfectly illustrated in the life of Christ. As God in human flesh, He dwelt among us "full of grace and truth" (John 1:14). Further, He was a walking revelation of God's glory and lives today in repentant hearts.

Presently, my spirit wrestles with many hindrances to lasting revival—among them, a powerful and sometimes shaky ego. I need to let go and let God take full control. I need to be a "miniature Christ," reflecting His glory. When I die to self, He will assume His rightful place as Conductor of my life, and I will hear the full symphony of His favor, promised to the faithful.

■ **Personal prayer**   *O God, my Savior, reflect Your glory in me today. May my ego decrease as Your attributes increase in my life today!*

David's Prayer   For Mercy

■ **Theme**   *Hear, O* LORD, *and answer me, for I am poor and needy.
Guard my life, for I am devoted to you. You are my God; save your servant
who trusts in you. Have mercy on me, O Lord, for I call to you all day
long. Bring joy to your servant, for to you, O Lord, I lift up my soul. You
are forgiving and good, O Lord, abounding in love to all who call to you.
Hear my prayer, O* LORD; *listen to my cry for mercy. In the day of my
trouble I will call to you, for you will answer me (vv. 1–7).*

■ **Development**   I really admire David. Here is a man who doesn't
mind admitting his weaknesses, and in doing so, demonstrates his
strength. Three times in these few verses, the verb *call* is used (vv. 3,
5, 7). David doesn't just pray; he calls to God, "crying out in a loud
voice."

When I'm under intense pressure, I tend to question God rather
than call out to Him. My life gradually becomes layered with anxiety.
Before long, fear has a firm grip on my soul, and my prayer is more a
pathetic whimper than a strong plea.

Not David! He speaks to the Lord with all the authority of his
convictions and in the expectation of an affirmative answer: "Hear,"
"Answer," "Guard," "Save," "Have mercy." Then he congratulates
the Lord for His kindness and forgiveness, His abounding love and His
tender mercy.

David's song is a perfect balance of petition and praise. This form
provides a model not only for my meditations, but for the full measure
of my days. How very simple! How profoundly rewarding!

234

■ **Personal prayer**   *Hear my prayer, O Lord, as You heard King
David's. Give me the same bold conviction, the same simple faith, the same
childlike trust. May I never petition until I've taken time to praise!*

David's Prayer

For an "Undivided" Heart

■ **Theme**   *Among the gods there is none like you, O Lord; no deeds can compare with yours. All the nations you have made will come and worship before you, O Lord; they will bring glory to your name. For you are great and do marvelous deeds; you alone are God. Teach me your way, O LORD, and I will walk in your truth; give me an undivided heart, that I may fear your name. I will praise you, O Lord my God, with all my heart; I will glorify your name forever. For great is your love toward me; you have delivered me from the depths of the grave (vv. 8–13).*

■ **Development**   Though David sometimes prays and writes in bold strokes, this passage has an almost ethereal quality. How magnificently he expresses God's sovereignty! How tenderly he caresses the Name of the Lord who loves him and preserves his life!

In these lines I hear traces of the impressionists—Debussy, Ravel, Delius. I hear muted strings and harp glissandi. I hear transparency, sheen, and range of mood from turbulence to serenity.

With all the verbal artistry at his command, David pours out his love song to the Lord. But for me, the climax of the piece comes in verse 11, when he prays, "Give me an undivided heart."

Suddenly I am startled out of my reverie, brought up short, reduced to tears. I, who never cry! "An undivided heart"! I know that line—that hauntingly familiar refrain. I understand so well how a heart can be ripped open and laid bare, fragmented, broken. Yet I rarely share this kind of intimate pain, but bury it beneath a facade of cool indifference.

So David knows that agony too! Yet there is no hint of self-pity. From the heights of ecstasy to the "depths of the grave," he keeps on singing!

■ **Personal prayer**   *Hear my prayer, O Lord. Make my life an artistic statement that magnifies and glorifies Your Name and celebrates Your incomparable greatness.*

David's Prayer For Strength

■ **Theme** *The arrogant are attacking me, O God; a band of ruthless men seeks my life—men without regard for you. But you, O LORD, are a compassionate and gracious God, slow to anger, abounding in love and faithfulness. Turn to me and have mercy on me; grant your strength to your servant and save the son of your maidservant. Give me a sign of your goodness, that my enemies may see it and be put to shame, for you, O LORD, have helped me and comforted me (vv. 14–17).*

■ **Development** I must admit I'm sometimes morose and unpredictable. David too is a man of many moods. Like most creative people, David shifts quickly from passion to pathos, from biting sarcasm to tender lyricism.

Harmony directly affects the emotions. Try watching a suspenseful program on television . . . with the sound turned down! Much of the edge, the drama, is lost. John Williams, composer of the scores for "Star Wars," "E.T." and "Superman," is a master of film scoring. Here is a lyric full of potential for a Christian composer.

● *Forte*—In loud and positive terms, David here profiles the "ruthless" enemies who oppose him and defy everything for which he stands. Not only do these "arrogant" men attack David, they have utter contempt for the Lord as well (v. 14).

● *Affetuoso*—The mood changes to one of warmth and affection as David catalogs the virtues of his Lord—compassion, grace, patience, love, faithfulness, mercy, strength, goodness. Such a God will not fail him in this time of imminent danger (vv. 15–16).

● *Spiritoso*—With rising vigor and a sense of urgency, David cries out for mercy and for "a sign . . . that my enemies may see it and be put to shame" (v. 17).

● *Rallentando*—As the tempo slows, there is implicit trust in David's final words; "You, O LORD, have helped me and comforted me" (v. 17). Whether David was anticipating God's early response to his request or whether he is reflecting on past favors, he's confident that God acts in his behalf.

236

■ **Personal prayer** ● *Largo*—My Lord and my God, I bow in acknowledgment of Your mercies. Come to my rescue today and deliver me as much from myself as from false friends and enemies.

Processional to Zion

■ **Theme**   *He has set his foundation on the holy mountain; the* LORD *loves the gates of Zion more than all the dwellings of Jacob. Glorious things are said of you, O city of God. . . . As they make music they will sing, "All my fountains are in you" (vv. 1–3, 7).*

■ **Development**   I love to hear people really sing—so that the walls vibrate and the air currents get moved around! I remember hearing some kids sing like I'd never heard before. About a hundred of them were jammed into a small, white brick chapel at Hampden DuBose Academy. Under the baton of Miss Dorothy Hill and accompanied by two grand pianos, they lifted the roof! There have been other memorable times and places . . . the Praise Gathering in Indianapolis, Indiana . . . Christian Artists' Retreat at Estes Park, Colorado . . .

But the music we'll hear in the celestial city will far surpass anything we'll ever hear on this earth. "The city of God" mentioned in these verses written by the Sons of Korah is both a geographical location—Jerusalem—and a symbolic one—heaven.

Zion, which encompasses Jerusalem and surrounding hills, was the earthly dwelling place of God—the chosen object of His love (Psalm 78:68). With its towers, gates, bulwarks, and palaces, it stood as proof of eternal reconciliation with God. The very enemies who pursued David most of his life—Rahab (Egypt), Babylon, Philistia, Phoenicia, Tyre—will be recorded by the Lord Himself in His register (v. 6).

In the New Jerusalem, that heavenly city, the population will be composed of peoples from all nations and ages. Music will be the language of praise!

As a Christian whose name is recorded in the Lamb's Book of Life, I look forward to that glorious reunion. I will become part of the music and dancing of eternity. I will sit down with the saints at God's banquet table. Today I march onward and upward to Zion!

■ **Personal prayer**   *O Lord, keep my eyes firmly fixed on my future home. Don't let the hindrances and strongholds of the Enemy rob me of rewards and joy in that great day when I will see You face to face.*

Song of Suffering
Heman's Complaint

■ **Theme**   O LORD, *the God who saves me, day and night I cry out before you. May my prayer come before you; turn your ear to my cry. For my soul is full of trouble and my life draws near the grave. I am counted among those who go down to the pit; I am like a man without strength. I am set apart with the dead, like the slain who lie in the grave, whom you remember no more. . . . You have taken from me my closest friends and have made me repulsive to them. I am confined and cannot escape; my eyes are dim with grief* (vv. 1–5, 8–9a).

■ **Development**   Physical suffering, the irrational emotions that accompany it, and the seeming injustice of "bad things happening to good people" is a bewildering reality. Sensitive scholars have grappled with these questions. (See *The Problem of Pain*, C. S. Lewis; *Why Me, Lord?*, Warren Wiersbe; *Where Is God When It Hurts?*, Philip Yancey.)

This psalmist isn't afraid to ask hard, penetrating questions. Heman the Ezrahite, a gifted and sensitive musician (1 Chronicles 25:1), has composed one of the saddest passages in all the Bible. Since youth, he has been afflicted with some kind of debilitating disease that has not only sapped his strength (v. 4), but has separated him from the comfort of his closest friends. He is actually "repulsive to them" (v. 8). In his lonely isolation, he feels like a forgotten man.

He handles his pain by praying day and night. "O LORD, the God who saves me . . . turn your ear to my cry!" (vv. 1–2).

I'm reminded of another Man who suffered not only physical torture, but also bore the weight of my sin. He too cried out in His pain: "My God, my God, why have you forsaken me?" (Mark 15:34). Jesus, though sinless and perfect, experienced unimaginable shame and agony . . . for me.

■ **Personal prayer**   *Father, when I'm called upon to suffer, may I cry out to You in patient prayer. Deliver me from bitterness and remind me always of the One who suffered so cruelly in my behalf!*

Song of Suffering
Heman's Conclusion

■ **Theme**   *I call to you, O LORD, every day; I spread out my hands to you. Do you show your wonders to the dead? Do those who are dead rise up and praise you? Is your love declared in the grave, your faithfulness in Destruction? . . . But I cry to you for help, O LORD; in the morning my prayer comes before you. Why, O LORD, do you reject me, and hide your face from me? From my youth I have been afflicted and close to death; I have suffered your terrors and am in despair* (vv. 9b–10, 13–15).

■ **Development**   Like many a modern-day counterpart, this ancient psalmist is full of mind-boggling questions about his condition: If I die, can I praise God from the grave? Why have I suffered so long? Is God deaf? Why have my friends and loved ones been taken from me?

This deeply emotional psalm is a mini-version of the Book of Job. As in that masterpiece, Heman's questions are left unanswered. Yet I'm convinced that Job—and perhaps Heman too—found comfort in the very process of prayer. Job concluded, "Though he slay me, yet will I hope in him" (Job 13:15)! Not being in control, they were driven to trust in God's sovereignty.

God alone knows the answers to the puzzling circumstances of life, though prayer itself, as an act of worship, does bring a measure of relief. *Personal introspection* is not the total answer. *Personal projection* in faith toward the Lord is the beginning of divine resolution.

239

■ **Personal prayer**   *O Lord, I thank You for the release I find in prayer and for the fact that I am not overwhelmed by my pain in any final sense. Help me to continually choose to exercise faith in You . . . even when I see no visible solutions.*

Covenant-Maker   God's Promises

■ **Theme**   *I will sing of the* LORD's *great love forever; with my mouth I will make your faithfulness known through all generations. . . . You said, "I have made a covenant with my chosen one, I have sworn to David my servant, 'I will establish your line forever and make your throne firm through all generations.'" . . . "If his sons forsake my law and do not follow my statutes, if they violate my decrees and fail to keep my commands, I will punish their sin with the rod, their iniquity with flogging; but I will not take my love from him"* (vv. 1, 3–4, 30–33a).

■ **Development**   In the music industry, contracts are vital for spelling out the agreement between the publisher and the artist. What responsibilities will each party be expected to fulfill?

One of the greatest contracts ever written is between two parties, God and His servant David. "I have made a covenant with my chosen one," God says. "I have sworn to David my servant, 'I will establish your line forever and make your throne firm through all generations.'" (vv. 3–4).

Still, a contract is only as valid as the integrity of the persons negotiating it. God is faithful and trustworthy (v. 1), while He acknowledges that the human weakness of David and his line will cause them to be capable of violating the terms of the agreement. "If his sons forsake my law and do not follow my statutes . . . I will punish their sin with the rod . . . but I will not take my love from him [David]" (v. 30–33). This covenant of love, faithfulness, and blessing is inviolable, eternal, and based on God's holiness.

Ethan, the wise man who wrote this psalm, grapples with one apparent contradiction in God's contract with King David. God has promised blessing to future generations, yet the king is in imminent danger of death from his enemies almost daily!

The psalmist reminds the Lord of His own nature and character. In essence he says, "Lord, I believe You are loving and faithful. You haven't delivered David from his enemies *yet*, but I believe You will!" (v. 1).

If only my faith could soar on such wings!

240

■ **Personal prayer**   O Lord, I cling to Your precious promises, fully confident that You who made the promises are able to keep them!

Covenant-Keeper   God's Faithfulness

■ **Theme**   *I will declare that your love stands firm forever, that you established your faithfulness in heaven itself. . . . The heavens praise your wonders, O LORD, your faithfulness, too, in the assembly of the holy ones. For who in the skies above can compare with the LORD? Who is like the LORD among the heavenly beings? . . . You are mighty, O LORD, and your faithfulness surrounds you. . . . "Nor will I ever betray my faithfulness. I will not violate my covenant or alter what my lips have uttered. Once for all, I have sworn by my holiness—and I will not lie to David—that his line will continue forever and his throne endure before me like the sun; it will be established forever like the moon, the faithful witness in the sky"* (vv. 2, 5–6, 8b, 33b–37).

■ **Development**   Contracts are no longer taken very seriously. Legal loopholes are found and exercised every day. Marriage vows are violated and families ripped apart. Promises between friends are broken.

Only One can be counted on to keep His Word. "His [David's] throne will endure before me like the sun; it will be established forever like the moon, the faithful witness in the sky" (vv. 36–37). Even the heavens bear witness to His faithfulness!

The Lord doesn't approve of broken promises and casual contracts. I long to uphold my part of His covenant of grace and follow Him faithfully.

241

■ **Personal prayer**   *O Lord God Almighty, may I honor all vows and keep all contracts, remembering that You consider such agreements sacred and binding.*

August

PSALMS 89–105

He opened the rock, and water gushed out;
like a river it flowed in the desert. —Psalm 105:41

Covenant-Breaker   God's Memory

■ **Theme**   *How long, O LORD? Will you hide yourself forever? How long will your wrath burn like fire? Remember how fleeting is my life. For what futility you have created all men! What man can live and not see death, or save himself from the power of the grave? O Lord, where is your former great love, which in your faithfulness you swore to David? Remember, Lord, how your servant has been mocked, how I bear in my heart the taunts of all the nations, the taunts with which your enemies have mocked, O LORD, with which you have mocked every step of your anointed one. Praise be to the LORD forever! Amen and Amen (vv. 46–52).*

■ **Development**   There are times when I'm tempted, like the writer of this psalm, to wonder if God has forgotten His promises. Surely the Lord will remember His covenant to King David, Ethan agonizes, though it seems doubtful at the moment. Despite God's promises, the king has suffered humiliating defeat—rejection, anger, renunciation, plunder, scorn, and shame.

Ethan, the Levite musician renowned for his remarkable wisdom, writes of divine wrath and holy anger. He is moved by the futility of life and the inevitability of the grave. He appeals to God's infinite love and great faithfulness. He asks God to honor His word, then ends his prayer with a moving doxology which concludes Book III (Psalms 73–89).

If I take only the immediate point of view, life often appears unfair and futile. But if I appeal to God's love and faithfulness, I begin to approach life from the divine perspective. The final step is to follow Ethan's lead in praising God for *everything that happens.* "Praise be to the Lord forever! Amen and Amen."

■ **Personal prayer**   *O Lord God Almighty, I know You keep Your promises, but time passes and I can't always see the answers to my prayers. Give me steadfastness and faith to believe in Your perfect faithfulness. The only covenant-breakers are Your people!*

Moses' Masterpiece
Contrasting Images: Transitory Man Versus Everlasting God

■ **Theme** *Lord, you have been our dwelling place throughout all generations. Before the mountains were born or you brought forth the earth and the world, from everlasting to everlasting you are God. You turn men back to dust. . . . For a thousand years in your sight are like a day that has just gone by, or like a watch in the night. . . . You have set our iniquities before you, our secret sins in the light of your presence. All our days pass away under your wrath; we finish our years with a moan. The length of our days is seventy years—or eighty, if we have the strength; yet their span is but trouble and sorrow, for they quickly pass, and we fly away. . . . Teach us to number our days aright, that we may gain a heart of wisdom (vv. 1–4, 8–10, 12).*

■ **Development** As a child, I loved blowing bubbles. They would float in the air like iridescent Christmas ornaments, only to disappear a second later. I had a similar experience with cotton candy. With great expectation, I would bite into the tantalizing pink bouquet, only to have it dissolve in my mouth almost immediately. I learned early how many things in life are merely fleeting illusions.

In this masterful blend of contrasting images, Moses teaches us that our earthly existence is like that sparkling bubble or that frothy confection. Human beings are "dust" that is soon swept away in "the sleep of death" or new grass that springs up in the morning, but withers away by nightfall (v. 5).

Though mankind is transitory, God is eternal. "Before the mountains were born . . . you are God" (v. 2). Man may be finite, but God is infinite, "from everlasting to everlasting" (v. 2). Nor does He measure time as we do, for "a thousand years . . . are like a day that has just gone by, or like a watch in the night" (v. 4).

Moses pleads with his fellow mortals to recognize the fleeting quality of life, "to number their days" (v. 12). I must reorder my priorities and plan strategically so that every moment of every day will be spent wisely and in preparation for the glorious life to come!

245

■ **Personal prayer** *Lord, I praise You for Your infiniteness and constancy. I thank You that, even though my days on this earth are brief, I will sing Your praises for eternity!*

Moses' Masterpiece
Contrasting Images: Affliction Versus Affirmation

■ **Theme**   *Relent, O LORD! How long will it be? Have compassion on your servants. Satisfy us in the morning with your unfailing love, that we may sing for joy and be glad all our days. Make us glad for as many days as you have afflicted us, for as many years as we have seen trouble. May your deeds be shown to your servants, your splendor to their children. May the favor of the Lord our God rest upon us; establish the work of our hands for us—yes, establish the work of our hands (vv. 13–17).*

■ **Development**   The human mind can only conceive of things in contrasts. For example, love would be unintelligible if there were no such thing as indifference. Francis Schaeffer, noted theologian, used to refer to this idea as "a" and "non-a," or the law of contradiction. The arts use contrasts in a similar fashion. The tension between unity and diversity produces high art.

In the same way, we can't fully appreciate the splendor of a sunrise without the darkness of night (v. 14), or vibrant good health without a little pain (v. 15), or the satisfaction of a job well done without some failures (v. 17).

Living out the changing textures of my life, I discover new depth in my growing relationship with my Lord. As He meets my deepest needs for love and acceptance, for healing, for relief from persecution, for meaningful work, I find inspiration for music-making. Out of a heart filled with gladness and gratitude, I will write, sing, and play songs of praise to Him.

When I am plagued by uncertainty about the future, insecurity about the present, and guilt about the past, I need to focus on the unchanging nature of God. My moods may shift like quicksilver, but God remains ever the same—omnipotent, infinite, and eternal. I rest on these granite peaks of His personality.

■ **Personal prayer**   *O Lord, I long to compose a masterpiece to You. Against the drab backdrop of my own sin, sickness, and despair, I am inspired to write of Your everlasting, unfailing love!*

Song of Shelter and Security
Promise of Protection

■ **Theme**   *He who dwells in the shelter of the Most High will rest in the shadow of the Almighty. I will say of the LORD, "He is my refuge and my fortress, my God, in whom I trust." . . . For he will command his angels concerning you to guard you in all your ways; they will lift you up in their hands, so that you will not strike your foot against a stone. You will tread upon the lion and the cobra; you will trample the great lion and the serpent. "Because he loves me," says the LORD, "I will rescue him; I will protect him, for he acknowledges my name. He will call upon me, and I will answer him; I will be with him in trouble, I will deliver him and honor him. With long life will I satisfy him and show him my salvation" (vv. 1–2, 11–16).*

■ **Development**   Because I live in a fallen world, I am constantly exposed to evil. Seen and unseen dangers lurk in every shadow.

This magnificent psalm is a testimony to the security found only in the "Most High," the Sovereign God of the universe. The Creator has posted a guard of angels around the psalmist to protect him "in all [his] ways" (v. 11).

Some angelic beings are created to praise God continually (i.e., seraphim). Whole choirs of angels sing "Holy, holy, holy." (See Isaiah 6:3; Revelation 4:8; 5:9–12.) Others are assigned to guard duty (Psalm 91:11). Still others serve God as agents of His mighty works (Job 38:7; Acts 7:53). Some are ministering spirits sent to defend God's people (Psalm 34:7). Another special ministry of angels is to assist the saints at the time of death. Angels carried Lazarus to Abraham's bosom (Luke 16:22).

Verses 14–16 are precious promises from God Himself. By His divine authority, God declares, "I will rescue . . . protect . . . answer . . . be with him in trouble . . . deliver and honor . . . satisfy with long life . . . and show him my salvation."

Everything I need for a full and prosperous life is promised "because [I] love [Him] . . . and acknowledge [His] name" (v. 14). I can heave a big sigh of relief. I'm safe in Him!

247

■ **Personal prayer**   *O Most High, the Almighty, help me to become fully aware that I have complete safety and security because You are my hiding place and I dwell in the shadow of Your wings.*

Song of Shelter and Security
Freedom from Fear

■ **Theme** *Surely he will save you from the fowler's snare and from the deadly pestilence. He will cover you with his feathers, and under his wings you will find refuge; his faithfulness will be your shield and rampart. You will not fear the terror of night, nor the arrow that flies by day, nor the pestilence that stalks in the darkness, nor the plague that destroys at midday. A thousand may fall at your side, ten thousand at your right hand, but it will not come near you. You will only observe with your eyes and see the punishment of the wicked. If you make the Most High your dwelling—even the LORD, who is my refuge—then no harm will befall you, no disaster will come near your tent* (vv. 3–10).

■ **Development** Can it be true? As a believer, will I really be spared suffering? Will the "deadly pestilence" (disease) and "plague" pass over my house and strike my unsaved neighbor? Can I avoid the "fowler's snare"—those insidious attempts to damage my reputation—just because I'm a Christian? How do I trust in the Lord when pain and death and treachery are real?

The key to my understanding lies in verses 4 and 5: "He will cover you with his feathers, and under his wings you will find refuge. . . . You will not fear. . . ."

Does this passage mean, then, that I will never suffer pain or loss? I don't think so, though I choose to believe the truth of this psalm. Through the power of the Holy Spirit, I believe that, if I take refuge in the Lord, I will not be afraid *in spite of my circumstances*. I become aware that the deep inner core of my personality—the real me—cannot be touched or harmed by evil unless I permit it. Pressure and pain give me an opportunity to flex my spiritual muscles. I can choose to trust the Lord to deliver me from fear, or I can be victimized by it.

In time, I experience the miracle of triumph through my tears, peace in the midst of the storm.

■ **Personal prayer** *O Most High, the Almighty, I praise You for protecting my real self—the part of me that will live forever—from all danger including death. I can live unafraid, knowing that You are with me always.*

Doxology of Praise   *Declaration*

■ **Theme**   It is good to praise the LORD and make music to your name, O Most High, to proclaim your love in the morning and your faithfulness at night, to the music of the ten-stringed lyre and the melody of the harp. For you make me glad by your deeds, O LORD; I sing for joy at the works of your hands. How great are your works, O LORD, how profound your thoughts! The senseless man does not know, fools do not understand, that though the wicked spring up like grass and all evildoers flourish, they will be forever destroyed (vv. 1–7).

■ **Development**   This psalm is music to a musician's ears! The psalmist declares that it is good to praise the Lord, from morning till night (v. 2). I am to make music to His name, an outpouring of praise to be accompanied by the ten-stringed lyre and the melody of the harp.

What motivates me to praise is the impact of the Lord's works— not only His acts in history but also His personal supernatural work in my life. I don't need to play semantic games or to psych myself into a fake piety or phony joy. The Lord really has done some profound and amazing things! His thoughts are infinite and astonishing. I want my life to be captivated by His greatness and grandeur. What cause for singing, playing, and dancing!

■ **Personal prayer**   Great are You, Lord! I want to make music to Your name all day long!

Doxology of praise   Exaltation

■ **Theme**   But you, O LORD, are exalted forever. For surely your enemies, O LORD, surely your enemies will perish; all evildoers will be scattered. You have exalted my horn like that of a wild ox; fine oils have been poured upon me. My eyes have seen the defeat of my adversaries; my ears have heard the rout of my wicked foes. The righteous will flourish like a palm tree, they will grow like a cedar of Lebanon; planted in the house of the LORD, they will flourish in the courts of our God. They will still bear fruit in old age, they will stay fresh and green, proclaiming, "The LORD is upright; he is my Rock, and there is no wickedness in him" (vv. 8–15).

■ **Development**   Can you imagine "winter without Christmas?" Yet that's exactly how C. S. Lewis described the state of the unsaved. The enemies of God have nothing to look forward to!

Boldly contrasting with this bleak metaphor is the eternal condition of the believer. The righteous will flourish like a stately palm tree or like a cedar of Lebanon, remaining "fresh and green" into old age and still bearing fruit.

So life is perceived in simple, basic terms. I can choose to live solo—apart from God, independent and autonomous. Or I can draw near Him and develop a finely tuned intimacy, vulnerability, and dependence. He lets me play my instrument in my own style. But as I follow Him, the Master Conductor, I become part of His score.

One person follows the path to self-destruction; another follows the way to mature, productive faith and exquisite harmony!

> Praise God, from whom all blessings flow;
> Praise Him, all creatures here below;
> Praise Him above, ye heavenly host;
> Praise Father, Son, and Holy Ghost. Amen.

Music by Louis Bourgeois. Words by Thomas Kerr.

■ **Personal prayer**   O Lord, Most High, You are exalted forever. I confess my utter dependence and vulnerability before You. Satisfy my thirst for You today.

Our God Reigns

■ **Theme**   *The LORD reigns, he is robed in majesty; the LORD is robed in majesty and is armed with strength. The world is firmly established; it cannot be moved. Your throne was established long ago; you are from all eternity. The seas have lifted up, O LORD, the seas have lifted up their voice; the seas have lifted up their pounding waves. Mightier than the thunder of the great waters, mightier than the breakers of the sea—the LORD on high is mighty. Your statutes stand firm; holiness adorns your house for endless days, O LORD (vv. 1–5).*

■ **Development**   I remember being overwhelmed the first time I heard Beethoven's "Hallelujah" from *The Mount of Olives* when I was still in high school. I'll never forget the power, the majesty, the dignity of that piece. I wondered if the music of heaven would sound like that!

Psalm 93 echoes that immortal music, celebrating the day when the Lord will reign forever and ever. This poetic form—the enthronement psalm or theocratic psalm—was used in temple worship to extol God's sovereignty. It soars majestically to the Lord, "robed in majesty" and "armed in strength" (v. 1), whose throne is high above the oceans.

The ancients—the Canaanites in particular—were terrified of the sea. Baal, their god, was authenticated by struggling with and overcoming Yam, the sea god in Canaanite mythology. But in verses 3–4 the sea is a metaphor of God's strength and might—"pounding waves," "thunder of the great waters," "mightier than the breakers of the sea."

I can live today in anticipation of His future reign on this earth when final justice will prevail. In the meantime, I need have no fear of the awe-inspiring forces of nature, but can exult in them as evidence of the power of Almighty God. Such incredible beauty and might are but a reflection of His character and strength.

■ **Personal prayer**   *Dear Lord, I worship You whose voice thunders above the crashing waves and rolling breakers. Please focus Your power on solving my small problems today as I wait in eager expectation of that day when all nature sings.*

Soliloquy on Security
My Inheritance—God's Award

■ **Theme**   O LORD, the God who avenges . . . shine forth. Rise up, O
Judge of the earth; pay back to the proud what they deserve. . . . Does he
who disciplines nations not punish? Does he who teaches man lack
knowledge? The LORD knows the thoughts of man; he knows that they are
futile. Blessed is the man you discipline, O LORD; the man you teach from
your law; you grant him relief from days of trouble, till a pit is dug for the
wicked. For the LORD will not reject his people; he will never forsake his
inheritance. Judgment will again be founded on righteousness, and all the
upright in heart will follow it (vv. 1–2, 10–15).

■ **Development**   It is with great ambivalence that I attend award
ceremonies. Admittedly, it's a thrill to be nominated and win. After
all, peer approval is something to be appreciated at any age! But if I
don't win or, worse, if I'm not even nominated, I feel a certain
rejection.

It seems so innocent—this compulsion we have to prove
ourselves, to earn recognition, to accumulate awards. Yet, at the root
of these ambitions is that subtle and seductive monster, pride, that
seeks to elevate self rather than God.

Selfish ambition has no place in the life of the believer, nor is it
necessary, for I am already guaranteed a precious legacy. As Christ's
co-heir, I will share in His glory (Romans 8:18). Instead of gold
medallions and lavish trophies conferred by my peers, I'd rather work
for the "prize for which God has called me heavenward in Christ Jesus"
(Philippians 3:14). On that day of judgment and reward, I want to
receive His "Well done!" Such a commendation will far surpass all the
tarnished gold the world has to offer.

■ **Personal prayer**   Dear Lord, forgive my preoccupation with triviali-
ties—the recognition of my peers and the acclaim of the world. Crush any
proud place in me and help me focus on receiving an award of merit from
You, bestowed after the grand finale of time.

Soliloquy on Security
My Consolation—God's Loyal Love

■ **Theme** *Who will rise up for me against the wicked? Who will take a stand for me against evildoers? Unless the LORD had given me help, I would soon have dwelt in the silence of death. When I said, "My foot is slipping," your love, O LORD, supported me. When anxiety was great within me, your consolation brought joy to my soul (vv. 16–19).*

■ **Development** I can relate to this psalmist whose foot is "slipping" and whose knees are buckling beneath him. He is weighted down with performance pressure and negative criticism. At such times even the godly can stumble.

I remember vividly the first time I had a memory lapse in a public performance. I was playing Mendelssohn's "Rondo Capriccioso" as a piano solo at Word of Life Island. Up to that time I'd never gone blank in my life! But here, before an audience of five hundred people, I forgot the notes. That sinking sensation came flooding back as I watched Debi Thomas stumble on the ice during the Olympic figure skating competition. It takes a lot to be able to get up and go on with your career after that kind of public embarrassment!

In this psalm the psalmist is outnumbered and overpowered. Human resources are inadequate. He has no back-up. . . .

In music, back-up is critical. Once, while conducting several hundred Baptist teenagers in John Peterson's and my musical, "I Love America," to the accompaniment of a tape track, someone accidently kicked out the plug! I was mortified, but we continued *a cappella.*

At last the psalmist remembers the Lord—His help (v. 17), His love (v. 18), His consolation (v. 19). Belief in one's own ability alone produces a false sense of security. Faith in God results in consolation, comfort, and inner strength.

■ **Personal prayer** *Dear Lord, I thank You for lifting me up when I stumble. When I'm filled with anxiety and "stage fright," I'm a prime candidate for Your comfort!*

Invention of Praise

First Part—Praising God's Sovereignty

■ **Theme**   *Come, let us sing for joy to the LORD; let us shout aloud to the Rock of our salvation. Let us come before him with thanksgiving and extol him with music and song. . . . Come, let us bow down in worship, let us kneel before the LORD our Maker; for he is our God and we are the people of his pasture, the flock under his care* (vv. 1–2, 6–7).

■ **Development**   The psalmist almost explodes with praise in this stirring enthronement psalm. He sings for joy to the Lord and worships the One who provides security and deliverance. He moves on to celebrate God's marvelous wide-ranging creativity, for He is the "great King above all gods" who made the mountain peaks, the sea, and the depths of the earth.

In the tradition of Abraham and other spiritual forefathers, I am compelled to fall face down before my Lord. Merely bowing or kneeling will just begin to express my heart's adoration in the presence of such majesty. Yet He is also my tender Shepherd and desires to have intimacy with the people of His pasture.

■ **Personal prayer**   *O Great King and Gentle Shepherd, I can scarcely believe that You who created the world desire fellowship with one of Your lowly sheep. Praise your Name forever!*

Invention of Praise
Second Part—Warning Against Unbelief

■ **Theme**   *Today, if you hear his voice, do not harden your hearts as you did at Meribah, as you did that day at Massah in the desert, where your fathers tested and tried me, though they had seen what I did. For forty years I was angry with that generation; I said, "They are a people whose hearts go astray, and they have not known my ways." So I declared an oath in my anger, "They shall never enter my rest"* (vv. 8–11).

■ **Development**   As the first movement in this symphony of praise ends, bringing the believer to his knees in worshipful adoration, there is an abrupt change of pace.

I can almost hear the rich, somber tones of the horns here. God is issuing a stern ultimatum: "Do not harden your hearts!" He is referring, of course, to the obstinate children of Israel who had murmured in the wilderness, sounding like the random notes of an orchestra tuning up. But His warning has my name on it. I often become critical and negative, and my whining sounds like a kid learning to play the violin!

The names of key geographical locations in Israel tell the story: "Meribah" (strife—like the fuzzy tones on an electric guitar); "Massah" (testing—like the critical shaping of the oboe's double reed). At those memorable sites, His rebellious children pushed the Lord to the limits of His patience. As a result, they never made it to the Promised Land. This whole episode feels romantic, German, and Wagnerian to me—so intense, so sad, so earthy.

Suddenly I hear a trumpet fanfare signaling God's desires for me: "Be warned! I will give you abundant opportunity to follow where I lead, but you must obey—instantly, without argument or complaint!"

This warning, in stark and striking measures, climaxes the symphony, and the lingering cadences resonate in my heart and mind: Unbelief and resistance cost the children of Israel their promised rest in the land flowing with milk and honey. Will I be faithful to the end? Will my performance disintegrate, or will I reach the finale?

255

■ **Personal prayer**   *O Great God King, soften my heart toward You and turn my murmurings into a melody of praise.*

Greater Is He
All the Earth Praises His Majesty . . .

■ **Theme**   *Sing to the LORD a new song; sing to the LORD, all the earth. Sing to the LORD, praise his name; proclaim his salvation day after day. Declare his glory among the nations, his marvelous deeds among all peoples. For great is the LORD and most worthy of praise; he is to be feared above all gods. For all the gods of the nations are idols, but the LORD made the heavens. Splendor and majesty are before him; strength and glory are in his sanctuary (vv. 1–6).*

■ **Development**   What makes a song publishable? First, the content must be fresh and biblical—presenting God's truth in a new way. Too many songs are imitative and derivative and seem to be cloned from secular sources.

A wonderful song should be eternal, dealing with a universal theme that has cosmic significance and presented in a form that is contemporary and natural.

Certain themes are especially pleasing to the Lord: salvation (v. 2), His glory (v. 3), His marvelous deeds (v. 3). Thematically, in both life and music, we must declare His attributes and His acts, reflect His majesty, and celebrate history—His story!

Pondering His majesty, splendor, strength, and glory should lead us to spiritual ecstasy. *Our Lord made the heavens and spun the galaxies into space!* Out of this should come art that is worthy of His praise. The alternative is the lifeless, toneless, sounds of the pagan world.

Powerful, life-changing music will never be initiated by monetary concerns or ego needs, for human genius without a focus on God is sterile. Until He does a deep work in our lives, we really don't have anything to write about!

■ **Personal prayer**   *I worship You, Sovereign Lord, with all the creativity at my command. Inspire me to write and sing Your praises and to live my song!*

Greater Is He

Nations and Nature Praise His Majesty . . .

■ **Theme**   *Say among the nations, "The LORD reigns." The world is firmly established, it cannot be moved; he will judge the peoples with equity. Let the heavens rejoice, let the earth be glad; let the sea resound, and all that is in it; let the fields be jubilant, and everything in them. Then all the trees of the forest will sing for joy; they will sing before the LORD, for he comes, he comes to judge the earth. He will judge the world in righteousness and the peoples in his truth (vv. 10–13).*

■ **Development**   When I was still in graduate school, I had a marvelous opportunity to participate in a revival in Mexico City. The evangelist was Luis Palau, the Billy Graham of Latin America; the song leader was Bruce Woodman, the Cliff Barrows of that continent; the organist was yours truly. I can still hear those thousands of Latin people singing God's praises in their own language. Because I don't speak fluent Spanish, I recognized only a few phrases, but the name of "Je-sus" provided a common denominator.

The apostle Paul tells of a day, perhaps very soon, when Christ will be exalted and every creature from every nation on earth will acknowledge Him. Today's reading from the Psalms is the Old Testament counterpart of a magnificent passage in Philippians: "Therefore God exalted him to the highest place and gave him the name that is above every name, that at the name of Jesus every knee should bow, in heaven and on earth and under the earth, and every tongue confess that Jesus Christ is Lord, to the glory of God the Father" (2:9–11).

On that day, the curse on nature will be lifted, and God will pour out His blessing. The heavens and earth will be glad, and all of creation will tremble with joy and music. The sea will "resound, and all that is in it" (v. 11); the fields will be jubilant (v. 12), and "all the trees of the forest will sing for joy" (v. 12).

If even inanimate objects are moved to praise, how much more should my tongue be loosed to join in the universal chorus!

■ **Personal prayer**   *Dear Lord, I sing Your precious Name, for "Jesus is the sweetest Name I know!" I rejoice with people of all nations and with all of nature in the majesty and glory of that Name.*

Epiphany of Glory
Vision of the Lord's Glorious Coming

■ **Theme**   *The LORD reigns, let the earth be glad; let the distant shores rejoice. Clouds and thick darkness surround him; righteousness and justice are the foundation of his throne. Fire goes before him and consumes his foes on every side. His lightning lights up the world; the earth sees and trembles. The mountains melt like wax before the LORD, before the Lord of all the earth. The heavens proclaim his righteousness, and all the peoples see his glory (vv. 1–6).*

■ **Development**   Reading the prophetic words of this psalm excites my imagination. My Lord is coming again to rule and to reign! In light of that dynamic truth, all the petty frustrations of this life seem ridiculously unimportant.

The sublime poetry of these verses describes in figurative language the Lord's glory. In their broadest interpretation, they also depict His coming reign and remind me of prophecies in both Old and New Testaments. When He comes, He will be surrounded by clouds. (See Revelation 1:7.) "Fire goes before him and consumes his foes." (See Isaiah 66:15–16.) Not only do men fear Him, but nature trembles as well. "His lightning lights up the world." (See Luke 17:24.) "The mountains melt like wax." (See Micah 1:4.) "The heavens proclaim his righteousness, and all the peoples see his glory" (v. 6).

If I knew Jesus were coming one week from today, how would I change my life and ministry? I'd go on a crash course to know my Lord a lot better. I'd put house-hunting on hold and wait for that mansion in glory! I'd double-check with certain relatives about their relationship with the Lord, and if necessary I'd share the gospel more honestly and passionately with them. I'd spend more time in the Word, allow the Holy Spirit to control me more completely, and draw closer to my brothers and sisters in Christ. If I had any extra time, I'd concentrate on making some music to the praise and glory of God!

258

■ **Personal prayer**   *O Lord, I feel like a child at Christmas when I anticipate Your coming again! Order my priorities to conform to Your plan for my role in Your kingdom. Give me a fresh vision!*

Epiphany of Glory
A Call to Righteous Living and Faithfulness

■ **Theme**   *All who worship images are put to shame, those who boast in idols—worship him, all you gods! Zion hears and rejoices and the villages of Judah are glad because of your judgments, O LORD. For you, O LORD, are the Most High over all the earth; you are exalted far above all gods. Let those who love the LORD hate evil, for he guards the lives of his faithful ones and delivers them from the hand of the wicked. Light is shed upon the righteous and joy on the upright in heart. Rejoice in the LORD, you who are righteous, and praise his holy name (vv. 7–12).*

■ **Development**   How do we define idolatry in contemporary terms? The "images" mentioned in biblical times refer to physical objects made with hands. But idolatry also means "clinging attachment or devotion." In Christian terms idolatry refers to anything or anyone that comes "between God and me." It takes many subtle forms—making heroes out of celebrities, getting carried away with my own gifts, being unduly impressed with personal status symbols, education, or expertise.

The emptiness and foolishness of idolatry is exposed when the radiant glory of God penetrates the fog. This super ego that blinds us to our own sin, these works of our own hands are then laid bare, and we recognize the "Most High over all the earth" (v. 9).

With the Lord of Glory as my reference point and His righteous reign as my context, I need to learn how to discern idolatry— especially in myself—and hate it as much as He does. I need to trust in His deliverance from wickedness, then rest secure because "he guards the lives of his faithful ones."

On this—my birthday—I want to celebrate by creating a new work of praise to His glory. He is the Author of life, the Composer of the music of my days, my Songmaker!

259

■ **Personal prayer**   *Dear Lord, trample any idols I may have foolishly erected. As You crush them, may the sweet perfume of my love and gratitude rise before You and may the melody of my heart be a sacrifice of praise.*

Sing to the Lord a New Song
The Lord Has Made His Salvation Known

■ **Theme**   *Sing to the LORD a new song, for he has done marvelous things; his right hand and his holy arm have worked salvation for him. The LORD has made his salvation known and revealed his righteousness to the nations. He has remembered his love and his faithfulness to the house of Israel; all the ends of the earth have seen the salvation of our God (vv. 1–3).*

■ **Development**   When I read of God's covenant with Israel, His loyal love and faithfulness to His chosen people, I don't feel excluded, but greatly blessed. Spiritually I too am Jewish—part of the spiritual seed of Abraham (Galatians 3:28–29)!

As that concept impacts my life, I am moved to make music to this God who has included me in His marvelous plan. Saved and sealed by His Spirit, I sing and proclaim His salvation to "all the ends of the earth." As nonbelievers overhear my songs of praise, they will be drawn to His irresistible love.

This psalm motivated Isaac Watts to write the familiar carol "Joy to the World" that is sung each Christmas to Lowell Mason's heroic melody:

> Joy to the world! the Lord is come!
> Let earth receive her King;
> Let every heart prepare Him room,
> And heaven and nature sing.
>
> He rules the world with truth and grace,
> And makes the nations prove
> The glories of His righteousness
> And wonders of His love.

260

■ **Personal prayer**   *O Lord, I long to compose carols of joy, celebrating the marvelous things You have done in my life.*

Sing to the Lord a New Song
He Will Judge the World in Righteousness

■ **Theme**   Shout for joy to the LORD, all the earth, burst into jubilant song with music; make music to the LORD with the harp, with the harp and the sound of singing, with trumpets and the blast of the ram's horn—shout for joy before the LORD, the King. Let the sea resound, and everything in it, the world, and all who live in it. Let the rivers clap their hands, let the mountains sing together for joy; let them sing before the LORD, for he comes to judge the earth. He will judge the world in righteousness and the peoples with equity (vv. 4–9).

■ **Development**   There is nothing subdued or restrained about the message of this psalm! It's a toe-tapper! How can we be still when we are exhorted to "burst into jubilant song" (v. 4), "shout for joy before the Lord" (v. 5), and "make music . . . with trumpets and the blast of the ram's horn" (v. 6)!

My former neighbor, Dr. Bill Reus, has hunted long-horn rams on all the major continents of the world. When I first saw these fierce-looking horns mounted over his fireplace, I was reminded of the ancient orchestra. At the inauguration of Solomon's temple, 120 priests blew rams' horns, accompanied by other Levites singing and playing cymbals, harps, and lyres (2 Chronicles 5). No wonder the Lord says, "Make a joyful noise!"

All of nature joins in a cacophony of sound and motion. "Let the sea resound. . . . Let the rivers clap their hands. . . . Let the mountains sing together for joy" (vv. 7–8).

What inspires this explosion of joy? What induces this liberated worship in song? The Lord is coming! And when I think of all that will mean, I am inspired to mix all the rich colors available to me in this palette of praise and pour out my own "new song."

261

■ **Personal prayer**   Dear Lord, unleash my spirit today and set me free to create music worthy of Your praise. Let my imagination soar as I lift up Your Name!

Sing to the Lord a New Song

Sing to the Lord a new song,
Sing to the Lord all day long;
Break out in praise and sing the refrain;
Our Lord will come to rule and reign.

He saved us with His holy hand,
Announced His truth to every land;
In love and truth He watched His own,
To all the earth His grace was shown.

With shouts of joy before your King,
With happy voices, anthems sing;
Join all in rapturous symphony,
And worship Him in harmony.

Vast seas and oceans roar with acclaim,
People of earth, His worth proclaim;
Let rivers clap their hands in glee,
And hills sing songs spontaneously.

Words and music by Don Wyrtzen.
© 1974 by Singspiration Music.

Holy, Holy, Holy   *The Lord is Holy*

■ **Theme**   *The LORD reigns, let the nations tremble; he sits enthroned between the cherubim, let the earth shake. Great is the LORD in Zion; he is exalted over all the nations. Let them praise your great and awesome name—he is holy. The King is mighty, he loves justice—you have established equity; in Jacob you have done what is just and right. Exalt the LORD our God and worship at his footstool; he is holy (vv. 1–5).*

■ **Development**   Dr. Karl Menninger, internationally celebrated psychiatrist, has asked the question: "Whatever became of sin?"

The ugly reality of sin fades away when we lose our vision of the dazzling holiness of God (Isaiah 6). In our modern perception, the shed blood seems cannibalistic and barbaric, the price of forgiveness is cheapened, and the Good News is relegated to the "religion" section of the local newspaper.

This psalm inspires us to recover the truth of God's character. He alone is holy—"perfectly pure and worthy of profound reverence." This is the pillar—the *sine qua non*—upon which everything in Christianity rests!

> *Holy, holy, holy! Lord God Almighty*
> *Early in the morning our song shall rise to Thee;*
> *Holy, holy, holy! Merciful and mighty!*
> *God in three persons, blessed Trinity!*
>
> *Holy, holy, holy! All the saints adore Thee,*
> *Casting down their golden crowns around the glassy sea;*
> *Cherubim and seraphim falling down before Thee,*
> *Who wert and art and evermore shalt be.*

Words by Reginald Heber. Music by John B. Dykes

■ **Personal prayer**   *Dear Lord, I praise Your great and glorious Name because You alone are holy.*

Holy, Holy, Holy
The Lord Answers Prayer

■ **Theme**   *Moses and Aaron were among his priests, Samuel was among those who called on his name; they called on the LORD and he answered them. He spoke to them from the pillar of cloud; they kept his statutes and the decrees he gave them. O LORD our God, you answered them; you were to Israel a forgiving God, though you punished their misdeeds. Exalt the LORD our God and worship at his holy mountain, for the LORD our God is holy (vv. 6–9).*

■ **Development**   The Lord has dramatically steered my passage through life. In high school I wanted to attend a particular college, but God chose Moody Bible Institute. (If I hadn't listened to His voice, I probably wouldn't have met Karen!) After Moody, I planned to study at Juilliard, but God wanted me at King's. (If I hadn't obeyed, I probably wouldn't be involved in the world of Christian music.) After college I had my sights set on graduate school at Columbia University, but God led me to Dallas Theological Seminary. (If I had followed my own inclination, I probably wouldn't have written this book!) These career turning points all came out of wrestling matches with the Lord. It is only as I look back that I can see the providential hand of God on our lives.

Our Lord has a history of answering the prayers of His saints. In ancient times, Moses (Exodus 3, 4), Aaron (Exodus 4:27–31; 7:6), Hannah (1 Samuel 2), Samuel (1 Samuel 3), and Nehemiah (Nehemiah 1) called on the name of the Lord, and He answered. They were rewarded for their obedience. Though God punished Israel for misdeeds, He also forgave them and regularly answered their prayers.

Why don't more people pray more often, believing that God really hears and answers? Maybe it's because they have bought into the system that claims we are self-sufficient beings, perfectly capable of taking care of ourselves and, at the extreme, that we're even evolving into gods! Yet it only takes one turning point like mine, one gigantic crisis, one moment of unresolved conflict to realize how frail and vulnerable we are. We need Him every hour!

■ **Personal prayer**   *Dear Lord, I know You hear and answer today just as You did in the days of Moses, Aaron, and Samuel. May I always call on You rather than relying on my puny human resources.*

The Old One-Hundredth

■ **Theme**   *Shout for joy to the* LORD, *all the earth. Worship the* LORD *with gladness; come before him with joyful songs. Know that the* LORD *is God. It is he who made us, and we are his; we are his people, the sheep of his pasture. Enter his gates with thanksgiving and his courts with praise; give thanks to him and praise his name. For the* LORD *is good and his love endures forever; his faithfulness continues through all generations (vv. 1–5).*

■ **Development**   A brilliant example of an ancient musician at his best is contained in this enduring psalm. Perhaps only the Twenty-third is more widely known and loved in all of Christendom.

The things that are most familiar to us, however, often lose their deepest meaning. To rediscover the rich mother lode of treasure in these verses, I've asked myself why this passage has remained one of the best-loved in all the Bible.

There are at least five reasons: First, the Lord is God—Creator, Sustainer, Redeemer (v. 3). Second, He made me and I belong to Him. My identity is in Him. I'm not a faceless nonentity, floating through the impersonal cosmos, but *a child of God*, "the sheep of his pasture" (v. 3). Third, the Lord is good. He wishes me good, not evil (v. 5). Fourth, He loves me with an endless love because I am infinitely precious to Him (v. 5). Finally, His covenant of love extends to my children—D.J. and Kathy—and to any grandchildren they may give me someday! (v. 5).

Such good news fills me with joy and a desire to "enter His gates with thanksgiving and His courts with praise."

■ **Personal prayer**   *Dear Lord, help me to shout for joy today, to worship You with gladness, and to come before You with joyful songs.*

Sing Joyfully Before the Lord!

Sing joyfully before the Lord,
Obey Him gladly on the earth;
Rejoicing, take Him at His Word,
Before Him sing with joy and mirth!

Go through His open gates with joy,
Go to His courts with deepest praise;
Let grateful songs your tongue employ,
And bless His name for endless days!

Because the Lord is always good,
His faithfulness forever sure,
His truth for endless ages firmly stood,
And will for ages still endure.

Words and music by Don Wyrtzen.
© 1971 by Singspiration Music.

Psalm of Integrity

■ **Theme** *I will sing of your love and justice; to you, O LORD, I will sing praise. I will be careful to lead a blameless life—when will you come to me? I will walk in my house with blameless heart. I will set before my eyes no vile thing. . . . No one who practices deceit will dwell in my house; no one who speaks falsely will stand in my presence. Every morning I will put to silence all the wicked in the land; I will cut off every evildoer from the city of the LORD (vv. 1–3, 7–8).*

■ **Development**   I've given a lot of thought lately to the question of personal and professional ethics. Rumors of corruption in government have always been rife; business empires crumble in the face of fraud and embezzlement at the level of top management; politicians and preachers alike succumb to greed and lust. How can I guard my own integrity in these perverse times?

David's psalm gives me some cues to managing my personal and professional life. Unique among the rules of the ancient Near East, David was a man whose lifestyle and reign were marked by integrity. He was scarred, fallen, and flawed like the rest of us, yet he submitted to God's authority over his life. Here is the character by which he ruled.

First, he pledged himself to be "careful to lead a blameless life," realizing that the attitude of one's heart dictates his actions (vv. 2–3). Second, he warned the people that he would tolerate no shady deals, no under-the-counter maneuvers, no ethical hanky-panky (vv. 4–6). More than that, he threatened to deal sternly with those who violated sound principles of moral conduct (vv. 7–8), and then God allowed David to experience the consequences of his own actions!

David chose justice over popularity, integrity over peace at any price. He boldly confronted evil in his empire and set the standard by his strong commitment to personal purity.

Nor can I abdicate my responsibility as God's man in my own world. He calls me to authenticity—not just image—both in the office and at home.

■ **Personal prayer**   *O Lord, keep me pure and blameless as I move from the realm of my business dealings to my God-ordained position as head of my home.*

Ballad of Burnout   *Burned Out*

■ **Theme**   *Hear my prayer, O LORD; let my cry for help come to you. Do not hide your face from me when I am in distress. Turn your ear to me; when I call, answer me quickly. For my days vanish like smoke; my bones burn like glowing embers. My heart is blighted and withered like grass; I forget to eat my food. . . . All day long my enemies taunt me; those who rail against me use my name as a curse. . . . My days are like the evening shadow; I wither away like grass (vv. 1–4, 8, 11).*

■ **Development**   I know what it's like to run dry, both spiritually and creatively. The symptoms the psalmist describes in these verses are all too familiar. One day blends, facelessly, into another, with nothing to show for it. Unbridled emotions produce almost physical pain before plunging me into a state of feeling almost nothing at all. I have no heart for my work, no inspiration. To top it all off, I suffer from periodic insomnia and, occasionally, even loss of appetite!

Psychologists diagnose this problem as "burnout." Authors call it the "blank page syndrome." Musicians sometimes refer to it as a creative dry spell. I call it low-grade motivation or no motivation at all. The psalmist feels that life itself is over.

But there's a flip side to this record of griefs. This afflicted believer is doing the only thing he knows to do, thereby setting the pace for every depressed believer who has ever lived. He calls on the Lord! He cries out to him and groans in His presence.

Inspiration for victorious living and for creative music-making have a common source—intimacy with the Lord. One way to nurture intimacy with Him and beat the cycle of despair is to begin with an uninhibited outpouring of raw and honest emotion. To deny these overwhelming feelings is to concede defeat. Pretending is fantasy; honesty produces reality. The psalmist's way, though painful, is the only sure route to healing, wholeness, and renewed creativity.

■ **Personal prayer**   *Hear my prayer, O Lord. I'm burned out, dried up, and spiritually depleted. I turn to You—Savior, fellow Sufferer, Songmaker.*

Ballad of Burnout   Worn Out

■ **Theme**   *The nations will fear the name of the* LORD, *all the kings of the earth will revere your glory. For the* LORD *will rebuild Zion and appear in his glory. He will respond to the prayer of the destitute; he will not despise their plea.* . . . *"In the beginning you laid the foundations of the earth, and the heavens are the work of your hands. They will perish, but you remain; they will all wear out like a garment. Like clothing you will change them and they will be discarded. But you remain the same, and your years will never end. The children of your servants will live in your presence; their descendants will be established before you"* (vv. 15–17, 25–28).

■ **Development**   My wife Karen is an astonishingly beautiful lady whose clothes make an artistic statement. A person with a strong sense of style and color, her tastes run from sporty and classic to elegant and sophisticated. With her fair Nordic coloring, I love to see her in pink. In any gathering she stands out, and I'm always proud of her. Whatever the occasion, she's always appropriately dressed.

But clothing, no matter how fine the fabric or how well-constructed, eventually wears out or becomes outdated. In this passage, the psalmist calls our attention to the fact that even the heavens, that vast canopy covering the earth, will "wear out like a garment" (v. 26). The Lord will change them (heaven and earth) "like clothing" and "they will be discarded" (v. 26).

Karen is no clotheshorse. While she enjoys dressing in good taste and with a kind of flair, she's a person of great spiritual sensitivity and depth. She knows as well as this psalmist that the only covering that will endure is Jesus Christ, who clothes us in His righteousness.

We can have confidence that the Lord knows the deepest needs and desires of our heart and will respond accordingly. Styles may change—in fashion and in other art forms, including music! Only our great God remains the same, from generation to generation, world without end!

■ **Personal prayer**   *Lord, Karen and I bring our pitiful wardrobe to You. In Your sight our garments are as filthy rags. We rejoice that we will be dressed in Your righteousness throughout all eternity!*

Bless the Lord, O My Soul!
Praising the Lord for His Benefits

■ **Theme**   Praise the LORD, O my soul; all my inmost being, praise his holy name. Praise the LORD, O my soul, and forget not all his benefits—who forgives all your sins and heals all your diseases, who redeems your life from the pit and crowns you with love and compassion, who satisfies your desires with good things so that your youth is renewed like the eagle's (vv. 1–5).

■ **Development**   This exalted work is the definitive answer to the problems so honestly enumerated in Psalm 102.

David's artistic soul erupts in uninhibited praise. From the core of his being, from the focal point of his soul, he praises the holy name of the Lord. And he has good reason to celebrate!

The Lord has given David a cornucopia overflowing with gifts of His grace. He has forgiven David's sins (v. 3). He has healed his sickness (v. 3). He has delivered David from the grave (v. 4). He has enriched David's life with gifts of loyal love and tender compassion (v. 4). He has satisfied David's deepest desires with good things (v. 5).

Instead of being grounded by despair, David can now soar like an eagle. Instead of a weak, anemic faith, he is blessed with vigorous spiritual health that vibrates in his songs of praise.

■ **Personal prayer**   I praise You and thank You, O Lord, for all of Your blessings to me: Your forgiveness, Your healing, Your deliverance, Your love, Your compassion, and for fully satisfying my inner being with Yourself.

Bless the Lord, O My Soul!

Praising the Lord for His Compassion

■ **Theme**　The LORD . . . *made known his ways to Moses, his deeds to the people of Israel: The LORD is compassionate and gracious, slow to anger, abounding in love. He will not always accuse, nor will he harbor his anger forever; he does not treat us as our sins deserve or repay us according to our iniquities. For as high as the heavens are above the earth, so great is his love for those who fear him; as far as the east is from the west, so far has he removed our transgressions from us. As a father has compassion on his children, so the LORD has compassion on those who fear him; for he knows how we are formed, he remembers that we are dust. . . . But from everlasting to everlasting the LORD's love is with those who fear him, and his righteousness with their children's children—with those who keep his covenant and remember to obey his precepts (vv. 6–14, 17–18).*

■ **Development**　Whenever I read this psalm cataloging the virtues of God, I feel like Moses must have felt when standing in His presence on Mount Sinai (Exodus 34:6–7). Moses was allowed to view the back of God, and in that intimate exposure, the great man of God found out what our Lord is like!

He is compassionate and not only feels our pain and sorrow, but stands ready to alleviate it. He is gracious, choosing not to punish our sins in proportion to their seriousness (v. 10). He is loving and even-tempered (vv. 7–8). He does not hold grudges (v. 9). His love is infinite; His forgiveness, totally effective and complete (vv. 11–12).

Of all these divine attributes, the one that resounds in my spirit like the clash of cymbals is His love. It is incomprehensible and inexhaustible. It is "wide and long and high and deep," and when I begin to grasp it, my inner being is strengthened by the Holy Spirit (Ephesians 3:16–21). I am changed from the inside out.

My imagination fired, I want to write a concerto, using God's incomparable love as my theme!

■ **Personal prayer**　*I am grateful, Lord, that Your mercy, love, and compassion temper the anger and judgment that should rightfully fall on me. Praise be to the Lord of love and grace!*

Bless the Lord, O My Soul!
Praising the Lord for His Dominion

■ **Theme**   The LORD has established his throne in heaven, and his kingdom rules over all. Praise the LORD, you his angels, you mighty ones who do his bidding, who obey his word. Praise the LORD, all his heavenly hosts, you his servants who do his will. Praise the LORD, all his works everywhere in his dominion. Praise the LORD, O my soul (vv. 19–22).

■ **Development**   At various stages of my life, I have exercised authority in a number of arenas. I have been a church music director, head of a music department in a Christian college, editor-in-chief of a music company, and instructor in a theological seminary. Musicians and writers sometimes consult me for musical and theological advice. At home, God has assigned me the roles of husband to Karen and father to D.J. and Kathy.

But God's domain has no such limitations or restrictions. The entire universe is under His dominion. All of creation is obligated to bow before Him. "Angels and mighty ones . . . do his bidding and obey his word" (vv. 20–21). Heavenly hosts praise Him and servants do His will.

If the whole creation is expected to worship the Lord, then I must bless the Lord in my personal life as well. Neglecting worship and praise will shrink my soul and reduce the margins of my life and influence. If I desire fulness, richness, and abundance, I'll spend my days adoring the King of the universe—the only One worthy of concentrated service and worship.

■ **Personal prayer**   I praise You and thank You, O Lord, for Your sovereignty and authority over all creation. I want to join the heavenly hosts in praising Your name today. Teach me some "melodious sonnet."

His Glorious Creation
The Glory of the Creator

■ **Theme**   *Praise the LORD, O my soul. O LORD my God, you are very great; you are clothed with splendor and majesty. He wraps himself in light as with a garment; he stretches out the heavens like a tent and lays the beams of his upper chambers on their waters. He makes the clouds his chariot and rides on the wings of the wind. He makes winds his messengers, flames of fire his servants. He set the earth on its foundations; it can never be moved. You covered it with the deep as with a garment; the waters stood above the mountains. . . . He makes springs pour water into the ravines; it flows between the mountains (vv. 1–6, 10).*

■ **Development**   Psalm 104 focuses on the glory of the Creator revealed in His majesty, His care of creation, and His rule.

The exalted poetry of these verses portrays God as light. He wraps Himself in a garment of radiance. The skies over the earth are envisioned as a tent, covering nomadic dwellers. His personal dwelling place is pictured above the waters of the sky, attended by the elements—winds and flames of fire.

God's glory is also observed in His perfect maintenance of creation. He waters the animals from freshly made springs. He provides grassy meadows for cattle to graze in and for men to cultivate. Out of the rich resources of the ground come wine, oil, and bread. He provides stately trees as a home for birds and majestic mountains as havens for wild goats.

He establishes the intricacies of the vernal equinox and the summer solstice and marks out the precise pathway of all the stars. He allows the sun and moon to rule the days, the nights, and the seasons. The circadian rhythms of men and animals, predetermined by these heavenly bodies, give meaning and variety to life, and further indicate the glory and imagination of the Creator.

■ **Personal prayer**   *Praise the Lord, O my soul! I praise You for Your majesty, Your creativity, Your care, and Your rule. As the seasons change and as each day fades into night, I'm continually reminded of Your glory in creation.*

His Glorious Creation
The Glory of His Creation

■ **Theme**   *How many are your works, O LORD! In wisdom you made them all; the earth is full of your creatures. There is the sea, vast and spacious, teeming with creatures beyond number—living things both large and small. There the ships go to and fro, and the leviathan, which you formed to frolic there. These all look to you to give them their food at the proper time. . . . I will sing to the LORD all my life; I will sing praise to my God as long as I live. May my meditation be pleasing to him, as I rejoice in the LORD. But may sinners vanish from the earth and the wicked be no more. Praise the LORD, O my soul. Praise the LORD (vv. 24–27, 33–35).*

■ **Development**   The psalmist bursts into passionate praise, celebrating God's creation. An earth full of creatures, teeming seas, and overarching heavens was brought into being where nothing had existed before! Only God can do that.

   Dr. Harold Best, dean of Wheaton College Conservatory, says, "Creativity is the ability both to imagine (think up) something and to execute it." He feels that creativity, craftsmanship, technique, and skill are often confused. The *special* quality of creativity "lies in the thinking up, the *imagining.*"

   Man takes raw materials which God has made and fashions them into useful items (i.e., trees become lumber; lumber becomes houses or furniture). In the same way a Christian musician uses the laws of nature (i.e., the harmonic series) to produce music. The composer must fashion the building blocks of music into ideas, themes, and melodies that become vehicles of praise.

   The psalmist is so stirred by these lofty thoughts that he vows to sing praise to the Lord as long as he lives, *in a manner pleasing to the Lord.* I too want to please God—not my colleagues or my competition—through the works of my mind and my hands. Though I have written approximately two hundred anthems and songs, only those will endure that have been inspired by the heart of God.

   I echo the psalmist who concludes with a mighty "Hallelujah!" and "Amen!"

274

■ **Personal prayer**   *I praise You, Lord, for Your creativity and Your artistic control over creation. I, like every other living creature of earth, am totally vulnerable and dependent upon You for inspiration and for life itself! Hallelujah!*

How Great Thou Art!
His Greatness

■ **Theme** *Give thanks to the LORD, call on his name; make known among the nations what he has done. Sing to him, sing praise to him; tell of all his wonderful acts. Glory in his holy name; let the hearts of those who seek the LORD rejoice. Look to the LORD and his strength; seek his face always. Remember the wonders he has done, his miracles, and the judgments he pronounced. O descendants of Abraham his servant, O sons of Jacob, his chosen ones. He is the LORD our God; his judgments are in all the earth* (vv. 1–7).

■ **Development** Throughout the entire history of Israel, God has revealed His greatness through His loyal, covenant love. The psalmist inspires his audience to call on the name of the Lord and to give thanks. He urges them to proclaim to the nations the Lord's mighty miracles in history.

I need this kind of spiritual motivation. I need a stirring preacher to remind me that the Lord has worked miraculously on my behalf. Why? Because I tend to take for granted His continual intervention in my life and to get so wrapped up in myself that I forget how great He is!

■ **Personal prayer** *Dear Lord, prod my memory when I forget Your miracles! Write them on my heart and stir me to sing about Your goodness!*

How Great Thou Art!
His Faithfulness

■ **Theme**   He remembers his covenant forever, the word he commanded, for a thousand generations, the covenant he made with Abraham, the oath he swore to Isaac. . . . He brought out Israel, laden with silver and gold, and from among their tribes no one faltered. Egypt was glad when they left, because dread of Israel had fallen on them. He spread out a cloud as a covering, and a fire to give light at night. They asked, and he brought them quail and satisfied them with the bread of heaven. He opened the rock, and water gushed out; like a river it flowed in the desert (vv. 8–9, 37–41).

■ **Development**   Certain key words leap from the pages of the Psalms—words used repeatedly to speak of the enduring quality of God's covenant with His people—words and phrases such as "forever," "for a thousand generations," "everlasting" (vv. 8–10).

In this psalm the musician is praising the Lord for taking His promises seriously. Unfortunately, we contemporary Christians use these words and phrases pretty casually. In fact, our list of synonyms is extensive: eternal, always, evermore, unending, endless, ceaseless, continual, perpetual. But do we really grasp the meaning of forever?

In reviewing this passage, I see again the "forever" faithfulness of God in keeping His covenant with Israel. First, He protected them as aliens in foreign lands, keeping His eye on Abraham wherever he went—Chaldea, Haran, Canaan, Egypt, and the Negev (vv. 12–15). Second, the Lord guided His people to Egypt and promoted Joseph to rule over them (vv. 17–22). Third, the Lord blessed His oppressed people with productivity (v. 24). Fourth, the Lord used Moses and Aaron to deliver them from Egypt (vv. 26–36). Finally, the Lord was faithful in providing for them, while they were in the wilderness (vv. 39–41). So even when Israel was "following afar off," God was faithful in meeting their needs (vv. 42–45).

If I were to trace the steps of my own pilgrimage, there would be many parallels, because God's character never changes. It is this kind of endless love and provision He promises me today.

276

■ **Personal prayer**   Dear Lord, I thank You for providing for Israel's needs in the ancient world. Because Your character never changes, I know You will care for me unceasingly, always, forever!

September

PSALMS 105–119

*Needing closeness, not remoteness, I almost
lost the joy of His priceless song. But when I
choose the Lord, He erases past error and teaches
me to sing again! —Psalm 118*

How Great Thou Art!   Freedom

■ **Theme**   *For he remembered his holy promise given to his servant Abraham. He brought out his people with rejoicing, his chosen ones with shouts of joy; he gave them the lands of the nations, and they fell heir to what others had toiled for—that they might keep his precepts and observe his laws. Praise the LORD (vv. 42–45).*

■ **Development**   This shrinking world of ours has given me a new appreciation for this passage from Psalm 105. America has never fallen into enemy hands, nor has any other nation stormed the streets of our cities and carried our people into captivity. Still, I read newspaper accounts and see telecasts of this kind of tyranny in the world today.

When the Lord remembered His "holy promise" to Abraham, He "brought out" His people from the bondage of Egypt to the security of the Holy Land "that they might keep his precepts and observe his laws" (v. 45). The bottom line of deliverance is freedom to obey and praise His holy Name.

How ironic that "captives" are often freer than many Americans who practice shallow and casual Christianity. Tatiana Goricheva, author of *Talking About God Is Dangerous: Diary of a Russian Dissident,* is a recent emigrant who claims, "My life only began when God found me." Even in atheistic Russia, her faith was growing strong and vibrant before her arrival in this country. Upon viewing a Western TV evangelist for the first time, however, she observed, "What this man said on the screen was likely to drive more people out of the church than the clumsy chatter of our paid atheists. Dressed up in a posh way . . . he was a boring, bad actor with mechanical and studied gestures. . . . For the first time I understood how dangerous it is to talk about God. Each word must be a sacrifice—filled to the brim with authenticity. Otherwise it is better to keep silent." God demands our praise, but it must be genuine!

■ **Personal prayer**   *O Lord, may every word I write and every song I sing be a sacrifice of praise to Your holy Name!*

Chaconne of Confession
Confessing Inconsistency

■ **Theme**   Praise the LORD. Give thanks to the LORD, for he is good; his love endures forever. Who can proclaim the mighty acts of the LORD or fully declare his praise? Blessed are they who maintain justice, who constantly do what is right. Remember me, O LORD, when you show favor to your people, come to my aid when you save them, that I may enjoy the prosperity of your chosen ones, that I may share in the joy of your nation and join your inheritance in giving praise (vv. 1–5).

■ **Development**   In baroque music, a composition consisting of the repetition of a short theme or succession of harmonies in slow triple meter is called a "chaconne." Johann Sebastian Bach said, "The end and goal of thorough bass is nothing but the honor of God." Here we have the psalmist's chaconne of confession.

Musically speaking, confession is the groundbass around which this psalm is structured. Far from "constantly doing what is right," Israel was more often ungrateful and rebellious. Depraved humanity exhibited itself regularly in her history. The ancient prophets, including Ezekiel and Isaiah, sounded a stern warning, urging her to confess and forsake her evil ways. (See Nehemiah 9, Isaiah 64, and Ezekiel 20.)

The psalmist strikes a major chord by praising God's goodness and constancy, as evidenced in the mighty acts He has performed in Israel's behalf. On that same note he moves on to pronounce a blessing on those who are consistently just and fair, progressing to a chord of concern for his personal accountability before the Lord.

Emotionally I'm capable of pretty severe mood swings, but I worship the living God of the universe who never changes. Sunrise and sunset, summer and winter, in adversity and prosperity—He parades past me the evidence of His unchanging nature. Even when the unthinkable happens and I'm caught off guard by crisis or tragedy, He is there to blend those dissonant chords into the musical pattern of His plan.

■ **Personal prayer**   I praise You, Lord, today for Your constancy. When all of life crumbles in around me, I can count on Your faithful love to orchestrate a symphony of joy.

Chaconne of Confession
Confessing Sin

■ **Theme**   *We have sinned, even as our fathers did; we have done wrong and acted wickedly. When our fathers were in Egypt, they gave no thought to your miracles; they did not remember your many kindnesses, and they rebelled by the sea, the Red Sea. Yet he saved them for his name's sake, to make his mighty power known. . . . But they soon forgot what he had done and did not wait for his counsel. . . . They defiled themselves by what they did; by their deeds they prostituted themselves (vv. 6–8, 13, 39).*

■ **Development**   It has been said that the curse of Christianity is a short memory! Why can't we learn? Why must we continue to make the same mistakes? Don't we know the consequences of following our spiritual ancestors who sinned in the very same ways as their fathers before them?

I listen to the psalmist's litany of sins and feel deep empathy with those ancient brothers and sisters who stumbled through the wilderness. Over and over again—at the Red Sea, at Peor, at Meribah—they resisted God's guidance. How could they have made such arrogant demands to be fed, then complain when the menu never varied? How could they forget all those miracles so soon and begin their murmuring and complaining? How dared they to provoke God to anger, so much so that He would have killed them had it not been for Moses' intercession? Yet Moses himself was no paragon of virtue. His disobedience cost him the dream of his life—entering the Promised Land.

Pride, arrogance, complaining, disobedience. Guilty as charged—my spiritual forebears . . . and me! I stand condemned before the God of Abraham and Moses "without one plea, but that Thy blood was shed for me."

■ **Personal prayer**   *I'm just like my fathers, Lord! Those people just couldn't learn. Neither can I. My soul is also a litany of disobedience and rebellion, but I'm glad 1 John 1:9 is still in the Book!*

Chaconne of Confession
Seeking Forgiveness

■ **Theme**   *Therefore the LORD was angry with his people and abhorred his inheritance. He handed them over to the nations, and their foes ruled over them. Their enemies oppressed them and subjected them to their power. Many times he delivered them, but they were bent on rebellion and they wasted away in their sin. But he took note of their distress when he heard their cry; for their sake he remembered his covenant and out of his great love he relented. . . . Praise be to the LORD, the God of Israel, from everlasting to everlasting. Let all the people say, "Amen!" Praise the LORD (vv. 40– 45, 48).*

■ **Development**   God is neither distant nor deaf. He did not turn His face from faithless Israel, nor does He fail to hear our cries of distress, though it may seem that way sometimes.

In His anger, God turned Israel over to heathen nations for punishment. Under their foreign taskmasters, the chosen people soon cried out for deliverance, and God answered.

Suddenly a majestic fanfare soars above the confessional—the harmonic changes for which I've been listening: "For their sake he remembered his covenant and out of his great love he relented" (v. 45). Despite their stiff-necked rebellion and the pitiful waste of their lives, God still loved them and wouldn't let them go!

Time after time He sent judges to lead them back to Him. Time after time they were faithful for a season and then fell back into their old ways. He was forced to discipline these delinquent children. "Those whom I love I rebuke and discipline" (Revelation 3:19).

At last! The great resolution! The people of God will return to Him, where they will remain in His presence "from everlasting to everlasting." The psalmist ends Book IV of the Psalter with a doxology of praise to the God of Israel. And all the people said, "Amen!"

■ **Personal prayer**   *O Lord my God, I thank You for not closing the door permanently when I sin. Like my ancient brothers and sisters, I can approach You with a contrite heart and find forgiveness and restoration.*

Descant of Deliverance
A Simple Theme

■ **Theme**   Give thanks to the LORD, for he is good; his love endures forever. Let the redeemed of the LORD say this—those he redeemed from the hand of the foe, those he gathered from the lands, from east and west, from north and south. Some wandered in desert wastelands, finding no way to a city where they could settle. They were hungry and thirsty, and their lives ebbed away. Then they cried out to the LORD in their trouble, and he delivered them from their distress. . . . Let them give thanks to the LORD for his unfailing love and his wonderful deeds for men. Let them sacrifice thank offerings and tell of his works with songs of joy (vv. 1–6, 21–22).

■ **Development**   A descant is a soaring counter-melody, usually sung by a few sopranos. The theme of this passage is the simple declaration of God's goodness and enduring love. His nature demands that He act on that love and He has done so. You might try reading these parts alternately with someone else.

> **Descant: He gathers His chosen people from all corners of the earth.**
>
> Theme: The Lord is good; His love endures forever.
>
> **Descant: He has redeemed us—paid our ransom, bought us back, covered our debt.**
>
> Theme: The Lord is good; His love endures forever.
>
> **Descant: He delivers us from distress.**
>
> Theme: The Lord is good; His love endures forever.
>
> **Descant: He satisfies our hunger and thirst with living water and good things.**
>
> Theme: The Lord is good; His love endures forever.
>
> **Descant: He brings us out of darkness into His marvelous light.**
>
> Theme: The Lord is good; His love endures forever.
>
> **Descant: He heals all our diseases and rescues us from the grave.**
>
> Theme: The Lord is good; His love endures forever.
>
> **Descant: He will still every storm of life to a whisper and guide us to our haven of rest.**

282

■ **Personal prayer**   Lord, I praise You for Your unfailing love and incomparable deeds of kindness.

Descant of Deliverance
A Soaring Descant

■ **Theme**   *He turned rivers into a desert, flowing springs into thirsty ground, and fruitful land into a salt waste, because of the wickedness of those who lived there. He turned the desert into pools of water and the parched ground into flowing springs; there he brought the hungry to live, and they founded a city where they could settle. . . . But he lifted the needy out of their affliction and increased their families like flocks. The upright see and rejoice, but all the wicked shut their mouths. Whoever is wise, let him heed these things and consider the great love of the* LORD *(vv. 33–36, 41–43).*

■ **Development**   The southeastern region, where I now live, recently experienced four years of drought. Interestingly enough, weather fronts skirted middle Tennessee many times, bringing storms and showers to neighboring counties, but not a drop to Nashville and Williamson County! There was a great deal of speculation as to the reasons—our geographical configuration, changes in prevailing winds, even the ozone layer.

Wiser heads, seeking counsel from the Scriptures, concluded that only God holds the answer, since He alone can "turn the desert into pools of water and the parched ground into flowing springs" (v. 35). The governor of a sister state suffering from the same drought called for a day of prayer for rain. Within twenty-four hours, the whole state was enjoying the first good downpour in weeks!

The Lord gives and withholds blessing according to the faithfulness of His people. Since all products come from resources in the earth, all of humanity is dependent upon God's providential care.

Just as He controls nature, He is also fully capable of ordering human experience. He may choose to humble the arrogant or to exalt the poor and needy. He can silence the wicked and inspire the redeemed to sing His praises. The psalmist suggests, "Whoever is wise, let him heed these things and consider the great love of the LORD" (v. 43).

283

■ **Personal prayer**   *As I meditate on Your great love, O Lord, I long for showers of blessing on the barren soil of my life.*

Toccata of Triumph
Celebrating His Love and Faithfulness

■ **Theme**   *My heart is steadfast, O God; I will sing and make music with all my soul. Awake, harp and lyre! I will awaken the dawn. I will praise you, O LORD, among the nations; I will sing of you among the peoples. For great is your love, higher than the heavens; your faithfulness reaches to the skies. Be exalted, O God, above the heavens, and let your glory be over all the earth (vv. 1–5).*

■ **Development**   I love to improvise on the piano—to sit down at the keyboard and to freely associate musically, to wing it! The term "toccata" comes from the Italian *toccare*, "to touch" (the keys), and is an early keyboard form designed to showcase the resources of the instrument, the ingenuity of the composer, and the technical virtuosity of the performer.

Part of the extraordinary body of King David's creative work is this toccata of triumph in praise of the Lord's loyal love of Israel. The theme is repeated for emphasis from Psalm 57:7–11.

Being the virtuoso he is, David is not interested in a dull, lifeless recital as he worships, but brings his whole being into the experience. He begins the day with a spontaneous outburst of song, depending not on prepared material, but on the flow of the Spirit to inspire both words and melody.

David's theme is the unsurpassed greatness of God's love which is "higher than the heavens" and His marvelous faithfulness which "reaches to the skies." He exalts his Lord who dwells in the heavens and desires that His glory will pervade the earth.

King David possessed not only a healthy mindset but the fullness of God in the deep recesses of his being. Because he was in touch with eternity, he was able to interpret reality and to live his life with freedom and authenticity. He beautifully fulfilled and pre-lived Christ's words in John 10:10: "The thief comes only to steal and kill and destroy; I have come that they may have life, and have it to the full."

284

■ **Personal prayer**   *O God, I want to sing and make music with all my soul today. I lift up my worship to You because of Your great love and faithfulness.*

Toccata of Triumph
Pleading for God's Help

■ **Theme**   *Save us and help us with your right hand, that those you love may be delivered. God has spoken from his sanctuary: "In triumph I will parcel out Shechem and measure off the Valley of Succoth. Gilead is mine, Manasseh is mine; Ephraim is my helmet, Judah my scepter. Moab is my washbasin, upon Edom I toss my sandal; over Philistia I shout in triumph." Who will bring me to the fortified city? Who will lead me to Edom? (vv. 6– 10).*

■ **Development**   Our do-it-yourself society has developed another dimension over the past few decades—professions geared to *helping* us do it ourselves. All of these professionals—financial advisors, tax consultants, career counselors, psychologists, family and children's service personnel, marriage counselors—are in business for the primary purpose of adding input to our decision-making. These advisors, especially if they are Christians, are generally motivated by genuine concern for people, and we benefit from their training and expertise.

Solomon, the wisest man who ever lived, said, "Plans fail for lack of counsel, but with many advisers they succeed" (Proverbs 15:22). There are times when tragedies, crises, or life changes create tension in an individual or a family. Professional Christian counselors who listen with empathy and a strong commitment to confidentiality can help untangle our knotty problems. Karen and I have both benefited from this kind of godly counsel. (I heartily recommend the counseling model of Dr. Larry Crabb of the Institute of Biblical Counseling.)

But David sounds a warning note: "Is it not you, O God? . . . Give us aid against the enemy [fear, financial reverses, family crises], for the help of [godless] man is worthless" (v. 12).

The Lord is the source of all personal strength and confidence and the ultimate answer to every problem we face in life. Sensitive counselors are often instruments of help and healing, but "with God we will gain the victory!" (v. 13).

285

■ **Personal prayer**   *O God, I thank You for Your trained representative of personal healing and deliverance, but may I never make the mistake of placing all my faith in human counsel. Your right hand is my strength!*

Chant of Curses Cursing the Wicked

■ **Theme** *O God, whom I praise, do not remain silent, for wicked and deceitful men have opened their mouths against me; they have spoken against me with lying tongues. . . . Appoint an evil man to oppose him; let an accuser stand at his right hand. When he is tried, let him be found guilty, and may his prayers condemn him. May his days be few; may another take his place of leadership. May his children be fatherless and his wife a widow. May his children be wandering beggars, may they be driven from their ruined homes. . . . May the iniquity of his fathers be remembered before the LORD; may the sin of his mother never be blotted out. May their sins always remain before the LORD, that he may cut off the memory of them from the earth (vv., 1–2, 6–10, 14–15).*

■ **Development** David, the man "after God's own heart," is never seen in his true humanity more graphically than in this psalm. On the surface he appears vindictive and cruel. His rhetoric is sharp and his attitude toward his enemies is harsh. David minces no words in letting God know how to dispose of his persecutors. He wants them blotted off the face of the earth! Exterminated! X'd out!

In explosive terms the psalmist describes the scenario as he'd like to see it played out. He asks that these wicked and deceitful men be opposed, accused, found guilty, condemned, yanked from positions of leadership, their families made fatherless and husbandless, and their children left to become homeless scavengers of society. As if that isn't enough, David goes on to suggest that their sins be *remembered* while they themselves be *forgotten!*

How do we mesh this diatribe with the New Testament imperative to "turn the other cheek" Luke (6:29)? One must bear in mind that David anticipated an earthly kingdom dedicated to righteousness. He did not have the full biblical revelation we possess today. Heathen peoples in the ancient world were corrupt and licentious, and David's righteous stance stood in bold contrast to their debauchery. What we have here is bold, passionate poetry cursing sin and immorality and defending righteousness and morality. David does not deny his angry feelings but freely vents them!

286

■ **Personal prayer** *O God, I learn from David that, if I must let off steam about my circumstances, I can do it safely in Your presence!*

Chant of Curses   Praying for Help

■ **Theme**   *But you, O Sovereign LORD, deal well with me for your name's sake; out of the goodness of your love, deliver me. For I am poor and needy, and my heart is wounded within me. . . . Help me, O LORD my God; save me in accordance with your love. Let them know that it is your hand, that you, O LORD, have done it. . . . With my mouth I will greatly extol the LORD; in the great throng I will praise him. For he stands at the right hand of the needy one, to save his life from those who condemn him (vv. 21–22, 26–27, 30–31).*

■ **Development**   The violent enemy David so vividly portrays here spews forth curses until he wears them like a black shroud about himself. I have a hard time condemning David for feeling the way he does about this guy! In fact, I admire his honesty.

   David is in no condition to avenge or even to protect himself from further insult and injury. He simply doesn't have the resources, physically or emotionally. His body is weakening because of fasting and lack of appetite, and his gaunt appearance serves only to bring on more ridicule.

   Realizing his helpless condition, David's prayer is up front, candid and forthright. He submits to the Lord's sovereignty, appealing to His goodness and love and asking for deliverance.

   The key to his prayer resounds like the chord from a great organ echoing in an empty cathedral: "Let them know that it is *your* hand, that *you*, O LORD, have done it" (v. 27). Now David's true motives are clearly seen. By a supernatural work of the Lord, his enemies will know the Source of real power!

   I am sometimes guilty of trying to crank up a worship experience without an intense awareness of any supernatural work of God in my life. An honest, vulnerable appraisal provides the rich soil for God to work creatively. I wonder how often my own self-deception, denial, and defensiveness have kept me from a deep work of God in my life. Real need motivates intense prayer. Passionate prayer prompts the Holy Spirit to produce miracles. When I experience a miracle—God's unmistakable touch on my life—I burst out in genuine praise!

287

■ **Personal prayer**   *O God, I too extol You. You work daily in my life and continually meet my needs, and I can't help bursting out in praise to Your Name!*

Messianic Masterpiece
His Sovereignty

■ **Theme**   The LORD says to my Lord: *"Sit at my right hand until I make your enemies a footstool for your feet."* The LORD *will extend your mighty scepter from Zion; you will rule in the midst of your enemies. Your troops will be willing on your day of battle. Arrayed in holy majesty, from the womb of the dawn you will receive the dew of your youth. The LORD has sworn and will not change his mind:* "You are a priest forever, in the order of Melchizedek" (vv. 1–4).

■ **Development**   This psalm is quoted many times in the New Testament (Matthew 22:44, Mark 12:36, Luke 20:42, Acts 2:34–35, and Hebrews 1:13). In fact, Jesus Himself quoted this psalm often. The Holy Spirit inspired it, David wrote it, and it is definitely messianic.

By "listening" carefully, I can "hear" the voice of God speaking to His Son, who would not be born for yet another thousand years! David says: "The LORD (Yahweh) says to my Lord (David's Lord, the Messiah): 'Sit at my (the Father's) right hand until I make your (the Son's) enemies a footstool for your feet.'" Messiah is seated at the right hand of God—the place of authority. At the end of time the Messiah will wield His holy scepter, ruling all peoples righteously, and His enemies will consequently become His footstool. Vigorous young warriors, adorned in holiness, will fight in a massive battle against the forces of evil.

Yahweh has proclaimed that the Messiah will be an eternal Priest in the order of Melchizedek. (See Hebrews 5, 6, and 7.) Priest and King will be united in One Person, Israel's true Messiah. As Priest, Christ became His own sacrifice when He died on the cross. As King, He is destined to rule and reign righteously at the end of time.

In a few lines of exquisite Hebrew poetry, the Lord gives us a glimpse into some of the mysteries of His glorious plan of redemption. Old Testament history is full of motifs which will only find their fulfillment at the end of time in Messiah's reign.

288

■ **Personal prayer**   *Dear Lord, because of the sacrifice of Your Son, I have eternal life. Because of His predicted rule and sovereign reign, my future is secure!*

Messianic Masterpiece
His Conquest

■ **Theme** *The Lord is at your right hand; he will crush kings on the day of his wrath. He will judge the nations, heaping up the dead and crushing the rulers of the whole earth. He will drink from a brook besides the way; therefore he will lift up his head (vv. 5–7).*

■ **Development** From my perspective there's something wrong with just about everything these days! But these verses assure me that someday soon everything will be set straight, the books will be balanced, and the enemies of God defeated once and for all!

Without the revelation of the New Testament, however, we would be in the dark about this passage. Later witness from God informs us that Christ will come again, accompanied by saints of all ages, to reign on the earth. At that time He will rule from His position of sovereign authority at the right hand of God, the Father. From that vantage point, He will crush kings and judge earthly rulers (v. 5). He will be refreshed (from a lovely country brook) and exalted (v. 7).

These are lofty thoughts. What do I learn from all of this? I learn that wickedness will give way to righteousness, that suffering will succumb to good health, that war will be replaced by perennial peace, that unfairness will be supplanted by justice, and that righteousness will reign on the earth.

I derive enormous security from the fact that all conflicts—from international and national to relational and personal—will be finally and ultimately resolved. Only the Lord can do that. Bless His holy Name!

■ **Personal prayer** *Dear Lord, I look forward to the dawn of a new day, when You will make all things right. The glorious prospect of the future gives me hope as I face the frustrations of today.*

Paean of Praise

Because of Who He Is . . .

■ **Theme** *Praise the* LORD, *I will extol the* LORD *with all my heart in the council of the upright and in the assembly. Great are the works of the* LORD; *they are pondered by all who delight in them. Glorious and majestic are his deeds, and his righteousness endures forever. He has caused his wonders to be remembered; the* LORD *is gracious and compassionate (vv. 1–4).*

■ **Development** Using an artistically controlled art form—the acrostic—the psalmist celebrates the nature of God. Each line begins with a letter of the Hebrew alphabet, extolling God's glory and majesty, His righteousness, His grace and compassion.

Volumes have been written on knowing about God. We can know all *about* someone, yet never come to know that person intimately. As a kid, I almost worshiped the musical flair and expertise of Ralph Carmichael, noted songwriter, arranger, and composer. I bought his records, corresponded with him, borrowed his scores, and closely followed his brilliant career. But I never got to meet him personally until I was in graduate school. Now I know him as a good friend and colleague. It is that kind of *knowing* that Dr. J. I. Packer intended when he wrote his classic work, *Knowing God.*

We can read about God, study about Him, sing to Him, even pray to Him—without really *knowing* Him. But when we recognize Him for who He is—our Creator and Redeemer—then our spirits cry out, "Abba, Father!"

■ **Personal prayer** *I praise You, Lord, not just for the wonderful things You have done in my life, but because of who You are!*

Paean of Praise
Because of What He Does . . .

■ **Theme**   *He provides food for those who fear him; he remembers his covenant forever. He has shown his people the power of his works, giving them the lands of other nations. The works of his hands are faithful and just; all his precepts are trustworthy. They are steadfast for ever and ever, done in faithfulness and uprightness. He provided redemption for his people; he ordained his covenant forever—holy and awesome is his name. The fear of the LORD is the beginning of wisdom; all who follow his precepts have good understanding. To him belongs eternal praise (vv. 5–10).*

■ **Development**   The psalmist develops his theme very specifically here. Our compassionate and gracious Lord has expressed Himself by helping His people—by providing a daily supply of food, by remembering His covenant and keeping His promises to make them victorious in conquest, by bequeathing to them the heathen lands around them, by revealing His power. And wonder of wonders, when they continued to grumble and complain against Him, He provided a way back to Him—a plan of redemption and forgiveness!

My Lord is no less active in my life today. He provides for my basic needs—food, shelter, clothing—by allowing me to serve Him through meaningful and fulfilling work. He has blessed me with rich personal relationships with my family and intimate friends. To guide me in facing the hassles of daily living, He has sent His Holy Spirit, and I find myself clinging to Him every day.

The conclusion of this psalm reminds me of Proverbs 1:7: "The fear [awesome respect] of the LORD is the beginning of knowledge." It seems that following His precepts in obedience should be the obvious outcome of my gratitude for all He's done for me!

■ **Personal prayer**   *I pray that You will fill me with an awesome respect for You, Lord, so that it will be the most natural thing in the world to obey Your rules for right living!*

Portrait of a Godly Person

What does a godly person look like?

■ **Theme**   *Praise the* LORD. *Blessed is the man who fears the* LORD, *who finds great delight in his commands. His children will be mighty in the land; the generation of the upright will be blessed. Wealth and riches are in his house, and his righteousness endures forever (vv. 1–3).*

■ **Development**   God has always sought out strong individuals who are willing to commit themselves to courageous leadership. The need has never been more desperate than now! Psalm 112 suggests the prototype for this kind of leader.

What does this person look like?

First, you can usually spot a godly man or woman by his *happy* countenance. I don't mean a perpetual ear-to-ear grin or some kind of slaphappy euphoria, but a stillness, a serenity, a relaxing of the facial muscles that is rare in this world of uptight urbanites. Only the indwelling Spirit of God can bring that unearthly peace and joy—a joy that is promised to the one "who finds great delight in [passionate love for] His [the Lord's] commands" (v. 1).

C. S. Lewis, internationally celebrated author said, "God cannot give us happiness and peace apart from Himself because it is not there. There is no such thing." Peace is found in a cause or a person greater than oneself. Christ is that quintessential Person.

Second, the godly person is *prosperous* (vv. 2–3). This Old Testament promise for Israel suggests that this godly leader's children will make their mother and father proud, that the family will enjoy agricultural prosperity, and that right living will result in long life.

Our contemporary culture defines prosperity more narrowly in terms of money and financial independence only. I want to be God's man, but I limit the Lord's blessings if I anticipate a financial windfall. I'll take any blessing He chooses to give me—family harmony, spiritual growth, effectiveness in ministry, knowing Him more intimately!

■ **Personal prayer**   *O Lord, let me be a godly person in a hostile world. Don't let me settle for our cultural definition of prosperity, but open my spiritual eyes to see that Your desires for me are infinitely more satisfying than my limited dreams.*

Portrait of a Godly Person
How Does a Godly Person Act?

■ **Theme**   Even in darkness light dawns for the upright, for the gracious and compassionate and righteous man. Good will come to him who is generous and lends freely, who conducts his affairs with justice. . . . The wicked man will see and be vexed, he will gnash his teeth and waste away; the longings of the wicked will come to nothing (vv. 4–5, 10).

■ **Development**   Whenever I think of a man of God, I inevitably think of my dad. A man marked by conviction, consistency, and energy, he has been my greatest role model.

A man of great strength and generosity, he derives enormous pleasure from being involved with people. He has stood behind my music and has been a real encouragement to me. He is living proof of the paradox in Christianity that when you give much, it will be multiplied to you (Luke 6:38). His happiness is in direct relation to his active caring for others.

Dad has rock-solid faith. Even when my mom died, he was unflappable. So deep were his spiritual roots that, when the winds of adversity blew, the branches of that mighty oak swayed, but the taproot held firm. "He will have no fear of bad news" (v. 7). Because his faith is steadfast, his security system could not be taken away. He is acutely aware that the Lord has already conquered the worst possible thing that can happen. His phobias and icy fears melt in the warm sunshine of God's love. Unlike secular man "who will gnash his teeth and waste away" (v. 10), my dad is part of the unshakable kingdom.

The French have an interesting word, *creneau*. It means "hole" or "opening." To be successful, a businessman has to look for holes or openings in the marketplace. There is a huge *creneau* in the Christian marketplace for godly leaders who have the strength to be role models. The world desperately needs such persons—joyous and prosperous (effective), compassionate and generous, stable and secure. These attributes belong to the kingdom man!

293

■ **Personal prayer**   Lord, I want to be a kingdom man! I'd like to model for others what my father has modeled for me.

Anthem of Angels   Call to Worship

■ **Theme**   Praise the LORD. Praise, O servants of the LORD, praise the name of the LORD. Let the name of the LORD be praised, both now and forevermore. From the rising of the sun to the place where it sets, the name of the LORD is to be praised (vv. 1–3).

■ **Development**   Musically inclined or not, have you ever pictured yourself in heaven, singing with the angelic choir? You may not be able to carry a tune now, but if you're a believer, your voice will blend one day with countless millions of others in a glad "Hallelujah!"

The word *hallelujah* comes from two beautiful Hebrew words: *hallel*, "Praise," and *jah*, referring to "Yahweh," Jehovah. So, "hallelujah" means "praise the Lord." Taken from the "hallel," a collection of songs sung at the great Jewish festivals—Passover, Pentecost, and Tabernacles—Psalms 113–118 are music for a heavenly choir performance. Our Lord joined in shortly before His death (Mark 14:26).

This psalm begins and ends with an exhilarating call to worship. Praising the Lord is a divine imperative, not an option for the servants of God. You can't plead a case of laryngitis or skip rehearsal. The command is clear. Praise the Lord—"now and forevermore" from "the rising of the sun to its setting" (vv. 2–3).

Only Yahweh—whose name was too sacred even to be uttered aloud by ancient worshipers—is worthy of continual praise. Yet how blithely and flippantly we speak that glorious Name. As we move toward colloquial speech in our prayers, sermons, and lyrics, we need to guard against irreverence and disrespect. We need to speak His sacred Name as if we were breathing a prayer.

Am I praising Him continually—by every action of my life as well as with my vocal chords? Am I praising Him in prayer? Am I praising Him in front of my children as well as in private moments of meditation? It's time for the angelic choir rehearsal to begin! He's coming soon!

294

■ **Personal prayer**   Beginning now, O Lord, keep me accountable for my praise to You. Let it be unending . . . beginning now!

Anthem of Angels   *Cause for Praise*

■ **Theme**   *The LORD is exalted over all the nations, his glory above the heavens. Who is like the LORD our God, the One who sits enthroned on high, who stoops down to look on the heavens and the earth? He raises the poor from the dust and lifts the needy from the ash heap; he seats them with princes, with the princes of their people. He settles the barren woman in her home as a happy mother of children. Praise the LORD (vv. 4–9).*

■ **Development**   In this descriptive praise psalm, two great themes will echo for eternity through the halls of heaven: God's greatness (vv. 4–5) and His grace (vv. 6–9).

God is great. There is no lord like our Lord. He is unique, over all, above all. He sits enthroned on high. In this context, study the magnificent lyric poetry of Isaiah 40:12–41:4. Our view of man tends to be overblown and our view of God, to be disproportionately small. When our vision of God enlarges, our problems will shrink to size.

God is grace. He manifests grace (unmerited favor) to us in three ways:

First, from His exalted position in the heavens, He stoops to survey all of creation. God the Father "made himself nothing, taking the very nature of a servant, being made in human likeness [Jesus the Son]" (Philippians 2:6–7).

Second, God honors the poor and seats them with the nobility. Our position in the heavenly community will not depend on earthly status or recognition by our peers, but on His grace.

Third, God settles the barren woman in her home "as a happy mother of children." Sarah's miraculous pregnancy was the joy of the ancient world (Genesis 18, 21). Hannah's humiliation was transformed into jubilation (1 Samuel 2). This psalm links the song of Hannah (1 Samuel 2:1–10) with the Magnificat of Mary (Luke 1:46–55).

The psalm concludes with a final hallelujah—praise the Lord! Who is like the Lord, our God? He is unique—equally at home above the heavens or at the side of the lowliest and loneliest creature.

■ **Personal prayer**   *I praise You, Lord, for stooping to lift me up, for seating me at Your banquet table, and for settling me forever in Your home in glory.*

Celebration of Deliverance
The Earth Trembles

■ **Theme**   *Why was it, O sea, that you fled, O Jordan, that you turned back, you mountains, that you skipped like rams, you hills, like lambs? Tremble, O earth, at the presence of the Lord, at the presence of the God of Jacob, who turned the rock into a pool, the hard rock into springs of water* (vv. 5–8).

■ **Development**   The psalmist doesn't attempt to answer the questions posed in verses 5 and 6. Instead, he commands the earth to tremble in the presence of the Lord, the God of Jacob. Why? Because only He can turn desert rocks into refreshing pools of water. Only He can transform inanimate stones into wells of gushing water. Only He can take my parched, meaningless life and restore it with springs of living water!

The revelation of God's power over nature was the only thing that encouraged Job when he was hurting. God led him through a painfully revealing process of counseling through such questions as: "Do you know the laws of the heavens? Can you set up God's dominion over the earth? Can you raise your voice to the clouds and cover yourself with a flood of water? Do you send the lightning bolts on their way? . . . Who endowed the heart with wisdom and gave understanding to the mind? Who has the wisdom to count the clouds? Who can tip over the water jars of the heavens when the dust becomes hard and the clods of earth stick together?" (Job 38:33–38).

The Lord has sovereign control over nature. Man can't lift a finger to influence nature. It's unruly, violent, and disobedient; it can only be manipulated and rearranged. But if God can, even on a whim, control the forces of nature, He can exert control over my seemingly unpredictable life. When I am helpless and lack courage and confidence, I can place unwavering trust in His incomparable power and might.

■ **Personal prayer**   *O God of Jacob, refresh and renew my life today. Lead me out of the barren desert to an oasis of Your care!*

Contrasts   *Spirituality Versus Idolatry*

■ **Theme**   *Not to us, O LORD, not to us but to your name be the glory, because of your love and faithfulness. Why do the nations say, "Where is their God?" Our God is in heaven; he does whatever pleases him. But their idols are silver and gold, made by the hands of men. They have mouths, but cannot speak, eyes, but they cannot see; they have ears, but cannot hear, noses, but they cannot smell; they have hands, but cannot feel, feet, but they cannot walk; nor can they utter a sound with their throats. Those who make them will be like them, and so will all who trust in them* (vv. 1–8).

■ **Development**   While heathen nations ask, "Where is their God?" our Lord is going about doing whatever He pleases.

Pagan idols are inanimate—having never possessed life—and obviously impotent. Made by man from the metals of the earth, they are unable to see, to hear, to smell, to feel, to speak, or to move about. God Himself is responsible for the raw materials from which they are molded! Interestingly, the psalmist observes that the artisans who make idols, as well as those who trust in them, will be "like them"—powerless and useless.

We tend to become "like" the people we idolize, the environment we live in, even the music we hear! We absorb like a sponge the personalities and mannerisms of the people we admire. As mentors and models, they dramatically alter and influence our lives. It's also true that our minds are somewhat like computers. If we program them with junk, junk comes out! And if any of these people or things become more important to us than God, then we become idolators!

In short, there is only one authentic, infinite, personal God of the universe. Counterfeit gods are not only disappointing, but dead. What a pathetic waste when a person bestows his allegiance on worthless pieces of junk—whether they be carved images or compact discs! We must focus on the "things that are excellent" (Philippians 4:8).

■ **Personal prayer**   *O Lord, not to us, but to Your name be the glory and honor.*

Contrasts   Life Versus Death

■ **Theme**   *May the LORD make you increase, both you and your children. May you be blessed by the LORD, the Maker of heaven and earth. The highest heavens belong to the LORD, but the earth he has given to man. It is not the dead who praise the LORD, those who go down to silence; it is we who extol the LORD, both now and forevermore. Praise the LORD (vv. 14–18).*

■ **Development**   Why don't we sing? The Maker of heaven and earth has given us everything to delight us, but so many people move through the measure of their days like marionettes, with painted smiles and no music in their hearts.

Why don't we sing? There are three primary reasons.

First, the pressures and complexities of modern life can take the song right out of the heart. Contemporary lifestyles often destroy intimacy, the soil in which artistry grows.

Next, we are overexposed to music, especially "elevator music." Second-rate sounds flood the airwaves at home, in the car, in the office, in restaurants. It's like musical wallpaper, so we become spectators rather than participants.

Third, "it is not the dead [persons without the Lord]" who praise Him. The psalmist tells us that they go to a place of *silence* (v. 17). There is no singing there!

Against the backdrop of pagan idolatry, the psalmist pleads with the house of Israel, the house of Aaron, and all who fear the Lord, to place their trust in the Lord and to lift their voices in praise. "Extol the Lord, both now and forevermore" (v. 18).

■ **Personal prayer**   *O Lord, help me to trust and praise You endlessly. May I personally and with full self-awareness experience Your blessing.*

Personal Song of Thanksgiving   *Deliverance from Death*

■ **Theme**   *I love the LORD, for he heard my voice; he heard my cry for mercy. Because he turned his ear to me, I will call on him as long as I live. The cords of death entangled me, the anguish of the grave came upon me; I was overcome by trouble and sorrow. Then I called on the name of the LORD: "O LORD, save me!" . . . For you, O LORD, have delivered my soul from death, my eyes from tears, my feet from stumbling, that I may walk before the LORD in the land of the living (vv. 1–4; 8–9).*

■ **Development**   I'll never forget the day I discovered that our senior editor at Singspiration Music, Norman Johnson, was terminally ill. I watched him cope with the vicissitudes of suffering for eight years as he battled Lou Gehrig's disease. He died while listening to Handel's *Messiah*. The "Hallelujah Chorus" was beautifully and victoriously rendered at his memorial service in an arrangement he penned. My dear friend, Norm, went out in a blaze of glory!

Once you've stared Death in the face, he is no longer the fearsome specter that lurks in childhood dreams. In fact, at that moment, God's reality and ultimate victory over death are never more evident.

The bad news of this psalm is that the psalmist, nearing death, was overcome with self-pity and defeat. Briefly, during this episode, life was the pits. The good news is that he didn't rely on human resources to pull him through. Though there is a place for medicine and Christian ministry to the hurting, this psalmist went beyond all such aid and directly into the presence of the Great Physician, the Wonderful Counselor. Furthermore, the Lord heard and answered, choosing to demonstrate His graciousness and compassion (vv. 8–9).

A certain responsibility accompanies great deliverance. For the rest of his life this psalmist won't forget God's loving mercy. Adversity has enriched his life. Suffering has purged him of superficiality. Like Job, he can say, "But he knows the way that I take; when he has tested me, I will come forth as gold" (Job 23:10).

299

■ **Personal prayer**   *O Lord, I don't have to experience serious illness to know Your mercy and grace. You are the Lord of my life . . . and the Victor over death!*

Personal Song of Thanksgiving *Promise to Praise*

■ **Theme**   *How can I repay the LORD for all his goodness to me? I will lift up the cup of salvation and call on the name of the LORD. I will fulfill my vows to the LORD in the presence of all his people. Precious in the sight of the LORD is the death of his saints. O LORD, truly I am your servant; I am your servant, the son of your maidservant; you have freed me from my chains. I will sacrifice a thank offering to you and call on the name of the LORD. I will fulfill my vows to the LORD in the presence of all his people, in the courts of the house of the LORD—in your midst, O Jerusalem. Praise the LORD (vv. 12–19).*

■ **Development**   "How can I repay the LORD for all his goodness to me?" This question asked by my ancient colleague rings true for me today. He answers with four "I wills." First, *I will pray.* "I will lift up the cup of salvation and call on the name of the LORD" (v. 13). Second, *I will praise the Lord publicly.* "I will fulfill my vows to the LORD in the presence of all his people" (v. 14). Third, *I will offer sacrifice.* "I will sacrifice a thank offering to you" (v. 17). True worship doesn't come cheap. The psalmist concludes by repeating, *"I will fulfill my vows to the LORD in the presence of all his people,"* adding "in the courts of the house of the LORD—in your midst, O Jerusalem" (v. 19).

He is overwhelmed that the Lord has delivered him from his miserable existence and from death. He is conscious of his servanthood and his sonship. He has become unshackled—freed from the confinement of his chains. He is filled with joy in the awareness that the Lord cares about the death of His saints (v. 15). God's children are safe and secure even at this ultimate moment.

"How can I repay the LORD for all his goodness to me?" I can pray, praise, and offer my life as a living sacrifice. The only fitting conclusion is again, "Hallelujah! Praise the Lord!"

300

■ **Personal prayer**   *Thank You, Lord, that I can trust You to be with me and take care of me in life . . . and in death.*

All Glory, Laud, and Honor

■ **Theme**   Praise the LORD, all you nations; extol him, all you peoples. For great is his love toward us, and the faithfulness of the LORD endures forever. Praise the LORD (vv. 1–2).

■ **Development**   I've never been invited to the White House. President Gerald Ford, however, was presented a copy of our musical, "I Love America," and wrote a wonderful letter extolling that patriotic work.

Psalm 117 is a miniature invitation to people everywhere. The purpose is praise; the place is wherever God's people gather. The reasons for this adulation are given in verse 2. The Lord is to be praised because of His great love and His abiding faithfulness.

The Lord is to be worshiped for who He is—for His character, for His attributes. His covenant love (hesed) is loyal and eternal; it is not subject to mood swings and emotional vacillation. His faithfulness is based on truth (emet). Because the Lord's Word is true or reliable, He is faithful. Loving and faithful. What an apt description of our Lord! The psalmist's response is again, "Hallelujah!—Praise the Lord!"

Whatever my mood today, I know my Lord is *loving and faithful*. Whatever adverse circumstances I face today, I know my Lord is *loving and faithful*. Whatever physical ailment I experience today, I know my Lord is *loving and faithful*. Whatever business reverses occur today, I know my Lord is *loving and faithful*. Whatever domestic tension I feel today, I know my Lord is *loving and faithful*. Why worry and fret? He invites me to remember that He is loving and faithful. Praise the Lord!

301

■ **Personal prayer**   Lord, I may be unpredictable and moody, but You can be counted on to be loving and faithful . . . no matter what!

Festal Procession
Praising His Loyal Love

■ **Theme**   Give thanks to the LORD, for he is good; his love endures forever. Let Israel say: "His love endures forever." Let the house of Aaron say: "His love endures forever." Let those who fear the LORD say: "His love endures forever" (vv. 1–4).

■ **Development**   The ancient Israelis sang this psalm—the final song in the "Hallel"—as they marched to the sanctuary to worship the Lord. It was used during the Passion Week of our Lord (Matthew 21:9), and it may have been sung in the Upper Room (Matthew 26:30). It was God's loyal love that energized the Israelite army to defeat the surrounding nations.

The wording suggests that these first few verses were either spoken or sung antiphonally. If we read the passage that way, the phrases spring to life:

Congregation: "His love endures forever."
Worship leader: "Let Israel say . . ."
Congregation: "His love endures forever."
Worship leader: "Let the house of Aaron say . . ."
Congregation: "His love endures forever."
Worship leader: "Let those who fear the Lord say . . ."
Congregation: "His love endures forever."

Though I can't understand how this truth meshes with obvious injustices in the world today, I know that God is loving and good. Though I see only a small slice of history, I know that God's wisdom encompasses all of time and eternity. I'm learning to accept by faith His mysteries.

■ **Personal prayer**   Lord, this psalm causes me to consider how Your loyal love extends to our nation, to the Wyrtzen household, and to all the community of believers who fear your Name. I praise You for Your enduring love!

Festal Procession

Acknowledging His Deliverance from Distress

■ **Theme**   *In my anguish I cried to the* LORD, *and he answered by setting me free. The* LORD *is with me; I will not be afraid. What can man do to me? The* LORD *is with me; he is my helper. I will look in triumph on my enemies. It is better to take refuge in the* LORD *than to trust in man. It is better to take refuge in the* LORD *than to trust in princes (vv. 5–9).*

■ **Development**   The stunning thought occurs to me that I've already made most of the major decisions I'll make in this life—choice of spouse, education, profession, Lord and Savior. But some choices present themselves again and again, and I have to decide what I'm going to do about them.

The psalmist is in the same boat. He can either trust his friends, or he can take refuge in the Lord. He can even consult with "princes" (authorities and experts), or he can cry out to the Lord in his dilemma. Human resources or divine power? Which shall it be?

There is so much room for error. I've made some mistakes through the years; a few have been trivial, others have had more devastating consequences. The choices come again. I can trust in secular philosophy, humanistic psychology, and modern science and technology. I can cast my lot with the scholars and experts of human opinion. Or, I can take the often unpopular stance of placing my faith in the Lord. When I choose the Lord, He erases past errors and teaches me to sing again!

■ **Personal prayer**   *Lord, I'm so prone to human error without Your constant guidance. Help me always to look to You—not to man-made systems—to define my life and to bring back the music when I falter.*

Teach Me to Sing Again

In my wandering, my heart hardening,
In such little things I made the wrong choice;
And for many days, in such little ways,
My life went astray from your still, small voice.

Ever straying, disobeying,
Rarely praying, not judging right from wrong!
Needing closeness, not remoteness,
I almost lost the joy of Your priceless song.

Teach me to sing again, light up my face again,
Help me to trust again, dear Lord, today;
Teach me to sing again, lifting my praise again,
Free me to love again, dear Lord, I pray.

Words and music by Don Wyrtzen.
© 1985 by Singspiration Music.

Festal Procession
Exulting in Confidence, Triumph, and Joy

■ **Theme** *I was pushed back and about to fall, but the* LORD *helped me. The* LORD *is my strength and my song; he has become my salvation. Shouts of joy and victory resound in the tents of the righteous: "The* LORD*'s right hand has done mighty things! The* LORD*'s right hand is lifted high; the* LORD*'s right hand has done mighty things!" (vv. 13–16).*

■ **Development** The psalmist is down for the count! Heathen nations swarm around him like bees, ready to crush and destroy. They have pushed him back until he is ready to fall.

The mighty conjunction *but* signals a dramatic change. "*But* the LORD helped me!" (v. 13). Three times this psalmist has called on the name of the Lord. The Lord's response is to "cut them off." The Hebrew terminology is pretty graphic here. "Cut them off" means to circumcise them (vv. 10–12). Our Lord is not namby-pamby nor squeamish in dealing with evil. Now the shouts of victory can resound throughout the "tents of the righteous."

A hard-won battle isn't something you can keep to yourself! It's natural to exclaim and exult when a victory is won. This ancient colleague grows eloquent in his praise: "The Lord is my strength and my song; he has become my salvation" (v. 14). I felt much the same way when I wrote "Jesus Is My Music!"

> My life was out of tune and happiness eluded me,
> My life was dissonant and missing inner harmony;
> But then I met the Savior and received His gift of grace,
> And now my heart sings melody.
>
> Jesus is my music, Jesus is my song,
> Jesus is my music, I want to sing His praises all day long.

Words and music by Don Wyrtzen. © 1977 by Singspiration Music.

■ **Personal prayer** *Lord, help me to go forth in Your Name. You are my strength, my salvation and my song!*

Festal Procession
Anticipating the Coming Kingdom

■ **Theme**   Open for me the gates of righteousness; I will enter and give thanks to the LORD. This is the gate of the LORD through which the righteous may enter. I will give you thanks, for you answered me; you have become my salvation. The stone the builders rejected has become the capstone; the LORD has done this, and it is marvelous in our eyes. This is the day the LORD has made; let us rejoice and be glad in it (vv. 19–24).

■ **Development**   Karen and I experienced the excitement that is Israel on our trip to the Holy Land. We were deeply moved to see Gethsemane, Golgotha, the Lord's tomb, and so many other biblical settings and scenes. One of the greatest thrills of the trip was entering Jerusalem through one of the many gates in the wall surrounding the ancient city. In fact, we even walked on the walls. While the present wall and buildings were erected in the sixteenth century A.D., the pilgrim feels a sense of expectancy upon seeing those gates!

The topmost stone of each Gothic or Romanesque arch is called the "capstone"—a vital piece of architecture that knits the rest of the stones together. In this psalm the "stone" takes on a symbolic meaning. "The stone the builders rejected [Jesus Christ, the Messiah] has become the capstone" (v. 22). The builders symbolize the Jewish leaders who not only rejected Him but schemed to have Him put to death (Matthew 26:3–5). Therefore, God would invite others into His kingdom (Matthew 21:43). The psalmist, overjoyed with this new development, bursts into song: "This is the day the LORD has made; let us rejoice and be glad in it" (v. 24).

Most of us try to fill the crowning point of our lives with people or things, but it can only be adequately fulfilled by one Person and that is Jesus Christ. Things, in time, prove to be worthless. Relationships are often broken or grow routine. Achievement may seem meaningless. Only Jesus, our Capstone, can hold our lives together and give them eternal significance.

306

■ **Personal prayer**   Lord, You are the Stone which the builders rejected, but I want You to be the Capstone of my life.

Praise for the Word of God
Trust and Obey

■ **Theme** א Aleph. *Blessed are they whose ways are blameless, who walk according to the law of the LORD. Blessed are they who keep his statutes and seek him with all their heart. They do nothing wrong; they walk in his ways. You have laid down precepts that are to be fully obeyed. Oh, that my ways were steadfast in obeying your decrees! Then I would not be put to shame when I consider all your commands. I will praise you with an upright heart as I learn your righteous laws. I will obey your decrees; do not utterly forsake me (vv. 1–8).*

■ **Development** Psalm 119 is a *magnum opus*, a mighty hymn of praise for the Word of God. The writer of this psalm lived under a lot of pressure—both internal and external. Men of earthly consequence persecuted him and ridiculed his beliefs. The severe test of his faith only strengthened him in his inner man. He became strong and resilient because he placed his faith in the Word of God and meditated on it day and night. The Word became his comfort and his ultimate resource for emotional strength.

This work is also an artistic masterpiece. Its structure is simple, elegant, and precise. This is the consummate alphabet psalm in which each line of each paragraph of eight verses starts with the same letter of the Hebrew alphabet. Verses 1–8 begin with the first letter of the Hebrew alphabet; verses 9–16 begin with the second, etc.

As he celebrates the value, worth, and magnificence of the Law, the psalmist almost runs out of words—*commandment, statute, judgment, precept, testimony, way, path. . . .*

The person who trusts in God's Word and obeys it is happy (vv. 1–2). Obedience brings stability and leads to righteousness.

The secular environment or worldly system we live in is diametrically opposed to the Word of God. Its philosophy and value system are poles apart from Christian beliefs, yet even believers are far more influenced by our materialistic culture than they realize. This psalm stops me short: Am I more deeply affected by the world or by the Word?

■ **Personal prayer** *Dear Lord, forgive me for not trusting and obeying You. My lack of faith has caused pain and unhappiness for myself and others. As I meditate again on Your Word, fill me with deep joy and peace.*

Praise for the Word of God
Memorizing the Word

■ **Theme**   ⊐ Beth. *How can a young man keep his way pure? By living according to your word. I seek you with all my heart; do not let me stray from your commands. I have hidden your word in my heart that I might not sin against you. Praise be to you, O LORD; teach me your decrees. With my lips I recount all the laws that come from your mouth. I rejoice in following your statutes as one rejoices in great riches. I meditate on your precepts and consider your ways. I delight in your decrees; I will not neglect your word* (vv. 9–16).

■ **Development**   How can a young person in this decadent society hope to lead a pure life? How can one avoid wandering from the truth? How can one be protected from committing sin? By mastering God's Word. By allowing it to control his or her life. The way to master the Word is to memorize it—just the way a good symphony conductor memorizes a score. Then when the spiritual battles come, the Sword of the Spirit can be wielded at a moment's notice, without fumbling for words!

The psalmist asks the Lord's help in learning the divine decrees, then publicly recites God's magnificent Law. He rejoices in following the Lord's statutes as one exults in great riches. At work during the day or in his bed at night, he runs these precepts through his mind. He doesn't intend to neglect them, because God's Law is his delight!

The Word has impacted this psalmist's mindset. He has not programmed his mind with trash and pornographic material which feed lust and lead to unhealthy fantasizing. He doesn't have to live with the pressure and pain caused by an unbalanced, sick mental attitude. His life is pure because his thoughts are pure.

■ *Personal prayer*   *O Lord, don't let me neglect Your Word. As I hide it away in my heart like nuggets of gold, I am enriched. As I follow its precepts, I'm strengthened for the battle.*

October

PSALMS 119–125

Older saints have learned that dependence upon the Lord and His Word is the secret to perfect freedom. —Psalm 119

Praise for the Word of God
Open My Eyes

■ **Theme** ‎ג Gimel. *Do good to your servant, and I will live; I will obey your word. Open my eyes that I may see wonderful things in your law. I am a stranger on earth; do not hide your commands from me. My soul is consumed with longing for your laws at all times. You rebuke the arrogant, who are cursed and who stray from your commands. Remove from me scorn and contempt, for I keep your statutes. Though rulers sit together and slander me, your servant will meditate on your decrees. Your statutes are my delight; they are my counselors (vv. 17–24).*

■ **Development**　Living is not just a meaningless vacuum for this author-composer. The goal of his life is to keep God's Word. Is this legalism—a slavish adherence to the letter of the Law? No! The psalmist is depending on God's truth for strength and sustenance. This Word is supporting him as a life raft supports a drowning man on a storm-tossed sea. This concept is repeated often in this psalm (vv. 24, 37, 40, 50, 77, 88, etc.).

He prays that his eyes will be opened to behold "wonderful things" out of the Law. He prays for insight and illumination so that God's commandments will not be hidden from him. So intensely involved is he in this quest that his soul "is consumed with longing" for the Law "at all times" (v. 20).

What "wonderful things" do I find for living life in this troubled twentieth century? I love to read the Word aloud; it gets my ear involved as well as my eye. Recently, I read the whole book of Ephesians aloud in one sitting. Often, I put outstanding passages on 3 x 5 cards and carry them around with me for ready reference. Second Corinthians 12:9 helps me with feelings of inadequacy and incompetence. Jeremiah 29:11 helps me regarding uncertainty about the future. First Chronicles 28:20 gives me encouragement in my work. Occasionally I make Scripture songs out of these key concepts. Then the Scripture, combined with music, comforts and sustains me.

■ **Personal prayer**　*O Lord, open my eyes that I may behold "wonderful things" from Your Word today.*

Praise for the Word of God
Song of the Soul Set Free

■ **Theme** ד Daleth. *I am laid low in the dust; preserve my life according to your word. I recounted my ways and you answered me; teach me your decrees. Let me understand the teaching of your precepts; then I will meditate on your wonders. My soul is weary with sorrow; strengthen me according to your word. Keep me from deceitful ways; be gracious to me through your law. I have chosen the way of truth; I have set my heart on your laws. I hold fast to your statutes, O Lord; do not let me be put to shame. I run in the path of your commands, for you have set my heart free (vv. 25–32).*

■ **Development**   Rich in contrasts, this passage displays the positive against the negative. First, a mournful tone is heard: "I am laid low"; "My soul is weary"; "Keep me from deceitful ways"; "Do not let me be put to shame" (vv. 25, 28, 29, 31).

Then, on a rising crescendo, the psalmist realizes the possibilities available to him through God's Word—renewal, strength, truth, freedom! As he begins to understand these precepts, he is filled with wonder.

Jesus articulated this truth in John 8:31–32: "To the Jews who had believed him, Jesus said, 'If you hold to my teaching, you are really my disciples. Then you will know the truth, and the truth will set you free.'"

This kind of freedom is the definitive answer to bondage, to obsessive-compulsive behavior. After receiving my new nature as God's gift of grace, I was inspired to write one of my first songs, "The Day That I Met Jesus"—a song that was later recorded by Jerome Hines of the Metropolitan Opera and arranged by noted songwriter, Kurt Kaiser.

■ **Personal prayer**   *O Lord, set my heart free as I adhere to Your truth and hold fast to Your commands.*

Praise for the Word of God
Not for Selfish Gain

■ **Theme**   ה He. *Teach me, O LORD, to follow your decrees; then I will keep them to the end. Give me understanding, and I will keep your law and obey it with all my heart. Direct me in the path of your commands, for there I find delight. Turn my heart toward your statutes and not toward selfish gain. Turn my eyes away from worthless things; preserve my life according to your word. Fulfill your promise to your servant, so that you may be feared. Take away the disgrace I dread, for your laws are good. How I long for your precepts! Preserve my life in your righteousness* (vv. 33–40).

■ **Development**   What drives me? What hidden desires motivate me to perform? What goals beckon me? Part of being imperfect, human, and fallen is the struggle with mixed motives. I want my life to bring glory to God, but I also want some other things—personal fulfillment, meaningful work, the recognition of my peers, financial success, domestic tranquility. O how easy it is to be deceived, to rationalize, to be a self-preservationist! I want to be "in the world but not of it," yet, to be honest, secular culture carries a punch that the Word often doesn't.

This psalmist puts me to shame! He observes the Law wholeheartedly (vv. 33–35), then begs God to purge him of any unworthy motives—"selfish gain," "worthless things" (vv. 36–37). Then he gives us the key to proper motivation for the study of God's Word as well as for all other endeavors undertaken by the believer. "Direct me in the path of your commands" (v. 35). With divine direction, the psalmist knows he can't miss a beat.

If I live to fulfill my own goals and desires or even to satisfy the expectations of others—no matter how worthy—I'll miss the greater blessing of living my life to please God. Obeying His Word is the premiere goal that drives me now!

312

■ **Personal prayer**   *O Lord, turn my heart toward Your statutes today. May I not live my life for selfish gain, but to please You!*

Praise for the Word of God
I Will Speak of Your Statutes

■ **Theme** ┐ Waw. *May your unfailing love come to me, O LORD, your salvation according to your promise; then I will answer the one who taunts me, for I trust in your word. Do not snatch the word of truth from my mouth, for I have put my hope in your laws. I will always obey your law, for ever and ever. I will walk about in freedom, for I have sought out your precepts. I will speak of your statutes before kings and will not be put to shame, for I delight in your commands because I love them. I lift up my hands to your commands, which I love, and I meditate on your decrees (vv. 41–48).*

■ **Development** Down through the ages, some have dared to proclaim the Word of God at the risk of endangering their lives or reputations. In 1521 Martin Luther was excommunicated by Pope Leo X. Charles V, emperor of the Holy Roman Empire, ordered him to appear before the Diet (meeting) of princes, nobles, and clergymen at Worms, Germany. They demanded that Luther recant his beliefs, but he refused. "Unless I am convinced by the testimony of the Scriptures or by clear reason (for I do not trust either in the pope or in councils alone, since it is well known that they have often erred and contradicted themselves), I am bound by the Scriptures . . . and my conscience is captive to the Word of God. I cannot and I will not retract anything!"

This psalmist vows to "speak of [the Lord's] statutes before magistrates and kings" (v. 46). In his day that would have been a dangerous thing to do, as it is in some parts of the world today.

Several other bold personal assertions are made in these verses: "I trust in your word" (v. 42). "I have put my hope in your laws" (v. 43). "I will always obey your law" (v. 44). "I delight in your commands because I love them" (v. 47).

Here is a person with a passion for God's Word. He is obsessed with it. He thinks about it constantly. As the Word dominates his thoughts, it changes his life and frees him to face life unafraid.

■ **Personal prayer**   *O Lord, let me become so immersed in Your Word that I share it freely wherever I go—whether in the company of colleagues or kings!*

Praise for the Word of God
Precious Promises

■ **Theme**   ז Zayin. *Remember your word to your servant, for you have given me hope. My comfort in my suffering is this: Your promise preserves my life. The arrogant mock me without restraint, but I do not turn from your law. I remember your ancient laws, O LORD, and I find comfort in them. Indignation grips me because of the wicked, who have forsaken your law. Your decrees are the theme of my song wherever I lodge. In the night I remember your name, O LORD, and I will keep your law. This has been my practice: I obey your precepts* (vv. 49–56).

■ **Development**   "Your decrees are the theme of my song!" What a mandate for the Christian musician! What a mission statement for a godly artist! As Christopher Smart said in 1763, "Glorious the song, when God's the theme." The content of our art must be the magnificence of God's truth. Yet it is so easy to water it down, leave it out, or yield to the temptation to explore other areas of thought that are more appealing, more commercial.

This servant had discovered the rock of God's truth during a particularly painful time of suffering and opposition. The precious promises contained in God's Word had given him hope and comfort. Even in the depths of his dark night, he remembered these promises and recited them. The habits of holiness he had developed sustained him at the time of his greatest need. Therefore, because God's Word has been tried and tested in his life, these precepts now occupy all of his thoughts. There is no room for lesser interests!

My theme song is that which consumes me because it has been tested and proven. As I experience the truth of God's Word daily and am convicted by its power, my goal or mandate is to set God's truth to music in simple, powerful form.

■ **Personal prayer**   *O Lord, Your promises preserve my life and comfort me. May Your decrees be the theme of my song for the rest of my days.*

Praise for the Word of God
With All My Heart

■ **Theme**   ח Heth. *You are my portion, O LORD; I have promised to obey your words. I have sought your face with all my heart; be gracious to me according to your promise. I have considered my ways and have turned my steps to your statutes. I will hasten and not delay to obey your commands. Though the wicked bind me with ropes, I will not forget your law. At midnight I rise to give you thanks for your righteous laws. I am a friend to all who fear you, to all who follow your precepts. The earth is filled with your love, O LORD; teach me your decrees (vv. 57–64).*

■ **Development**   I remember my high school days when, under pressure to perform, I wanted to be left alone. The result was an unfulfilled inner life, a personal emptiness, and a passionless Christianity. I followed at a distance, because there was little delight and joy in my relationship with the Lord.

This psalmist is committed, dedicated, passionately involved. "I have sought your face *with all my heart*" (v. 58), he declares. Nothing lackadaisical about this man's approach to Bible study! In fact, we'd say that this person is "on fire for the Lord." So strong is his devotion that, even if the wicked were to bind him with ropes, he will not forget the law (v. 61).

Not only does he make all kinds of declarations about what he plans to do in the future, but he has already put feet to his intentions. He takes stock of his actions and chooses to follow God's law (v. 59). He prays, giving thanks for the good guidance of God's Word (v. 62). He befriends fellow believers who share his love and reverence for the Lord (v. 63).

Where is this level of commitment and dedication today? Which of us, living in the midst of a secular society, gives this kind of intense devotion and concentration to spiritual matters? We wake up in the middle of the night, besieged with worries and anxieties. The psalmist wakes up and praises the Lord with all his heart!

315

■ **Personal prayer**   *O Lord, help me to seek Your face with all my heart!*

Praise for the Word of God
It Was Good for Me to Be Afflicted

■ **Theme**   ʊ Teth. *Do good to your servant according to your word, O LORD. Teach me knowledge and good judgment, for I believe in your commands. Before I was afflicted I went astray, but now I obey your word. You are good, and what you do is good; teach me your decrees. Though the arrogant have smeared me with lies, I keep your precepts with all my heart. Their hearts are callous and unfeeling, but I delight in your law. It was good for me to be afflicted so that I might learn your decrees. The law from your mouth is more precious to me than thousands of pieces of silver and gold* (vv. 65–72).

■ **Development**   What kind of man is this psalmist? He thanks God for adversity and affliction! He must be sado-masochistic!

Reading on, I understand. "Before I was afflicted, I went astray, but *now* I obey your word" (v. 67). The painful consequences of sin have driven him to the Word of God and now he considers "the law from [the Lord's] mouth . . . more precious . . . than thousands of pieces of silver and gold" (v. 72).

We contemporary Christians prefer simple answers to very complex issues. We all seem to think there must be an easier way to personal depth and spiritual maturity. But the nature of reality is like a tapestry with knots underneath, a symphony containing dissonance, or a play enhanced by dramatic tension. When I wonder why life with the Lord can't be easier, I am reminded of the song, "No Easier Way," that I wrote with Claire Cloninger.

■ **Personal prayer**   *O Lord, let me learn to praise You for the hard times that drive me to my knees, and to remember that Your suffering paid the price of my eternal security!*

No Easier Way

Why can't I live my life without losing it?
Why can't I grow without pain?
Why can't I live for You, Lord, without dying?
There must be an easier way!

There was no easier way for You,
There was no easier thing You could do;
The cost of my life
Was the cross and the grave,
There was no easier way!

Words by Claire Cloninger and Don Wyrtzen. Music by Don Wyrtzen.
© 1984 by Singspiration Music.

Praise for the Word of God
Living the Law

■ **Theme**　'Yodh. *Your hands made me and formed me; give me understanding to learn your commands. May those who fear you rejoice when they see me, for I have put my hope in your word. I know, O LORD, that your laws are righteous, and in faithfulness you have afflicted me. May your unfailing love be my comfort, according to your promise to your servant. Let your compassion come to me that I may live, for your law is my delight. May the arrogant be put to shame for wronging me without cause; but I will meditate on your precepts. May those who fear you turn to me, those who understand your statutes. May my heart be blameless toward your decrees, that I may not be put to shame* (vv. 73–80).

■ **Development**　This ancient believer-musician places his complete hope in the Word, since the Lord has delivered him from pain and has made of him an example and encouragement to other believers.

He is acutely aware that his very life has come from God. Infinitely powerful hands have made and formed him. He is not a product of chance. Now he requests understanding to learn God's Law so that others will be filled with joy when they observe his life.

The staggering truth dawns that I am the only Bible some people will ever read! Am I living its precepts faithfully so that unbelievers "rejoice when they see me," or are the pages of my life so marred with my own errors that they are difficult to read? Is the music of my life flat, dull, and boring?

I cry out to the Lord for compassion! I need another chance to live out His Word before the world so I will point others to Him.

■ **Personal prayer**　*Thank You, Lord, for forming me, for forgiving me, and for sending me as Your love letter to the world. May the words and music of my life be consistent with Your truth.*

Praise for the Word of God
A Wineskin in the Smoke

■ **Theme**   ⊃ Kaph. *My soul faints with longing for your salvation, but I have put my hope in your word. My eyes fail, looking for your promise; I say, "When will you comfort me?" Though I am like a wineskin in the smoke, I do not forget your decrees. How long must your servant wait? When will you punish my persecutors? The arrogant dig pitfalls for me, contrary to your law. All your commands are trustworthy; help me, for men persecute me without cause. They almost wiped me from the earth, but I have not forsaken your precepts. Preserve my life according to your love, and I will obey the statutes of your mouth* (vv. 81–88).

■ **Development**   With dramatic imagery, the psalmist compares himself to "a wineskin in the smoke." In the heat of severe persecution and harassment, his soul is shriveled up like a goatskin, and his eyes, "looking for the promise," grow red and watery.

Then he uses a startlingly modern phrase: "They almost wiped me from the earth" or "wiped me out" (v. 87)! Arrogant persecutors are digging his grave in anticipation of an early death.

Even in these unbelievably adverse circumstances, the psalmist's faith in God's Word is immovable. He continually voices his hope and trust in God's divine "decrees," His trustworthy "commands," His "precepts," and "statutes." The emphasis is on God's Word—not on the wrongs that have been committed.

I can understand this ancient musician's impatience. I have experienced deep hurt, searing anger, and dark despair. I've sometimes wondered where I fit in and where God is when I've needed Him. I've even rebelled and come awfully close to dropping out. Yet, when I allow God to perform on the keys of my life, music comes forth! Like the psalmist, I choose to put my hope in the Word, to honor the Lord, and to wait patiently for Him to work more obviously and directly in my life.

■ **Personal prayer**   *O Lord, help me, even when under intense pressure and pain, to learn to wait for You to do Your deep work in my life.*

Praise for the Word of God

In All Perfection I See a Limit

■ **Theme** ל Lamedh. *Your word, O LORD, is eternal; it stands firm in the heavens. Your faithfulness continues through all generations; you established the earth, and it endures. Your laws endure to this day, for all things serve you. If your law had not been my delight, I would have perished in my affliction. I will never forget your precepts, for by them you have preserved my life. Save me, for I am yours; I have sought out your precepts. The wicked are waiting to destroy me, but I will ponder your statutes. To all perfection I see a limit; but your commands are boundless* (vv. 89–96).

■ **Development**   I'm a perfectionist by nature. I probably use perfectionism defensively in uncomfortable situations to distance myself from other people. We use all kinds of devices like armor to protect ourselves—humor (being too funny), intellectualization (being too smart), superficiality (being too sweet). Sometimes achievement is an attempt to prove ourselves worthy in the eyes of others and ourselves.

This psalmist has a more realistic view. He promotes the faithfulness of God and His eternal Word. It's settled in heaven, therefore he can stake his life on its immutable perfection. These qualities of the Word have supported the struggling psalmist in persecution and affliction. Through it all, he's clung to the one sure thing he knows—the Word of God. It has become his delight, his salvation, and his stable reference point.

This section ends with a beautiful, original insight. "To all perfection I see a limit" (v. 96). No matter how high the level of excellence one might attain, the product of human creativity is short-lived at best. Works of art, clever creations, powerful empires—all are temporal. Only the Word is perfect, boundless, and eternal!

■ **Personal prayer**   O Lord, I praise You for the absolute reliability of Your Word. Help me to recognize the short-term duration of any work I may accomplish, including songwriting. May I look to Your Word for perfection and not to myself.

Praise for the Word of God
I Have More Insight Than All My Teachers

■ **Theme** ם Mem. *Oh, how I love your law! I meditate on it all day long. Your commands make me wiser than my enemies, for they are ever with me. I have more insight than all my teachers, for I meditate on your statutes. I have more understanding than the elders, for I obey your precepts. I have kept my feet from every evil path so that I might obey your word. I have not departed from your laws, for you yourself have taught me. How sweet are your words to my taste, sweeter than honey to my mouth! I gain understanding from your precepts; therefore I hate every wrong path* (vv. 97–104).

■ **Development** I can recall some teachers and professors who profoundly impacted my life. Mrs. Lillian Gearhart taught me piano; Jay Ciser and Carl Hamilton taught me art; Dr. Charles Horne taught me apologetics; Prof. Howard Hendricks taught me Bible study methods; Dean Arlton taught me music history; Dr. Bruce Waltke taught me the Psalms and Hebrew; Dr. Charles Ryrie taught me theology; Dr. Francis Schaeffer taught me about culture. Dr. John F. Walvoord, D. J. DePree, and Bob Steed have been father figures and mentors to me. What a foundation they gave to me!

But this psalmist claims that he has more "insight" than all his teachers, "more understanding than the elders" (v. 100), for "you yourself [the Lord] have taught me" (v. 102)!

I too have learned that reading the Word with my intellect alone is inadequate. As R. A. Torrey said, "No amount of mere human teaching, no matter who our teachers may be, will ever give us a correct and exact and full apprehension of the truth. . . . We must be taught directly by the Holy Spirit. The one who is thus taught will understand the truth of God better, even if he does not know one word of Greek or Hebrew, than the one who knows Greek and Hebrew thoroughly . . . but who is not taught of the Spirit."

I also must submit to the Holy Spirit as my teacher. I need His comfort and counsel. Otherwise, the undertow of secular society may pull me down.

■ **Personal prayer** *O Lord, Your Word is "sweeter than honey." Feed me by Your Holy Spirit so I may know the truth.*

Praise for the Word of God
Your Word Is a Lamp unto My Feet

■ **Theme**   ⫯ Nun. *Your word is a lamp to my feet and a light for my path. I have taken an oath and confirmed it, that I will follow your righteous laws. I have suffered much; preserve my life, O LORD, according to your word. Accept, O LORD, the willing praise of my mouth, and teach me your laws. Though I constantly take my life in my hands, I will not forget your law. The wicked have set a snare for me, but I have not strayed from your precepts. Your statutes are my heritage forever; they are the joy of my heart. My heart is set on keeping your decrees to the very end (vv. 105–112).*

■ **Development**   How well I remember taking my son, D.J., on a camping trip to northern Michigan. Just the two of us, a small tent, a crackling fire, some fishing poles, and a raft. Wanting to spend quality time with my son, I left my books at home. But just before we went to sleep, D.J. pulled out a flashlight and a book he had brought along. In the pitch dark, the glow of the campfire and the beam from the flash gave us all the light we needed.

Without the searchlight of God's Word, we'd be left to flounder in the dark, looking for the way. But His Law points out the snares of the wicked, and we can avoid stumbling into their traps.

The psalmist has vowed to follow God's righteous decrees, so there is nothing to fear from visible or invisible foes. When the darkness closes in, he has the enlightenment of the Word and cannot stray from these rock-like precepts (v. 110).

Not only does this ancient one have light for his present difficulties, but God's statutes are his "heritage forever." He can look forward to life in the light now and throughout eternity. As a result, he offers the "willing praise" of his mouth (v. 108) and obedience to the Word "to the very end" (v. 112).

What the psalmist did not have was an intimate relationship with the Light of the World, who came to banish darkness forever. I walk in the increased illumination of the Messiah—the prophecy fulfilled!

322

■ **Personal prayer**   *O Lord, I thank You for sending Christ, the living Word, who walks with me to point out hidden dangers and to shepherd me through the canyons and ravines of my life.*

Praise for the Word of God
I Stand in Awe

■ **Theme** *HW ẕ Samekh. I hate double-minded men, but I love your law. You are my refuge and my shield; I have put my hope in your word. Away from me, you evildoers, that I may keep the commands of my God! Sustain me according to your promise, and I will live; do not let my hopes be dashed. Uphold me, and I will be delivered; I will always have regard for your decrees. You reject all who stray from your decrees, for their deceitfulness is in vain. All the wicked of the earth you discard like dross; therefore I love your statutes. My flesh trembles in fear of you; I stand in awe of your laws (vv. 113–120).*

■ **Development**   Awesome! If I've heard that word once, I've heard it a thousand times. With two teenagers and their friends around the house, I've become convinced that this word is basic to the vocabulary of young America.

Still, *awesome* is a perfectly good word. *Random House Dictionary* defines it as "characterized by awe—an overwhelming feeling of reverence, admiration, and fear produced by that which is grand, sublime, extremely powerful, or the like." The psalmist certainly feels this kind of reverence for God's laws.

Because of the sublime Word of God, the psalmist has a holy hatred for duplicity and doublemindedness. He is opposed by wicked men, who use pretense and illogical reasoning to bolster their position. In God's eyes, however, they are "dross"—waste materials that will be removed by His smelting process.

This psalmist isn't gullible enough to believe that he is immune to the seductive wiles of the wicked and prays earnestly for strength to stay true to God's awesome decrees. He actually trembles in God's presence!

Modern-day believers often try to be too cozy, too familiar with God. We sing superficial songs and engage in cliché-ridden, repetitive prayers. Many of us know the *traditions* but never have been moved by the *truth*. We've never felt our flesh quiver in awe as we behold the majesty of God's eternal Word!

■ **Personal prayer**   *O Lord, when I open Your Word, I'm standing on holy ground. Teach me to tremble in Your presence!*

Praise for the Word of God
I Am Your Servant

■ **Theme**   ע Ayin. *I have done what is righteous and just; do not leave me to my oppressors. Ensure your servant's well-being; let not the arrogant oppress me. My eyes fail, looking for your salvation, looking for your righteous promise. Deal with your servant according to your love and teach me your decrees. I am your servant; give me discernment that I may understand your statutes. It is time for you to act, O* LORD; *your law is being broken. Because I love your commands more than gold, more than pure gold, and because I consider all your precepts right, I hate every wrong path* (vv. 121–128).

■ **Development**   Most of us living in affluent America know very little about servanthood. We expect excellent and efficient service from others, and accept it as our due. It is so much more human to desire stardom than servanthood!

Three times in this passage, however, the psalmist—likely a person of honor and prestige in the community—professes his status as a lowly servant before God: "Ensure *your servant's* well-being" (v. 122). "Deal with *your servant*" (v. 124). "I am *your servant*; give me discernment" (v. 125). He isn't too proud to admit his need to be educated in the royal decrees or to seek divine wisdom for decision-making.

Ancient believers, overcome by the greatness of God and their own worthlessness, often prostrated themselves before the Lord in abject humility (Psalm 5:7). We do well to get on our knees even once in a while.

Yet Jesus, God incarnate, willingly left the glories of heaven to walk the dusty pathways of this earth. He owned no property, sought no public office, accumulated no possessions. "The Son of Man did not come to be served, but to serve, and to give his life as a ransom for many" (Matthew 20:28). He came to serve . . . and to die for my sins!

Such love compels me to fall on my face. "I am your servant; give me discernment that I may understand your statutes" (v. 125).

■ **Personal prayer**   *Speak, Lord! Your servant is listening!*

Praise for the Word of God
Your Word Is Wonderful

■ **Theme**   ℶ Pe. *Your statutes are wonderful; therefore I obey them. The unfolding of your words gives light; it gives understanding to the simple. I open my mouth and pant, longing for your commands. Turn to me and have mercy on me, as you always do to those who love your name. Direct my footsteps according to your word; let no sin rule over me. Redeem me from the oppression of men, that I may obey your precepts. Make your face shine upon your servant and teach me your decrees. Streams of tears flow from my eyes, for your law is not obeyed (vv. 129–136).*

■ **Development**   God's Word is wonderful—marvelous, extraordinary, remarkable! The word *wonderful* literally means "to generate wonder." Even the simple, the unintelligent, the uneducated can grasp its truth when instructed by the Holy Spirit. Its inspiration exceeds that of Shakespeare, Mozart, Milton, Bach, and the greatest poets and composers who have ever lived.

So amazing is the power of these statutes and commands that the psalmist opens his mouth and "pants" for understanding. His deep personal longing for the truth is like gasping for breath after running the Boston Marathon.

As I read these verses, I'm reminded of "Wonderful Words of Life," Dad's theme song for the Word of Life Hour. I grew up hearing it.

> *Sing them over again to me,*
> *Wonderful words of life;*
> *Let me more of their beauty see,*
> *Wonderful words of life.*

Words and music by Philip P. Bliss.

■ **Personal prayer**   O Lord, teach me to love Your truth and see the wonder of Your words!

Praise for the Word of God
Your Word Is Righteous

■ **Theme**   צ Tsadhe. *Righteous are you, O LORD, and your laws are right. The statutes you have laid down are righteous; they are fully trustworthy. My zeal wears me out, for my enemies ignore your words. Your promises have been thoroughly tested, and your servant loves them. Though I am lowly and despised, I do not forget your precepts. Your righteousness is everlasting and your law is true. Trouble and distress have come upon me, but your commands are my delight. Your statutes are forever right; give me understanding that I may live (vv. 137–144).*

■ **Development**   The psalmist is filled with deep love and reverence for the Law. Because the Lord is righteous, His Word is also fully trustworthy. The Lord's promises are fully reliable because they have been thoroughly tried, tested, and proven.

But all is not well here. The psalmist is almost worn out with zeal. His enemies ignore the Word of God. He is feeling lowly and despised. Arnold Schoenberg said, "Dissonances are more difficult to comprehend than consonances." Horace labeled it "harmony in discord." The psalmist is alluding to the "discordant harmony" of his existence.

But his depression cannot obliterate his memory of the law. Continual trouble and distress do not snatch away his ingrained delight in the Lord's commands. No matter how lonely or how oppressed he feels, God's Word stands unaffected.

What a comfort to know beyond a shadow of a doubt that the Word of God is absolutely trustworthy and reliable! May we not let technological change, moral relativism, scientific advances, or intellectual pride rob us of our confidence in God's eternal Word!

■ **Personal prayer**   *O Lord, I praise You and thank You for Your flawless Word!*

Praise for the Word of God

Long Ago I Learned from Your Statutes

■ **Theme**   ק Qoph. *I call with my heart; answer me, O* LORD, *and I will obey your decrees. I call out to you; save me and I will keep your statutes. I rise before dawn and cry for help; I have put my hope in your word. My eyes stay open through the watches of the night, that I may meditate on your promises. Hear my voice in accordance with your love; preserve my life, O* LORD, *according to your laws. Those who devise wicked schemes are near, but they are far from your law. Yet you are near, O* LORD, *and all your commands are true. Long ago I learned from your statutes that you established them to last forever* (*vv.* 145–152).

■ **Development**   Some of the Scripture songs I learned as a kid have supported me in times of crisis such as those described by this psalmist (i.e., "Thy Word Have I Hid in My Heart," "Thy Word Is a Lamp unto My Feet"). My mom taught me that music comforts. I remember her singing around the house some of Norman Clayton's lovely songs: "Now I Belong to Jesus" and "We Shall See His Lovely Face."

As trouble sweeps in like a flood, the psalmist gets up before daybreak to pray. Then, at night, restless and sleepless, he meditates on God's promises, likely committed to memory when he was younger. Because he knows the Word, the psalmist can call on it instantly for help in any emergency. He promises to keep the divine statutes (v. 146), to continue to hope (v. 147), and to rest his destiny on the Lord's loyal love and His Law (v. 149). This musician feels close to the Lord because God's Word is lodged firmly in his mind and heart!

Scripture songs are like tapes that play over and over in our minds. Because more of our senses are involved in learning them, they bring God's truth to the forefront of our consciousness. What a glorious wedding when the Word is united with music!

■ **Personal prayer**   *O Lord, thank You for my mom who taught me hymns and gospel songs when I was young. Now these Scripture songs and biblical promises hold me steady in times of trouble.*

Praise for the Word of God
Your Compassion Is Great, O Lord

■ **Theme**   ⸷ Resh. *Look upon my suffering and deliver me, for I have not forgotten your law. Defend my cause and redeem me; preserve my life according to your promise. Salvation is far from the wicked, for they do not seek out your decrees. Your compassion is great, O LORD; preserve my life according to your laws. Many are the foes who persecute me, but I have not turned from your statutes. I look on the faithless with loathing, for they do not obey your word. See how I love your precepts; preserve my life, O LORD, according to your love. All your words are true; all your righteous laws are eternal (vv. 153–160).*

■ **Development**   How prone we human beings are to panic when the pressure builds. Our faith shrinks and we're even tempted to avoid unpleasant confrontations at all costs—in other words, to run in the other direction!

The ancient songwriter must have known that trapped feeling. Three times he reminds the Lord of His promise to renew and preserve life: "Preserve my life according to your promise" (v. 154). "Preserve my life according to your laws" (v. 156). "Preserve my life, O LORD, according to your love" (v. 159).

Suddenly the theme of this song sounds above the discord of defeat like the clear, sweet note of a lark: "Your compassion is great, O LORD!" (v. 156). The Lord not only knows the feelings of our infirmities and sympathizes with us, but He *desires to alleviate the pain or remove its cause altogether!*

I can't begin to comprehend the love and compassion of the Lord. Under intense emotional pressure, I either abandon it or forget it. Yet He is faithful to supply His mercies in rich abundance if I follow the example of my ancient counterpart and ask for it!

■ **Personal prayer**   *O Lord, I thank You for Your great love and compassion. Revive my life on the basis of Your truth today!*

Praise for the Word of God
I Rejoice in Your Promise

■ **Theme** ‎ש Sin and Shin. *Rulers persecute me without cause, but my heart trembles at your word. I rejoice in your promise like one who finds great spoil. I hate and abhor falsehood but I love your law. Seven times a day I praise you for your righteous laws. Great peace have they who love your law, and nothing can make them stumble. I wait for your salvation, O LORD, and I follow your commands. I obey your statutes, for I love them greatly. I obey your precepts and your statutes, for all my ways are known to you* (vv. 161–168).

■ **Development** What a sunny, bright, and joyful passage! The psalmist has the distinction of having both loved and kept the Law. Now the music in his heart spills across the page in a lilting progression of praise: "I rejoice in your promise" (v. 162). "I wait for your salvation" (v. 166). "I obey your statutes, for I love them greatly" (v. 167). I'm reminded of the tumbling, dancing counterpoint in a Bach invention or fugue.

This musician has taken his stand for God's Law and has consequently suffered persecution at the hands of heathen rulers. He is not driven by selfish ambition nor is he achievement-oriented. He is not experiencing a mid-life crisis. Rather, he's exulting in the "great spoil" he has found in God's Word. This "find" far surpasses earthly treasures—masterpieces of art and literature, wealth and possessions, even great music! God's Word has turned his life inside out.

I long to be radically changed—to know the psalmist's peace and stability, his patience and personal obedience. I want to love and follow the Word so that I'll be turned inside out!

329

■ **Personal prayer** *O Lord, may my heart rejoice in Your Word! Let me learn to love You with an intensity that is reflected in everything I do or write or sing!*

Praise for the Word of God
My Lips Overflow with Praise

■ **Theme**   ת Taw. *May my cry come before you, O LORD; give me understanding according to your word. May my supplication come before you; deliver me according to your promise. May my lips overflow with praise, for you teach me your decrees. May my tongue sing of your word, for all your commands are righteous. May your hand be ready to help me, for I have chosen your precepts. I long for your salvation, O LORD, and your law is my delight. Let me live that I may praise you, and may your laws sustain me. I have strayed like a lost sheep. Seek your servant, for I have not forgotten your commands (vv. 169–176).*

■ **Development**   This magnificent psalm ends with a very beautiful but humble prayer, encompassing a cluster of pleas for insight and help. Its tone is "the grace of thankfulness."

Five requests rise before the Lord, each of the five movements more beautiful than the last: "May my cry come before you" (v. 169). "May my lips overflow with praise" (v. 171). "May my tongue sing of your word" (v. 172). "May your hand be ready to help me" (v. 173). "May your laws sustain me" (v. 175).

The psalmist, awed by the magnitude and depth of the divine revelation, recognizes his own need for renewal and revival.

In some ways I'm like that other musician. He knows he's not out of danger yet. He's like a sheep that has strayed from the shepherd's side (v. 176). Lost, he longs to be found and restored to the fold. At least he knows his weakness, and that's the beginning of strength.

The psalm concludes at the end of the Hebrew alphabet, but the song plays on . . . in overflowing praise to God for His exquisite, awe-inspiring, magnificent Law!

■ **Personal prayer**   *O Lord, may my lips overflow with praise today and may my tongue sing of Your Word!*

Imperial March *War*

■ **Theme**   *I call on the LORD in my distress, and he answers me. Save me, O LORD, from lying lips and from deceitful tongues. What will he do to you, and what more besides, O deceitful tongue? He will punish you with a warrior's sharp arrows, with burning coals of the broom tree (vv. 1–4).*

■ **Development**   Why does our Christian pilgrimage seem to be uphill so much of the time? It was the same for the early believers, who faced a tough climb, literally as well as symbolically.

This "pilgrim song" was sung by ancient Israelis as they journeyed up to Jerusalem for their annual feast days. Psalms 120–134 are also identified as "songs of ascent."

The psalmist has been "burned" by lying lips and deceitful tongues. This personal verbal attack made by warlike adversaries is probably only the beginning of more direct assaults. Still, the sting of a slanderous tongue is enough to launch full-scale war.

In verse 3 he addresses his foes with a question: "What will he do to you, O deceitful tongue?" then answers with vibrant imagery. The wicked will be slain with a "warrior's sharp arrows" and "with burning coals" (v. 4). The broom tree is mentioned because its excellent firewood burns bright, long, and hot!

From these verses I learn that God does not deal lightly with untamed tongues. He hates slander, lying, deceit, and gossip! Because individuals are made in the image of God, they are to be treated with dignity and respect, and we are not allowed to speak in an unrestrained manner about them. How typical it is to run rough-shod over God's precious children. Paul speaks against "obscenity, foolish talk, and coarse joking" (Ephesians 5:4). He tells us they are out of place for the Christian and ought to be replaced by thanksgiving-talk!

■ **Personal prayer**   *Bridle my tongue, Lord, and keep me from speaking irreverently or thoughtlessly. Keep a song on my lips rather than shallow speech.*

Imperial March Peace

■ **Theme**   *Woe to me that I dwell in Meshech, that I live among the tents of Kedar! Too long have I lived among those who hate peace. I am a man of peace; but when I speak, they are for war (vv. 5–7).*

■ **Development**   War and peace have long been the topic of lively discussions among political analysts, writers, and thinkers of all generations. But even in peacetime, believers are not at home in this world. Until Jesus comes, there will be, at best, an uneasy truce between the forces of good and evil.

The psalmist laments that he dwells among peoples with whom he has nothing in common. Meshech, located southeast of the Black Sea, was a remote, barbaric tribe (Genesis 10:2). Kedar, south of Damascus in the Syrian desert, was about as far from Meshech as one could get. He was saying, in effect: "I'm surrounded by warlike, nomadic, Ishmaelites!" He has lived with these vexing people for too long and ends his song in clashing discord: "I am a man of peace, but when I speak, they are for war" (v. 7).

If we are to be salt and light in a hostile world, we can expect the same kind of opposition. But we have the consolation of a Friend who walks and talks with us and who will make us special, distinctive, and unique as we live in our secular culture.

> This life can be a crowded arcade—
> A busy thoroughfare;
> Yet quiet appointments can be made
> With Jesus anywhere.
>
> I'll walk and talk with Him today
> Relating as friend to Friend;
> My Lord will lead me through life's way
> As I walk and talk with Him today.

Words and music by Don Wyrtzen.
© 1975 by Singspiration Music.

■ **Personal prayer**   *Lord, as I dwell in "Meshech and among the tents of Kedar," may I keep quiet appointments with You for strength and solace in this foreign land.*

Pilgrim Song of Assurance
Thesis: The Lord Is My Help

■ **Theme**   *I lift up my eyes to the hills—where does my help come from? My help comes from the LORD, the Maker of heaven and earth (vv. 1–2).*

■ **Development**   Last summer, while on vacation in New York state, I decided to climb Mount Colden, one of the steepest peaks in the Adirondacks. Along with several relatives, I started out, and by late afternoon, we had covered approximately ten miles to the top and back! Even though I could barely walk for the next three days, the exhilarating rush of achievement and the view from the top of the mountain were worth a little temporary discomfort!

Mountains were significant in the life of Israel. Not only did they provide natural fortifications against invading armies, but the mountains were places of comfort and security. Since Jerusalem rested on a cluster of hills, the whole area came to be associated with the Holy City—the dwelling place of Yahweh.

On his way to Jerusalem, this pilgrim observes the surrounding mountains. "Where does my help come from?" (v. 1) he asks, then answers his own question: "My help comes from the LORD, the Maker of heaven and earth" (v. 2). Part of that creation was the thrusting up and heaving of the earth to form the rounded hills and majestic mountains. Noticing His dramatic creation prompts us to remember the Creator.

Vicarious exposure to nature doesn't take the place of being there. Watching National Geographic documentaries on TV or videotape will never produce the same heady effect as breathing in fresh, clean air and seeing the view from the top! We need these reminders of the permanence of God's creative care and His help.

■ **Personal prayer**   *Precious Lord, remove the cataracts from my eyes. May I be reminded of Your comfort and security when I behold the grandeur of Your mountains!*

Pilgrim Song of Assurance
Development: Helping in All Eventualities

■ **Theme**   *He will not let your foot slip—he who watches over you will not slumber; indeed, he who watches over Israel will neither slumber nor sleep. The LORD watches over you—the LORD is your shade at your right hand; the sun will not harm you by day, nor the moon by night. The LORD will keep you from all harm—he will watch over your life; the LORD will watch over your coming and going both now and forevermore (vv. 3–8).*

■ **Development**   The Divine Watchman! This psalm of assurance gives me a fresh glimpse of God as the One who keeps watch over His children night and day. In the words of the old spiritual, "He never sleeps, He never slumbers."

Perhaps a Levite priest, accompanying the pilgrim on his journey, is speaking here. Note the change in pronouns from *I* and *my* to *you*. He reassures the traveler of the Lord's divine protection as he walks the rugged terrain. We can feel the same sense of protection on crowded superhighways, in high-crime neighborhoods, and on the streets of the inner city. The priest also suggests that God—unlike the Canaanite fertility gods—never goes off duty or takes a nap on the job.

The Lord Himself guards us—not some common soldier on night watch! He "watches over" every aspect of our lives—our "comings and goings," our times of rest and recreation. He whose eye is on the sparrow promises to keep an eye on me!

■ **Personal prayer**   *Precious Lord, thank You for Your guidance in all circumstances at all times. I can rest, knowing You neither slumber nor sleep.*

Pilgrimage to Jerusalem
The Splendor of the Holy City

■ **Theme**   *I rejoiced with those who said to me, "Let us go to the house of the LORD." Our feet are standing in your gates, O Jerusalem. Jerusalem is built like a city that is closely compacted together. That is where the tribes go up, the tribes of the LORD, to praise the name of the LORD according to the statute given to Israel. There the thrones for judgment stand, the thrones of the house of David (vv. 1–5).*

■ **Development**   Do we drag our heels on Sunday morning, or do we look forward to worship services? Do we expect to meet God there, or do we fail to find Him in our empty ritual and meaningless form?

David has an entirely different attitude as he approaches the gates of Jerusalem. His heart is filled with joy and expectancy. "I rejoiced with those who said to me, 'Let us go to the house of the LORD'" (v. 1). He loves the capital city and looks forward to participating in one of the great festivals of worship there.

Located within the walls are the royal palace, administrative buildings, and sturdy homes of prominent citizens. The entire complex is solidly and compactly constructed. The psalmist also praises it as a civic and spiritual center, where justice is administered and the tribes congregate to praise the name of the Lord.

Jerusalem, teeming with people and activities of all kinds, was an exciting place to visit. One day the New Jerusalem will be the gathering place of people of all nations, and the Lord will be glorified forever! For a look at the New Jerusalem, turn to Revelation 21 and read about the Holy City "coming down out of heaven from God as a bride beautifully dressed for her husband."

■ **Personal prayer**   Lord, make Your house an exciting place for me to visit. May our worship together become an enriching, exhilarating experience.

Pilgrimage to Jerusalem
Prayer for Peace

■ **Theme**   Pray for the peace of Jerusalem: "May those who love you be secure. May there be peace within your walls and security within your citadels." For the sake of my brothers and friends, I will say, "Peace be within you." For the sake of the house of the LORD our God, I will seek your prosperity (vv. 6–9).

■ **Development**   Ancient Israelis were not only to take pride in their capital city, but also to pray for its security. Jerusalem has been a focal point, a hot spot, for centuries. Here David prays for the welfare of his beloved city and for the personal security of others who love her. He prays that there will be peace within the walls and security within the citadels—the two outside limits of the city.

More important than the city or its inhabitants, however, is the house of the Lord. David prays for its prosperity. The King James phrase, "I will seek thy good" (v. 9), is rendered by Luther, "I will seek what is best for you."

We live in a rootless society. Many factors contribute to rootlessness—mobility, industrialization, domestic upheaval, isolation, alienation, etc. The foundations are crumbling. We have downplayed community and stressed individualism. Our identities are threatened. We feel lost. We have become a society of vagabonds!

David's roots were in his Lord, his nation, his city, his family. He was not a loner—isolated from culture and tradition, nor was he insulated from regular interaction with people. He was part of a congregation of believers, and his unselfish prayer stretches beyond the bounds of his day to embrace believers of all generations. We are reminded to pray for the peace of Jerusalem.

336

■ **Personal prayer**   Lord, as I pray for the peace of Jerusalem, fill me also with Your serenity and security.

Song of the Slave   *Submission to God*

■ **Theme**   *I lift up my eyes to you, to you whose throne is in heaven. As the eyes of slaves look to the hand of their master, as the eyes of a maid look to the hand of her mistress, so our eyes look to the LORD our God, till he shows us his mercy (vv. 1–2).*

■ **Development**   Maclaren, internationally celebrated Scottish pulpiteer, called this psalm "a sigh and an upward gaze and a sigh!"

In this brief passage, a slave lifts his eyes to God and cries out for mercy and deliverance from contempt. He places himself in complete submission to God with the faith that the One who sits enthroned in the heavens can help him. He finds his confidence in the exalted majesty of God. As a slave looks to his master and as a maid looks to her mistress, so also do "our eyes look to the LORD our God, till he shows us his mercy" (v. 2).

Many times I'm unaware that I need help until some crisis or tragedy sharply reminds me that I am very human and needy! Even then, I often go to the wrong sources of help. Experts have their place, but they can never substitute for trust in the Lord who is our ultimate Help.

One of Mom's favorite songs was "There Is No Problem." When I play it, I think of her and of her loving counsel.

> There is no problem that Jesus cannot solve
> And not a need He cannot satisfy;
> There is no heartache He cannot understand,
> He is omniscient and knows the reasons why.
> There is no pain my Lord has never known—
> Because He's Lord, I lay my burdens at His throne.

Words and music by Don Wyrtzen.
© 1981 by Singspiration Music.

■ **Personal prayer**   *May I lift up my eyes to You, today, O Lord, and lay my burdens at Your throne.*

Song of the Slave
Release from Contempt

■ **Theme**   Have mercy on us, O LORD, have mercy on us, for we have endured much contempt. We have endured much ridicule from the proud, much contempt from the arrogant (vv. 3-4).

■ **Development**   This is an earnest plea for deliverance from contempt and ridicule. Wounded and hurting, the author cries out, "LORD, have mercy on us!" (v. 3).

At times, an agonized cry for mercy is the only recourse we can take. Christians in all walks and circumstances of life have had to take it on the chin for their faith.

The apostle Paul had more than his share: "Five times I received from the Jews the forty lashes minus one. Three times I was beaten with rods, once I was stoned, three times I was shipwrecked, I spent a night and a day in the open sea, I have been constantly on the move. I have been in danger from rivers, in danger from bandits, in danger from my own countrymen, in danger from Gentiles; in danger in the city, in danger in the country, in danger at sea. . . . I have labored and toiled and have often gone without sleep; I have known hunger and thirst and have often gone without food; I have been cold and naked" (2 Corinthians 11:24–27).

This missionary martyr suffered for *doing* God's will; he didn't suffer for *not doing* God's will. Under abnormal stress and pressure, he reached unscaled heights of achievement, exploits, and excellence— not the least of which was writing almost half of the New Testament!

For it was Paul who also said, "I consider that our present sufferings are not worth comparing with the glory that will be revealed in us" (Romans 8:18).

The Lord must laugh at our complaints. We're soft! We need to toughen up and learn how to take anything the Enemy can dish out because "the one who is in you is greater than the one who is in the world" (1 John 4:4).

338

■ **Personal prayer**   O Lord, I'm ashamed when I read the recital of injustices and wrongs committed against the great saints of the ages. Help me to shape up as Your man in my own hostile environment.

Deliverance in the Dorian Mode *First Motif: Protection*

■ **Theme** *If the LORD had not been on our side—let Israel say—if the LORD had not been on our side when men attacked us, when their anger flared against us, they would have swallowed us alive; the flood would have engulfed us, the torrent would have swept over us, the raging waters would have swept us away (vv. 1–5).*

■ **Development** The dorian mode is a musical scale which sounds somewhat like minor. Melodies written in this mode have a somber feeling. David has narrowly escaped grave danger, and his song gives the impression that he is still gasping for breath! If the LORD had not delivered him, the surrounding nations would have "swallowed [him] alive" (v. 3).

Not only is David's life in jeopardy, but the entire nation of Israel is at risk. Enraged heathen nations pursue God's precious jewel like a flash flood that can swiftly destroy everything in its path.

These verses comprise more than a footnote in ancient history. This is a crisis of major proportions—a situation in which an entire nation can be obliterated from the earth! But God intervened and protected them.

I haven't yet been asked to put my life on the line for my faith, but I have felt the flood waters of emotional pressure engulfing me. I know what it's like to feel pain from crisis in close personal relationships and from trauma related to upheaval in the circumstances of life. These verses are a reminder to me that God is always with me to sustain and uphold me. Since the Lord is on my side, I will never be swallowed up or destroyed. Nothing and no one can harm me. I'm safe!

■ **Personal prayer** *I praise You for being on my side and for Your protection in all kinds of danger—internal and external.*

Deliverance in the Dorian Mode *Second Motif: Help*

■ **Theme** *Praise be to the LORD, who has not let us be torn by their teeth. We have escaped like a bird out of the fowler's snare; the snare has been broken, and we have escaped. Our help is in the name of the LORD, the Maker of heaven and earth (vv. 6–8).*

■ **Development** I probably don't realize just how spiritually destitute I am! To add more stress, I sometimes ponder the uncertainty of the future. What in the world can give me hope and help?

David's metaphor of the bird in the fowler's net is so appropriate. Israel was that "bird" enmeshed in the strands of the net, ripe to be torn by the teeth of wild animals (v. 6). The Lord broke the framework and allowed the bird to fly free, suggesting the utter helplessness of the trapped one and the need for radical intervention from the outside.

No wonder David bursts forth with thanksgiving and praise! "Praise be to the LORD" (v. 6) who has marvelously revealed His power to come to the aid of the weak. Because He is the great Creator of heaven and earth, He is also quite competent to sustain His creation and to hear the helpless cries of His creatures.

David ends his song with a simple declaration of faith. I return to my own original question: "What in the world can give me hope and help?" Maybe that's just it! True intervention and help don't exist "in the world." David's overwhelmingly satisfying answer is good enough for me: "My help is in the name of the LORD, the Maker of heaven and earth" (v. 8). I claim that promise!

340

■ **Personal prayer** *May I place complete confidence in Your ability to help me today, O Lord, whatever I may be facing.*

Hymn of Trust   Security

■ **Theme**   *Those who trust in the* LORD *are like Mount Zion, which cannot be shaken but endures forever. As the mountains surround Jerusalem, so the* LORD *surrounds his people both now and forever more. The scepter of the wicked will not remain over the land allotted to the righteous, for then the righteous might use their hands to do evil (vv. 1–3).*

■ **Development**   This is a beautiful hymn about the inner security of believers—both in the time of David and for today.

The nation Israel is in grave danger of being dominated by foreign powers, but the Lord promises His people that He will not allow this scepter of wickedness to remain over them as long as they place their trust in Him (v. 3). A New Testament quotation comes to mind: "God is faithful; he will not let you be tempted beyond what you can bear. But when you are tempted, he will also provide a way out so that you can stand up under it" (1 Corinthians 10:13).

If Israel will just trust in the Lord, they will be blessed with a deep sense of inner security and unshakability. They will be like Mount Zion which is solid and immovable. They will be like a mountain rooted deeply in the bedrock of the earth. The Lord's protective care will encircle them at all times like the mountains surrounding Jerusalem. He will be for them an impregnable wall of defense.

My sense of security cannot be based on quality in human relationships or the relative stability of life's circumstances. It must rest squarely on the Lord Himself who is immutable and unchanging. He is my mountain! I must believe that, apart from the irrationality of my feelings. Then I will be secure . . . whether I feel like it or not!

■ **Personal prayer**   *I thank You, Lord, that my security is like Mount Zion, unshakable and deeply embedded in Your attributes.*

November

I always wanted to please my dad—
to perform well in recital, to achieve
so that he would be proud of me.

Hymn of Trust
Prayer for Personal Integrity

■ **Theme**   Do good, O LORD, to those who are good, to those who are
upright in heart. But those who turn to crooked ways the LORD will banish
with the evildoers. Peace be upon Israel (vv. 4–5).

■ **Development**   Here the psalmist contrasts the "upright" (straight-
as-an-arrow, honest, unswerving in principle) with the "crooked"
(bent, devious, dishonest, untrue). God calls me to "be real" in my
relationship with Him. He expects me to stay true and not to deviate
from the course He has assigned me. Genuine godliness will be
blessed, while those who "bend" His rules will be "banished with the
evildoers" (v. 5).

I struggle to remain perfectly true to my calling as a Christian
musician in a world that loves artificiality and pretense—"a good
show." But the applause of the crowd, while sweet to the ear, is short-
lived. On the other hand, God's reward for arrow-straight, true-pitch
living is eternal life in His presence and His "Well done!"

> To be what You want me to be, dear Lord,
>   I'll live for eternity;
> To be more like Your Son, dear Lord—
>   I've only just begun
>
> To be what You want me to be, dear Lord,
>   I'll live for eternity;
> To be more like Your Son, dear Lord,
>   Until the race is won.

Words and music by Don Wyrtzen.
© 1972 by Singspiration Music.

344

■ **Personal prayer**   Give me a vision of You, Lord—unshakable,
unchangeable, and secure. Keep me true and straight!

A Brief Jubilate   Joy and Restoration

■ **Theme**   When the LORD brought back the captives to Zion, we were like men who dreamed. Our mouths were filled with laughter, our tongues with songs of joy. Then it was said among the nations, "The LORD has done great things for them." The LORD has done great things for us, and we are filled with joy (vv. 1–3).

■ **Development**   Anyone who has ever experienced the loss of a loved one, financial reverses, serious illness, or imprisonment of any kind will treasure this psalm. The first few verses vibrate with the sheer joy of deliverance after long years of burden-bearing and captivity!

Most likely, the psalmist is referring to the time immediately after the return of the nation Israel from its exile in Babylon (537 B.C.). Happiness and exuberance reign supreme. God's people probably have to pinch themselves to believe they are really free! Laughter comes easily. Jubilant shouting is heard often. The Israelites release their pent-up feelings in a flood of healing, restorative praise.

The Gentile outsiders looking on say in amazement, "The LORD has done great things for them!" (v. 2). No nation has ever been restored after deportation. It is as incomprehensible to these ancient people as it would be if the Soviet Union suddenly decided to release all their political prisoners!

It is this euphoric sensation of delight and joy that should seize me every time I meditate on all the great things the Lord has done for me. If I spent more time dwelling on God's major triads—"the great things"—there would be less time for the minor irritations and frustrations of life!

■ **Personal prayer**   Remind me, O Lord, of the major triumphs You have accomplished in my behalf—my salvation, my eternal security, my constant protection—and don't let my song lapse into a minor mode!

A Brief Jubilate
Hope and Full Deliverance

■ **Theme** *Restore our fortunes, O* LORD, *like streams in the Negev. Those who sow in tears will reap with songs of joy. He who goes out weeping, carrying seed to sow, will return with songs of joy, carrying sheaves with him (vv. 4–6).*

■ **Development** Unless you know something of the topography of Israel, you can't fully understand the faith demonstrated by the psalmist in this prayer.

The Negev—the desert south of Judah—contains many "wadis" that are bone-dry eleven months of the year. But in the twelfth month, during the rainy season, these dry stream beds quickly fill with water and become raging torrents. This psalm cries out for that kind of dramatic change in the history of Israel as the captives flow back to their native land.

The second metaphor is equally graphic. Before irrigation, sowing and reaping in this barren part of the world were extremely difficult. Seed was often sown with little prospect of harvest. Yet the ancient musician believes that God will send life-giving rains and, even after long neglect, that the desert will bloom once more. The weeping sowers will return "with songs of joy" to greet the returning captives.

What a comfort to know that the Lord can take my dried-up, unproductive life and drench it with His showers of blessing! All the self-improvement courses and how-to books in the world combined with herculean human effort cannot begin to match the incomparable grace and mercy of God!

■ **Personal prayer** *Lord, change the dry, barren riverbeds of my life into raging streams in the desert.*

Solomon's Pilgrim Psalm
Futility of Work Apart from God

■ **Theme**   *Unless the* LORD *builds the house, its builders labor in vain. Unless the* LORD *watches over the city, the watchmen stand guard in vain. In vain you rise early and stay up late, toiling for food to eat—for he grants sleep to those he loves (vv. 1–2).*

■ **Development**   Solomon, the wisest man who ever lived and one of the greatest kings of Israel, teaches us that it is useless to attempt anything without God's approval and blessing whether it be building a house, making a home, guarding a city, earning a living, or even trying to get a decent night's sleep!

There is a simple interdependence in all of life—a basic theme that underlies the complex movements of our daily existence. That theme is the sovereignty of God—the fact that as Number One in the universe, He has everything under His control.

A building contractor can erect a house, but whether he acknowledges it or not, he's dependent upon the Lord for the right weather conditions, raw materials for building supplies, and strength to build. A couple can get married and start a family, but unless they practice faith in the Lord, there is less than a 50 percent chance that their marriage will survive. An army can be mustered to defend cities and countries, but true peace comes only from God. Inspiration for worthwhile artistic achievement is God's gift. The ability to earn a living—both talent and drive as well as health and stamina—are His gifts. And even relief from one's labors—refreshing sleep—comes from the hand of a loving Father.

Diligence without divine blessing is an exercise in futility. For me to attempt anything without God's help is like trying to get my sailboat to tack by blowing into the sail. I have to wait for the breath of God!

■ **Personal prayer**   *Lord, I confess my utter dependence on You. Teach me to wait on inspiration from You in all my endeavors.*

Solomon's Pilgrim Psalm
Reward of Children Sent from God

■ **Theme**   *Sons are a heritage from the LORD, children a reward from him. Like arrows in the hands of a warrior are sons born in one's youth. Blessed is the man whose quiver is full of them. They will not be put to shame when they contend with their enemies in the gate (vv. 3–5).*

■ **Development**   Many young couples in our society seem to be content to remain childless. Their two-paycheck incomes buy a lot of convenience and a lot of "stuff." But few of them realize how children can enrich life by forcing us outside our self-centered routines. Few of them understand that children stretch our horizons and prompt us to higher goals. Few of them ever consider how lonely they'll be in old age. And almost nobody ever mentions the importance of bringing up godly children to build a dynamic Christian community that can impact our culture and civilization.

Part of the current erosion of the family is simply that children are undervalued. They are often viewed as excess baggage, an inconvenience. They seem to get in the way of career aspirations, creating pressure on the woman, robbing her of youth and beauty and sapping her energy. They are considered by some as more of a liability than an asset.

How different from the Hebrew point of view! Children were seen as "a heritage from the LORD," (v. 3), a reward, and tokens of His grace. Furthermore, the possibility of becoming the mother of the Messiah was the coveted goal of young Hebrew women.

To the Hebrew man, adult children were regarded as a means of defense—"arrows in the hands of a warrior" (v. 4) and support—"when they contend with their enemies in the gate" (v. 5). Cases were tried and business was transacted at the gates of the city, and if a man were to encounter difficulty, he could count on his grown sons to lend strength to his argument.

A few years ago I expressed my dreams for my own family in a prayer song entitled, "Bless Our Home."

348

■ **Personal prayer**   *Dear Lord, I thank You for D.J. and Kathy and for the love and support they give me.*

Bless Our Home

Bless our home with grace from above,
May we know the shelter of Your precious love.
Be the center of our family.
May You live with us in all Your majesty.

Fill each room with Christian love and cheer,
And the peace of knowing You are very near;
Bless with special joys that You provide,
May Your holy name be always glorified.
    Amen.

Words and music by Don Wyrtzen.
© 1986 by Singspiration Music.

Count Your Many Blessings
Present Blessings

■ **Theme** *Blessed are all who fear the* LORD, *who walk in his ways. You will eat the fruit of your labor; blessings and prosperity will be yours. Your wife will be like a fruitful vine within your house; your sons will be like olive shoots around your table. Thus is the man blessed who fears the* LORD *(vv. 1–4).*

■ **Development** "Blessed (supremely happy) is the person who has meaningful work and a fruitful family." This paraphrase of Psalm 128 reduces the abundant life to its simplest terms. Yet many in our contemporary society, including Christians, take such humble gifts for granted and expect more!

Solomon, in all of his brilliance and wisdom, takes us back to the basics. Fearing God (reverencing and obeying Him) will bring blessing, he states. Then he enumerates the gifts of grace that follow: food to sustain life, productive work, and family. The wife and mother is depicted as a "fruitful vine"; the children, little "olive shoots" (v. 3). This metaphor of a bountiful table is God's true picture of prosperity and happiness, not material wealth.

■ **Personal prayer** *Lord, help me to fear You and walk in Your way today. Give my wife and children a special touch of Your grace so they may bask in the happiness of Your presence with them.*

Count Your Many Blessings
Future Blessings

■ **Theme**   *May the LORD bless you from Zion all the days of your life; may you see the prosperity of Jerusalem, and may you live to see your children's children. Peace be upon Israel (vv. 5–8).*

■ **Development**   The psalmist moves now from individual happiness in the context of a single family to national prosperity within the context of the nation of Israel. He longs to see Jerusalem, the City of Zion, prospering and flourishing all the days of his life. From her, blessings will flow out to all nations on earth.

The young father pictured earlier in the psalm is now a grandfather, observing the blessings of the Lord falling on many generations. We make much of the sins of the fathers being visited on future generations, but fail to speak of the blessings of the righteous filtering down through the generations (vv. 3, 4, 6).

I remember well my paternal grandparents. They both died when I was seven years old. However, since they lived in our home during their latter years, they left an indelible impression of security and godliness.

The psalmist concludes with a lovely benediction: "Peace be upon Israel!" Thus, he expresses for all of us the deepest longing of our hearts—peace. Deep personal peace doesn't come from things. It flows from warm, intimate relationships and from a close walk with God.

■ **Personal prayer**   *Dear Lord, as we learn to walk more consistently by Your side, give us the peace that passes human understanding. If You don't come soon, may I live to hear my grandchildren singing Your praises!*

Opus of Oppression   Deliverance

■ **Theme**   *They have greatly oppressed me from my youth—let Israel say—they have greatly oppressed me from my youth, but they have not gained the victory over me. Plowmen have plowed my back and made their furrows long. But the LORD is righteous; he has cut me free from the cords of the wicked (vv. 1–4).*

■ **Development**   We desperately need to grapple with a theology of suffering. Many Christians are surprised and even shocked when they're called upon to experience any degree of pain. This leads to a feeling of displacement, dislocation, even disinheritance. We may be confused and feel a profound sense of injustice. We may feel that more was promised than was delivered. Our doubt, anger, and resentment may even shake the foundations of our faith.

This psalmist laments, in a kind of summary, all of the national disasters that have befallen his people and prays for the overthrow of their enemies. Israel has suffered indignity, ignominy, and hostility for generations. She has been besieged continuously by the Canaanites, the Aramaeans, the Ammonites, the Edomites, the Philistines, the Assyrians, and the Chaldeans. The psalmist remembers many such attacks from his youth, but he also recalls that the enemy has never prevailed against him for long.

The literary figure is gripping! Israel is pictured as a poor wretch lying face down on the ground as plowmen cut deep furrows in the tender flesh. This gives us some ideas of the extreme suffering and severe pain that was commonplace for that nation.

But the psalmist does not dwell on these inhumane acts. He praises the righteous Lord who has delivered his people. He has "cut them free from the cords of the wicked" (v. 4).

Perhaps we need to learn about adversity from ancient Israel. Perhaps we need to remember that suffering is part of being human in a fallen world, that ungodly people suffer too. And perhaps we need to remind ourselves that our God is a righteous God. Justice will ultimately prevail. He has promised victory and deliverance—if not immediately—then in the world to come!

352

■ **Personal prayer**   *I thank You, Lord, for Your righteousness. I pray that You will execute justice in my life and by Your mercy cut me free from the cords of wickedness.*

Opus of Oppression   Vindication

■ **Theme**   *May all who hate Zion be turned back in shame. May they be like grass on the roof, which withers before it can grow; with it the reaper cannot fill his hands, nor the one who gathers fill his arms. May those who pass by not say, "The blessing of the LORD be upon you; we bless you in the name of the LORD" (vv. 5–8).*

■ **Development**   Why does it seem as if the nonbelievers in this world get all the breaks and have all the fun? They live fast, hard, and, it appears, free!

But we can take great comfort in the promise of this psalm. No matter how it may seem, the wicked are doomed to failure. (See Psalm 37:1–2.) This psalmist has the big picture, and our confusion stems from our limited and cloudy vision.

Still, my ancient colleague covers all his bases and prays for the vindication of his people. He pictures the Israel-haters as tufts of grass on a Palestinian roof. They wither even before the owner has a chance to pluck them. They're not worth the time it takes to weed them out! He'll leave them to the blazing sun of God's wrath.

The psalm ends with a strong suggestion to fellow Israelites to withhold blessing from passersby on the street. It has always been customary in Israel to greet people by invoking God's blessing on their lives. In this case, the passionate musician/poet holds out for silence: "Don't say, 'The blessing of the LORD be upon you'" (v. 8).

When Karen and I visited Israel, the people often greeted us with a friendly "Shalom"—"Peace be unto you." They're still looking for the fulfillment of prophecy. Justice will prevail in the end, and Israel will be utterly and finally vindicated. It also follows that, if I am suffering unjustly, I can expect satisfaction from a just God. In the meantime, I need to concentrate on my Savior, whose suffering I will never be able to imagine or comprehend in this life.

■ **Personal prayer**   *I thank You, Lord, that You are the answer to all injustice and inhumanity in this world and that You are still in control. Help me to trust in the fulfillment of that prophecy just as my Israeli neighbors do.*

Motet of Mercy   Forgiveness

■ **Theme**   *Out of the depths I cry to you, O LORD; O Lord, hear my voice. Let your ears be attentive to my cry for mercy. If you, O LORD, kept a record of sins, O Lord, who could stand? But with you there is forgiveness; therefore you are feared (vv. 1–4).*

■ **Development**   When I think of God's accounting ability, I cringe, much like the author of this psalm. Suppose every unkind word I had ever spoken, every lie I had ever told, every shortcut I had ever taken, every word of gossip that ever passed my lips, every lustful thought I had ever entertained, every sin I've ever committed, were recorded on audio and videotape to be played back at will?

My fellow musician sums it up succinctly: "Who could stand?" (v. 3).

Though I am saved by grace, I am constantly engaged in a wrestling match between the old sinful nature and the new man. As the apostle Paul complained: "I know that nothing good lives in me, that is, in my sinful nature. For I have the desire to do what is good, but I cannot carry it out. For what I do is not the good I want to do; no, the evil I do not want to do—this I keep on doing" (Romans 7:18–19).

There is a way out, however. It's a one-word answer. Forgiveness. In His infinite mercy, God chooses to pardon the penitent sinner (Isaiah 55:6–7). If He did not, we would all be destroyed by His judgment. Because we have been forgiven much, we are able to respond in grateful praise. We will be moved to revere and respect Him, to worship and adore Him, to follow and obey Him!

■ **Personal prayer**   *I cry out of the depths to You for mercy, O Lord! I need Your forgiveness again and again.*

Motet of Mercy   Hope

■ **Theme**   I wait for the LORD, my soul waits, and in his word I put my hope. My soul waits for the Lord more than watchmen wait for the morning. . . . O Israel, put your hope in the LORD, for with the LORD is unfailing love and with him is full redemption. He himself will redeem Israel from all their sins (vv. 5–8).

■ **Development**   There are several musical terms for "pause" or "rest." Pauses in music, the cessation of sound, affect the flow of a piece and create variety and diversity. Delay, anticipation, build-up are all crucial in musical dynamics.

This pilgrim psalmist understands the value of patient waiting. Thoroughly familiar with the holy writings of the Old Testament prophets, he trusts the Lord for ultimate fulfillment of His promises— God's unfailing love and His full redemption. Lawrence Richards, in his work, *Expository Dictionary of Bible Words*, says, "It is striking to note that in all the Old Testament's exploration of the meaning of *padah* ("redeem or ransom"), only in Psalm 130:7–8 is this concept associated with redemption from sin." God's sovereign hand is not forced by human entreaties unless the time is right. He hears prayer, then acts according to His own schedule.

In ancient times watchmen were posted atop the broad gates of Jerusalem to sound the alert if signs of imminent danger were observed. The night watches were long and arduous. If the watchmen could make it until the first rays of the rising sun, they could rejoice in their security for yet another night. Waiting in darkness merely emphasized the glory of the sunrise!

As I wait in the darkness of uncertainty and human inadequacy, I rest in the fact of His sunrise that is surely coming . . . tomorrow!

355

■ **Personal prayer**   Lord, I'm waiting as patiently as I know how. And in the process of waiting, I find a blessing, for I am looking forward to Your glorious coming and to an eternity spent in Your presence!

Harmony of Humility

■ **Theme**   *My heart is not proud, O* LORD, *my eyes are not haughty; I do not concern myself with great matters or things too wonderful for me. But I have stilled and quieted my soul; like a weaned child with its mother, like a weaned child is my soul within me. O Israel, put your hope in the* LORD *both now and forevermore (vv. 1–3).*

■ **Development**   David's reign as Israel's greatest king was matched by his contributions to art and literature, including the most profound psalm lyrics ever written. While he extended Israel's borders to their limit, made Jerusalem the capital city, and founded an eternal dynasty of which our Lord, the Messiah, descended, he was also a virtuoso harpist and led a sweeping renaissance of Israeli culture. He accomplished this through building instruments, teaching music, and composing the temple liturgy.

With all his worldly "success," David was a humble man with a childlike faith in God. His soul was still and quiet (v. 2) because he was not neurotically driven by selfish ambition. He wrote: "He makes me lie down in green pastures, he leads me beside quiet waters" (Psalm 23:2). As a weaned child no longer needs its mother's milk, he learned to receive his nurture from the Lord: "You prepare a table before me" (Psalm 23:5). His value system was founded on God's eternal principles, not on ego-driven materialism.

The Bible stresses humility. To the humble, God gives salvation (Psalm 18:27), sustenance (147:6), and grace (Proverbs 3:34). The Lord hates arrogance and pride, which result in overwhelming self-confidence and insensitivity to others. This attitude is self-destructive. David is the consummate model of a creative artist and successful entrepreneur who didn't let his notoriety and fame go to his head. Trusting in the Lord is the opposite of pride and the only route to deeply satisfying human fulfillment.

■ **Personal prayer**   *O Lord, "lead me beside quiet waters" and give me rest from my obsessive behavior. I'm tired of the pressure I impose on myself. Help me to trust in You today for everything I need.*

Recitative of Remembrance
Remembering David

■ **Theme** O LORD, *remember David and all the hardships he endured. He swore an oath to the LORD and made a vow to the Mighty One of Jacob: "I will not enter my house or go to my bed—I will allow no sleep to my eyes, no slumber to my eyelids, till I find a place for the LORD, a dwelling for the Mighty One of Jacob"* (vv. 1–5).

■ **Development** It is impossible to overestimate the contribution made by Bill and Gloria Gaither to the gospel music field. Bill's down-to-earth wisdom, combined with Gloria's reflective lyricism, has produced some of our best contemporary songs and hymns—"Because He Lives," "Something Beautiful," "There's Something About That Name," "The Family of God," "Let's Just Praise the Lord," and hundreds more. I love the passion they bring to their work. Bill has been a friend, advisor, and encourager to me.

David was such a leader, and this psalm celebrates his devotion to the nation he served and the Lord he worshiped. The nation had been restored from exile in Babylon, and its people were keenly aware of David's legacy.

He evidenced his commitment by swearing an oath that he would not rest until he found a place of worship in which the Lord could dwell. This oath most likely referred to David's intense desire to build the temple (2 Samuel 7). So fervent was this desire that he vowed neither to enter his house nor to sleep until his mission was accomplished (vv. 3–5). Because of this single-minded devotion, God made a covenant (contract) with David. This covenant, with future implications, was extremely significant, particularly during the leadership of Ezra and Nehemiah.

What a mentor David is to me! His commitment to the Lord resulted in concrete action. David was much more than a sentimental, romantic leader; he was serious and committed, and God dealt with him accordingly. What a crying need there is for leaders like this today!

357

■ **Personal prayer** O Lord, *deepen my commitment and conviction. I want to be deadly serious about Your business and my relationship with You.*

Recitative of Remembrance
Resolving to worship

■ **Theme** *We heard it in Ephrathah, we came upon it in the fields of Jaar: "Let us go to his dwelling place; let us worship at his footstool—arise O LORD, and come to your resting place, you and the ark of your might. May your priests be clothed with righteousness; may your saints sing for joy." For the sake of David your servant, do not reject your anointed one (vv. 6–10).*

■ **Development** Ephrathah? Jaar? What are these places with the strange-sounding names? They were towns where the ark (covenant box) rested in limbo until David moved it to Zion (2 Samuel 6). Ephrathah was an old name for Bethlehem, where our Lord was born. Jaar was also known as Kiriath Jearim—the "city of forests," one of the four leading cities of the Gibeonites (Joshua 9:17).

The ark was God's earthly dwelling—His footstool, in the sense that it was His earthly throne. Because it symbolized the awesome presence of God, the ark often went ahead of the Israeli army in battle.

The people are praying that God will reveal Himself again to them, that their priests will be "clothed with salvation," and that their saints will "sing for joy" (v. 16). The prayer concludes with a petition that David, the "anointed one," will not be rejected. The word *anointed* in Hebrew is *masiah* which is transliterated "Messiah, anointed one." Appearing only thirty-nine times in the Old Testament, this word is often a synonym for "royal office." It is used especially to identify the royal line of David (Psalms 2:2; 18:50; 24:9; 29:10; 132:10, 17).

These early saints were serious about their faith. Prayer and praise were not perfunctory, for worship was a priority in their lives. How human it is to take God for granted! Praise the Lord for the passionate leadership of King David!

■ **Personal prayer** *Clothe me with righteousness today, O Lord, that I may sing for joy!*

Recitative of Righteousness
Reiterating the Lord's Oath

■ **Theme** *The LORD swore an oath to David, a sure oath that he will not revoke: "One of your own descendants I will place on your throne—if your sons keep my covenant and the statutes I teach them, then their sons will sit on your throne for ever and ever." For the LORD has chosen Zion, he has desired it for his dwelling: "This is my resting place for ever and ever; here I will sit enthroned, for I have desired it—I will bless her with abundant provisions; her poor will I satisfy with food. I will clothe her priests with salvation, and her saints will ever sing for joy. "Here I will make a horn grow for David and set up a lamp for my anointed one. I will clothe his enemies with shame, but the crown on his head will be resplendent" (vv. 11–18).*

■ **Development** This psalm confirms that God's promises will be fulfilled no matter what the circumstances. God has made specific promises to King David about his dynasty—promises regarding the sanctuary and Mount Zion which would be blessed with food for the poor, salvation for the priests, and joy for the saints (vv. 15–16). Under David's reign the tiny land expanded ten times over, became a powerful nation, and occupied almost all the land God had promised to Abraham.

The "burning lamp" symbolizes the continuation of David's dynasty, which would come to a glorious culmination in David's greatest Son, the Messiah. The metaphor for the Messiah is the animal horn, an ancient symbol of strength and vigor. This horn, or powerful ruler, would sprout and flourish. In moving poetry the Lord reiterates His oath to David: From his line would come the Messiah, David's descendant and the Coming One, the ultimate Priest and King of Israel! David was God's prototype of the Messiah, His Son.

Whatever my circumstances right now, I can rest in the fact that God fulfills His promises. His covenant is solid and sure. His program is moving along right on schedule. Just as He blessed David, He is about to touch my life in a unique way.

359

■ **Personal prayer** *May I rest in the surety and certainty of Your promises today, O Lord.*

The Beauty of Unity

■ **Theme**   *How good and pleasant it is when brothers live together in unity! It is like precious oil poured on the head, running down on the beard, running down on Aaron's beard, down upon the collar of his robes. It is as if the dew of Hermon were falling on Mount Zion. For there the* LORD *bestows his blessing, even life forevermore (vv. 1–3).*

■ **Development**   When Israel celebrated her great religious festivals, families came together to worship the Lord. These "homecomings" were accompanied by colorful pageantry and moving music.

Last June we had a Wyrtzen family reunion. My sister Mary-Ann and her husband, Dave Cox, are the founders and directors of the Word of Life Seminary in Brazil. My sister Betsy teaches at Mountainside Christian Academy in Schroon Lake, N.Y. My brother David, with his wife Mary, pastors the Midlothian Bible Church in Texas. My brother Ron is a Christian businessman who sells precision ski boats. His wife, Christine, is a prominent recording artist. My mom went to be with the Lord a few years ago, but He provided a wonderful new wife for Dad. He and Joan are busy serving the Lord as the founder and first lady of Word of Life International. Each one unique, yet with a common bond of love and unity.

In this passage David agrees that it is "good and pleasant" when believers live in unity. He uses two striking word pictures to illustrate this idea: The oil of anointing ran down Aaron's beard and onto his breastplate. So also, the unity of worshipers in Jerusalem will consecrate the nation. Heavy mountain dew from the north fell on Zion, invigorating and nourishing the vegetation. So also, meaningful worship blesses the nation.

I need this reminder of the importance of family and community. In the press of publishing deadlines and concert commitments, I tend to lose touch with family members and even with the local church support group of believers. Strong, creative leaders need to feel part of a caring fellowship.

■ **Personal prayer**   *O Lord, someday we will all come together for a great Family Reunion. Teach me that I belong to the greater family of God, and make me accountable for keeping up family ties!*

Benediction to the Pilgrim Psalms

■ **Theme**   Praise the LORD, all you servants of the LORD who minister by night in the house of the LORD. Lift up your hands in the sanctuary and praise the LORD. May the LORD, the Maker of heaven and earth, bless you from Zion (vv. 1–3).

■ **Development**   I'm intrigued by the relationship between the act of leading people in worship and the boon of personal blessing spelled out in this psalm. This unusual benediction, given by the congregation to their leaders, exhorts the priests and Levites to keep up the good work!

These ministers are encouraged to continue their personal times of devotion in order to undergird their public ministry. Leaders who have to bear heavy burdens for others day and night (v. 1) are especially vulnerable to attacks from the Enemy. When they are physically and emotionally exhausted, their spiritual guard is down. It is imperative, then, that they be lifted up in prayer by members of their congregation, just as Aaron and Hur lifted up Moses' hands during the long hours of the battle with the Amalekites (Exodus 17:8–16).

The final words of this psalm flow like a soothing balm across troubled and tired spirits: "May the LORD, the Maker of heaven and earth, bless you from Zion" (v. 3). Our Lord, not the lifeless pagan gods of the ancient world—such as the Canaanite god, Baal—created the universe and can certainly strengthen His faithful representatives.

I am deeply touched by the significance of this psalm for my own life and work. First, I'm reminded that the effectiveness of my public ministry is dependent, to a great degree, upon keeping a vital and dynamic personal relationship with the Lord. I also have a number of close friends who regularly and faithfully pray for me (Nelson, Bill, Mrs. Meurlin), and a corps of choir members and church musicians who remember to pray for me when they see my name on a piece of music. I have no way of knowing what my life would be without this consistent, loving care and support!

361

■ **Personal prayer**   O Lord, thank You for the intercessory prayer of Christian friends. I am blessed, both by serving You and by the encouragement and concern of those who act as a link for refueling my tired spirit.

A Musical Mosaic
A Litany of Praise

■ **Theme**   Praise the LORD. Praise the name of the LORD; Praise him, you
servants of the Lord, you who minister in the house of the LORD, in the
courts of the house of our God. Praise the LORD, for the LORD is good; sing
praise to his name, for that is pleasant . . . O house of Israel, praise the
LORD; O house of Aaron, praise the LORD; O house of Levi, praise the
LORD; you who fear him, praise the LORD. Praise be to the LORD from Zion,
to him who dwells in Jerusalem. Praise the LORD (vv. 1–3, 19–21).

■ **Development**   Because this psalm is a compilation of quotations
from other Old Testament sources, the form is a musical mosaic of
praise based on the Law, the Prophets, and the Psalms.

How does a busy musician, husband, and father find time for
praise? I am not always physically present in the "house of the Lord,"
but somewhere in transit—torn between the roles I'm called to play.
But I can make praise a priority, spending those precious moments
meditating on God's goodness, greatness, and faithfulness—wherever
I am.

Having a daily quiet time with the Lord is vital. I've used many
different approaches over the years—reading the Bible through in one
year, reading five Psalms a day plus one chapter from Proverbs,
studying a book of the Bible in depth, or reading the Word aloud. A
special blessing comes when I read the Bible and pray with Karen.

No one is exempt from the roll call of the faithful. The houses of
Israel, Aaron, and Levi (vv. 19–20) include all who fear and
reverence the Lord. We are called to praise Him in the house where
He dwells—Jerusalem (Zion), for the ancient worshiper; our individual local churches, for the contemporary saint.

Praise is easy for a musician, you say, but what about the person
who's tone-deaf or can't carry a tune? Try singing along with a
Christian artist on cassette tape. Write down your thoughts about the
Lord, then share them with a friend.

A faithful heart, an earnest desire to please the Lord, a life
362 dedicated to His glory—these are the most eloquent songs of praise!

■ **Personal prayer**   I join with my ancient Levite brothers, Lord, in
praising Your name for Your goodness and faithfulness.

A Musical Mosaic
Longing to Praise

■ **Theme**   For the LORD has chosen Jacob to be his own, Israel to be his treasured possession. I know that the LORD is great, that our LORD is greater than all gods. The LORD does whatever pleases him, in the heavens and on the earth, in the seas and all their depths. He makes clouds rise from the ends of the earth; he sends lightning with the rain and brings out the wind from his storehouses. . . . Your name, O LORD, endures forever, your renown, O LORD, through all generations. For the LORD will vindicate his people and have compassion on his servants (vv. 4–7, 13–14).

■ **Development**   My dad, Jack Wyrtzen, has had an aura of authority about him for as long as I can remember. A man of unusual strength and energy, he founded Word of Life International from scratch. He now ministers in camps, Bible institutes, clubs, concerts, rallies, and through media all over the world.

As you might imagine, his presence has been strongly felt in our home. I always wanted to please him—to be the best I could be, to perform well in recital, to speak and teach effectively, to achieve so that he would be proud of me. His image in my concept of reality has profoundly affected my view of God, the transcendent Sovereign of the universe!

The motive behind the praise in this psalm is the sovereignty of God, who chose Israel as his "treasured possession" (v. 4), demonstrated His superiority over pagan deities (v. 5), and still orchestrates all the events of Israel's history—past, present, and future (vv. 8–13).

Knowing that God never changes and that He is as concerned with the daily agenda of Don Wyrtzen as with the affairs of mankind, I am moved to write songs of praise.

■ **Personal prayer**   Lord, I acknowledge You as Sovereign—my complete and ultimate authority. I long to please You in everything I think or do.

Our God Is in Control

Our God is in control,
Though pressures burden the soul;
He allows both major and minor
In His perfect harmony.

Yes, our God is in control,
Though pressures burden the soul;
His sovereign plan is a symphony
Which will sing for eternity.

As we place our faith in the Lord,
Our worry will decrease;
And when we delight ourselves with His Word,
We sense His perfect peace.

Words and music by Don Wyrtzen.
© 1976 by Singspiration Music.

A Musical Mosaic   Legacy of Praise

■ **Theme**   *He struck down the firstborn of Egypt, the firstborn of men and animals. He sent his signs and wonders into your midst, O Egypt, against Pharaoh and all his servants. He struck down many nations and killed mighty kings—Sihon king of the Amorites, Og, king of Bashan and all the kings of Canaan—and he gave their land as an inheritance, an inheritance to his people Israel (vv. 8–12).*

■ **Development**   Two Hebrew words are linked to the concept of inheritance—*yaras*, which means "to become an heir" or "to take possession," and *nahal*, which indicates "giving or receiving property." The Lord promised an unbelievable inheritance to Israel, and modern Israel's expansion is motivated by a strong belief in this ancient right. So far, Karen and I haven't lived long enough to inherit property, possessions, or money from parents or other relatives, so we have to use our imagination to grasp this.

But a forty-acre farm or $100,000 in bonds could never be compared to the inheritance of Israel. God's people would inherit "many nations" (v. 10)! And the legacy lives on, to be fulfilled only when the Lord returns to reign in the New Jerusalem!

Again, the historical events surrounding Israel's inheritance are catalogued—the "signs and wonders" God sent against the Egyptians, culminating in the killing of their firstborn (v. 8); God's leadership in the occupation of Canaan, including His divine intervention in the overthrow of heathen kings (vv. 11–12).

I share in this legacy of love and praise. I've been delivered from sin and have received God's gift of grace. I've felt His work in my life as He overthrows bastions of fear, insecurity, and depression. I've known the joy of walking in green pastures with my Lord. I've sensed His breath on my soul and have been inspired to compose songs and musicals to His glory. And someday I'll enter into the promised rest of Israel to enjoy Him forever!

■ **Personal prayer**   *Lord, as You performed signs and wonders in Israel, please work supernaturally in my life and bless me with Your inheritance of peace.*

Antiphonal Psalm of Love
Introit: Calling the Congregation to Praise

■ **Theme**   *Give thanks to the* LORD, *for he is good.* His love endures forever. *Give thanks to the God of gods.* His love endures forever. *Give thanks to the Lord of lords:* His love endures forever. . . . *Give thanks to the God of heaven.* His love endures forever (*vv. 1–3, 26*).

■ **Development**   In this marvelous antiphonal psalm, which was used in worship by ancient Israelis, one part of the congregation sang the theme and the other responded with the refrain. Twenty-six times the refrain—"His love endures forever"—is repeated. Today we would call this a "hook," the big idea, the major thesis, the central concept.

Because this was a favorite festival song and because its theme was predominant in the Old Testament, this psalm is often called "The Great Hallel."

In the first few verses the psalmist commands his listeners to praise the Lord by giving thanks. Basic to this thanksgiving is the awareness and conviction of the Lord's goodness. Because He is good, His loyal love continues forever. He is eternally bound to His people by virtue of His solemn covenant (contract) with them. And who is behind this covenant, the very nature of which is loyal love? "The God of gods" (v. 2). "The Lord of lords" (v. 3).

The original summons is restated in verse 26. "Give thanks to the God of heaven. His love endures forever." This is the only time in the Psalms where God is referred to as the "God of heaven," though Ezra and Nehemiah pick up the phrase in later writings. (See Ezra 1:2 and Nehemiah 1:4).

When I'm tempted to revel in self-revulsion, self-pity, feelings of worthlessness and despair, I need to remember that God loves me with a loyal love that will endure forever! This is the only strong, adequate basis for any positive feelings about oneself.

■ **Personal prayer**   *O Lord, I give thanks for Your goodness and for Your loyal love which stands forever firm, no matter how weak and indecisive I may be.*

Antiphonal Psalm of Love
Service of Praise: Praising the Lord for Creation

■ **Theme**   *To him who alone does great wonders,* His love endures forever. *who by his understanding made the heavens,* His love endures forever. *who spread out the earth upon the waters,* His love endures forever. *who made the great lights*—His love endures forever. *the sun to govern the day,* His love endures forever. *the moon and stars to govern the night;* His love endures forever *(vv. 4–9).*

■ **Development**   Preoccupied with business as usual, I have the tendency to sleepwalk through life, ignoring the beauties of creation around me. Television and films can dim our sight to a real visual experience, just as Muzak can jade our hearing so we don't really hear good music. Or I concentrate on biblical truth, while failing to observe God's testimony in nature. I believe it's possible to be too serious, too scholarly, too cognitive. Perhaps that's why so few people produce great art!

The psalmist is strongly motivated to give thanks because of his keen observation of God's magnificent creation. He alone "does great wonders" (v. 4). Mere man cannot even begin to fathom the genius and power necessary to fashion the heavens.

In poetic form the psalmist enumerates the splendors of nature—the land, the waters, the dazzling stars and planets—spread out like a diamond necklace against a black velvet curtain. All of these represent gifts of grace that contribute to our equanimity and well-being. Each one gives unique testimony to the eternally enduring love of God. We live in an ultimately benign cosmos, not a hostile universe, and behind it all is the unfathomable love of God.

Surprised by the full circle of a rainbow or the breathtaking sight of the aurora borealis, the great "northern lights," I am moved to praise. "His love endures forever!"

■ **Personal prayer**   *Lord, I thank You for the astonishing beauty of Your creation. Make me more aware of my surroundings as I brush against Your brilliant designs and help me to hear this silent song of Your love!*

Antiphonal Psalm of Love

Service of Praise: Thanking the Lord for His Acts in History

■ **Theme**   To him who struck down the firstborn of Egypt

> His love endures forever.

and brought Israel out from among them

> His love endures forever.

with a mighty hand and outstretched arm;

> His love endures forever.

to him who divided the Red Sea asunder

> His love endures forever.

and brought Israel through the midst of it,

> His love endures forever.

but swept Pharaoh and his army into the Red Sea;

> His love endures forever.

to him who led his people through the desert,

> His love endures forever.

. . . and gave their land as an inheritance,

> His love endures forever.

an inheritance to his servant Israel;

> His love endures forever.

to the One who remembered us in our low estate

> His love endures forever.

and freed us from our enemies,

> His love endures forever.

and who gives food to every creature.

> His love endures forever.

Give thanks to the God of heaven.

> His love endures forever.

(vv. 10–16, 21–26)

■ **Development**   God's loyal, enduring love extends to this century and to you and me on this special day. What greater cause for giving thanks?

■ **Personal prayer**   *O Lord, thank You for the thread of Your love in the tapestry of human history. Along with my ancient Israeli brother, I praise You today!*

Songs of Zion in a Strange Land
Weeping over Jerusalem

■ **Theme**   *By the rivers of Babylon we sat and wept when we remembered Zion. There on the poplars we hung our harps, for there our captors asked us for songs, our tormentors demanded songs of joy; they said, "Sing us one of the songs of Zion!" How can we sing the songs of the LORD while in a foreign land? If I forget you, O Jerusalem, may my right hand forget its skill. May my tongue cling to the roof of my mouth if I do not remember you, if I do not consider Jerusalem my highest joy (vv. 1–6).*

■ **Development**   Sometimes crying is more appropriate than singing. I find myself at times looking back with longing to the days when I was growing up on Word of Life Island, where we spent wonderful summers. Or the days when I was in public school in Maplewood, New Jersey. Or the beautiful high school campus of Hampden DeBose Academy in Zellwood, Florida. I can identify with these homesick Israelites.

The people of God are homesick for their beloved homeland. Captive in Babylon, hundreds of miles from Jerusalem, they lament the loss of their freedom. Even the tough Israeli spirit—known for its fervor and fire—is quenched, and all they can do is weep. They have been deeply hurt by slavery and oppression.

When their captors demand entertainment—"one of the songs of Zion"—they refuse and hang their harps on the poplar trees "by the rivers of Babylon" (vv. 1–3). Instead, the psalmist reminisces about Jerusalem. He vows to consider Jerusalem his "highest joy" (v. 6). Remembering will keep his zeal fresh.

This psalmist, like other musicians who despair over lost opportunities, is open to a deep work of God in his life. When the Lord restores His glory to Zion, there will be singing and dancing! But that will come later. Because God is good, the future will be good if we walk with Him!

■ **Personal prayer**   *O Lord, do an exciting and colorful work in my life also, and may I burst out in creative worship of Your mighty name and awesome power!*

Songs of Zion
in a Strange Land
Judging Israel's Captors

■ **Theme**   Remember, O LORD, what the Edomites did on the day Jerusalem fell. "Tear it down," they cried, "tear it down to its foundations!" O Daughter of Babylon, doomed to destruction, happy is he who repays you for what you have done to us—he who seizes your infants and dashes them against the rocks (vv. 7–9).

■ **Development**   The Jews have never been reticent about expressing anger. These verses reflect their deep mourning while in exile as they cry out to the God of justice to repay their enemies for cruel and barbaric treatment.

The Edomites are singled out first. These pagan people celebrated while Jerusalem was destroyed. (See Ezekiel 25:12–14 and Joel 3:19.) The Babylonians, guilty of a brutality that almost defies description, are next. Deep sadness and bitterness are poured out against these heathen oppressors who had smashed the Israelite children "against the rocks" (v. 9)! The victimized Israelites are demanding that God do the same to their enemies' children!

What do we have here? Certainly not the "turn the other cheek" ethic of the New Testament.

There is an honest facing up to the cold reality of violence and raw evil in the world. Apart from God's grace and His redemptive power in the human heart, people are capable of exacting terrible atrocities against their neighbors! Yet this psalm is, no doubt, a poetic catharsis. Pouring out bitterness and hurt can be the beginning of healing; pretending the hurt doesn't exist leads only to mental and physical illness.

I'm grateful for the honesty and candor of this ancient psalmist, but even more grateful for the New Testament revelation that there is forgiveness for me as well as for those who have wronged me!

■ **Personal prayer**   Lord, help me to acknowledge the deep inner pain in my life. I claim Your forgiveness and grace for my life today.

David's Vow of Praise
Praise for Boldness

■ **Theme**   *I will praise you, O LORD, with all my heart; before the "gods" I will sing your praise. I will bow down toward your holy temple and will praise your name for your love and your faithfulness, for you have exalted above all things your name and your word. When I called, you answered me; and you made me bold and stouthearted. May all the kings of the earth praise you, O LORD, when they hear the words of your mouth. May they sing of the ways of the LORD, for the glory of the LORD is great (vv. 1–5).*

■ **Development**   King David had a full-hearted faith which he expressed uniquely and creatively. In these deeply satisfying verses, David praises the Lord *before the gods of the pagans!*

Dr. Elton Trueblood, in his book, *Alternative to Futility,* says, "The basic defect of the Protestant churches lies not in their divided condition but in their insipidity. They show so little imagination. The same kind of dull and lifeless service is repeated endlessly, whatever the occasion. We are in a time of crisis when we need a dynamic fellowship to turn the world upside down. What we are offered is a stereotype. A man, having become convinced that we are in a race with catastrophe, may seek the very bread of life, but in practice he is forced to sing sentimental songs with words he does not mean, listen to some comforting platitudes, and finally shake the minister's hand at the door, because there is no other way to escape! In short, this kind of church illustrates Professor Whitehead's dictum perfectly. 'It is in full decay because it lacks the element of adventure.'"

We need "adventurous fellowship." Like David, we need to take our stand boldly "before the gods," declaring our faith and singing praise to the Lord!

■ **Personal prayer**   *I long to praise You, Lord, wholeheartedly, courageously, and creatively. As I bow before You, inspire me with songs of praise and worship.*

David's Vow of Praise
Prayer for Fulfillment

■ **Theme** *Though the LORD is on high, he looks upon the lowly, but the proud he knows from afar. Though I walk in the midst of trouble, you preserve my life; you stretch out your hand against the anger of my foes, with your right hand you save me. The LORD will fulfill his purpose for me; your love, O LORD, endures forever—do not abandon the works of your hands (vv. 6–8).*

■ **Development** I have long been intrigued with the idea of knowing God's will and have opened myself to His loving guidance and direction. He has led me specifically by His Word and His Spirit, and it is comforting to know that He cares more about my character than about my performance.

God is gradually teaching me about reality and values as well. Because I believe He desires intimacy with me, I pray about every detail of my life. Sometimes He uses friends, circumstances, even books to point me in the right direction. And because I have a passion for music and communication, He allows me to be involved in creative projects for His glory and honor.

I understand David's plea for fulfillment in this psalm. From the description of his boyhood, it is obvious that David had talent and quickly became proficient. He was a skillful harpist. (The Hebrew roots for *skill* and *wisdom* are the same!) He was a passionate lyricist, responsible for at least half of the Psalter. He was a man favored by God who "preserved" his life and gave it "purpose."

As one who is prone to melancholy, the last part of this passage comforts and encourages me: "The LORD will fulfill his purpose for me!" (v. 8). He designed me. He brought me into being. He is with me. He hasn't forgotten me. He hasn't overlooked me in the grand scheme of things. My life has a divine purpose and goal. I can stand with the apostle Paul and say, "Being confident of this, that he who began a good work in you will carry it on to completion until the day of Christ Jesus" (Philippians 1:6). What a promise!

372

■ **Personal prayer** *Thank You, Lord, for promising to fulfill Your purpose for my life! I believe it and claim it!*

Symphony of God's Attributes

First Movement: He Knows Everything (Omniscience)

■ **Theme**   *O LORD, you have searched me and you know me. You know when I sit and when I rise; you perceive my thoughts from afar. You discern my going out and my lying down; you are familiar with all my ways. Before a word is on my tongue you know it completely, O LORD. You hem me in— behind and before; you have laid your hand upon me. Such knowledge is too wonderful for me, too lofty for me to attain (vv. 1–6).*

■ **Development**   This magnificent psalm opens with a frightening assertion of God's omniscience. Omniscience is a lofty theological term which means that God knows everything—everything actual and everything possible. In fact, His knowledge covers both the realms of reality and the imagination.

God knew David inside out (v. 1). He knew what time he got up in the morning and what time he went to bed at night (vv. 2–3). He even knew David's thoughts before he framed them into words (v. 4).

The New Testament confirms this attribute of God. "He [Jesus] did not need man's testimony about man, for he knew what was in a man" (John 2:25). This is terrifying news to the one whose mind is riddled with sinful thoughts and who acts on those impulses.

But to the person who understands God's unconditional love and acceptance, His omniscience is good news! Gloria Gaither's profound phrase sums it up so well: "For the one who knows me best, loves me most." This maximum exposure of my personality, combined with my Lord's total acceptance of me, boggles my mind. It is also what makes the gospel so unbelievably thrilling!

373

■ **Personal prayer**   *Lord, you know everything about me, yet You love me anyway!*

Symphony of God's Attributes

Second Movement: He is Everywhere (Omnipresence)

■ **Theme**   *Where can I go from your Spirit? Where can I flee from your presence? If I go up to the heavens, you are there; if I make my bed in the depths, you are there. If I rise on the wings of the dawn, if I settle on the far side of the sea, even there your hand will guide me, your right hand will hold me fast. If I say, "Surely the darkness will hide me and the light become night around me," even the darkness will not be dark to you; the night will shine like the day, for darkness is as light to you (vv. 7–12).*

■ **Development**   Upon learning that God knows the worst about him, David's first impulse is to run! Fallen, sinful humanity always attempts to flee from the presence of the absolute holiness of God. But there is no place to hide, for God is everywhere! He's omnipresent!

God is everywhere, but He is not *in* everything. That's pantheism. He is infinite and personal, but He is self-contained and separate from His creation. Nothing escapes His notice.

The comforting thought is that, if He is everywhere, He is also immediately accessible! I can make contact with Him immediately and instantly. He is right here! Distance between God and me is created not by His initiative, but by my sin and guilt. Where God is, there can be no evil. Light and darkness do not coexist at the same place at the same time.

Martin Luther once said, "Music is one of the greatest gifts that God has given us: it is divine and, therefore, Satan is its enemy. For with its aid many dire temptations are overcome; the devil does not stay where music is."

I am newly encouraged to make music. For where God is, there can be no evil. Where God is, there is music!

■ **Personal prayer**   *O Lord, I'm happy that I'm can't flee from Your presence. I'm comforted by the fact that You are everywhere and that music is praise to Your name!*

Fearfully and Wonderfully Made

Fearfully and wonderfully made,
I'm unique, one of a kind,
Fearfully and wonderfully made,
My beginning was God's design.

He was with me before my birth
And formed my being with care;
I'm a person of infinite worth—
A masterpiece beyond compare!

Fearfully and wonderfully made,
I'm woven as His tapestry;
Fearfully and wonderfully made,
I'm created for eternity.

His imprint is seen everywhere,
And He has plans for me;
In secret He knew I was there—
A mystery of God's decree!

Fearfully and wonderfully made,
I'm woven as His tapestry;
Fearfully and wonderfully made,
I'm created for eternity.

Word and music by Don Wyrtzen.
© 1985 by Singspiration Music.

Symphony of God's Attributes

Third Movement: He Is All-Powerful (Omnipotence)

■ **Theme** *For you created my inmost being; you knit me together in my mother's womb. I praise you because I am fearfully and wonderfully made; your works are wonderful, I know that full well. My frame was not hidden from you when I was made in the secret place. When I was woven together in the depths of the earth, your eyes saw my unformed body. All the days ordained for me were written in your book before one of them came to be. How precious to me are your thoughts, O God! How vast is the sum of them! Were I to count them, they would outnumber the grains of sand. When I awake, I am still with you (vv. 13–18).*

■ **Development**   God is all-knowing, ever-present, and *all-powerful!*

Aware that the darkness could not hide him from God (vv. 12–13), David was moved to meditate on God's supernatural superintendence, which extended to the most private depths of his mother's womb!

These verses describing reproduction are among the most touching and tender in all the Bible. David considers God's orchestration of his own conception and development: "You knit me together in my mother's womb. . . . My frame (skeleton) was not hidden from you when I was made in the secret place. . . . your eyes saw my unformed body" (vv. 13, 15–16).

God is fully cognizant of the union of sperm and egg, the attachment of the embryo to the uterine lining, and the development of that tiny life.

This passage gives every human being a remarkable basis for self-worth. From the moment of conception, God is present, and through every phase of development thereafter. The human embryo is not the result of a biological accident, no matter what the circumstances. Rather, it embraces the image of God and is not to be equated with trash to be discarded! Because God presides over the mysteries of human reproduction, all life has meaning and eternal significance.

376

■ **Personal prayer**   *O Lord, I praise You for creating my inmost being. I praise You because I am fearfully and wonderfully made.*

December

PSALMS 139–150

He spreads the snow like wool and scatters the frost like ashes. —Psalm 147:16

Symphony of God's Attributes
Finale: David's Response

■ **Theme**   *If only you would slay the wicked, O God! Away from me, you bloodthirsty men! They speak of you with evil intent; your adversaries misuse your name. Do I not hate those who hate you, O LORD, and abhor those who rise up against you? I have nothing but hatred for them; I count them my enemies. Search me, O God, and know my heart; test me and know my anxious thoughts. See if there is any offensive way in me, and lead me in the way everlasting (vv. 19–24).*

■ **Development**   Piano tuning is a fine art. A piano has three strings for each tone. If the instrument is flat, the strings must be tightened; if it is sharp, the strings must be loosened. The piano tuner always has a point of reference—"A-440"—using either a tuning fork or an electronic device called a strobe tuner. But he also depends on his ear—perfect pitch or good relative pitch—and a thorough acquaintance with harmonic intervals.

After cataloging the sins of God's enemies, who are consequently his as well, David focuses on himself. Unlike those who "misuse" the name of the Lord, David prays, voluntarily submitting himself to God's tuning fork: "Search me"; "Test me"; "See if there is any offensive way in me" (vv. 23–24). In effect, he is saying: "LORD, let me know if my life is out of tune!"

As is true so many times in the Psalms, David meets trouble with an expression of faith in the nature of God. He is both infinite and personal, transcendent and immanent—far above to watch over us, yet within to guide us. He knows how it feels to be human, because He came in the flesh and walked where we walk (John 1:1, 14).

David finds a deep wellspring of comfort and serenity in these harmonious attributes.

As the tuning fork is applied to my life, I can "hear" the flat keys. The Master Tuner may have to tighten the strings, thus producing temporary pain and stress. But the final result will be a beautifully voiced instrument of praise, fit for a heavenly concerto!

378

■ **Personal prayer**   *O Lord, let me know if my life is out of tune! Search me, test me and check me out. I long to sing and play in perfect harmony with Your plan!*

Imprecatory Impromptu
David Prays for Justice

■ **Theme**   Rescue me, O LORD, from evil men; protect me from men of violence, who devise evil plans in their hearts and stir up war every day. They make their tongues as sharp as a serpent's; the poison of vipers is on their lips. Keep me, O LORD, from the hands of the wicked; protect me from men of violence who plan to trip my feet. Proud men have hidden a snare for me; they have spread out the cords of their net and have set traps for me along my path. O LORD, I say to you, "You are my God." Hear, O LORD, my cry for mercy. O Sovereign LORD, my strong deliverer, who shields my head in the day of battle—do not grant the wicked their desires, O LORD; do not let their plans succeed, or they will become proud (vv. 1–8).

■ **Development**   Again, David vents his emotions, hence the title for this psalm. An "imprecation" is a curse on the wicked. An "impromptu" is a musical piece played extemporaneously. David is spontaneously engaging in an emotional outburst in song. The tone is harsh, strident, and dissonant.

In his opening prayer, David prays for justice and protection from the wicked. He then proceeds to curse them for their vicious character. Their tongues are poisonous; their hands do evil things; their minds devise all kinds of cunning plots to trap David and take him off the scene.

In verses 6–8, he praises God's sovereignty, using military imagery to affirm His protective power. David then concludes this section by praying for the divine restraint of the wicked.

David's prayer life is marked by honesty and openness. He never denied the reality of internal pressure. He is obviously fearful and his emotions are churning, but he feels perfectly free to dump all of this junk on God. God is certainly big enough to take it!

The great psalmist is very objective about his suffering, but because he acknowledges it and works through it, he is able to cope, with God's help. I can do the same!

379

■ **Personal prayer**   O Strong Deliver, I pray that You will protect me from the cunning schemes of ungodly persons. I pray also that You will protect me from myself and deliver me from unnecessary guilt and fear.

Imprecatory Impromptu
David's Response to His Enemies

■ **Theme**   *Let the heads of those who surround me be covered with the trouble their lips have caused. Let burning coals fall upon them; may they be thrown into the fire, into miry pits, never to rise. Let slanderers not be established in the land; may disaster hunt down men of violence. I know that the LORD secures justice for the poor and upholds the cause of the needy. Surely the righteous will praise your name and the upright will live before you (vv. 9–13).*

■ **Development**   God is holy, righteous, and pure. Man is evil, unfair, and deceitful. The morality is clear-cut and unrelenting. Because I desperately want to give people the benefit of the doubt, I sometimes tend to be "marshmallowy" about ethics.

David's intimate walk with God produced an objectivity that enabled him to see things in black and white. Thinking in grays doesn't work in the area of personal morality. This kind of reasoning results in a naive and shallow view of sin. We need to learn how to hate evil as much as God does, but we are more addicted to happiness than committed to holiness.

While David's prayer may seem a little shocking to those of us living in a society tainted by secular humanism, we must bear in mind that his enemies were malicious men. They were as annoying as insects, as repulsive as reptiles, and as lethal as sharks. They were cunning and predatory—out to kill!

He responds with equal passion. He prays that the poisonous words of the wicked will boomerang. He prays that "burning coals" will fall on their heads like volcanic residue from Sodom and Gomorrah (Genesis 19). He prays that their slander will be self-defeating and that disaster will pursue them and bring them down.

Like the clash of cymbals, a stunning thought strikes my consciousness; *David's righteous wrath was not directed against his enemies, but poured out to God in a prayer song!* When I am most troubled by injustice and unkindness, I can "talk it out" with God through music rather than "taking it out" on others!

380

■ **Personal prayer**   *O Lord, I'm glad David was a passionate person too! And I've learned today that I don't have to act on my negative impulses, but can pour them out before You in healing, restorative prayer and praise!*

Evensong   *Song of Protection*

■ **Theme**   *O LORD, I call to you; come quickly to me. Hear my voice when I call to you. May my prayer be set before you like incense; may the lifting up of my hands be like the evening sacrifice. . . . But my eyes are fixed on you, O Sovereign LORD; in you I take refuge—do not give me over to death. Keep me from the snares they have laid for me, from the traps set by evildoers. Let the wicked fall into their own nets, while I pass by in safety (vv. 1–2, 8–10).*

■ **Development**   For many people prayer is a one-liner beginning with "Gimme." For others, it's a hasty "thank you" mumbled over meals, or a bedtime blessing left over from childhood. For David, prayer was a way of life.

Here David bows before the Lord during the evening sacrifices. We're allowed to peer over his shoulder as he observes this meaningful ritual. First, he calls on the name of the Lord—a name that, in its very use, promises power. His words rise like sweet perfume because they flow from a sincere heart. He lifts his hands in a posture of praise and commitment and prays, with open eyes fixed on his Lord.

The prayer itself is spelled out in specific terms—for the presence of the Lord (v. 1), for preservation of life (v. 8), for supernatural discernment of snares set by the wicked (v. 9), for vindication (v. 10).

I am reminded of the life of Queen Esther (Esther 1–10). Haman, the highest noble under King Xerxes, had a vendetta against the Jews, especially Mordecai, Esther's guardian. He even erected a gallows, seventy-five feet high, on which to hang Mordecai. Instead, Esther acted responsibly, God acted sovereignly, and the tables were turned!

What a comfort there is in the knowledge that God has a plan for us that will not be thwarted by the worst the wicked can do!

■ **Personal prayer**   *O Lord, I know You hear my prayers just as You heard King David's. Don't let me fall into the traps set by the world, but let this humanistic society hang itself by its own rope while "I pass by in safety."*

Evensong   *Song of Sanctification*

■ **Theme**   *Set a guard over my mouth, O LORD; keep watch over the door of my lips. Let not my heart be drawn to what is evil, to take part in wicked deeds with men who are evildoers; let me not eat of their delicacies. Let a righteous man strike me—it is a kindness; let him rebuke me—it is oil on my head. My head will not refuse it. Yet my prayer is ever against the deeds of evildoers; their rulers will be thrown down from the cliffs, and the wicked will learn that my words were well spoken (vv. 3–6).*

■ **Development**   David had the right idea. His aspirations were lofty; he was just too human to attain them! Still, he longed to be pure, blameless, and sanctified (set apart).

In this passage he submits three parts of his body to the Lord for cleansing—his lips and mouth, lest he speak evil (v. 3); his heart, lest he become involved in sensual pleasures (v. 4); his head, lest his mind toy with the evil schemes of the wicked (v. 4). In fact, he asks for corrective support from godly friends.

God never intended for us to face life alone. If we isolate ourselves from real, down-to-earth relationships, the Enemy will subtly distract us, seduce us, and then devour us. My close friends—Nelson Bennett, Bill Rigg, and Bob Steed—regularly pray for me, communicate with me, and generally hold me accountable. Karen and I also attend a small group Bible study, where we experience rich Christian fellowship in a private setting. Without this support, we would be depriving ourselves of one of the greatest blessings the Lord gives us— intercessory prayer.

In unity there is strength to endure temptation, to make a frontal attack on societal sins, and to stand firm against the Enemy. God has set me apart for His ministry, but He has also blessed me with godly friends who pray for me and point out possible dangers I am too blind to see.

■ **Personal prayer**   *O Lord, I thank You again for such prayer warriors as my dad and his wife, Joan; Karen's mom, Ruth Parr, and a few others who faithfully hold me up in prayer. I know You have brought these people into my life to help me fight the battle . . . and win!*

Longing and Lament
I Cry Aloud to the Lord

■ **Theme**   *I cry aloud to the* LORD; *I lift up my voice to the* LORD *for mercy. I pour out my complaint before him; before him I tell my trouble. When my spirit grows faint within me, it is you who know my way. In the path where I walk men have hidden a snare for me. Look to my right and see; no one is concerned for me. I have no refuge; no one cares for my life* (*vv.* 1–4).

■ **Development**   David's circumstances couldn't be worse! He is hiding out in a cave with the murderous King Saul in hot pursuit. David is utterly helpless and alone.

His prayer is more of a demand than a polite request. He is crying "aloud," literally shouting at God!

Every trail and road is mined and booby-trapped, and David is spooked. He's afraid to make a single move! Not only is he in a position of grave physical danger, but he's psychologically bankrupt as well. Isolated, he feels that "no one cares" (v. 4).

I understand this feeling. As long as I can remember, I've been quiet, introverted, high-strung, and overly sensitive. You probably wouldn't be able to tell from observing me, but deep inside is a very fragile persona. There are times when I feel that I might as well drop out because no one cares. It's the price one pays for having the volume turned up too high on life!

David has "no refuge" (v. 4)—no place and no one but God. Actually, that's exactly where the Lord wants us. The best place is to be in a position of absolute dependence upon God. Most of us still believe we can make it in our own strength, that we make life work on our own. The real truth is that *He* gives us the power to do everything we do. "You may say to yourself, 'My power and the strength of my hands have produced this wealth for me.' But remember the LORD your God, for it is he who gives you the ability to produce wealth, and so confirms his covenant" (Deuteronomy 8:17–18). Some people aren't blessed because they're depending too much on their own talent.

■ *Personal prayer*   *O Lord, I'm only too conscious of my weakness and vulnerability. Please show me Your strength at the point of my deepest need!*

Longing and Lament
They Are Too Strong for Me

■ **Theme**   I cry to you, O LORD; I say, "You are my refuge, my portion
in the land of the living." Listen to my cry, for I am in desperate need;
rescue me from those who pursue me, for they are too strong for me. Set me
free from my prison, that I may praise your name. Then the righteous will
gather about me because of your goodness to me (vv. 5–7).

■ **Development**   Contemporary Christians are suffering from spiritual
anorexia. Ignoring the Lord's bountiful feast spread out in His Word,
we're literally starving ourselves to death. And instead of being strong
and robust in the faith, we're weaklings, cowering in the face of real
conflict and adversity. Like David, we look at the opposition and say,
"They are too strong for me!" (v. 6).

How is it that a beautiful and gifted young woman like Karen
Carpenter could literally starve herself to death? Why did she try to
control her life through diet and exercise instead of turning to the Lord
for answers to her problems? Depth psychology may provide some
insights regarding the dynamics of this disease, but God's Word
penetrates the mysteries of human existence and provides final
resolution in Jesus Christ.

David did have the good sense to turn to the Lord. His consuming
desire was to be able to praise the Lord and thus present a strong
witness to other believers.

We don't have to fear the strength of our "enemies"—pride, out-
of-control ambition, destructive use of sexuality, craving for status and
things. The Lord has given us every resource needed to grow healthy,
to build up our sin-immune system. We need to move from milk to
meat! "Anyone who lives on milk, being still an infant is not
acquainted with the teaching about righteousness. But solid food is for
the mature, who by constant use have trained themselves to
distinguish good from evil" (Hebrews 5:13–14).

As we continue to eat heartily from God's Word, we'll be filled
with His goodness and Spirit. Seeing the change, the righteous will
"gather about" in open-mouthed wonder and praise to God!

384

■ **Personal prayer**   O Lord, when there is so much rich food available for
our spirits, why do we starve ourselves? Lead me to the banquet table and let
me feast on Your Word so my brothers and sisters in Christ may be fed and
encouraged.

Pathetique Sonata

First Movement—My Spirit Grows Faint within Me

■ **Theme**   O LORD, hear my prayer, listen to my cry for mercy; in your faithfulness and righteousness come to my relief. Do not bring your servant into judgment, for no one living is righteous before you. The enemy pursues me, he crushes me to the ground; he makes me dwell in darkness like those long dead. So my spirit grows faint within me; my heart within me is dismayed (vv. 1–4).

■ **Development**   In this age of focus on physical fitness, I wonder if we give nearly as much thought to the condition of our spirits. The body can look pretty good on the outside, while spiritual rigor mortis is in the process of setting in. Too many of us are "faint." We're spiritual wimps!

I'm impressed all over again with David's brutal honesty about himself. He doesn't attempt to project positive images or to numb himself into relief through positive mental attitudes. He's forthright and objective. His lament is real and rich in its intensity. Emotionally, he has pulled the blanket of dark despair over his head. Because he's spiritually impoverished, he's ready for a mighty work of God in his life.

And he desperately needs one. In verses 3 and 4, he tells us that his enemies are still pursuing him relentlessly and that he is being forced to entomb himself in desert caves for protection.

In this psalm, I don't hear the mighty warrior king of Israel. Instead, I hear the pathetic plea of one who recognizes that power comes, not from physical strength or military strategy, but in trusting the faithfulness and righteousness of God.

■ **Personal prayer**   O God, hear my prayer today. The macho image is not for me. I confess my inability to work out the details of my life or even to protect myself! Be merciful to me.

Pathetique Sonata

Second Movement—My Spirit Faints with Longing

■ **Theme**   *I remember the days of long ago; I meditate on all your works and consider what your hands have done. I spread out my hands to you; my soul thirsts for you like a parched land. Answer me quickly, O LORD; my spirit faints with longing. Do not hide your face from me or I will be like those who go down to the pit (vv. 5–7).*

■ **Development**   David was no stranger to suffering. It became the foundation upon which the Lord erected a rich, intimate relationship with him.

The psalmist is now rescued through reminiscence. He considers God's mighty acts in history. He meditates on His supernatural works. These thoughts begin to restore and renew him.

Before, David's personality resembled a dry, parched land. Now, he recognizes his inner thirst and longing for God and reaches out to his heavenly Father. His request is of the utmost urgency. He feels as if he is about to die, to "go down to the pit" (v. 7). Perhaps his most horrifying thought is that the Lord will overlook him!

Spiritual pain is often the catalyst for change and growth. As I reach the end of my own limited resources, I grope toward God in desperation. He closes that great gap with His own presence and lets me know that He has not overlooked my need.

■ **Personal prayer**   *O Lord, please look beyond my fault to see my need. My soul thirsts for You like a parched land. Refresh me with the rains of Your love.*

Pathetique Sonata
Third Movement—May Your Good Spirit Lead Me on Level Ground

■ **Theme**   Let the morning bring me word of your unfailing love, for I have put my trust in you. Show me the way I should go, for to you I lift up my soul. Rescue me from my enemies, O LORD, for I hide myself in you. Teach me to do your will, for you are my God; may your good Spirit lead me on level ground. For your name's sake, O LORD, preserve my life; in your righteousness, bring me out of trouble. In your unfailing love, silence my enemies; destroy all my foes, for I am your servant (vv. 8–12).

■ **Development**   At the moment of rebirth, when the human spirit is "yielded and still," the Holy Spirit moves in to make His home and to provide assistance for our pilgrimage with God.

Even David anticipated something of this divine exchange, I think. His despairing prayer, filled with strong, virile verbs, is the night sky against which the dazzling stars of God's grace through His Spirit are displayed.

Guide—David prays, "Show me the way" (v. 8), sensing that God's guiding Spirit will not leave him stranded, nor remove him from the unfailing love that is everlasting.

Enabler—"Rescue me from my enemies" (v. 9), he continues. It is the Spirit of God who enables and empowers. David's many military coups were a result of divine intervention by the Enabler.

Teacher—"Teach me to do your will . . . may your good Spirit lead me on level ground" (v. 10). The Holy Spirit is our Teacher/Interpreter. It is He who explains spiritual mysteries and levels the ground of our understanding.

Comforter—"For your name's sake, O LORD, preserve my life . . . bring me out of my trouble" (v. 11). God's Spirit whispers words of encouragement and calls to our minds His mighty works in our behalf. He banishes discouragement and puts a song in our hearts!

387

■ **Personal prayer**   O Lord, fill me with Your Spirit today. Guide me, enable me, teach me, comfort me. I need help as I continue my pilgrimage.

Imperial March
David in Combat: Celebrating the Past

■ **Theme**   *Praise be to the LORD my Rock, who trains my hands for war, my fingers for battle. He is my loving God and my fortress, my stronghold and my deliverer, my shield, in whom I take refuge, who subdues peoples under me. O LORD, what is man that you care for him, the son of man that you think of him? Man is like a breath; his days are like a fleeting shadow* (vv. 1–4).

■ **Development**   David was the General MacArthur of his day—a conquering hero. He begins this stirring psalm by remembering past victories and enemies who have been subdued under him. But who forged David's career? Who gave him genius for military strategy? Who trained his hands for war and his fingers for battle? The Lord!

David had a personal relationship with God, who is strong, solid, and immovable, yet warm, loving, and intimate. He was David's Fortress, Stronghold, Deliverer, and Shield (v. 2). David went forth in God's strength to crush his enemies in battle. We are to do the same! (See Ephesians 6.) God's character—His nature and attributes—sustained David and made him bold and courageous—a winner!

What is almost incomprehensible to me is that this mighty God of war invites me—weak and wandering though I be—into His presence to receive the same kind of strength that He gave David. He promises to be my Shield and Deliverer in the spiritual battles I must fight. Like David, I can be a conquering hero . . . in Him!

388

■ **Personal prayer**   *O Lord, be my Rock, my Fortress, my Deliverer, and my Shield today. My battles are not as obvious as David's but they are just as deadly!*

Imperial March
David in Combat: Pleading for Help in the Present

■ **Theme**   *Part your heavens, O L*ORD*, and come down; touch the mountains, so that they smoke. Send forth lightning and scatter the enemies; shoot your arrows and rout them. Reach down your hand from on high; deliver me and rescue me from the mighty waters, from the hands of foreigners whose mouths are full of lies, whose right hands are deceitful. I will sing a new song to you, O God; on the ten-stringed lyre I will make music to you, to the One who gives victory to kings, who delivers his servant David from the deadly sword. Deliver me and rescue me from the hands of foreigners whose mouths are full of lies, whose right hands are deceitful (vv. 5–11).*

■ **Development**   David set his faith firmly in divine intervention rather than in human strategy. He longed for a dazzling supernatural display of God's power! He wanted to see the heavens illuminated by holy fireworks (v. 5)! He knew that when God sent forth lightning, enemies were scattered (v. 6), and when God sprung His bow and shot His arrows, villains were put to rout (v. 6).

What inspiration for music! In ancient Israel the creative process worked like this:

Genuine need—God's people were backed against the wall.

Imminent danger—They faced the possibility of being wiped out.

Honest lament—They groaned and cried out to the Lord for salvation and deliverance. Whole families clothed themselves in sackcloth and ashes, fasted, and prayed.

Divine intervention—The Lord heard their cry and supernaturally delivered them.

Genuine praise—They worshiped God for His mighty works!

We often do it all backward today—cranking up a praise experience while nothing is happening in our lives! Yet David was so confident of success that he wrote this psalm of victory *before the fact!* Considering the unchanging nature of God and His faithfulness, I can begin *now* to compose music in gratitude for who He is and what He is going to do for me!

389

■ **Personal prayer**   *O Lord, even before You do Your next exciting work in my life, may I burst forth in creative worship of Your mighty name and power!*

Imperial March
David in Combat: Anticipating Peace and Prosperity

■ **Theme**   *Deliver me and rescue me from the hands of foreigners whose mouths are full of lies, whose right hands are deceitful. Then our sons in their youth will be like well-nurtured plants, and our daughters will be like pillars carved to adorn a palace. Our barns will be filled with every kind of provision. Our sheep will increase by thousands, by tens of thousands in our fields; our oxen will draw heavy loads. There will be no breaching of walls, no going into captivity, no cry of distress in our streets. Blessed are the people of whom this is true; blessed are the people whose God is the LORD (vv. 11–15).*

■ **Development**   Only a survivor or a veteran of war in some strife-ridden part of the world can really appreciate the absence of conflict. In this psalm David is projecting a future when world-wide peace will reign once more.

Insulated from most wartime violence as we are in America, I don't have to be concerned that my son, D.J., or my beautiful Kathy will be shot by invaders. I don't have to fear that bombs will destroy the farms of our country so that there will be no food in the supermarket (v. 13). I don't spend much time wondering if I'll be captured and exiled by foreign invaders (v. 14). For His own reasons, God has blessed America . . . for now!

But David reminds us of the divine condition for peace and prosperity: "Blessed are the people whose God is the LORD" (v. 15). There are definite signs of disintegration in our society: Families are in crisis, our economy is shaky, and war is still possible in many parts of the world. Could it be that we've forsaken the Lord?

■ **Personal prayer**   *O Lord, I long for Your blessing of world peace. Take control of our economy, our national security, and international affairs, so that all nations will know that You are our God!*

Praise to the King
His Attributes and Acts

■ **Theme**   I will exalt you, my God the King; I will praise your name for
ever and ever. Every day I will praise you and extol your name for ever and
ever. Great is the LORD and most worthy of praise; his greatness no one can
fathom. One generation will commend your works to another; they will tell
of your mighty acts. They will speak of the glorious splendor of your majesty,
and I will meditate on your wonderful works. They will tell of the power of
your awesome works, and I will proclaim your great deeds. They will
celebrate your abundant goodness and joyfully sing of your righteousness
(vv. 1–7).

■ **Development**   This noble praise psalm begins the grand doxology
(Psalms 145–150) of the entire Psalter, bringing this anthology of
ancient worship songs to a mighty crescendo. Excitement builds,
erupting in a fulfilling climax of praise in Psalm 150—the Old
Testament Hallelujah Chorus!

David begins by extolling God the King. He covenants with the
Lord to praise His name on a daily basis. He vows to keep the
relationship fresh, not taking anything for granted.

The psalmist praises the Lord for both His attributes and His acts.
Only God is worthy of praise because of His divine personality and
unprecedented acts in history. God is not an absentee landlord of His
universe! Future generations will tell the stories revealing His glorious
splendor and majesty.

What a model for my own praise experience! I need to daily
celebrate the Lord's attributes and actions in my life. How does His
character affect me personally? Can He ever act toward me in an
unloving way? Is He capable of upholding and sustaining me?

These are the concepts I must meditate on. These are the things I
must pray about. These are the images and pictures of God I must
write down to preserve for future generations of believers. What
poems, songs, and holy literature should spring forth from these
exalted thoughts!

■ **Personal prayer**   My God and King, You alone are worthy of daily and
forever praise! I exalt and declare Your goodness to all generations.

Praise to the King　His Love

■ **Theme**　The LORD is gracious and compassionate, slow to anger and rich in love. The LORD is good to all; he has compassion on all he has made. . . . The LORD is faithful to all his promises and loving toward all he has made. The LORD upholds all those who fall and lifts up all who are bowed down. The eyes of all look to you, and you give them their food at the proper time. You open your hand and satisfy the desires of every living thing (vv. 8–9, 13b–16).

■ **Development**　When I think of God's Fatherlove, I see His grace and compassion (v. 8), His goodness and mercy (v. 9), His faithful promises (v. 13), and *his open hand* (v. 16).

　　Our God is not stingy, but lavish in His gift-giving. He is a God of extravagance. He delights in caring for His children. Over and over again in His Word we are reminded of His gracious provision, both physically and spiritually: "They feast on the abundance of your house; you give them drink from your river of delights" (36:8). "You crown the year with your bounty, and your carts overflow with abundance" (65:11). "The LORD is my shepherd, I shall not be in want" (23:1). The refrain is echoed in the New Testament: "I have come that they may have life, and have it to the full" (John 10:10).

　　That greatest Gift was God Himself in human flesh!

■ **Personal prayer**　My Father God, I thank You for Your open hands which have satisfied the deepest desires of my heart through Jesus Christ . . . and keep on giving every day of my life!

Praise to the King   His Glory

■ **Theme**   *All you have made will praise you, O LORD; your saints will extol you. They will tell of the glory of your kingdom and speak of your might, so that all men may know of your mighty acts and the glorious splendor of your kingdom. Your kingdom is an everlasting kingdom, and your dominion endures through all generations (vv. 10–13).*

■ **Development**   I read the words of this passage and try to envision the kingdom described here—its glory, its splendor, its everlastingness!

God's kingdom—not made with hands—is filled with His glory and reflects His power and might. At the center–radiant and brighter than the sun—is the King Himself. His dominion is not transitory; it is an everlasting kingdom, enduring through all generations (v. 13).

So moved am I that I break forth into a song of praise:

> You are my God and King,
> Of Your greatness I will sing;
> I will thank You all my days
> And through eternity give You praise.
>
> I sing of Your wondrous fame
> And bow before Your name;
> For You rule in sovereignty
> And reign in glorious majesty.
>
> I give thanks for Your goodness
> And celebrate Your kindness.
> I bow in humility
> Before all You've done for me.
>
> Then someday when You come for me
> I'll be caught up to glory,
> And I'll join the angelic train
> To sing of Your sovereign reign.

Words and music by Don Wyrtzen.
© 1980 by Singspiration Music.

393

■ **Personal prayer**   *King of kings, I praise You for Your mighty deeds in my life and look forward to joining that "angelic train" in glory!*

Praise to the King   His Listening Ear

■ **Theme**   The LORD is righteous in all his ways and loving toward all he has made. The LORD is near to all who call on him, to all who call on him in truth. He fulfills the desires of those who fear him; he hears their cry and saves them. The LORD watches over all who love him, but all the wicked he will destroy. My mouth will speak in praise of the LORD. Let every creature praise his holy name for ever and ever (vv. 17–21).

■ **Development**   Picture the Lord. What image do you see? He's a perfect King—infinitely powerful and totally just. But He is also a loving Father—intimately near, warm, and personal. He is just exactly what each of us needs. How sad that many of us try to keep Him at arm's length most of the time!

King and Father. It may be easier to accept the image of God as King than as Father. Some, whose childhood memories are scarred by thoughts of unloving, insensitive parents, need to learn the definition of *father* by studying this psalm. This Father is never inattentive, neglectful, or too busy.

Even to those of us who were blessed with godly fathers, this concept may seem foreign to us. We're so busy declaring our independence, toughing it out alone, and proving ourselves that we lose sight of the truth that self-sufficiency never results in lasting satisfaction. We need to learn that we are most satisfied and safest in the arms of our heavenly Father. He is "near to all who call on him" (v. 18). How amazing!

■ **Personal prayer**   My God and King, I'm so glad You showed me something of Your heart through my dad and that I have only to turn to your Word to be further reminded of Your active love and care.

The Ultimate Priority
Praising His Greatness in Creation

■ **Theme**   Praise the LORD. Praise the LORD, O my soul. I will praise the LORD all my life; I will sing praise to my God as long as I live. Do not put your trust in princes, in mortal men, who cannot save. When their spirit departs, they return to the ground; on that very day their plans come to nothing. Blessed is he whose help is the God of Jacob, whose hope is in the LORD his God, the Maker of heaven and earth, the sea, and everything in them—the LORD, who remains faithful forever (vv. 1–6).

■ **Development**   Music has always been as necessary to me as breathing. A moving praise song such as "His Name Is Wonderful" evokes a whole range of feelings, memories, and associations. Certain songs, such as "In the Sweet By and By," "O That Will Be Glory for Me," and "When We All Get to Heaven" remind me of friends and loved ones who are waiting for us there—my mom, Karen's dad, the Barclays, Tim Walvoord, Louis Paul Lehman, and others. For me, music is a big part of the rhythm and meaning in life, and like David, I want praise to be the top priority of my life.

It's easy to praise the Lord when I see Him at every turn—at the seaside, in the mountains, in the snow frosting the trees outside the window of my study.

But God's unshakability is appreciated even more when seen against the backdrop of human weakness and transience. As David pointed out, "Mortal men . . . cannot save" (v. 3). Their final destiny is the grave; on the day of death their well-strategized plans come to nothing.

As the year draws to a close, I need to reevaluate my commitment to the Lord. Have I kept my priorities in order? Have I praised the Lord every day through meditating on His Word, through prayer, through music? Have I let the plastic things made by humans blind me to authentic masterpieces created by God? Have I cultivated a sense of His presence, so that I can know Him whom I've never seen? Am I worshiping Him with my whole person or with my head? Objective knowledge is a poor substitute for intimacy and involvement!

395

■ **Personal prayer**   Dear Lord, I want to praise You as long as I live. Make me sensitive to Your beauty in creation and may I move from an awareness of Your power and might to a warm, personal relationship with You.

The Ultimate Priority
Praising His Grace in Provision

■ **Theme**   He upholds the cause of the oppressed and gives food to the hungry. The LORD sets prisoners free, the LORD gives sight to the blind, the LORD lifts up those who are bowed down, the LORD loves the righteous. The LORD watches over the alien and sustains the fatherless and the widow, but he frustrates the ways of the wicked. The LORD reigns forever; your God, O Zion, for all generations. Praise the LORD (vv. 7–10).

■ **Development**   The Lord is to be praised, not only for His greatness in creation, but also for His provision on behalf of His people. He shows His loving favor in many ways. He helps the oppressed, feeds the hungry, sets prisoners free, makes the blind see, lifts up the fallen, loves the righteous, watches over aliens, sustains the homeless, and frustrates the wicked.

There are many prophetic allusions to the marvelous gifts of God's grace. (See Isaiah 42:6–8.) The New Testament records the fulfillment of this prophecy: "The Spirit of the Lord is upon me, because he hath anointed me to preach the gospel to the poor; he hath sent me to heal the brokenhearted, to preach deliverance to the captives, and recovering of sight to the blind, to set at liberty them that are bruised" (Luke 4:18 KJV). Indeed, the whole purpose of God's redemptive plan in history was "to the praise of his glorious grace" (Ephesians 1:6).

God's grace was personified through His Son, the Lord Jesus Christ. It is through Him and Him alone that we can be saved (Ephesians 2:8–9). He is the only true hope for fallen man.

The psalmist concludes by reminding us that the Lord reigns forever. He ends as he began—with a paroxysm of praise, "Hallelujah!"

396

■ **Personal prayer**   Dear Lord, I thank You for Your "glorious grace" and what it has done in my life. I thank You for the Lord Jesus Christ who personifies Your grace—Your undeserved favor.

A Very Personal Doxology
He Heals Me . . .

■ **Theme** Praise the LORD. How good it is to sing praises to our God, how pleasant and fitting to praise him! The LORD builds up Jerusalem; he gathers the exiles of Israel. He heals the brokenhearted and binds up their wounds. He determines the number of stars and calls them each by name. Great is our Lord and mighty in power; his understanding has no limit. The LORD sustains the humble but casts the wicked to the ground (vv. 1–6).

■ **Development** I've both experienced and observed "brokenheartedness," and it's a devastating blow either way. The holidays, when families come together to make memories, are especially poignant and difficult for some of us who are still grieving. It's so hard to accept the fact that I will never again see Mom or Karen's dad on this earth.

That's why this passage from Psalm 147 is so timely. David is referring, of course, to the exiled captives of Israel when he says, "He [the Lord] heals the brokenhearted and binds up their wounds" (v. 3), but he might be speaking of any broken heart anywhere.

Sometimes the "wounds" are caused by some significant "other" in one's life; sometimes they are self-inflicted through sin. But God loves to restore and rebuild. Just as He rebuilt Jerusalem after the Babylonian exile, He accepts any penitent sinner for remodeling. The only prerequisites are honesty, humility, and homage. The believer (or unbeliever) who truly repents and returns from sin is fully forgiven, restored, and radically rebuilt!

When we honestly face our grief or our sin and submit it to the Lord, He responds in grace by forgiving and healing. This profound, personal work then becomes the basis for authentic praise. I face an extravagant future with the Lord in glory, when I will see Mom and Karen's dad again. We'll have a lot of catching up to do!

■ **Personal prayer** Praise the Lord! I join in praising Your holy, precious name. I praise You for healing the brokenhearted and for setting us free to sing praise!

A Very Personal Doxology
He Delights in Me . . .

■ **Theme**   *Sing to the* LORD *with thanksgiving; make music to our God on the harp. He covers the sky with clouds; he supplies the earth with rain and makes grass grow on the hills. He provides food for the cattle and for the young ravens when they call. His pleasure is not in the strength of the horse, nor his delight in the legs of a man; the* LORD *delights in those who fear him, who put their hope in his unfailing love (vv. 7–11).*

■ **Development**   There are some things a father never forgets—his child's first steps, the first words, the first Christmas. I'll always remember the rush of pride I felt when our son, D.J., got the music award as a senior at Brentwood Academy. I felt the same deep emotion when his sister, Kathy, became the spelling champion of her class in Grand Rapids. My kids have delighted me on many occasions. Last Christmas, I was especially proud of D.J. when he visited the Heaston family every day to see their daughter, Heather, who was recovering from the auto accident that took the life of her sister, Leesha.

Though it blows my mind, I know how the Lord must feel when His children do well! "He delights in those who fear him" (v. 11). God is unimpressed by brute strength, but He "takes great pleasure and enjoyment in" the reverence of His children. We are created to praise, and when we learn to do that well, we know we're pleasing Him.

As we become aware of God's delight, we'll experience the gift of His glorious grace. We, in turn, will delight Him—a wondrous, intimate interplay between God the Father and His children.

■ **Personal prayer**   *Praise the Lord! I thank You and praise You for delighting in me. I place my confidence in Your glorious grace and unfailing love today.*

A Very Personal Doxology
He Gives Me Peace . . .

■ **Theme** Extol the LORD, O Jerusalem; praise your God, O Zion, for he strengthens the bars of your gates and blesses your people within you. He grants peace to your borders and satisfies you with the finest of wheat. He sends his command to the earth; his word runs swiftly (vv. 12–15).

■ **Development** David and the other psalmists had long been buried with their fathers when the angels sang the first Christmas carol: "Glory to God in the highest, and on earth peace to men on whom his favor rests" (Luke 2:14). How those ancient songwriters would have rejoiced at the coming of the Messiah—the "Prince of Peace" whom Isaiah foretold! (Isaiah 9:6).

Here the psalmist exhorts the inhabitants of the Holy City to praise the Lord. I can hear the harmony of soprano, alto, tenor, and bass as the "voices" blend in a choral anthem of peace.

Soprano—The high notes soar: "He strengthens the bars of your gates" (v. 13). These people need not fear invasion or attack. The Lord Himself stands at the gate to turn back any who should not enter.

Alto—Providing mellow, rich support is another voice: "And blesses your people within you" (v. 13). Blessing comes from His presence within. "Be born in me tonight," I echo.

Tenor—A strong male voice takes the lead and the song continues on a rising note of joy: "He grants peace to your borders" (v. 14). Peace! Peace! Where is peace in this chaotic world?

Bass—Deep and vibrant comes the reassuring word: "[He] satisfies you with the finest of wheat. . . . He sends his command to the earth; his word runs swiftly" (vv. 14–15). The Lord provides. Not only does He satisfy our hunger for food, but He sends His Word—the written Word and the living Word! Jesus Christ is born! He lives to bring peace!

■ **Personal prayer** Praise the Lord! I thank You for the gift of Your Word which sustains me. But I thank You even more for the gift of Your Son, Immanuel—God with us!

A Very Personal Doxology
He Sustains His Word

■ **Theme**   *He spreads the snow like wool and scatters the frost like ashes. He hurls down his hail like pebbles. Who can withstand his icy blast? He sends his word and melts them; he stirs up his breezes, and the waters flow. He has revealed his word to Jacob, his laws and decrees to Israel. He has done this for no other nation; they do not know his laws. Praise the* LORD *(vv. 16–20).*

■ **Development**   What a wondrous wintertime scene is painted in this passage! The greatness of the Lord is perceived by the effect of His Word. He speaks, and the elements of nature obey. When He commands, blizzards occur. "He spreads the snow" and "scatters the frost" (v. 16). "He hurls down his hail like pebbles" (v. 17). The icy blast is almost felt as well as seen in this graphic word picture.

Similarly, at His command, the spring thaw sets in, rivers run, like the melting of an icy heart in the warmth of His love. His Word is inviolable, authoritative, and sure.

The most powerful display of His grace was the gift of His written Word. The magnificence of the Mosaic Law and the earth-shattering ethical insights of His decrees were His special gift to Israel. No other nation then possessed the glory of His commandments.

Through Israel His Word comes down through the generations. It was the Word of God that sustained King David throughout his turbulent life. It is His Word that sustains us. Through His precious Word we receive His gifts of grace. Praise the Lord!

■ **Personal prayer**   *O Lord, I praise You for the gift of Your written Word which sustains and quickens my spirit.*

Canticle of Praise
All Creation Sings Praise

■ **Theme**   Praise the LORD. Praise the LORD from the heavens, praise him
in the heights above. Praise him, all his angels, praise him, all his heavenly
hosts. Praise him, sun and moon, praise him, all you shining stars. Praise
him, you highest heavens and you waters above the skies. Let them praise the
name of the LORD, for he commanded and they were created. He set them in
place for ever and ever; he gave a decree that will never pass away (vv. 1–
6).

■ **Development**   On this night of nights, all creation erupts in a
cosmic explosion of joy: "Hallelujah!" The psalmist's poetic expression
is intensified by the use of personification. The luminaries in the
heavens praise the Lord (v. 1). The angels—heavenly hosts—praise
the Lord (v. 2). All the elements of nature praise the Lord (vv. 3–4).

What motivates all of creation to praise the Lord? The fact that its
very existence is based on the Word and decree of the Lord. On this
night, hundreds of years after this psalm was written, the Word
became flesh and dwelt among us—like a candle igniting a forest fire
that would banish the darkness forever! (Luke 2).

But what if Jesus had not come?

401

■ **Personal prayer**   Jesus, I'm so glad You came! I join with all creation
in singing Your praises!

Canticle of Praise
Earthly Hosts Sing Praise

■ **Theme**   *Praise the LORD from the earth, you great sea creatures and all ocean depths, lightning and hail, snow and clouds, stormy winds that do his bidding, you mountains and all hills, fruit trees and all cedars, wild animals, and all cattle, small creatures and flying birds, kings of the earth and all nations, you princes and all rulers on earth, young men and maidens, old men and children. Let them praise the name of the LORD, for his name alone is exalted; his splendor is above the earth and the heavens. He has raised up for his people a horn, the praise of all his saints, of Israel, the people close to his heart. Praise the LORD (vv. 7–14).*

■ **Development**   All nature sings praise to the Lord! The list of members in the great universal choir is a kaleidoscope of animate and inanimate creatures—sea creatures, lightning and hail, snow and clouds, small creatures and flying birds, kings and princes, rulers and nations, young men and maidens, old men and children—all crying out with joy, all praising the Lord together!

Why do they praise Him? First, they are responding to the glory of His name (v. 13). Second, they realize that His glory transcends His creation (v. 13). Third, they are praising Him in gratitude for the king He has given Israel (v. 14)—a prelude to the coming of Christ!

Why do I, who now know the Messiah, often neglect praise? Why is my heart sometimes unresponsive? Could I be guilty of worshiping the creation rather than the Creator (Romans 1:25)? How do I alter this condition? By bowing again before His cradle throne, by cherishing this Gift from the Father, by adoring Him!

■ **Personal prayer**   *O Lord, I adore You! I cherish the gift of Your salvation and commit myself again to You with full fervor and joy!*

Motet for the Meek
Motivation for Praise

■ **Theme**   Praise the LORD. Sing to the LORD a new song, his praise in the assembly of the saints. Let Israel rejoice in their Maker; let the people of Zion be glad in their King. Let them praise his name with dancing and make music to him with tambourine and harp. For the LORD takes delight in his people; he crowns the humble with salvation. Let the saints rejoice in this honor and sing for joy on their beds (vv. 1–5).

■ **Development**   How quickly we forget! Once the gift is unwrapped and we exclaim over it, we lay it aside for a bigger and shinier one! What have I done with the gift of God's Son and the salvation that cost Him so dearly?

The psalmist prods my conscience when he calls on the people of Israel to "sing a new song" even while they are resting (v. 5)! I shouldn't have to be reminded. My joy in the Lord should be so full that it spills over in spontaneous praise!

Then I read on and am convicted all over again. Israel is commanded to express her joy with dancing and instrumental performance (v. 3). Not only are we to use our voices and musical instruments, but also our bodies in complete, free, and uninhibited rejoicing. Yet dancing is an art form virtually unheard of in today's worship services! It is foreign to our culture, by and large, yet when we are too proper, too controlled, we may miss some of the blessings God has in store for us.

Consistent and creative praise keeps faith alive and growing. I must envision God as loving, caring, and delighting in me. Then I will be inspired to use all the gifts He has given me in exuberant praise!

■ **Personal prayer**   Teach me a new song, Lord, and may I learn to express my joy with unrestrained enthusiasm!

Motet for the Meek
Summation of Praise

■ **Theme**   May the praise of God be in their mouths and a double-edged sword in their hands, to inflict vengeance on the nations and punishment on the peoples, to bind their kings with fetters, their nobles with shackles of iron, to carry out the sentence written against them. This is the glory of all his saints. Praise the LORD (vv. 6–9).

■ **Development**   God calls on Israel not only to praise His name but also to execute vengeance on the nations. The Israelites were to worship Him, yes, but they were also to stand for God's justice and to put down evil in the world. They would be praising with their mouths while brandishing a double-edged sword in their hands!

The psalmist gives us no romanticized view of God. He calls for the annihilation of heathen nations, for wicked kings to be fettered, and for His absolutely just sentence to be carried out. As His saints obey the Lord, they experience His glory.

What a study in contrasts—worship and vengeance, praise and power! If this seems strange, it may be because we are comfortable with doublemindedness. We want to be intimate with God while "cozying up" to evil on the side. The Lord wants us to be "wise about what is good, and innocent about what is evil" (Romans 16:19). We're open to praising God, but we're not as interested in balancing our worship with a holy hatred of sin. He calls us to praise and to prophesy. He needs some young Vance Havners who have the conviction to write and speak out against hypocrisy and evil. He needs worship leaders— "Praise spokesmen"—but He also summons contemporary prophets— "praise motivators"—who will cry out against injustice and sin in our world.

404

■ **Personal prayer**   May I have the inner strength not only to praise You, Lord, but to take a stand for righteousness in the circles where I live and work.

The Hallelujah Chorus
The "Where" of Praise

■ **Theme**   Praise the LORD. Praise God in his sanctuary; praise him in his mighty heavens (v. 1).

■ **Development**   This psalm is an orchestra of praise—every instrument imaginable poised and lifted up in worship, celebrating God's incomparable excellence.

Wherever His creatures live, God should be praised, the psalmist says. First, he encourages believers to praise the Lord in the sanctuary. Second, he urges the angels to praise the Lord in the sky, the vault of heaven. Since God's glory fills the universe, His praise must do no less!

Many of us organize our lives into neat, convenient categories—business, domestic, spiritual. We find it hard to think about praising the Lord at work, or while swimming or playing tennis, or at home with the family. Worship is slotted in on Sundays and Wednesday nights. Many of us have fallen into the sacred versus secular dichotomy, which robs us of spontaneity and vitality in our relationship with the Lord. Such a narrow concept of praise leads to a life of truth without beauty which, in turn, can result in legalism, disillusionment, or even rebellion.

We need to learn to praise the Lord wherever we are. We ought to try standing around the dinner table, holding hands with our loved ones, and singing the doxology together. We ought to dare humming the tune to a hymn at break in the office. We ought to join some major community choir in the Easter or Christmas season and sing the "Hallelujah Chorus," and allow ourselves to lose control of our emotions, letting the tears flow down our cheeks and the chills run up our spines. That will be a preview of heaven when we join the angelic choir of millions upon millions! Hallelujah!

■ **Personal prayer**   Dear Lord, may I be bold enough to praise You wherever I am today—at home, in the office, in the midst of recreation, or at church. You inhabit praise, so my joyful heart is Your "sanctuary."

The Hallelujah Chorus
The "Why" of Praise

■ **Theme**   *Praise him for his acts of power; praise him for his surpassing greatness (v. 2).*

■ **Development**   Why should believers praise the Lord? The answer is simple: Because He deserves it!

He spoke the world into being, established the first couple in their garden home, then provided redemption for all mankind when they sinned. The Redeemer paid for your sins and mine on a Roman cross thousands of years later. We honor and extol Him for these mighty deeds and saving acts. That's reason enough to praise Him.

But there is more. If He did nothing at all, there would still be necessity for praise. We are created for communion with God. We are His admiring audience, His fans, who applaud Him for the glory of His attributes and the beauty of His character.

We must move on from knowing the facts about Him to knowing *Him*. We must move from distance to intimacy. Then we can truly join the heavenly band in singing:

> *Gloria in excelsis Deo!*
>
> *Angels we have heard on high,*
> *Sweetly singing o'er the plains,*
> *And the mountains in reply,*
> *Echoing their joyous strains.*
>
> *Gloria in excelsis Deo!*

406

■ **Personal prayer**   *Gloria in excelsis Deo! I'm eager to praise You in celestial language, Lord. Teach me to sing like the angels!*

The Hallelujah Chorus
The "Who" of Praise

■ **Theme**   Let everything that has breath praise the LORD. Praise the LORD (v. 6).

■ **Development**   Who should praise the Lord? The psalmist answers in verse 6. "Everything that has breath" should praise the Lord. All of creation should be involved (Psalm 148:7–12). Infants and children are included (8:2). Even animals are not left out (Job 38–41). Worship is not the exclusive province of pastors, Christian celebrities, or worship leaders. All believers should join the creation in exalting and honoring the Lord. It's a privilege and joy!

In fact, when we sing, our Lord sings with us! When we worship, He worships with us (Psalm 22:22; Hebrews 2:12). The believer has no higher calling!

> We bow and worship Him, our Lord and King—
> Forever and ever His praise we'll sing;
> To Him all honor, love, and thanks we bring—
> And to His attributes we'll cling.
>
> He is deserving of all thanks and praise
> With joy overflowing our hearts we raise;
> We'll sing and sing of Him for endless days—
> This is our sacrifice of praise!

Words and music by Don Wyrtzen.
© 1973 by Singspiration Music.

■ **Personal prayer**   Dear Lord, may I praise You with every breath I take! And may I so inspire others with the music You give me that all creation will join in the chorus!

The Hallelujah Chorus
The "How" of Praise

■ **Theme**   *Praise him with the sounding of the trumpet, praise him with the harp and lyre, praise him with tambourine and dancing, praise him with the strings and flute, praise him with the clash of cymbals, praise him with resounding cymbals (vv. 3–5).*

■ **Development**   We are to praise Yahweh with every kind of musical form and instrument available!

In ancient times, great national feasts and sacred occasions were ushered in by the fanfare of the trumpet (2 Chronicles 5:1–14). These trumpets were most likely rams' horns, primitive versions of modern valve trumpets and flugelhorns (Psalm 150:3).

Timbrels (tambourines), strings, and flutes are mentioned as vehicles of praise in verse 4. Joyous celebrations of victory were marked by the use of these instruments accompanied with dancing (149:3). Dancing was an integral part of Hebrew worship. Miriam danced to the tambourine (Exodus 15:20–21). So also did the women who greeted Saul and David in their moments of victorious celebration (1 Samuel 18:6–7). King David was so elated by the return of the ark of the covenant to Jerusalem that he broke into dancing (2 Samuel 6:14–16).

In verse 5, clashing cymbals are mentioned. So we see that every kind of instrument, form, and sound is called upon to praise God—solemn and festive, percussive and melodic, gentle and strident, dissonant and consonant, fast and slow, stirring and meditative.

The church is just beginning to take advantage of the technological revolution—synthesizers, multi-track recording techniques, etc. Our challenge is to praise the Lord with our whole being and with every instrument at our disposal. We are to take the message of the gospel and translate it into the language of today. Luther did it in the sixteenth century. Sankey did it in the nineteenth century. Rodeheaver did it in the early twentieth century. Let us follow in their footsteps and in the steps of David, that great musician of the ancient world!

■ **Personal prayer**   *Dear Lord, help me to praise you with my whole being—heart, soul, mind, and body—and with all the instrumental forms, sounds, and inventions available to me.*
SOLI DEO GLORIA!

Postlude

What I've learned from the Psalms

A *Musician Looks at the Psalms* revels in three-part form. Each day of the journal has been divided into an exposition of the theme, a development of the theme, and a prayer (or recapitulation). The book itself also follows a three-part structure: prelude, body of work, and postlude.

A postlude is a closing piece of music, often an organ voluntary at the end of a worship service. I would like to use this postlude to share with you what I have learned from the Psalms. I can synthesize it into one big idea:

Only the Lord gives us a clear, accurate picture of reality. Without His divine revelation we don't have an adequate basis for our identity, our values, or our morality.

To elaborate I will state seven basic principles I have learned from my study of the Psalter, the ancient hymnbook of Israel. They give beautiful, sensitive answers to the meaning of life and form the architecture of a Judeo-Christian philosophy of life.

■ **First, my being and existence have eternal value because I am made in God's image.** I have learned that God "created my inmost being" and that "I am fearfully and wonderfully made" (Psalm 139:13–14). I am a person of infinite worth and dignity—"a little lower than the angels" and "crowned with glory and honor" (8:4–5). In Genesis

409

1:27 the Word explicitly says that God created me "in His own image." I am never to believe the Enemy's incessant message that I am valueless and worthless. Indeed, rather I am crowned with meaning and majesty!

■ *Second, my deepest longings to be loved and to be special are met in the Lord.* I've learned that His loyal love endures forever (Psalm 136). Nothing I could ever experience can keep me from God's love (Romans 8:38–39). Based on this love, I am safe and secure in Him (Psalm 16). But not only do I possess inner security in the Lord, I am also adequate and unique because of Him. I am to rule over God's glorious creation (8:6). Only the Lord defines the universe and brings meaning to the particulars of life. Only He has it all together. Therefore, when I experience deep longings—hunger and thirst— they are met in the Lord. "As the deer pants for streams of water, so my soul pants for you, O God" (Psalm 42:1, see Isaiah 55:1–2). Therefore, I don't need to distort reality or distract myself from pain because my Lord ultimately gives me all I need. My inner core is only satisfied in Him!

■ *Third, my mind can be renewed and refreshed by mediating on the Word.* My study of the Psalms has taught me that the real battles of life are fought in the mind. One's perception of reality determines his response to life. The Jewish nation was distinctive among the heathen peoples of the ancient world because their minds were filled with the magnificence of the law. I have the capability of running video-tapes in my brain that either tear me down or lift me up. I can think negatively or positively. You see, our lives can only be "transformed by the renewing of our minds" (Romans 12:1–2).

Joy comes from a refreshed and renewed mind. This is a major theme in the Psalter. "The law of the LORD is perfect, reviving the soul. The statutes of the LORD are trustworthy, making wise the simple. The precepts of the LORD are right, giving joy to the heart. The commands of the LORD are radiant, giving light to the eyes" (Psalm 19:7–8). Our thoughts, our cognitions govern our lives. They affect our choices and our choices predetermine our feelings. We all bear scars from the fall of man. One of our major wounds is to think inaccurately about moral truth. This is why we desperately need daily exposure to and immersion in God's Word.

410 ■ *Fourth, my life can have direction and purpose through obedience to God's truth.* The whole subject of the will of man and how it relates to the sovereignty of God is very complex. But we can all grasp the fact that our choices are based on our thoughts. We will not choose to go God's way until we begin to think His thoughts. Our minds function on a cybernetic principle: we are goal-oriented. We

will passionately pursue goals that we believe will give our lives meaning. The psalms teach us that the only ultimate meaning and deep personal fulfillment come from obedience to God's Word. The old hymn says it so simply, yet profoundly: "Trust and obey, for there's no other way to be happy in Jesus but to trust and obey" (John Sammis). David, the chief musician says, "But from everlasting to everlasting the LORD's love is with those who fear him, and his righteousness with their children's children—with those who keep his covenant and remember to obey his precepts" (103:17–18, 20). We can choose to praise, adore, and worship the Lord, whatever our circumstances.

■ *Fifth, my feelings can be experienced and expressed without fear or guilt.* The Psalter expresses two major motifs that are repeated again and again: *Life is tough but God is good.* These psalmists, ancient songwriters, lived in a period of severe adversity and upheaval. They knew what it was like to suffer, to groan and to cry out, but they worshiped a God who was big enough to handle their problems. Therefore, they poured out their souls to Him. Their prayers were moments of catharsis: "Out of the depths I cry to you, O LORD; O LORD, hear my voice. Let your ears be attentive to my cry for mercy" (130:1–2). They knew that "weeping may remain for a night, but rejoicing comes in the morning" (30:5). We are called to be holy, not happy. But many of us are addicted to happiness rather than committed to holiness. We gladly trade ultimate joy for short-term relief. The psalmists teach us to face life squarely—to look life right in the eye! In the nature of reality we will experience suffering and joy, pain and peace, adversity and felicity. Right now, we're pilgrims— "just a passin' through." This world is *not* our home. It's abrasive. We're not comfortable here. We're not totally at home yet, not fully satisfied. We're restless until we find God because we were made for eternity! We can allow ourselves to lament individually and nationally.

■ *Sixth, reality can only be grasped when I intimately embrace Jesus Christ as my Lord and Savior.* Because the apostle Paul had further revelation from God, he knew more about the gospel than did King David. Yet, even in the Psalms, we see the gospel taking shape in seedling form. Here are the key ideas. I would encourage you to think about them, apply them to your own life, and then make some concrete decisions about them.

411

I'm a precious person made in God's image.
God "created my inmost being." "I am fearfully and wonderfully made" (Psalm 139:13–14; see Genesis 1:27).

I will live forever.

David said that he would "dwell in the house of the LORD forever" (Psalm 23:6).

I have sinned.

But David himself was flawed and sinful. He says, "Have mercy on me, O God, according to your unfailing love; according to your great compassion blot out my transgressions. Wash away all my iniquity and cleanse me from my sin" (Psalm 51:1–2).

I need a Savior.

I believe that Jesus Christ is the Messiah of the Psalms. Listen to the mournful music of these moving words: "My God, my God, why have you forsaken me?" That's a *direct quote* from Psalm 22:1. Those exact words were spoken by Christ as He bore the sins of the world on a Roman cross (Matthew 27:46)!

I must choose to accept Him or reject Him.

Why must I choose? Why must I personally decide? Because "the LORD watches over the way of the righteous, but the way of the wicked will perish" (Psalm 1:6). I must accept Christ as my Savior and must simply ask Him to come into my life. "Yet to all who received him, to those who believed in his name, he gave the right to become children of God" (John 1:12). What gave Him the authority? He rose from the dead! (See Psalm 16:9–10 and Acts 2:31.) Why don't you choose to accept Him right now as your Lord and Savior? He is the supreme Answer to the question of life.

■ *Seventh, my being and personality will live forever, either with the Lord or apart from Him.*

David talks about being led "in the way everlasting" (Psalm 139:24). He says that he will be pursued by goodness and love all the days of his life. And he concludes the most sublime lyric ever written by saying, "I will dwell in the house of the LORD forever."

J.S. Bach signed his works in a unique way. It is an apt closing, a perfect signature, to this journal.

Soli Deo Gloria!
"To God alone be the glory!"

Psalm to Jesus

As a stream to the desert sand,
    As a rain to the vine;
As a shade to the barren land,
    So Your heart is to mine.

As a beam to the darkest night,
    As a calm to the sea;
As a kiss to the frightened child,
    So Your love is to me.

Yet, my heart longs for more,
    Lord, my soul thirsts for more—
My spirit hungers for more of You.

As a rose in the summer sun,
    So my heart longs for more of You!

Words by Nan Allen. Music by Don Wyrtzen.
© 1988 by Singspiration Music.